MW01484806

RICHARD RODGERS

YALE UNIVERSITY PRESS / NEW HAVEN AND LONDON

WILLIAM G. HYLAND

RICHARD
RODGERS

Frontispiece: Richard Rodgers, 1930s.

Published with assistance from the foundation established in memory of Philip Hamilton McMillan of the Class of 1894, Yale College.

Designed by Nancy Ovedovitz and set in Postscript Joanna type by Tseng Information Systems, Durham, North Carolina. Printed in the United States of America by Edwards Brothers, Ann Arbor, Michigan.

Library of Congress Cataloging-in-Publication Data
Hyland, William, 1929–

Richard Rodgers / William G. Hyland.
    p.   cm.
Discography: p.
Includes bibliographical references and index.
ISBN 0-300-07115-9 (alk. paper)
1. Rodgers, Richard, 1902–79.
2. Composers—United States—Biography.
I. Title.
ML410.R6315H95   1998
782.1'4'092—dc21
[B]   97-41161

A catalogue record for this book is available from the British Library.

The paper in this book meets the guidelines for permanence and durability of the Committee on Production Guidelines for Book Longevity of the Council on Library Resources.

10   9   8   7   6   5   4   3   2   1

For James, John, Victoria, and William

CONTENTS

OVERTURE

Richard Rodgers was a musical genius. He proved it time and again during his sixty-year career as a composer for the American stage. His first professional song was performed on Broadway when he was only seventeen, his last in a Broadway show six decades later, shortly before he died. In the intervening years he wrote well over a thousand songs and the musical scores for more than forty shows. When he began his career, he joined the ranks of such luminaries as George Gershwin, Jerome Kern, Vincent Youmans, Sigmund Romberg, Cole Porter, and Irving Berlin. When he wrote his last notes, in 1979, all these colleagues were dead or had retired. He had become an icon—and a relic.

But his career was not just an endurance test. Even if he had retired much earlier, the melodies he wrote to Lorenz Hart's words would earn him a niche in the history of American popular music. By 1942, when their partnership ended, Rodgers and Hart had created a cornucopia of songs that would forever qualify as standards, songs that would be played and enjoyed even into the 1990s.

In Rodgers and Hart's first great song hit, "Manhattan," the lyrics proclaimed, "We'll have Manhattan, the Bronx and Staten Island too." And of course they did take Manhattan. Their shows — *A Connecticut Yankee in King Arthur's Court*, *Simple Simon*, *Jumbo*, *On Your Toes*, *Babes in Arms*, *The Boys from Syracuse* — were fun, if not so well remembered. But the songs are memorable, though only a few aficionados can recall who sang what in which show or under what circumstances. In *Babes in Arms* the diminutive Mitzi Green — playing a character named Billie who wants to prove that she is one of the gang — introduced "The Lady Is a Tramp." Now the song is better recalled in performances by, say, Frank Sinatra or Lena Horne.

His later shows were a different story. As the partner of Oscar Hammerstein, Richard Rodgers became more than a fine songwriter. R&H, as they became known, created a new art form: the musical play. Not a play with music added, but an integration of music, lyrics, dialogue, characters, and plot in an originally conceived entity. The form began during World War II with *Oklahoma!*

With some obvious exceptions, most Broadway shows, even those created by the great songwriters, have faded. But this has not been true for Rodgers' shows: *Oklahoma!*, *Carousel*, *South Pacific*, and *The King and I* are still magical names. They are revived periodically, recorded by each new generation of singers, and seen regularly on television.

It would be romantic if the life story of such a major force in American musical history had been a rags-to-riches tale of a determined young man banging out tunes for Tin Pan Alley on a beat-up old upright piano until he was discovered. Rodgers' life was anything but that. He often said that his career might have prospered earlier if, like Irving Berlin, he had been a singing waiter around Union Square in lower Manhattan.

In fact, Richard Rodgers was born into an affluent Jewish family and grew up in Manhattan. Music came easily to him; both of his parents were musically inclined, and he may well have inherited their talent. His daughters, Mary and Linda, were also talented; Mary continued the tradition of writing for Broadway (*Once Upon a Mattress*), as did his grandson, Adam Guettel (*Floyd Collins*).

Rodgers' music studies were sporadic. His talents were so ingrained — he had a perfect ear for music — that he chafed at instruction, studying only enough to navigate through the theatrical world. As far back as he could remember, he had wanted to write for the theater. Rodgers loved everything about it, from the tumult of out-of-town tryouts to the incandescence of a Broadway opening night.

Richard Rodgers enjoyed three careers. The first was with Lorenz Hart, and the second with Oscar Hammerstein. When Hammerstein died, Richard Rodgers, then in his late fifties, could have retired with numerous laurels. But those who knew him best could not conceive of Richard Rodgers outside the theater. He began his third and final career by writing the lyrics to his own music, to prove that he could do it—and he succeeded. Then he found himself collaborating with a new generation: Stephen Sondheim, Sheldon Harnick, and Martin Charnin. Although his talents were still very much in evidence, he was frequently ill. Nevertheless, at the age of seventy-six he embarked on a new show, I Remember Mama. Unfortunately, it was not a success. A few months later, however, just before he died, the lights of Broadway proudly hailed yet another revival of Oklahoma!—a fitting coda.

Like many men and women of great creative ability, Rodgers was not easy to understand. In the theater he could be intimidating, but he was also a source of reassurance and stability during the taxing weeks of rehearsals and out-of-town tryouts. He was humorous and quick with a quip. His coworkers respected him but inevitably regarded him with a certain awe. He became extraordinarily successful in his work, enjoyed a privileged life, and shared two Pulitzer Prizes. He was also unhappy and depressed much of the time.

Of modest height, with a trim figure, he was attractive to women. In 1930, Rodgers married the charming Dorothy Feiner. They were married for almost fifty years, even though he was "tough to live with," had a tendency to hypochondria, and for a period drank to excess. In the 1950s he suffered a mental breakdown, and in the next two decades he endured devastating illnesses.

Nothing seemed to affect his creativity, however. He was confident of his abilities and therefore not particularly competitive or envious of the success of his fellow songwriters. Stories of his musical feats—such as writing a hit song in five minutes—grew to the point that he was embarrassed, prompting rather long-winded explanations of how he was able to compose so quickly. His sure touch could even irritate his collaborators, who sometimes worked over lyrics for days and weeks.

Rodgers' monument is the theater on 46th Street in Manhattan that bears his name. A fitting epitaph came from an unusual source. Late in his career Rodgers wrote background music for a television series about the wartime career of Winston Churchill. Perhaps with that great British statesman in mind the essayist and social critic Lionel Trilling said of Richard Rodgers, "Few men have given so much pleasure to so many people." This is the story of that man and his music.

ACKNOWLEDGMENTS

I never met Richard Rodgers, but I have known and admired his music for fifty years. During the late 1940s I spent summers playing in small combos in hotels, resorts, and even a gambling casino; every leader believed the patrons would be impressed if we played a lot of Rodgers and Hart songs. At one point I even wrote some rudimentary arrangements of half a dozen of their songs for a small group auditioning at a posh St. Louis hotel. We didn't get the job, but Rodgers' melodies and harmonies, especially "There's a Small Hotel," stuck in my mind.

Over the years, while working for the U.S. government and living in Virginia near Washington, D.C. (and for a time in New York), I saw many of Rodgers' shows and all the movies that were made of them (my favorite is *The King and* I). Some years ago, in writing another book about popular songwriting, I read his autobiography, *Musical Stages*. When I looked for more information I found that much had been published about Rodgers and Hart, and Rodgers and Hammerstein, but about Rodgers alone I found only a few biographies written in the 1950s. So I began the research that led to this book.

I am indebted to a number of people for their help. First, I wish to acknowledge the help of my wife, who always believed that a biography of Richard Rodgers would be worth writing and that it would find interested readers who shared her enthusiasm for his music. At a crucial point I was encouraged by Harry Haskell of Yale University Press, who saw merit in a ragged manuscript. I attribute his acumen to the fact that he is from Kansas City (Missouri, of course), as I am. My rough draft was salvaged by the careful and comprehensive editing of Karen Gangel and Heidi Downey (and by the production editing of Margaret Otzel). Mark Horowitz, librarian in the Music Division of the Library of Congress, gave me invaluable assistance in using the Rodgers and the Oscar Hammerstein Collections. The Rodgers and Hammerstein Organization was a key element in bringing this book to fruition. I am particularly indebted to Theodore Chapin, Bert Fink, and Robin Alton; and to Flora Griggs, at Williamson Music. I owe a special debt to Mary Rodgers Guettel, Richard Rodgers' daughter. She courteously and patiently pointed me in the right direction and answered what must have seemed endless and foolish questions. Finally, I am indebted to Richard Rodgers, Lorenz Hart, and Oscar Hammerstein, whose words and music have been my steady diet for the past four years. There was surely a song in their hearts, as there is in mine.

I

CAMPFIRE DAYS

One Sunday in winter 1918–19 two young men from Columbia University took a jaunt along the Upper West Side of Manhattan to one of the stately brownstones on West 119th Street. They were greeted by a short, unshaven young man dressed in carpet slippers, tuxedo pants, a rumpled dress shirt, and a shabby robe. He invited the pair in, and shortly thereafter the younger of the two visitors, Richard Rodgers, sat down at an upright piano in the sitting room, where a Victrola had been blaring Jerome Kern's "Babes in the Wood." He ran through a few melodies that he had written while his host, Lorenz Hart, offered comments, including a spirited critique of the failings of the American musical theater. By the time Rodgers and his friend, Phillip Leavitt, bade farewell an hour later, the team of Rodgers and Hart had been born. For the next twenty-five years they would write some of the greatest melodies and lyrics of the American musical theater.[1]

Richard Charles Rodgers was the second son of Dr. William A. Rodgers and Mamie Levy Rodgers. Both the Rodgerses and the Levys were Russian Jews who had immigrated to America in 1860, well before the great wave of Jewish emigration from Eastern Europe in the 1880s and 1890s. The family of Dr. Rodgers' mother was French and had emigrated by way of Alsace. It was unusual for Jews to move freely within or to emigrate from Alsace, especially before 1871, when the area passed into the control of the Prussian Kingdom.

Once in the United States, the Rogazinsky family (later to become Rodgers) settled briefly in Holden, Missouri, a rural area near Kansas City. Although this is the official family version of those early years, repeated by Rodgers and his biographers, no one seems to know why this unusual site was chosen. William, the father of Richard Rodgers, was born in Missouri in 1871, the oldest of eight children. A Jewish immigrant family in remote Holden must have been uncommon, because even in Kansas City there lived only a handful of Jewish families. (One of them, the Guettel family, reappeared in the life of the Rodgerses decades later when Henry Guettel married Mary Rodgers, Richard Rodgers' older daughter.)

Some time after the birth of William Rodgers the family moved to New York. There, William's father, Abraham Rogazinsky, worked as a barber at the fashionable Delmonico's. Although his father died when William was young, William nevertheless managed to graduate from City College. By then the family name had been anglicized to Rodgers. William served as a customs officer to work his way through Bellevue Medical School. He graduated in 1895.

The following year the new doctor met and married Mamie Levy, the daughter of Rachel Lewine and Jacob Levy, a well-to-do Jewish merchant. Like William's parents, Rachel's and Jacob's families had left their native Russia in 1860. (Jacob was sponsored by his brother Mayer Levy.) Before his marriage Jacob had boarded with the Lewine family on the Lower East Side. A job with Klingenstein Brothers, a garment supplier and manufacturer on Greene Street, eventually turned into a lucrative partnership for Levy. The Lewine family was also in business, and by the standard of the times, Rachel was well educated. Jacob and Rachel Levy had three children; Mamie, born in 1873, was the first of two daughters. Like her mother, Mamie was privileged to receive a good education, including private piano lessons.

Mamie and William were married in November 1896. Following a brief honeymoon in Europe they returned to live with her parents at 816 Lexington Avenue, on the East Side of Manhattan, but far from the Jewish ghetto on the

Lower East Side. In 1898 Mamie bore her first son, Mortimer, and four years later, on June 28, 1902, a second son, Richard Charles. Richard Rodgers' birthplace was a large house on Brandreth Avenue, Hammels Station, near Arverne, Long Island, where the family was enjoying a summer home rented by Jacob Levy. At that time prosperous Jewish families often summered in Long Island to escape the city heat.

Rodgers and his family later moved to 3 West 120th Street, next to Mount Morris Park—oddly enough, near the homes of Lorenz Hart and Oscar Hammerstein II, his two future collaborators. The family of the future songwriter Frank Loesser also lived in this area. This elegant new neighborhood was still semirural and, unlike the tenements of the Lower East Side, offered residents separate five-story apartments. Eastern European Jews who were moving out of the ghetto made up a large percentage of the new arrivals. Then, as now, the area was known by its Dutch name, Harlem, and by 1900 it was the second largest Jewish settlement in New York.

The Rodgers family did not make up a happy household. William and Mamie had made a mistake by moving in with her parents, an error that Mamie acknowledged years later. But she had been reluctant to cut the cord to her domineering mother, and the economics of being newlyweds probably recommended the decision. The couple's life was marred by constant conflict between Rodgers and his mother-in-law. Rachel Lewine Levy was apparently liberated, well read, highly opinionated, and free and strident in her commentaries, which embraced most known subjects. She disdained her husband's failure to overcome his native Russian accent, and she mocked his Orthodox Judaism. Her grandson referred to her as a know-it-all: if one wanted to learn some fact, one had only to ask grandma, Richard Rodgers commented in his later years.

Sixty-five years later Rodgers recalled in his memoirs the atmosphere of conflict and tension in his family. What he described as sheer hell at dinner was obviously burned into his memory. Bickering, yelling, or unnatural silences were the norm. The situation left him with a "deep feeling of tension and insecurity," he wrote.[2] Such references provide a fertile source for speculation about his psyche and whether his upbringing had any effect on his musical creativity. Rodgers often mused about whether his musical talents were the result of heredity or environment. Modern clinical research suggests that genes are probably the source of musical abilities. On the other hand, music was Rodgers' means of escape when he was young.

Richard's relationships with each family member were relatively amicable. He was devoted to his father, a loving and attentive parent who played a "greater

Richard Charles Rodgers in 1903, at the age of one.
As a child he had a natural ear for music and
balked at the idea of formal piano lessons.

part" in his life than anyone else. In turn, his father doted on his successful son, carefully assembling scrapbooks of his achievements. He made no attempt to draw him into the medical profession, perhaps because the elder son, Mortimer, had decided to follow in his father's footsteps. William did offer Richard sound financial advice from time to time, but Richard's career choices were his own.

Rodgers would fondly remember receiving an occasional pat on the cheek from his impeccably dressed grandfather, who loudly complained whenever young Richard asked to borrow his evening paper but nevertheless treated him well. His grandmother's brother, the feather merchant Samuel Lewine, split his residence between this house and his men's club. According to Rodgers, Uncle Sam, who died in 1913, added a touch of glamour to the quarrelsome household.

Mamie Rodgers was small, shy, and constantly worried about her health— she passed on her hypochondriacal tendency to Rodgers. Although she would on rare occasions comfort her son by taking his hands in hers, displays of affection did not come easily to her—nor would they to her son when he became a father. Richard and Mortimer experienced the usual love-hate sibling rivalry. As the younger of the two, Richard was protected within the family, which left his older brother frustrated and belligerent. On the other hand, Richard was always being shooed away by Morty and his friends.

Like many songwriters of his era, Richard Rodgers' first musical influence was his own home. His father was fond of singing the latest songs from the Broadway productions that he attended with his wife. He would bring home the vocal selections, and Mamie would accompany her husband on the piano, playing songs from Oscar Strauss' *The Chocolate Soldier* or Franz Lehar's *The Merry Widow*. Richard Rodgers must have treasured these moments, for he kept the musical collections until the 1960s, when he donated them to the Juilliard School of Music. When Rodgers imitated his mother's playing he found that he could pick out the melodies and even supply some rudimentary harmony. His talent made him the darling of the household. The piano also was a source of pleasure at a time when he desperately needed it.

Some claim that Richard could finger his way through a melody by the time he was three years old. Rodgers himself said only that he learned to play as a toddler. He was given some formal instruction by his aunt Tily Rodgers but did not enjoy such lessons; he claimed that they were a "dismal failure" because his natural ear for music led him to reproduce what he heard and to ignore the dreary printed exercises for young pianists. By the time he was nine he was spending much of his spare time at the piano; in his memoirs he wrote of the trauma of having to interrupt his playing for several months after undergoing surgery on an infected finger. He never reached George Gershwin's heights as a pianist, but he played as well as most of the songwriters of his era. Later, after he had achieved fame on Broadway, he took piano lessons and improved his playing significantly.

His grandparents were fond of opera. His grandmother had a subscription to the Metropolitan Opera, and his grandfather took him to various productions. Rodgers attended *Carmen*, saw a Diaghilev ballet, and heard Josef Hoffman play Tchaikovsky's First Piano Concerto at Carnegie Hall. It is possible that he was in the same audiences as the Gershwin brothers. His grandfather introduced him to musical shows as well. Richard remembered that his entire family attended Victor Herbert's *Little Nemo*—an operetta about a child's fantasy produced at the New Amsterdam Theater—the family having been treated to seats in an upper left-hand box. His grandfather also took him to see the well-known singer and comedian Ina Claire. Rodgers saw her at the beginning of her career in *The Quaker Girl* (which opened in October 1911), a popular British transplant with music by Lionel Monckton. By then the young man was concocting his own tunes.

Rodgers remembered Harlem of the early 1900s as a pleasant area. Morris Park,

The Rodgers family in 1905, from left: Dr. William
Rodgers, Mortimer, Mamie Levy Rodgers, and Richard.
Richard's parents loved Broadway shows; his grand-
parents had a subscription to the opera.

with its imposing bell tower, was a "wonderful place." Families congregated on
the stoops of the apartment buildings, as they had done in the evening on the
Lower East Side, and children played in the streets. In early evening passersby
could hear the refrains of "Only a Bird in a Gilded Cage" being played on an
upright piano, which was part of most households. Nearby was the Harlem
Opera House, owned by Oscar Hammerstein I, where the entertainment might
be Fanny Brice or Sophie Tucker. A block to the west, on Seventh Avenue, were
neighborhood theaters that featured local versions of shows produced in the
major theaters downtown.

Rodgers began school at P.S. 10, at 117th Street and St. Nicholas Avenue. He also took religious instruction at the imposing Temple Israel, which had moved from Fifth Avenue to Harlem as the Jewish population shifted. The Rodgers household was divided over religion: Jacob Levy was a religious man, but Rachel Levy was an avowed atheist and highly critical of her husband's devotion. Mortimer Rodgers was bar mitzvahed, but not Richard. One of Richard Rodgers' most vivid early memories was the death of his great-grandmother Rodgers, who lived several blocks away. He remembered her being carried out in a plain pine coffin for a hurried funeral. Her death marked the end of the observance of Orthodox Jewish customs in the Rodgers household. From then on, Richard, Mortimer, and their parents were Jewish for socioeconomic reasons rather than out of conviction.

That Richard Rodgers would recall, at the very beginning of his memoirs, his great-grandmother's death and its religious significance for his family suggests his need to justify his own religious alienation. Richard became an atheist, and as a parent he resisted religious instruction for his children. According to his wife, Dorothy, he felt that religion was based on "fear" and contributed to "feelings of guilt."[3]

In spite of family feuds and religious conflicts, Rodgers seems to have had a normal, though not necessarily happy, childhood. He lived in a well-ordered household: the menu for each evening was prescribed by the day of the week, with no variations allowed: for example, pot roast was served only on Mondays. For Richard the bright spot was Sunday, when the family was treated to cold cuts from Pomerantz's delicatessen. During their summers on Long Island the family became acquainted with the family of Benjamin Feiner, a New York lawyer. Benjamin Feiner, Jr., was a patient of Dr. Rodgers, and Richard became his occasional playmate. The summer that Richard was seven he gazed on the Feiners' newest addition, a baby girl named Dorothy, his future wife.

In 1914 his entire family moved to 161 West 86th Street, between Columbus and Amsterdam Avenues. This neighborhood was the site of the grand apartment complexes that originated with the construction of the famous Dakota. Among the well-known residents of the area were Florenz Ziegfeld and Arturo Toscanini, both of whom lived in the elegant new Ansonia, at Broadway and 73rd Street. Rodgers graduated from P.S. 166, on West 89th Street, in January 1916. The graduation program included a "Medley of Operas" performed as a piano solo by Richard Rodgers.

Rodgers recalled the inspiration that he received from his elementary school music teacher, Elsa Katz, an attractive young woman who encouraged him to play at school functions. A would-be biographer who sought her out reported back to Rodgers that Elsa Katz did not remember him, though she would have been proud to take credit for his career. Rodgers took this news with good humor and still insisted on the importance of her encouragement.

Richard enrolled at the prestigious Townsend Harris Hall, a high school reserved for talented young boys (Ira Gershwin and E. Y. "Yip" Harburg had attended a few years earlier, and Frank Loesser was to attend a few years later). Academic pursuits did not attract Rodgers, however, and he transferred to the more pedestrian De Witt Clinton High School, where Lorenz Hart had been a student.

Summer camp was an important part of the lives of Jewish boys whose families could afford it, and campers formed friendships that would last well into their adult years. While still in elementary school Rodgers went to a summer camp sponsored by the Weingart Institute, a private grammar school. Alumni included Oscar Hammerstein II and his brother, Reggie, as well as Lorenz Hart, who edited the camp newspaper, *Review*. The camp catered mainly to well-to-do German-Jewish families. A camper who remembered the place from his youth noted that it was run along "strictly disciplinarian lines": the daily routine included bugle calls for reveille, personal as well as room inspection, and two hours of instruction every morning.

Later Rodgers went to Camp Wigwam in Harrison, Maine, and then to Camp Paradox, on Lake Paradox in the Adirondacks. Lorenz Hart and his brother had spent two summers at Camp Wigwam several years before Rodgers. Other campers included the Selznick brothers, David and Myron; Herbert Sondheim, the future father of Stephen Sondheim; and the son of Adolph Zukor, founder of Paramount studios. Although Rodgers, Hart, Hammerstein, and Loesser could have encountered one another at school, at camp, or in the neighborhood, their paths did not cross until they were adults.

On Sunday evenings the campers put on variety shows. Hart (who arrived at camp with a footlocker full of books) once read from *Hamlet*, to the catcalls and Bronx cheers of his fellow campers. By the time Rodgers attended Wigwam he was so intrigued with music that he spent hours playing the piano rather than swimming and hiking. In 1916, Rodgers composed a song called "Campfire Days," which, despite the meandering melody, was not a bad effort for a fourteen-year-old.[4]

One of the camp's musical instructors was Arthur Loesser, a professional concert pianist and the half-brother of Frank Loesser. Arthur went on to write *Men, Women, and Pianos: A Social History*. But Rodgers' musical mentor at camp was Robert K. Lippmann, a counselor who was only four years older than Rodgers and had some professional ability. Rodgers later acknowledged Lippmann's influence, though it is impossible to determine how he shaped Rodgers' development. During this time Lippmann wrote the music for a camp song, with lyrics by Lorenz Hart, and during his college days he collaborated with Oscar Hammerstein II on shows at Columbia University.

By the time America entered into World War I, Rodgers' musical interests were solidifying, and he was attending Broadway musicals. After or even during successful runs, Broadway shows moved uptown, on the so-called subway circuit, to the theaters on the West Side. It was there, at the Standard Theater, that Rodgers first heard the music of Jerome Kern, an experience that changed his life.

The performances of Kern's work that Rodgers eventually heard originated at the tiny Princess Theater, on West 39th Street. It was there that Kern, Guy Bolton, and P. G. Wodehouse inaugurated a series of intimate musicals. The first show, *Nobody Home* (1915), elicited no special critical reaction, but a later production, *Very Good Eddie*, was a comedy that Rodgers saw a number of times. It was a song from this show, "Babes in the Wood," that Hart was playing on his Victrola when he and Rodgers met. Commenting on Kern's *Oh, Lady, Lady!* Dorothy Parker wrote: "Bolton, and Wodehouse and Kern are my favorite indoor sport, anyway. I like the way they go about a musical comedy. I like the way that action slides casually into songs. I like the deft rhyming of the song that is always sung in the last act by two comedians and a comedienne. And oh, how I do like Jerome Kern's music."[5] Kern later scoffed at some of the extravagant claims for the Princess series. Nevertheless, theater historians have concluded that these were the first truly cohesive musicals—they depended on plot and character rather than gags and slapstick, and they integrated the music and lyrics into the librettos. Kern's style during this period was simple and natural but had a touch of sophistication that set it apart from the routine output of other composers. Rodgers eventually saw all the Kern shows. Kern's music also persuaded George Gershwin to become a Broadway songwriter.

Rodgers' musical talents were refined enough for him to realize that Kern's work was something different, not only in the music but in the entire staging. He did not copy Kern, but he did absorb some of Kern's style. The difference between them was that Kern's musical roots dated to the era of operettas, and his compositions reflected European traditions, whereas Rodgers was more influenced by the Jazz Age. Rodgers was also impressed by the appealing flavor imparted by Frank Saddler's innovative style of orchestration. The smaller pit orchestras, dictated by the economics of the Princess productions, gave the score a bright coloration by skillful use of only a few instruments, including the newly popular saxophone.

By age fifteen Rodgers had decided that the musical theater was to be his profession, and he never wavered from this. The Kern shows made him realize that he was witnessing a historic moment in the American theater: "Somehow I knew it and wanted desperately to be a part of it."[6]

He got the opportunity he wanted in Columbia University's famous Varsity Shows. Even before becoming a student Rodgers had savored these musical revues, which were produced by the Columbia University Players. His brother, Mortimer, a student at Columbia, took him to the March 1917 production of *Home, James* at the Hotel Astor. Robert Lippmann, Richard's friend, had written the music for the show, which must have impressed Rodgers. There was no particular plot, and the characters had such names as Benny Dictine, but the show was well received by the audience, and the critics appreciated its youthful vigor.

After the show Mortimer took his brother backstage to meet the law student who had written most of the libretto and had performed as a singing and dancing French waiter. His name was Oscar Hammerstein II. This encounter was historic for American musicals, but the meeting itself produced no notable memories—in fact, neither of the future partners could even recall what was said. Hammerstein would later claim in jest that Rodgers was in short pants and awed by an upperclassman. Rodgers denied this, insisting that he had already graduated to "longies." Rodgers probably was right—he was just a few months short of fifteen. Whatever transpired, that afternoon Richard Rodgers decided to attend Columbia University and to write a Varsity Show. He succeeded in doing both.

2

FLY WITH ME

Attending Columbia was an adventure for Richard Rodgers. At the turn of the century the university catered to the upper middle class; young Jewish men who were not so well off usually went to City College (for example, Ira Gershwin and E. Y. Harburg). Rodgers, however, had no trouble entering the university in the fall of 1919, a member of the class of '23. His brother was a student in the class of 1921. Among Mortimer's classmates were Bennett Cerf, the founder of Random House, and Max Schuster and Richard Simon, who founded Simon and Schuster. Mortimer Rodgers and Cerf were fraternity brothers of Oscar Hammerstein II, who was attending law school. Cerf remembered that the younger Rodgers was always hanging around his brother's friends.

One of the attractions of Columbia was its liberal arts faculty, especially that of the English department, which included Carl Van Doren and John Erskine. What attracted Richard Rodgers was the chance to write expanded scores for the school's musical revues. Columbia also brought him into contact with men who would become his colleagues and associates: Oscar Hammerstein II; Herbert Fields, the son of the vaudeville comedian Lew Fields; Roy Webb, a musician who introduced Rodgers to the more serious side of his profession; and Phillip Leavitt, who introduced him to Larry Hart.

The Columbia Varsity Shows originated in 1892, and by the time Oscar Hammerstein arrived in 1912 they had been taken over by the Players Club. The idea was to stage an annual musical comedy revue written, produced, and performed by students. The shows were staged in one of New York's hotel ballrooms and ran for as long as a week. One show even went on a short tour. Many of the luminaries of the musical, theatrical, and academic worlds apprenticed in these musicals.

Hammerstein's first show, staged in spring 1915, was entitled *On Your Way*. It was written and directed by an alumnus, Kenneth Webb, with music by his brother, Roy Webb. Reviewers noted the performance of Hammerstein, who had a speaking and singing part: "He danced like Al Jolson and had some original steps of his own."[1] The following spring Hammerstein performed in and helped write several sketches for the next Varsity Show, *The Peace Pirates*, most of which was written by Herman Mankiewicz, the future journalist and screenwriter. The cast featured Lorenz Hart, who was also the drama critic for the college newspaper, the *Daily Spectator*. Hart wrote that Hammerstein, who appeared in blackface, was "thoroughly original and distinctly funny." Hart himself performed an impersonation of Mary Pickford, and years later Hammerstein wrote that Hart skipped and bounced around the stage like an "electrified gnome." The *New York Times* (April 13, 1916) noted that "in lyrics, lines and specialties the young men showed they knew their Broadway. Lorenz M. Hart gave some easily recognizable imitations of Belle Blanche's imitations of Ethel Barrymore . . . while Oscar Hammerstein, grandson of Oscar the Immortal, was a gentleman of color whose mannerisms suggested those of a blackface favorite of the revues."[2]

Hart was born into a solid middle-class German-Jewish family in New York in 1895. His parents, Max and Frieda Hart, had emigrated from Hamburg with their families, both of whom settled on the Lower East Side. Like the Rodgers-Levy family, the Harts later moved uptown, to West 119th Street. Lorenz, always called Larry (except by his mother, who called him Lorry), was the eldest of two sons.

Hart, who attended the School of Journalism at Columbia, was indifferent to classroom routine but enjoyed performing in the university shows and writing for various student publications. He had a strong literary bent and was fluent in German, and his family claimed a relationship with the poet Heinrich Heine. Before entering Columbia, Hart spent a summer touring Germany. When he met Rodgers he was earning a living as a translator of German plays for the Shubert Organization. It was rumored that he had translated Ferenc Molnár's play Liliom, though as a ghostwriter he received no credit.[3] (Liliom was the basis for Rodgers and Hammerstein's Carousel.)

Before joining forces with Hart, Rodgers was enlisted by his brother to help write the music for an amateur show produced by an organization known as the Akron Club, a combination social-athletic club. To raise money for the New York Sun's Tobacco Fund, which provided cigarettes for soldiers, the club put on a revue called One Minute Please at the Plaza Hotel in December 1917. The book was by Ralph Engelsman, a student at Columbia, with lyrics by Engelsman and Rodgers. A "Musical Farce in Three Acts," it was produced and staged by Milton Bender, a close friend of Hart's. The fifteen-year-old Rodgers wrote the music and some of the lyrics, played the piano, and conducted a five-piece orchestra.

About this time one of Rodgers' girlfriends arranged for him to play for Louis Dreyfus, the brother of the better-known music publisher Max Dreyfus. Louis Dreyfus listened to him play and then advised him to come back after he finished school. But others were more encouraging, including Leonard Lie-bling, editor of the Musical Courier, and Nola Arndt, widow of the composer Felix Arndt, who wrote the perennial piano exercise "Nola." She encouraged him to remain in the theater rather than experiment with Tin Pan Alley.

Before beginning his studies at Columbia, Rodgers was involved in one more amateur production, Up Stage and Down, presented by the Infants Relief Society at the Grand Ballroom of the Waldorf-Astoria Hotel on March 8, 1919. Rodgers, the musical director of the show, set some of his music to lyrics by Oscar Hammerstein, whom he had met two years earlier through his brother. "There's Always Room for One More," the first Rodgers and Hammerstein creation, was a jaunty two-beat tune with a Kern-like melody. The refrain is only sixteen bars and quite repetitive, but that was the style in the era. Hammerstein's bland lyrics—"My heart is filled to the brim with you"—did not help. By then, however, Rodgers had met Hart, and the two began to work on a few songs. But in May 1919, when Up Stage and Down reopened at the 44th Street Theater under a new title, Twinkling Eyes, there were no songs by Rodgers and Hart. The program credits Rodgers for the music and lyrics and lists Hart as director. With this show Rodgers and Hart had begun to work together.

Mortimer Rodgers and Bennett Cerf both opposed Rodgers' joining Hart, because they considered Hart shiftless and disorganized. According to Cerf's recollection, they thought he would never amount to anything. But Rodgers was not deterred. He and Hart were convinced that the musical theater, as exemplified by the Princess Theater triumvirate of Kern, Bolton, and Wodehouse, "was capable of achieving a far greater degree of artistic merit in every area than was apparent at that time."[4] In spring and summer 1919 they wrote a number of songs together, although their grand ambition was to write the score for a complete production. They got that opportunity through Phillip Leavitt's friendship with the family of the comedian Lew Fields, of the famed team of Weber and Fields. Leavitt knew Lew Fields' daughter, Dorothy, a fledgling performer who became an outstanding lyricist. Her brother, Herbert Fields, was a student at Columbia and was casually acquainted with both Rodgers and Hart. Lew Fields had split up with his famous vaudeville partner and had turned to producing and acting occasionally in his own shows. He was struggling to keep alive his new show, A Lonely Romeo, as an Actors' Equity strike threatened to close the entire theater district. An advertisement for A Lonely Romeo announced: "We Are Positively Open." Dorothy and Herbert Fields apparently persuaded their father to listen to a few songs by Rodgers and Hart.

There are differing reports of this crucial audition for Lew Fields. Some say that both Rodgers and Hart arrived at the Fields' summer home in Far Rockaway, New York; others claim that Rodgers went alone, and to a different location. The Fields family remembered only Rodgers; moreover, it would have been typical of Hart to miss such an opportunity. In any case, Rodgers played several songs, leading off with "Venus," Hart's favorite (though it was never published and has since been lost). Fields was not impressed. Rodgers then played an incidental song they had written called "Any Old Place with You," which Fields offered to buy and interpolate in A Lonely Romeo.[5]

According to most accounts, including Rodgers' memoirs, the Broadway debut of this first Rodgers and Hart song took place on Tuesday, August 26, 1919. In fact, the Casino Theater closed on Saturday, August 23, because of the actors' strike. The song was probably heard either just before the strike began or shortly after it ended; the sheet music was published in December 1919 by Jerome H. Remick; on the cover was an illustration of A Lonely Romeo. Decades later Rodgers, who had an incredible memory for all his melodies, wrote of "Any Old Place with You": "I came up with a bouncy melody that was intended to simulate the carefree chug-chugging of a honeymoon express. . . . It was all pretty naive, I suppose."[6]

The music was based on a simple theme stated in the first bar and then re-peated at a higher and a lower interval. This device indicates Rodgers' awareness of what was fashionable, and like his first song with Hammerstein, it was a mod-est attempt to reproduce a popular pattern. Unfortunately, it was too repetitive, which did not necessarily reflect a lack of imagination; rather, the repetition was an effort to instill the main melody in the hope that the listener would buy the sheet music.

In this case the lyrics were more notable than the melody. Hart's geographi-cal tour explained a desperate boy's effort to overcome his girlfriend's coolness.

> We'll melt in Syria,
> Freeze in Siberia,
> Negligee in Timbuktu.

> In dreamy Portugal,
> I'm goin' to court you, gal.
> Ancient Rome we'll paint anew.

These lyrics by Hart contrast with Hammerstein's first lyric for Rodgers, "There's Always Room for One More":

> My heart is an airy castle
> filled with girls I adore.
> My brain is a cloud of memories,
> with peaches galore.

Rodgers' musical talents might have developed differently had he first joined with Hammerstein rather than Hart. The scintillating nature of Hart's lyrics was forecast by the line that rhymed Portugal with "court you, gal." Hammerstein's approach to lyrical expression was reflected in his early talent for imagery: an "airy castle" and a "cloud of memories." Judging from what has survived of this early period, Rodgers' livelier music was probably more appropriate for Hart's wit and irreverence than for Hammerstein's budding romanticism.

That spring Rodgers and Hart wrote their first full-fledged musical score, *You'd Be Surprised*, for another Akron Club show. The show played the Plaza's Grand Ballroom on March 6, 1920, with Dorothy Fields and Phil Leavitt in the cast. Herbert Fields wrote some of the lyrics. The book and direction were by Hart's friend Milton Bender, and Rodgers conducted.

The big event for Rodgers and Hart came two weeks later, with the opening of the 1920 Columbia Varsity Show. Because of the stiff competition for these shows, Rodgers and Hart decided to apply as a composer-lyricist team and to submit a libretto as well. One of the judges was Oscar Hammerstein. Rodgers and Hart were selected, but their script was rejected in favor of Milton Kroopf and Phil Leavitt's depiction of the plight of Manhattan following a Bolshevik takeover. The show, Fly with Me, opened on March 24, 1920, and ran for four nights at the Hotel Astor's Grand Ballroom.

The lyrics were by Hart, except for Rodgers and Hammerstein's "There's Always Room for One More" and "Weaknesses," both borrowed from Up Stage and Down. Rodgers and Hart also borrowed some of their music from You'd Be Surprised—or perhaps it was the reverse, since the melodies for both shows were actually written at about the same time. The dances were sketched out by Herbert Fields. Fly with Me was quite favorably received: the New York Times review (March 25, 1920) was headlined "Columbia's Play Bright," followed by "Sparkling Musical in 'Fly With Me' acted at the Astor." The acclaim continued: "Music that sparkled from the rise of the curtain to its last descent was the gayest feature of the Columbia University Players gay musical comedy, 'Fly With Me.' . . . The best songs were 'Peek-in Pekin,' 'Moonlight and You' and the rollicking finale 'A College on Broadway.' "

Fly with Me, which smacked of Jerome Kern, incorporated the lively rhythms of the day, along with a dash of syncopation for effect. Although nothing exceptional emerged from the score, it was on the whole a good one. The waltz "If I Were You" foreshadowed the waltzes that Rodgers would write with both Hart and Hammerstein. "Peek-in Pekin" was a light, rhythmic song of only sixteen bars, but with a four-bar tag; it also had a strong verse. "Dreaming of You" was reminiscent of Victor Herbert and the operatic love songs of the time. The best love song was "Moonlight and You."

Perhaps the best-remembered number was a rousing fight song, "A College on Broadway." The Bolsheviks have abolished the old-fashioned schools, and two of the characters are reminiscing about the good old days when there were colleges. This story line leads into Hart's witty parody on college songs, including a glancing blow at "Bulldog," Cole Porter's famous fight song for Yale:

> Bulldogs run around New Haven,
> Harvard paints old Cambridge red,
> Even poor old Philadelphia
> Really has a college, it is said,
> And Williamstown belongs to Williams,
> Princeton's tiger stands at bay,

Richard Rodgers reading the script of *Poor Little Ritz Girl* of 1920, the first show that Rodgers and Hart wrote for Broadway.

> But old New York won't let the world forget
> That there's a college on Broadway.

Lew Fields heard the show, liked it, and invited Rodgers and Hart to write an entire Broadway production, tentatively titled *Poor Little Ritz Girl*. This was a breakthrough: not only was Fields still a force in show business, but writing a full score was the very opportunity that Rodgers and Hart had been hoping for. For some reason—perhaps stage fright—Rodgers and Hart simply lifted much of their earlier work for this new show, with new lyrics, of course. "Don't Love Me Like Othello" was taken from *Fly with Me* and transformed into "You Can't Fool Your Dreams." (It had also been used in *You'd Be Surprised*.) Rodgers always cited this song as an early example of Hart's imaginative approach, because Freudian lyrics were a rarity. There were other melodies from *Fly with Me* that received new lyrics: "Peek-in Pekin" became "Love's Intense in Tents"; "Love Will Call" was originally "Dreaming True"; and "All You Need to Be a Star" was rewritten as "Inspiration." They also wrote eight new songs for this show.

The prospect of writing a Broadway score brought Rodgers his first mention in *Variety*, on May 21, 1920. The front-page notice read: "17-YEAR-OLD COMPOSER/ Richard E. Rodgers Writer of Fields' New Numbers." This show by Fields, which was scheduled to open out of town, "brings to light that Richard E. [sic] Rodgers is but 17 years of age. He came to the fore last year with his interpolated number in Fields' 'Lonely Romeo' production, 'Any Old Place With You.' George Gershwin had not reached his majority when he wrote 'La La Lucille,' but Rodgers goes him one better." Rodgers must have been walking on air after this rave notice—and may even have forgiven the use of the wrong middle initial.

Nevertheless, Rodgers and Hart were still naive about the hard-boiled world of show business. After the early rehearsals, Rodgers and Herbert Fields blithely departed for Camp Paradox to work as summer counselors, and Hart went to Brant Lake, where he was also a counselor that summer. Rodgers and Fields wrote the Sunday entertainment at their camp, and Rodgers acted in their humorous sketches (one in blackface). Rodgers composed songs with such titles as "My Tent in Paradox" and "Victory Chant" (a march in 6/8 time). Rodgers and Fields even wrote a parody of Jerome Kern's songs, entitled "The Land Where Good Camp Songs Go." Rodgers wrote an article for the camp newspaper (using the pseudonym "Victor Herbert Rodgers") explaining why young campers would rather eat and play games than study music. Imagine a mother's "hurt astonishment," he wrote, when "Sonny" returns from camp having forgotten "The Last Rose of Summer" but able to play "The Bell Hop Blues" by ear! One Sunday evening the camp newspaper reported that "blue lights and green leaves made a fairyland out of the ordinary wooden stage. Tommy [Farrell] sat in a canoe, and everything combined to give his songs the best possible effect. The verses to a new tune by Dick Rodgers were catchy and everyone caught them immediately."[7]

While Rodgers, Fields, and Hart were enjoying an idyllic summer, things turned sour during tryouts in Boston. Lew Fields grew concerned over the future of *Poor Little Ritz Girl* and ordered radical surgery, cutting songs and acts, restructuring the plot, hiring a new conductor, and, most significantly, enlisting the services of the composer Sigmund Romberg. All of this was done without the participation or knowledge of Rodgers and Hart, and the blissfully oblivious Rodgers and Fields were given a noisy send-off for their Broadway debut. When opening night revealed so little of their own work and so much of Romberg's, they were outraged and humiliated. Even their title song had been dropped and replaced with a Romberg song of the same title.

Poor Little Ritz Girl opened July 28, 1920, at the Central Theater and ran for three months to favorable reviews. Kenneth MacGowan noted in the New York Globe that "the music is about equally divided between Rodgers' hard, brisk tunes and Romberg's rich and syrupy melodies." Another reviewer found the music not particularly inspired but pleasantly lilting: Romberg's songs were in his best Viennese waltz style, and Rodgers had written "some good numbers."

Rodgers returned to camp a bruised conquering hero. Yet he had gained invaluable experience: He had written a great deal of music tailored for a major Broadway attraction. He had witnessed how such a production was assembled and put together—and how it could be changed. He had worked with old hands as well as bright new stars, including the comedian Lulu McConnell. He had heard his songs rendered by a professional orchestra. And, of course, he had seen his name printed in a Broadway program and favorably mentioned in the reviews.

Unfortunately, the show was not a turning point in his career. Indeed, his music was not heard again on Broadway for five years. That fall he returned to Columbia, and the following spring he and Hart wrote another Akron Club production, Say Mama, and their second Varsity Show, You'll Never Know, which was directed by Oscar Hammerstein. Like the previous one, the Varsity Show was a success, but largely because it featured a twelve-year-old polyglot marvel from Columbia, Edward Roche Hardy, who spoke several languages in the show. No memorable songs emerged, though Hart's lyrics continued to be sprightly and humorous. An abridged piano-vocal collection was published.

The music for this Varsity Show sounded more mature than it had just a year earlier, perhaps because Rodgers had borrowed some of it from Poor Little Ritz Girl. Whereas the score of Fly with Me had the aura of a college show, some of the music for You'll Never Know was much closer to Broadway in tone and spirit, especially the title song and "Chorus Girls Blues." Rodgers considered these shows important learning experiences. When asked later how to get started in show business, he often answered by listing these little-remembered shows.

By the summer of 1921 he had achieved his initial ambition of writing for the Columbia Varsity series. Now he was ready to move forward. At the time he was romantically involved with Helen Ford, an aspiring Broadway singer. She and another girlfriend—he was becoming something of a ladies' man—prodded him into approaching his parents with a proposition: he wanted to leave Columbia and enroll in the Institute of Musical Art. Expecting fierce resistance, he was pleased that his parents reacted positively and encouraged him. Only his grandfather noted rather cynically that songwriters never got paid. This observation was not altogether untrue: Lew Fields had purchased the songs for *Poor Little Ritz Girl* outright and thereby avoided having to pay royalties.

Rodgers was nineteen when he left Columbia for the institute, which later became the Juilliard School of Music. He kept his ties to his Columbia friends and continued to collaborate with Hart. The pair became increasingly involved with Herbert Fields, who began to write their librettos. From time to time they worked with others from Columbia, including Oscar Hammerstein, whose career was beginning to flourish. It was a lean and frustrating period for Rodgers, during which little of his work for the stage was produced. But it was during this time that he transformed himself musically from talented amateur into skilled professional.

3

MELODY MAN

Richard Rodgers had a great reservoir of natural talent, and for the average songwriter on Tin Pan Alley that was enough. Many successful songwriters could not even read music; some could play the piano just well enough to work out melodies that could be transcribed by others. Some could not even do that and had to have the tunes they hummed or sang transcribed by professionals.

The musical stage was a different realm. Writing a Broadway musical was complicated and challenging—a song had to match a performer's style, for example, which could mean transposing the song into the star's most comfortable key, altering it to fit the performer's range, or orchestrating an effective accompaniment. In addition, songs were sometimes reprised by the orchestra alone or used for a dance routine. Such challenges required intimate knowledge of musical techniques and created a considerable gap between Tin Pan Alley and the musical theater.

Of the various productions seen on Broadway, the musical revue was easier than a book musical for the songwriter. The revue had developed over the years into a combination of singing, dancing, and comedy. Usually the musical numbers were separate and distinct: a few bars of introduction were followed by the verse and refrain, typically repeated once or twice, and then it was on to the next comedy sketch. The so-called book musical was more complex. There was usually a plot of sorts that required not only songs ranging from the romantic to the comic but also specialized dances and even pseudoballets. Background music and song cues were inevitable amid the dialogue. If several different singers were involved, a change in key might be necessary from one refrain to the next. Such problems were usually handled by professional conductors and orchestrators who were trained and experienced in the various musical forms. Sometimes they were songwriters themselves, but more often they were highly skilled technicians. Most songwriters wisely decided not to become orchestrators, because scoring melodies for a full orchestra was an art in itself. As Rodgers admitted, he could have studied the range of the oboe with success, but there was little chance of equaling the skill of, say, Robert Russell Bennett, the great Broadway orchestrator. Nevertheless, Rodgers began to realize that he had to acquire more musical technique to augment his natural talents.

Rodgers then met Roy Webb, a Columbia graduate who was still active as a songwriter in the Varsity Shows. In about 1920, Webb began to tutor Rodgers in the techniques of conducting and musical notation. Webb, who became a professional musician, had studied music at Columbia as well as privately and had a foundation in classical forms and methods. But his interest was in the more popular light music. In 1921 he was asked to help orchestrate the Broadway show *Wildflower*, with music by the relative newcomer Vincent Youmans. The show also included lyrics by another newcomer, Oscar Hammerstein, a friend of Webb's from Columbia. Webb was a protégé of the conductor Victor Baravalle and through him was appointed conductor of the musical show *Stepping Stones*, written for the vaudevillian Fred Stone, with a musical score by Jerome Kern.

Webb and Rodgers had a close professional and musical relationship, and Rodgers undoubtedly learned a great deal from Webb. Later, Webb orchestrated and conducted several Rodgers and Hart shows. Webb, who met Rodgers when Rodgers was quite young, commented that "even then he was composing beautiful songs, but had no idea of how to put them down on paper."[1] Rodgers described Webb as not only experienced but "exceedingly patient and kind."

It was largely Webb's training that gave Rodgers the confidence to conduct the orchestra for *Fly with Me*. He continued his association with Rodgers until the late 1920s, when Webb migrated to Hollywood, where he wrote background music for more than three hundred films, both musicals and melodramas.

Webb's tutoring was certainly helpful when Rodgers enrolled in the Institute of Musical Art, founded in 1905 by Frank Damrosch, a member of the celebrated musical family. Damrosch's purpose was to fill a void in musical training by creating a high-quality faculty to prepare prospective performers for the concert stage. His school received financial support from the Loeb family, of the Wall Street house of Kuhn, Loeb.

His enterprise proved a major success, helped in part by the prominence of his brother, Walter Damrosch, the longtime conductor of the New York Symphony. The institute's enrollment in the mid-1920s reached about one thousand. The faculty, which numbered more than one hundred members, included several prestigious musicians. Franz Kneisel, who led the Kneisel String Quartet, one of the country's finest, taught violin. Piano instruction was supervised by Sigmund Stojowski. Theory was taught by Percy Goetschius, his protégé George Wedge, and Frank Robinson; Goetschius and Wedge taught composition as well. The venerable Henry Krehbiel, music critic of the *New York Tribune*, taught music history and criticism. When Rodgers enrolled, the institute was located at 120th Street and Claremont Avenue, near Columbia University.

For the young Rodgers the atmosphere at the institute was new and stimulating. He was, for the first time, immersed in music in all its dimensions. Perhaps his most important influence there was Goetschius, a widely respected teacher, a noted author on composition, and, above all, an innovative theorist of harmony. For a student such as Rodgers, Goetschius' classes provided a grounding in the classical and early romantic era of composition. Some of this must have been demanding for an aspiring songwriter, but it gave Rodgers a strong feeling for the relationship between melody and harmony, which Goetschius emphasized. Over the years Goetschius' influence would become evident in Rodgers' style. Following his training with Goetschius, Rodgers displayed an affinity for the traditional centrality of the tonic chord, pure and simple. He once said that he was suspicious of a songwriter who was afraid of a strong tonic chord. He risked banality with this traditional approach, but it imparted a pristine clarity to his melodies. In Rodgers' hands it was always fresh and compelling.[2]

Rodgers appreciated his training and often mentioned it favorably. He specifically cited Goetschius' injunction against using easy progressions, which he called pigs because they were lazy and obvious. Rodgers studied ear training with George Wedge, who also became a well-known theorist. Ear training allowed Rodgers to hear his songs in his mind and write them down without having to transcribe them from the piano. This talent was not unique, but most writers of popular songs preferred to hammer out their melodies on the piano as they went along. At the institute Rodgers also learned to indicate harmony with roman numerals (that is, I for the tonic; V for the dominant); he used this shorthand throughout his career.

By his own admission Rodgers did not thrive on competition and conflict, and in this sense he was the opposite of George Gershwin and Irving Berlin. Instead, he responded to sympathy and understanding, perhaps as a reaction to the quarrels he had experienced at home. This desire to avoid conflict may also explain why he was never drawn to Tin Pan Alley, where songwriters suffered repeated indignities in trying to sell their work. At the Institute of Musical Art he found the congenial atmosphere and understanding that he relished. The students and faculty did not condescend to him because of his ambition to succeed on Broadway rather than in the concert hall. Even Frank Damrosch was sympathetic to Rodgers' goals. The institute admired his talent and enlisted him for various student shows. Rodgers rubbed elbows with talented musicians, both faculty members and fellow students. The founder of the Kroll String Quartet, William Kroll, was among the students participating in one of Rodgers' jazz shows. And Rodgers was befriended by a cello student, Gerald Warburg, the son of the financier Felix Warburg, who was on the board of the Metropolitan Opera. Gerald even wrote a few popular songs with his classmate. Decades later Rodgers wrote, "My years at the Institute were far more beneficial to me than four years at college could possibly have been."[3]

Rodgers also found the lighter side of the institute engaging. At the end of every academic year, after final exams (conducted in black-tie), the class put on a musical show. Rodgers was the obvious choice for songwriter. His first show, in June 1921, was titled "Say It with Jazz," a takeoff on Rimsky-Korsakov, and subtitled "A Coq d'Or-Ian Fantasy." The score included a number of songs recycled from Rodgers' earlier amateur productions, with lyrics suitably altered by Larry Hart, plus a few new songs. It was so popular that it earned Rodgers a scholarship for the next term.

Rodgers' growing abilities were evident in another, more serious assignment. He was hired by Lew Fields as musical conductor of his new revue, *Snapshots of 1921*, and ended up writing a song for the show as well. This began as a mainline show starring Lulu McConnell, De Wolfe Hopper, and Nora Bayes. It was an immediate success on Broadway, but the high cost of the show forced it to close. Shortly after the closing Fields filed for bankruptcy, but a few months later he revived *Snapshots* and took a scaled-down version on the road. By the time Rodgers joined the road company the major stars were gone, except for Fields himself and Lulu McConnell. There was one newcomer, a comic named Fred Allen. Rodgers took over conducting duties in November 1921, working in Pittsburgh and then in Detroit and Chicago.

Conducting the pit orchestra for a Shubert-Fields production was invaluable training, especially because in each city he had to rehearse and conduct a new orchestra. But life was not all the serious work of learning his musical craft. Touring was exciting work, and as Rodgers provocatively put it, he "learned a lot about life beyond the confines of the orchestra pit." In his memoirs he acknowledged romantic involvements around this time with two young women. It was also rumored that he had a brief romantic attachment to Dorothy Fields.

Although Rodgers was beginning to find success, this period turned out to be bitter and frustrating for him. He was denied the breakthrough afforded other young songwriters — George Gershwin and Vincent Youmans, for example, both of whom had been given a chance to write for Broadway despite their relatively obscure status. The legendary music publisher Max Dreyfus did grant Rodgers an audition at the request of Lawrence Schwab, a potential producer seeking a musical team for a play he was planning. Dreyfus, a formidable figure in the world of music publishing, claimed to have discovered Jerome Kern and George Gershwin; he did, in fact, promote their careers. At the time of the audition he was the director of T. B. Harms Music. But Dreyfus simply added insult to injury when he dismissed Rodgers' music as having "nothing there" and instead touted his own protégé, Vincent Youmans. In the end Schwab did produce a play, *Sweet Little Devil*, but the score was supplied by George Gershwin. Ironically, Dreyfus later became Rodgers and Hart's publisher, and he and Rodgers became good friends.

Meanwhile, Rodgers continued to work on amateur shows, usually to benefit some special group. In addition to the Akron Club show *Say Mama* and the Columbia Varsity Show *You'll Never Know*, Rodgers wrote music for a play, *The Chinese Lantern*, presented in 1922 by the Benjamin School for Girls, with a cast that included Dorothy Fields.

The year-end revue for the Institute of Musical Art, *Jazz à la Carte*, featured Rodgers' music. The review in the *New York Times* (June 3, 1922) called the show "hilarious" and noted that "well known musicians laughed with the students" attending the show. It was described as a "new burlesque" with music by "Richard C. Rogers [sic]," who is "not unknown to Broadway," and Gerald Warburg, who "has written musical pieces for the Junior League." The lyrics were by Frank

Hunter; the satirical plot was by Dorothy Crowthers; the stage manager was Herbert Fields; and the musical director was William Kroll, who had won the institute's annual Loeb prize of one thousand dollars as the most promising student. The burlesques included takeoffs of Broadway shows: "White Shadow," "He Who Gets Vamped," and the most popular refrain, "Every Girlie Wants to Be a Sally," performed by a chorus of precocious children (Jerome Kern's popular *Sally* had opened in December 1920). Rodgers also used some of his earlier songs, including "Another Melody in F," from *Fly with Me,* and "Breath of Spring," from *You'd Be Surprised,* with lyrics by Hart. Once again he interpolated "There's Always Room for One More," with lyrics by Oscar Hammerstein.

In March 1923 came *If I Were King,* again for the Benjamin School for Girls. Rodgers was fond of the show, which had aroused some interest. A producer who was planning a similar show listened to some of Rodgers' music but ended up hiring Rudolf Friml; the show was *The Vagabond King.* Years later Rodgers speculated on how his career might have changed had he been assigned to write *The Vagabond King.*

Next came a slightly more ambitious show for the institute, *A Danish Yankee in King Tut's Court,* performed on May 31, 1923. The idea was based on what might have happened had Tutankhamen's tomb been found "more alive than dead." (This was four years before *A Connecticut Yankee in King Arthur's Court* became the basis for a Rodgers and Hart hit on Broadway.) There were the usual burlesques, this time of the operas *Orpheus, Rigoletto,* and *Cavalleria Rusticana,* and a grand finale entitled "Wake Up, Aida." Rodgers contributed several songs, collaborating on some with Dorothy Crowthers; also included was "Will You Forgive Me?" from *Poor Little Ritz Girl,* with lyrics by Hart.

Then came *The Prisoner of Zenda,* again for the Benjamin School, followed in March 1924 by *Temple Belles,* produced for the Park Avenue Synagogue as entertainment for the Purim holiday, with Herbert Fields as director. The scores for these shows were for the most part a reworking of earlier songs; very little new music resulted. Moreover, Rodgers and Hart had not yet formed a permanent and exclusive partnership; both were still writing occasionally with other partners.

Phillip Leavitt described the two young songwriters at work during this period:

> If Dick happened to improvise a good melody, Larry would turn like a pointer and rush to the piano to hear it played again. If they both liked it, Dick would sketch out the notes on [a] staff sheet, and Larry would make his own lead sheet. Sometimes Dick would say

"I think we need a waltz here," then sit at the piano and play one. Instantly Larry would start to build a lyric for it. . . . Dick changed from a shy diffident kid into a thoughtful and aware composer. That does not imply that he emerged from a chrysalis into a firebrand, but he developed sureness, confidence and poise.[4]

Rodgers got a potential break in March 1924 with the production of The Melody Man, a comedy with Lew Fields that starred the team of Sammy White and Eva Puck. It was in this show that Rodgers met the actor Fredric March, who became a lifelong friend. The show toured for several weeks, under the name Henky, until Fields ran out of money. It included two songs by "Herbert Richard Lorenz," the pseudonym that Rodgers, Hart, and Fields had adopted in trying to change their luck.

Hart and Rodgers persuaded Hart's friend Billy Rose to invest in the show, and it went to Broadway. Henky ran for fifty-six performances at the Ritz Theater (May 13–31) and then moved to the 49th Street Theater (June 2–28). The two Rodgers-Hart-Fields songs, "Moonlight Mama" and the comic "I'd Like to Poison Ivy" ("because she clings to me!"), were both published in April 1924 but aroused no interest. Finally, in February 1925 there was one last amateur benefit show, Bad Habits of 1925, for the Evelyn Goldsmith Home for Crippled Children; it included a number of recycled songs and one new one, "I'd Like to Take You Home to Meet My Mother," a takeoff on "Yes, We Have No Bananas."

Although Rodgers had been involved in thirty amateur productions by this time, he had little to show for his labors. Without realizing it, however, the team of Rodgers and Hart—now really a triumvirate because Herbert Fields had joined them in almost every endeavor—had laid the groundwork for their fame. In 1922 they concocted a full-scale book musical entitled Winkle Town. The book was by Fields, and Oscar Hammerstein helped rewrite the plot after hearing some of the music (his participation seemed to guarantee success). The team took it to several producers who turned it down, based on the suspicion that if the show was such a winner, Lew Fields would have produced it; the reality was that Fields was broke again.

In any case, Winkle Town was not produced and the songs were not registered for copyright, though they were reworked for subsequent shows. Had one song been registered, the entry might well have read: "We'll Have Manhattan," by Richard Rodgers and Lorenz Hart.

By this time Rodgers was twenty-three years old and no longer a college student, but he was still living at home without earning his way. He contemplated a job in the infants' wear business (at fifty dollars a week) while readily admitting that he would return to the theater at the first opportunity. His biographic sketches always mention that one of America's greatest songwriters almost ended his career to sell baby clothes! It is an interesting commentary on the vagaries of success that by this time Richard Rodgers had already written, though the public had not yet heard, the melodies to two of his future hits, "Manhattan" and "Here in My Arms."

One spring evening as he sat alone at his parents' home, "my youthful dreams of becoming a composer fading into the air," he received a call from Benjamin Kaye, a lawyer friend who dabbled in show business; Kaye had even collaborated with Rodgers on a song, "Prism, Plums and Prunes," for the show *Up Stage and Down*. Kaye had found an opportunity for Rodgers to write for a revue being put on by a group of young performers. At first Rodgers indignantly refused—no more amateur shows! He quickly recanted when informed that the youngsters were actually professionals from the Theatre Guild's company. They were putting on a musical comedy revue at the Garrick Theatre on an off night to raise money to buy tapestries for a new theater that the guild would soon occupy.

The Theatre Guild—this was by no means the Benjamin School for Girls! Rodgers knew that if he was accepted as composer, his music would be heard by an elite Broadway audience. His career and life were about to take a crucial turn.

4

THE GARRICK GAIETIES

The Theatre Guild had earned a reputation for producing somber, heavy dramas, often by foreign authors. The group, founded in 1918, had no experience with or affinity for musicals, even though its productions were staged in the old Garrick Theatre, the original home of Harrigan and Hart's nineteenth-century musicals. The aim of the guild was to "produce plays of artistic merit not ordinarily produced by the commercial managers." This required financial support, so some of the younger players decided to write a musical-comedy revue to stage on an off night. The guild put up a small amount of money for the show and offered the use of the Garrick. By spring 1925, rehearsals had started, though the group was still looking for someone to write some original music.

After his conversation with Benjamin Kaye, Rodgers auditioned for two cast members: Edith Meiser, who was to write the lyrics, and Romney Brent, one of the principal singers. Meiser and Brent traveled to the elegant West Side, as they put it, to the "spacious" apartment of Dr. William Rodgers. Richard Rodgers sat at an "enormous grand piano" in his living room and played a few songs from his Columbia Varsity Shows. Meiser was unimpressed until Rodgers played "Manhattan." Then they "flipped." She returned to the Garrick and announced, "I have found the boy." Rodgers then auditioned for the guild's directors, Theresa Helburn and Lawrence Langner, who were also impressed. Helburn remembered Rodgers as a modest young man, alone on center stage, playing his songs on an old upright. At Rodgers' urging they even agreed to let Hart write the lyrics.[1]

The Garrick Gaieties opened on the afternoon of May 17, 1925, a Sunday, when the theater was usually dark. Like most revues, the numbers alternated between music and comedy. The regular performance at the Garrick was Ferenc Molnár's The Guardsman, which starred the renowned Alfred Lunt and Lynn Fontanne. Members of the Gaieties cast were to become famous as well: Libby Holman, in her first appearance, had one song; Lee Strasberg, artistic director of Actors Studio, had a minor role, as did Sanford Meisner, who became one of Broadway's most famous drama teachers; and the writer Alvah Bessie appeared in a small part. The featured performers were Sterling Holloway, Betty Starbuck, June Cochrane, Romney Brent, and Edith Meiser. Philip Loeb was the director, and Harold Clurman the stage manager. Herbert Fields taught the cast a few dance steps.

Intended as a spoof of the Theatre Guild's serious pretensions, the Gaieties opened with the number "Soliciting Subscriptions," followed by "Gilding the Guild." Hart's lyrics began:

> We bring drama to your great metropolis.
> We are the little-theatre group.
> Each of us has built a small Acropolis
> To hold our little-theatre troupe.

The song continued in this vein of ridicule:

> We like to serve a mild dish
> Of folklore quaintly childish
> Or something Oscar Wilde-ish.

In the same spirit, Benjamin Kaye wrote a sketch entitled "They Didn't Know What They Were Getting," a parody of Sidney Howard's "They Knew What They

Wanted," a Theatre Guild production that had won a Pulitzer Prize. The big hit was a satire of President and Mrs. Coolidge by Morrie Ryskind. Later performances included another sketch by Ryskind, a satire of the Scopes trial, with the Rodgers and Hart song "And Thereby Hangs a Tale." In this parody two monkeys were played by Lee Strasberg and Sanford Meisner. Rodgers needled them ever after for this inauspicious debut.

William Jennings Bryan died later that year, and the Scopes number had to be dropped, but according to Harold Clurman, Rodgers and Hart quickly replaced it. He recalled that Rodgers produced a melody and hummed it to Hart, who disappeared. A half hour later he reappeared with a lyric scribbled on a piece of scrap paper. (This episode may well have happened, but the song is not further identified; it was probably "It's Quite Enough to Make Me Weep.")

There was also a "Jazz Opera," entitled the "Joy Spreader," which poked fun at Grand Opera; critics called it a howl, but it was later dropped, over Rodgers' objections. The first Rodgers and Hart ballad, "April Fool," was sung by Betty Starbuck and Romney Brent in the first act. It was a pleasant melody, in 2/4 time, but not special. Libby Holman's solo, "Black and White," followed shortly, but Rodgers thought that her singing was flat and later cut the song.

In the second act, Sterling Holloway and June Cochrane sang "Manhattan," which Rodgers described in his memoirs: "Its easygoing strolling melody and ingeniously rhymed lyric related all of the everyday pleasures to be found in New York and didn't require literal or even stylized reproduction. Though the stage was bare except for the two kids, the audience could see and feel everything the song conveyed and they ate it up. . . . If one song can be said to have 'made' Rodgers and Hart, it surely was 'Manhattan.'"[2] The composition was a standard thirty-two bars, and there was nothing unusual in the harmony. The melody emphasized a four-bar phrase that was the foundation for Hart's sparkling portrait of the ordinary sights and sounds of New York:

> We'll have Manhattan,
> The Bronx and Staten
> Island too.
> It's lovely going through
> The zoo.
> It's very fancy
> On old Delancey
> Street, you know.

At this point Rodgers shifted to a new melodic phrase:

The subway charms us so
When balmy breezes blow
To and fro.

He then returned to his basic musical theme:

And tell me what street
Compares with Mott Street
In July?
Sweet pushcarts gently gliding by.

Again Rodgers shifted and introduced a five-bar passage quite different from the preceding themes:

The great big city's a wondrous toy
Just made for a girl and boy.

And, finally, he returned to a restatement of the first four bars:

We'll turn Manhattan
Into an isle of joy.

As with many hit songs that have endured, the words and music have become inseparable. This composition is not only an early example of the symbiosis of the two writers but also a testimony to Hart's irrepressible gifts. One suspects that if the same melody had had an ordinary June-Moon lyric, it would have quietly disappeared. The song was apparently intended mainly for the stage, because there are four sets of lyrics for the refrain. In the third chorus, Hart could not contain himself, giving us:

The city's clamor can never spoil
The dreams of a boy and goil.

The Garrick Gaieties drew good reviews. After the finale, Rodgers wrote, the theater was in an uproar:

I turned around to look at the audience; everyone was standing. Not standing to leave, just standing. Not just standing, either. Standing and clapping, cheering, yelling, stomping, waving and whistling. I turned back to the orchestra and had the boys strike up "Manhattan." The cast sang it. The musicians sang it. Even the audience sang it. After about ten curtain calls, the houselights went on, but still no one wanted to go. At last, slowly and hesitantly, the audience filed out, as if unwilling to leave to memory an experience that was so vivid and exciting.[3]

The excitement continued backstage. Lorenz Hart was jumping up and down, rubbing his hands together, and shouting that the show would run a year. This shattered the mood, because the show was scheduled to run for only one more performance. The next morning, however, the reviews were impressive. The *New York Times* (May 18, 1925) reviewer wrote that "the lyrics were mature and intelligently contrived. Rodgers' music was tuneful and well adapted to the needs of the entertainment," though the review failed to mention "Manhattan." Ward Morehouse, writing for the *New York Herald Tribune*, commented: "Most of the lyrics are particularly bright, and the music is appealingly tuneful." Robert Benchley, who was romancing Betty Starbuck, reviewed the show for *Life*: "By miles the cleverest and most civilized show in town. Rodgers and Hart's music and lyrics, together with the burlesque sketches and the playing by a half dozen hitherto unknown youngsters, should be a standing taunt and source of chagrin to those uptown revue managers who keep putting on the same old thing each year."

Rodgers and Hart had arrived. The review in *Variety* (May 27, 1925) referred to Rodgers and Hart as the boys who had been "hitting around" Broadway for some time, "bright fellows" who had not been able to click with anything "smartly." This show gave them their outlet, and "their stuff clicked here like a colonel's heels at attention." The reviewer, however, only alluded to a "song kidding Manhattan as a summer resort." In a display of nerve often reserved for youth, Rodgers and others persuaded Theresa Helburn to close *The Guardsman* and mount a full-scale production of the *Gaieties*. After learning that the Lunts were about to leave in any case, Helburn agreed. The revised version reopened on June 8, 1925, and ran through November 28. Rodgers was paid eighty-nine dollars a week to work as the conductor and a flat fifty dollars for his songs. A second important Rodgers song, "Sentimental Me," was added in the renewed version, though it probably had been written earlier. On his original manuscript Rodgers wrote, "This is a duet and the rhythm should be rather well marked. We are going to plug this one."

Success breeds success. Rodgers and Hart were now in a position to disinter *Sweet Rebel*, which they had written the previous year. The show, about the Revolutionary War in New York, was inspired by an actual incident. Mrs. Robert Murray, of Murray Hill, had diverted the British generals Howe and Clinton by offering them tea and cakes, giving General Putnam's forces time to escape on the Bloomingdale Road to join George Washington on the Heights of Harlem.

Hart had one day spied the plaque at 37th Street and Madison Avenue commemorating the event and felt that there might be a musical in the story. It had the right elements: conflict, the tension of the war, and a fictitious love interest: Betsy, Mrs. Murray's niece, would fall in love with an aide to General Howe. The alleged tea party could be transformed into a formal ball.

The team had completed a script by September 1924, though finding financial backing for an eighteenth-century period piece in the middle of the Roaring Twenties was still a problem. Lew Fields had been approached but was unimpressed with the idea of a musical in costume. Helen Ford had also tried, unsuccessfully, to get backing from John Murray Anderson. Ford, a dainty, attractive blonde, had broken into Broadway in Oscar Hammerstein's first musical, *Always You*, in January 1920. She was married to George Denham Ford, a successful producer and author, though she and Rodgers had a romantic involvement. Ford was intrigued by the show, mainly because she would play the lead.

After the success of the *Gaieties*, Ford resumed her campaign to find support for *Sweet Rebel*. This time she approached her husband, who agreed to produce the show and help raise the financing. And this time Anderson agreed to direct. The show, now retitled *Dearest Enemy*, opened at the Knickerbocker on September 18, 1925, and ran for 286 performances.

It was an elaborate production, with a large chorus of British redcoats and women in eighteenth-century ball gowns. Ford, playing Betsy, actually entered clad only in a barrel, having been surprised by a British officer (played by Charles Purcell) while swimming. They, of course, fall in love.

The switch from a revue to a book musical was not without its risks. In the mid-1920s the revue was still a popular form, depending on little more than costumes, scenery, good music, and an occasional comic sketch. Sometimes a loose theme tied the acts together, but this was by no means necessary. According to the *New York Times* (October 17, 1926), the opening-night audience might include cosmopolitan first-nighters along with "wealthy gunmen, boulevardiers, the bootleggers, gamblers, and all the more affluent of Broadway's picturesque world." Book musicals were a different category. The audience usually had greater expectations and would be apt to be more critical and less demonstrative in their reactions. They expected some semblance of a plot, singers who could act a little, a splash of comedy, and some effort to integrate the songs and dances. The hit musical of that year was the lively but frothy *No, No, Nanette*, by Irving Caesar and Vincent Youmans.

The role of the director was obviously important, and Rodgers and Hart were lucky to recruit Anderson, who had been educated in Europe and had studied with Max Reinhardt. He was described as the type who knew "something about everything which goes into a show."[4] His reputation grew out of his sophisticated use of costumes, lighting, and scenery for his own *Greenwich Village Follies*. His contributions in this regard were duly noted in the favorable reviews of *Dearest Enemy*.

Two Rodgers and Hart songs were brought over from the remnants of *Winkle Town*, but the major hit was "Here in My Arms," which they had written for *Sweet Rebel*. It was sung three times during the show, which was risky because of the highly repetitive melody. But as Rodgers pointed out, the context changed each time: "Repetition should be used not merely to drum a song into an audience's collective, but to make the relationship between the leading characters more meaningful through music."[5]

This song was an early example of Rodgers' talents. It starts with a four-bar phrase (which tunesmith detectives pointed out was the same melody as "Nobody Knows the Trouble I've Seen"). Rodgers gave the melody a different harmony and introduced similar nuances in the bridge, which were enough to make the song memorable. Rodgers, like a good chef, had the knack of adding just the right touches of spice.

"Here in My Arms" was also an early example of Hart's approach to lyrics. He explained that he sought out the dominant musical figure, in this case the last beat of the second bar and the first three notes of the third bar. He then thought up a lyric or phrase to fit the emphasis of the music—what came to mind here was "a-dor-able"—and filled in around this basic word. The lyric for the four-bar theme runs: "Here in my arms, it's adorable."

The other love song of the show was "Bye and Bye," a rather ordinary melody that ascends and descends along the notes of an F major triad and then repeated a tone higher against a G minor chord. This shift of a phrase by one interval had been employed for years in popular songwriting. But the Rodgers melody is enhanced by Hart's extraordinary rhyming ability and a simple yet charming sentiment:

> Bye and bye,
> Not now but bye and bye,
> Somehow we'll try and buy
> A little nest.

The humor was supplied by a flashback to the founding of New York (New Amsterdam) and a sketch about its patron, Peter Stuyvesant. The song "Sweet Peter" was a clever play on words by Hart:

Sweet Peter, sweet Peter!
Had a wife and couldn't cheat her.

The reason for Peter's failure at infidelity was that he could not sneak off, because his wooden leg would "boom-boom-boom" and give him away.

The show was Hart's first full-blown exposure. Several songs were cut, but Hart's remaining lyrics established him not only as a clever manipulator of rhymes but as a master of cynical, bittersweet sentiments as well. In "War Is War," he wrote for the female chorus:

Hooray!
We're going to be compromised.

The critics liked the show.[6] It was closer to an operetta than to a musical, wrote the New York Times. It bloomed with a "fresh charm," although the humor was rather "banal." Rodgers and Hart's fellow Columbian Herman Mankiewicz, writing in the New Yorker, found the book "dull" but the lyrics and music "fascinating." The noted critic Alexander Woollcott pronounced the score "fresh and pleasing." Variety decided that, compared with several other current musicals, it was a "good buy at $3.30." The most sweeping praise came from Frank Vreeland of the New York Telegram, who wrote that Rodgers would go far as a composer and that the team of Rodgers, Fields, and Hart "someday . . . will form the American counterpart of the once-great triumvirate of Bolton, Wodehouse and Kern." The show lasted through the season and went on tour.

This success changed Rodgers' life. His income went from virtually nothing to several hundred dollars per week. He could now afford the best restaurants and nightclubs. He bought himself a new car, a La Salle coupe. And, according to one writer, all the women he dated were "beautiful, intelligent, dynamic in personality." His other new friends were among the elite of show business. Richard Rodgers was famous.

Later in his life he complained—only half-seriously—that it had all come too easily. For the sake of a romantic tale, he should have suffered: his parents should have bitterly opposed his career in show business; his first show should have failed. He repeated this litany often, and it may well be that the ease of his early successes made Rodgers too self-conscious and led him to assume a diffident air about his work (even though he took it quite seriously). That he did not suffer and that he was well educated and firmly grounded in music apparently made him somewhat resentful of the colorful stories of other composers. Hart once pointed to the tapestries in the lobby of the Theatre Guild's new home and commented that he and Rodgers were responsible for them. Rodgers countered, "Hell, they're responsible for *us!*"

Whatever his feelings, Rodgers did not rest on his achievements. Like Jerome Kern and Oscar Hammerstein, Rodgers and Hart were tied almost completely to the stage. Neither Hart nor Rodgers served an apprenticeship on Tin Pan Alley, nor did they try to write single hit songs. Instead, they devoted their efforts to the production at hand, whether a book musical or a revue. One unfortunate result was that for every solid, memorable song perhaps half a dozen songs fell by the wayside. Other theater composers were in the same situation. Because there were no cast albums in the 1920s, only the songs that popular performers chose to record had a life after the stage. These artists occasionally guessed wrong and recorded a melody that did not gain popular acceptance. Fortunately, one can hear some of the more arcane Rodgers and Hart selections in reissues of these recordings.

Having made their mark in 1925–26, Rodgers and Hart found themselves in the mainstream of the Jazz Age. They had missed the Ragtime era that had influenced Irving Berlin, George Gershwin, and even Jerome Kern. Rodgers and Hart were products of the Roaring Twenties, and their music and lyrics—witty and urbane, with a certain bounce and liveliness—showed it. In this sense they were closer to Cole Porter—or rather Cole Porter was closer to Rodgers and Hart, because he came back to Broadway two years later.

Their work was inventive but not yet innovative. The elegant match of words and music that was so perfect in "Manhattan" was repeated in song after song. Generally, Rodgers wrote the music first and then Hart set a lyric. Sometimes they agreed on a title, and occasionally Hart wrote a few lines first. Which was more important? Did it matter whether words or music was written first? Oscar Hammerstein, an interested witness, suggested the following: "Words are easier to analyze. Everyone speaks and writes words. Few can write music. Its creation is a mystery. . . . We are made sad or happy, romantic, thoughtful, disturbed or peaceful by someone else's singing heart. To me this is a most exciting and inexplicable phenomena."[7] Hammerstein also believed that Rodgers and Hart's quick success illustrated "how eagerly the public runs to meet something new and good, surfeited as they are with stale and imitative professionalism."

Nevertheless, the collaboration between the mismatched Rodgers and Hart was perplexing. Rodgers was likable and clearly enjoyed a good time, but he nevertheless tended to business, promptly and efficiently. As his successes grew, he tended to settle down. He was no prude, and he occasionally referred to "tearing up" the town. He drank, perhaps more than he should have, and he and Hart often attended the same parties. In the beginning at least, Hart was the senior partner, and his name came first on the program and sheet music. Later that would be reversed.

Both were serious about their work, but, as Hammerstein noted, Rodgers was a planner, Hart was the antithesis. Hart often referred to Rodgers as either the principal or the professor. One of Rodgers' nonmusical collaborators later caustically called him saintly. Rodgers did not seem to mind: he often quipped that he was the big s.o.b. of the duo. But later, when he worked with Hammerstein, he could say that he was the small s.o.b. A number of performers would bear witness to Rodgers' description of himself.

On the other hand, everyone was charmed by Hart. He was very short, with a large head and a small torso, and his gnomelike qualities endeared him to almost everyone who met him. Edith Meiser, their collaborator in *The Garrick Gaieties*, reminisced: "Dick we were very fond of, but Larry was adored. He was a pet. He was very, very special. That's not to downgrade Dick at all. We were terribly fond of Dick. In a funny way you wanted to protect Larry, this funny ugly little man who was so dear."[8] Richard Rodgers' wife, Dorothy, vividly remembered Hart. When she entered her apartment, the familiar smell of an Upmann cigar would warn her that her husband and Larry Hart were at work. "In my mind's eye I can see Larry, leaning against the wall of our living room, scribbling the lyrics in soft black pencil on yellow foolscap. His head, the paper and the lyrics were all slanted uphill." She recalled one occasion on which Hart stood before their studio window, gazing out, preoccupied, while his cigar burned a hole in her curtain. Whenever something like this happened, Hart was so apologetic that Dorothy Rodgers ended up feeling that it was somehow her fault.

More and more Hart showed signs of unhappiness. He drank too much, and those around him were aware of his homosexuality. He was apparently tormented by the thought that his mother, Frieda, a stolid German woman, would learn of his sexual orientation. The director Harold Clurman, who knew Hart from *The Garrick Gaieties*, later wrote that Hart was horrified by his own homosexuality and felt thoroughly disgraced, having been brought up in a stereotypical Jewish family where such things were unheard of. Clurman felt that Hart was determined to punish himself. Hart's homosexuality remains a source of controversy and mystery. Over the years Hart proposed to several women, all of whom turned him down. His lifestyle became more secretive and dissolute. He would disappear for weeks, his whereabouts often unknown.

Rodgers never publicly acknowledged Hart's homosexuality until well after Hart's death. And although Rodgers was the source of the oft-repeated stories that Hart would simply disappear for days at time, he admitted that he usually knew where Hart was during these famous long disappearances. Some years after Hart's death, Rodgers wrote that Hart took pride in only one thing: his theater work. He did not seem to care about his appearance, where he lived, or his social or financial status, but he did care "tremendously" about "the turn of a phrase and the mathematical exactness of an interior rhyme."

Once he completed a lyric, Hart was extremely stubborn about changing it. This unyielding quality led to arguments that Rodgers described as "furious, blasphemous and frequent," though both understood that the arguments were academic, not personal. Rodgers likened their relationship to "two volatile chemicals in a retort," but the "explosion" resulted in a series of great songs. There can be little doubt that Rodgers' melodies were enhanced by Hart's brilliant lyrics. Both artists were extremely competent, and both wrote quickly. Hart could work under almost any circumstances, and Rodgers was always bursting with energy and ideas. Rodgers claimed that he had to write the music first because that was the only way to force Hart to concentrate on their work.

As Hart's lyrics became more jaundiced, Rodgers seemed to compensate instinctively. Rodgers believed that the lyrics written by the more mature Hart were better than his earlier ones. Hart began to substitute warmth for wit, and although he did not know how not to be clever, he began to show off less. On the other hand, Rodgers' talent for creating bright melodies occasionally toggled Hart's fine sense of humor and ignited his incomparable rhyming ability, which in turn produced some of the funnier—and finer—moments in American popular music.

In other words, they were a perfect team.

5

THE GIRL FRIEND

The success of their first two major shows earned Rodgers and Hart a passport to the world of the musical theater. It was an arena for the talented and therefore a place where they were likely to succeed.

It was also an arena shaped by commerce. Few shows were produced because of their artistic merit or social message, at least not until the 1930s. Nor were songs published for their special grace or charm. What the public wanted were entertaining shows, singable lyrics, and danceable melodies, occasionally leavened by some comic novelties.

Popular music did not automatically flow from the stage to the hit parade. Most of the so-called hit songs came from the warrens of

Tin Pan Alley. The "Alley" referred to various locations in Manhattan, where many of the music publishing firms were housed. A reporter, who also happened to be a songwriter, had given the trade its colorful name around 1900, complaining that what he heard through the open windows around Union Square sounded like pounding on tin—a quaint story, if true. Tin Pan Alley was where talented young songwriters, such as George Gershwin, plied their trade, massaging their pianos in tiny cubicles where performers could stop and shop for new material. Vaudeville entertainers haunted the publishing houses, badgering the song pluggers and shopping for a hit that would be their ticket into the more ornate and respectable revues.

With the increasing sales of popular sheet music, the growth of 78 rpm recordings, and the explosion of radio, music was suddenly a lucrative business. Gone were the days when budding young songwriters had to sell their music for a few dollars. A single piece of sheet music usually sold for about twenty-five cents, a few cents of which went to the composer for royalties, depending on the arrangement with the publisher. Harms, Inc., brought out six songs from *Dearest Enemy* (on the sheet music, Hart's name is listed before Rodgers'), and the team began earning money that continued even after the show closed.

A remarkable number of memorable songs were written in the 1920s. The most popular were bright and bouncy, reflecting the optimism of the times. Milton Ager wrote Al Smith's and Franklin D. Roosevelt's political theme song, "Happy Days Are Here Again," and he also wrote "Ain't She Sweet." Like Irving Berlin, Ager was of Russian immigrant stock, but unlike Berlin he was a serious student of classical music. Lew Brown, a member of the trio of De Sylva, Brown, and Henderson, was also from a family of Russian immigrants. Ray Henderson studied at the conservatory of music in Chicago, which was no impediment to writing "Five Foot Two, Eyes of Blue." B. G. "Buddy" De Sylva, the son of a vaudeville performer and a sometime student at the University of Southern California, wrote the words to "If You Knew Susie" for Eddie Cantor and to "California, Here I Come" for Al Jolson. As George Gershwin's partner he wrote the lyrics for "Somebody Loves Me," produced for George White's *Scandals*. Earlier he had crafted the words to "Look for the Silver Lining," Jerome Kern's trademark.

These songwriters were obviously talented, and the best of them usually gravitated toward the musical theater. Many, however, if not on Tin Pan Alley as such, worked as independent songwriters who remained available for shows, vaudeville acts, and, later, the movies. Some of America's best songwriters of this era—including Richard Whiting ("Ain't We Got Fun") and Walter Donaldson ("Carolina in the Morning")—fit this category. Harry Ruby ("Three Little Words") was among those who graduated to Broadway and then to Hollywood; he wrote a score for the Marx Brothers.

Musical craftsmanship was not a prerequisite to success, nor was musical illiteracy necessarily a bar. What mattered was capturing the fickle tastes of the public. At the same time, popular music was settling into a formula. Usually the length of the songs was thirty-two bars, divided into what was called an A-A-B-A structure. The first eight bars were the major theme (A); this was repeated in the following eight bars (A); then came the release, or bridge (B), eight bars of a theme that differed strongly from the first theme and then gracefully returned to it for the final eight bars (A). Although songwriters did not relish these rules or forms, the potential success of the formula could not be denied. Its virtue was that because the melody was repeated three times, the more engaging ones stuck in the public's mind. This rigid model put a premium on musical talent, however. Too often the songs were merely repetitive. The literate Hart and the musically imaginative Rodgers were talented enough to exploit the standard forms when necessary. They had the skill to be innovative while remaining within the confines of public acceptability.

Fortunately for Rodgers and Hart, the popular appetite for songs changed radically during and after World War I. Popular music tended to reflect society, and before World War I the musical stage had been dominated by shows imported from Europe. The great influx of immigrants to the larger cities of the East Coast undermined this dominance, however, because musical theater was now open to talent of any variety—it was a world attractive to immigrants and Jews. Indeed, Eastern European Jews began to dominate all phases of popular music, including publishing, performing, and writing. At the same time, songwriters like Berlin, Kern, and Gershwin wanted to write about America: no more stories about merry widows or chocolate soldiers. Rodgers and Hart fit in comfortably. *Dearest Enemy* was, after all, about the American Revolution.

The European-derived operettas remained popular, mainly because of Sigmund Romberg's great melodic gifts. But there was also a restless urge for something new and different, and jazz came along to satisfy it. This new musical rage had all the right ingredients: it was hot enough to be ultramodern but was still danceable, singable, and, above all, American. Jazz, with its rhythms in 2/4 and 4/4, challenged the genteel traditions of older music and became the major force molding American popular music. The lyrics grew more daring and sophisticated, and strange-sounding harmonies occasionally jumped out at the listener. European popular music was smooth and romantic, comfortable and reassuring. American music was charged and eager; it was sharp rhythm and exaggerated syncopation. Ragtime had been syncopated, but, befitting its name, was rough and jerky. The new, smoother syncopation was used for surprise and emphasis, and it was played to a steadier and harsher rhythm.

The sound of this new music also changed performances. Syncopated rhythms simply did not sound right played on a violin. Jazz called for more trumpets, even more trombones, woodwinds, some drums, and, yes, that musical pariah, the saxophone. With the addition of a piano and perhaps a banjo, this new instrumental combination made even the old-time songs sound refreshed.

By 1925, when Rodgers and Hart made their breakthrough, the leading dance orchestras were being heard in, say, the Palmer House in Chicago and the Muehlebach Hotel in Kansas City; on the stages of the Orpheum circuit; and even at Aeolian Hall on 48th Street in Manhattan. Paul Whiteman crowned himself King of Jazz, and indeed his various orchestras did boast some genuine jazz artists, notably the legendary cornetist Bix Beiderbecke. In February 1924, Whiteman sought to prove his title when he staged "An Experiment in Modern Music," a jazz concert that traced the history of the form. It is remembered for a single twenty-minute piano piece by young George Gershwin, who, commissioned by Whiteman, composed and performed *Rhapsody in Blue* for the extravaganza.

Authentic jazz—that is, the music played largely by black musicians in small clubs often frequented by white patrons—was only a small part of the Jazz Age. Broadway was largely the preserve of white males. Of the few women songwriters, most were lyricists. All-black shows began to make an occasional appearance on Broadway, usually as revues, beginning with *Shuffle Along*, with music by Noble Sissle and Eubie Blake. Ironically, the music for the longest-running black show, *Blackbirds of 1928*, was by the white team Jimmy McHugh and Dorothy Fields, who wrote "I Can't Give You Anything But Love" for Bill "Bojangles" Robinson. Gradually jazz began to influence the sweeter-sounding orchestras, as evidenced by recordings of Beiderbecke and his "gang" from the Whiteman orchestra playing Rodgers and Hart's songs.

Rodgers and Hart, however, never made themselves part of the jazz culture. Rodgers was less influenced by jazz than were Gershwin or Berlin. He did not frequent jazz clubs, at least not to hear the music, or go to Harlem in "ermines and pearls," as one of Hart's lyrics put it. Unlike Harold Arlen, Rodgers showed no affinity for the blues and no interest in hot music. His focus was on the theater itself. Even so, his melodies became popular with jazz artists and were recorded by many small jazz groups. Such unsolicited popularity may have prompted Rodgers and Hart to write a song, some years later, entitled "I Like to Recognize the Tune." Rodgers even had the temerity to comment that he saw no difference between the clarinet playing of Ted Lewis and Benny Goodman! Nevertheless, rhythm was king, because faddish dances like the Charleston, the Bunny Hug, and the Black Bottom depended completely on the exaggerated emphasis on the first and third beats of a measure.

Catering to public taste was never important to Rodgers and Hart. Neither was drawn to the commercial aspects of their profession, and as long as they made enough money to cover their creature comforts they paid no special attention to business. Rodgers was eventually forced to treat finances more seriously as his success ballooned, bringing in substantial sums of money over the years.

As Rodgers and Hart frequently proclaimed, they were determined to write integrated musicals that tied together words, music, and plot, and thus to emulate the shows that Jerome Kern had inaugurated at the Princess Theatre. But from 1925 through 1930 harsh financial realities dictated that their shows be light-hearted comedies, which were what audiences wanted and what producers invested in. Fortunately, Rodgers and Hart were young enough and ambitious enough to adapt.

Their productions of the 1920s were not memorable and are seldom revived; most were considered successful only by the prevailing Broadway standards. A run of 200 performances usually meant a profit (*Dearest Enemy* ran for 286), and a show that ran for 400 or 500 was considered a hit. Jerome Kern's *Sunny*, the biggest hit of 1925, reached 511 performances, and Sigmund Romberg's *The Student Prince* was on the boards more than 600 times. What distinguished Rodgers and Hart's shows, along with the shows of the other major writers, was not the fluffy plots or cardboard characters but the scintillating melodies and the sharp, clever lyrics. This gift is what made Rodgers and Hart worthy competitors of Kern, Gershwin, and Berlin.

In the 1920s, Rodgers and Hart were only one of the many new teams vying for recognition among theater audiences. Sixty to seventy years later, of course, the preeminence they established is obvious. Rodgers and Hart even achieved a sort of cult status, much to the surprise of Rodgers, who could never quite understand why a college generation so far removed from his own continued to be entranced by their songs. He had long since taken their words and music for granted and had moved on with his life.

They realized that their chosen profession was a gamble. Songwriters knew that it was unnatural for a character to burst into song in the middle of a scene, and they risked embarrassment if the audience failed to make the mental leap into the world of words and music. The alternative was to abandon hope of integrating words and music and to insert an unrelated song simply as a vehicle for a star—someone like Al Jolson. In such cases the audience did not care, because they had paid to hear Jolson. Whether he was in a clown suit or blackface was incidental. Such an approach was definitely not what Rodgers and Hart wanted.

They chose the so-called book musicals that had become increasingly popular in the 1920s. The music on stage was meant to bear some relationship to the story. Jerome Kern had been striving for this but by and large had failed. Despite the monumental Show Boat of 1927, most of his shows were airy tales (with fabulous music, of course). Rodgers and Hart had failed too, with one notable exception: A Connecticut Yankee, which opened a month before Show Boat. Producers wanted either a show built around a star or a story loaded with hit songs. Rodgers and Hart found themselves writing for shows that were little more coherent or serious than the great hits of that era. The season that featured Dearest Enemy, for example, also included the opening of Rudolf Friml's operetta The Vagabond King and the Gershwin brothers' Tip Toes. Typical of the era was No, No, Nanette, with music by Vincent Youmans and lyrics by Irving Caesar, and their hit song from that show, "Tea for Two." The show would also be remembered for its financial backing: Harry H. Frazee, the show's producer as well as the owner of the Boston Red Sox, sold Babe Ruth to the New York Yankees to raise the money for his musical.

A prime example of the Broadway musical of the 1920s—and the competition that Rodgers and Hart faced—was Good News, which opened a month before A Connecticut Yankee. With its amusing plot and good music, it was the kind of show that might have been written by Rodgers and Hart. It was a good-humored, slightly zany story about the travail of students at good ol' Tait College, with book, lyrics, and music by De Sylva, Brown, and Henderson. Connie, a somewhat bookish coed, is dragooned into tutoring the school's leading athlete so that he can pass his courses and win the big game. They fall in love, but not before singing "The Best Things in Life Are Free" and "Lucky in Love." Along the way the chorus bangs out "Varsity Drag" and "Good News." It ran for 557 performances, rivaling Show Boat's 575 performances.

Lasting success was nevertheless elusive. The team of De Sylva, Brown, and Henderson lasted only a few years. Many songwriters and lyricists floated between shows and songs. George and Ira Gershwin were a notable exception, and Cole Porter and Irving Berlin, of course, were their own lyricists. Otherwise, even a successful team—such as Kern and Hammerstein—was broken off or diverted. Kern worked with several lyricists: he wrote six shows with Hammerstein and five each with Otto Harbach, Anne Caldwell, and P. G. Wodehouse. In 1929–30 the versatile lyricist Yip Harburg wrote songs with ten composers. In contrast, Rodgers and Hart's twenty years of collaboration is remarkable.

The musical scene was exploding. Ziegfeld and his elaborate *Follies*, then nearing its twentieth anniversary, were still going strong. Earl Carroll's *Vanities* was still playing each year, but the Shuberts' *Passing Show* had expired. George White's *Scandals* of 1925 featured the last of the five scores that George Gershwin wrote for that show, though the revues continued with new composers. Irving Berlin's *Music Box Revues* had closed after several successful years.

Sunny and *Show Boat*, *Oh, Kay!* and *Tip Toes*, *Cocoanuts* and *The Music Box Revues*; Kern, Hammerstein, the Gershwins, and Berlin; Marilyn Miller, Gertrude Lawrence, and Helen Morgan—this was the Broadway that Rodgers and Hart sought to conquer. Almost immediately following *Dearest Enemy* they plunged ahead with another show, also based on a book by Herbert Fields, but this time produced by Lew Fields, who had reentered their lives. The elder Fields had been wary of *Dearest Enemy* mainly because it was a period piece and, as such, held no opportunities for his brand of comedy. To please him and to gain his support, the trio of Rodgers, Hart, and Fields came up with a contemporary jazz theme. They worked together on the top floor of Fields' brownstone, all the while politely ignored by the older man. Nevertheless, he did decide to produce their new show, *The Girl Friend*, and he enrolled as a coproducer the owner of the Vanderbilt Theater, Lyle Andrews.

Rodgers and Hart devised their plot around the sport of six-day bicycle racing, a fad of the time. The show was designed to feature the talents of the comedy team of Sammy White and Eva Puck. Leonard, the aspiring bike racer, is a naive county boy, played by White; he is encouraged by his trainer and sweetheart, Mollie, played by Puck. Mollie, who is the daughter of a former bicycle champion, contrives to get the support of a well-known promoter to sponsor Leonard. Her artifice is exposed, and she is blackmailed by the promoter's sister and forced to give up Leonard. Of course, Leonard wins the great race and all ends well.

The production was supervised by Lew Fields, and the orchestrations were by Maurice de Packh, who later became an outstanding orchestrator in Hollywood. *The Girl Friend* opened March 17, 1926, at the Vanderbilt and became Rodgers and Hart's third straight success, running until December 4, 1926, for 301 performances. Two important songs emerged in the first act: Puck and White sang "The Girl Friend" and introduced the show's major hit, "Blue Room." The third notable song, "Why Do I?", was sung by June Cochrane, from *The Garrick Gaieties*.

The response was enthusiastic. The New York Times review had strong praise for Eva Puck and the show itself: "It is a generally captivating musical comedy. [Rodgers and Hart] have supplied a number of very agreeable tunes that contain probably what is known as a song hit or two and adroit and well-fashioned rhymes." Alan Dale, in the New York American, went further: "What I liked best was its music. This WAS music, instead of molasses. There was a ditty called 'The Blue Room' which should be sung to exhaustion, while 'The Girl Friend' has melody, quaint orchestration and decided lilt. . . . A nice cosy evening." Some reviewers went out of their way to note the deplorable state of the current musical scene. Robert Benchley wrote, "Those of us calamity howlers who have been worrying about the low state of musical comedy, were pleased by Rodgers and Hart." Abel Green, writing in Variety, concluded that "considerably more is anticipated from Rodgers and Hart, who, as a team, are touted as an American Gilbert and Sullivan." This was extraordinary praise for a team that had had only two modest successes. To put them even tentatively in the league of Gilbert and Sullivan was testimony to their talent.[1]

The critics were right in one respect: in this show the outlines of a unique Rodgers and Hart style began to appear. "Blue Room" was later singled out as the first wholly distinctive Rodgers song because of a stylistic device that would reappear throughout his career: the use of two or three repeated notes as a basic theme, with phrases built around them. In analyzing "Blue Room," Rodgers wrote that the repeated pattern coincided with Hart's repeated use of "room," as in blue room, new room, ballroom, and small room. Hart exploited the melody to give an added sharpness to the lyric; then, in the final eight bars, they abandoned this link, lest it become too repetitive.

Another dimension of this song is worthy of note: in the release they skillfully used a scale, stretching almost an octave, which builds in momentum and is finally relieved by a graceful phrase that eventually leads back to the refrain. Rodgers often resorted to some form of scale, whether ascending or descending; the verse of "Manhattan" is an example. "Blue Room" became a Rodgers and Hart staple. In its original performance it was somewhat livelier than in the silky versions of later years (it was revived to good effect in the 1950s by Mel Tormé, though Rodgers did not like that version). The year following its introduction Lorenz Hart himself lampooned its optimism in another song, "Where's That Rainbow?", which caustically asked, "Where's that blue room they sing about?" It seems likely that "Blue Room" was written during rehearsals of The Girl Friend, for it is not in the original libretto.

The title song had a contemporary sound, with a strong Charleston-like beat that builds around an ascending rhythmic phrase. It was an unusual composition for Rodgers, who wrote few songs with such a dominant rhythm. Along with Mack and Johnson's original "Charleston," "The Girl Friend" became a sort of theme song for the Roaring Twenties.

In spite of the favorable reviews, the box office returns were below expectations, which led Rodgers, Hart, and Fields to suspend their royalties in order to keep the show alive. Soon, however, the show caught on, in part because of the popularity of the songs. It was a success not only in its original Broadway incarnation but also as a road show. Londoners loved it even though the original score had been eviscerated for that production.

Even before they were assured of *The Girl Friend*'s future, Rodgers and Hart agreed, reluctantly, to try a new edition of *The Garrick Gaieties*. Rodgers had been dubious when Theresa Helburn proposed the idea, fearing that no sequel could measure up to the freshness of the original. Partly out of sentiment and partly out of gratitude for what they owed the Theatre Guild, they agreed to try a new revue. An early number in the new show, a song titled "We Can't Be as Good as Last Year," reflected their doubts:

> We've lost all that artless spirit
> With our Broadway veneer.
> Then it was play, but we're old hams today,
> So we can't be as good as last year.

The new show, again directed by Philip Loeb, opened at the Garrick Theatre on May 10 and ran until October 9, 1926. This time the stage manager was Lee Strasberg, who succeeded Harold Clurman from the first edition. The show, like the previous one, spoofed the Guild's more serious productions. The second edition opened with "Six Little Plays," a satire on Bernard Shaw's *Arms and the Man*. This skit was set to music, and Hart's lyrics were devastating. Hart set the tone in the main refrain:

> Each little play has passed away —
> Some died because the public
> scorned 'em.
> They met their fate
> And got the gate
> Though all the learned critics
> mourned 'em.

For *Arms and the Man* he wrote:

My pretty play,
Shaw's witty play,
Sighed like the rest,
Tried like the rest,
Died like the rest.

This time the skits were intended to be even more up-to-date, and there was more music. The musical director was Rodgers' sometime mentor Roy Webb, but Rodgers conducted opening night. The big number was a satire on current musical comedies, entitled "Rose of Arizona," needling *Rose Marie*. It included a parody of Jerome Kern's famous "Till the Clouds Roll By." Hart's comic version was called "It May Rain." The lyric of the refrain began: "It may rain when the sun stops shining." Another comic song in the mini-operetta was "Mexico," a takeoff on Rudolf Friml's *The Vagabond King*:

Onward, onward to the foe!
Here's to Pershing and to Coolidge,
And to H—! with Mexico!"

Rodgers and Hart were right to worry about comparisons of the first and second versions of the *Gaieties*. In the *New York Times* (May 11, 1926), Brooks Atkinson noted that the warning of the early song carried a grain of truth: the new edition, he wrote, "slumps badly in the second half." Other reviews were also tempered. One concluded: "This year their work seems inferior in quality. None of their numbers matches the excellence of the opening skit." John Mason Brown also believed that it was not up to the previous year's show. Some of the critics, however, trumpeted the second as even better that the first. The newspaper advertisements picked up on this sentiment, featuring a quote by Percy Hammond: "Excels in wit, humor and song any of Broadway's current and similar dissipations." And Atkinson ended his review by giving the show his seal of approval: "Nevertheless, even in its present form it is the most intelligent revue in town."[2]

The *New Yorker* reviewer noted that the second *Gaieties* was not as good as the first but also that the authors not only admitted it but even joked about it. The same reviewer also commented that the cast had assumed a slightly more high-brow air, now calling itself the "Theatre Guild Studio." This meant, the reviewer concluded, "that the music has been written by Richard Rodgersovsky, lyrics by Lorenz Hartachenko. The staging done by Philip Loebovitch and Herbert Field-sieff. And it all takes place in the Garrick Theatre, this side of the River Dnieper, along the retreat from Moscow." More seriously, the reviewer urged the reader to attend, guaranteeing an intelligently funny, tuneful, and brightly informal evening: "There is an elaborate travesty of the everyday musical comedy ["Rose of Arizona"]. At first gulp this sounds terrible. Especially when you have to refer to your program to be sure that it is a travesty. However, it turns out to be gorgeous. . . . The songs, written in that excellent flipperty style which is the outcome of the Rodgers (music) and Hart (lyrics) combination, are tossed about and danced against with great glee. Though none of them seems quite able to tap the inner ear so immediately as did some of the hits of last season."

The *Gaieties* was in danger of floundering, so, in response to criticism, some numbers were dropped and others moved. In June, Brooks Atkinson returned to see the show and wrote about the revisions: "To judge any revue on the basis of the first performance alone is obviously absurd." He found that the changes had in fact strengthened the show, which finally enjoyed a slightly longer run than the first *Garrick Gaieties*.

The one song from the show that endured was generally overlooked by the reviewers: "Mountain Greenery." It was sung by Sterling Holloway, who had introduced "Manhattan." "Mountain Greenery" concentrated on repeated notes more or less connected by scales, a device that had become Rodgers' signature. This oscillating movement created a strong rhythm somewhat akin to that of "The Girl Friend" but without the syncopation of the Charleston. Perhaps it was most noteworthy for Hart's interior rhymes: "beanery, keener-re-ception and greenery." The rest of the score did not survive.

Within two years a core of important Rodgers and Hart works had been created. "Mountain Greenery," "Manhattan," "The Girl Friend," "Blue Room," and "Here in My Arms" remain standards in every revival of the vintage, formative years of Rodgers and Hart. Both lyrics and music were different enough to draw attention. At about this time Rodgers humorously claimed that Hart had not really worked on polishing "Manhattan" but had written it in four minutes and twelve seconds on the back of a "dirty envelope," just before the show opened. Rodgers later offered a more serious anecdote concerning Hart's abilities: "I saw him write a sparkling stanza to 'The Girl Friend' in a hot smelly rehearsal hall, with chorus girls pounding out jazz time, and principals shouting out their lines. In half an hour he fashioned something with so many healthy chuckles in it that I just couldn't believe he had written it in one evening." [3]

In the summer of 1926, Rodgers turned twenty-four; he was several years younger than Jerome Kern was when he embarked on his legendary Princess Theatre series. Gershwin was twenty-six when he wrote *Rhapsody in Blue* and the score for *Lady Be Good*. Rodgers was keeping pace, despite several years of frustrating amateur shows. Although Hart's lyrics remain fascinating exercises, it is Rodgers' music that has endured. It is a tribute to their partnership, however, that they are always linked as Rodgers and Hart.

By the mid-1920s the trend was for American musicals to invade Britain, reversing several decades of British domination of American theater. British producers were now on the lookout for American productions, either to find established shows that could travel across the ocean or to recruit new talent.

The benefactors of Rodgers and Hart were two British stars, Jack Hulburt and his wife, Cicely Courtneidge. They were performing in New York in their own revue, *By the Way,* which had opened on December 28, 1925, the same night as the Gershwins' *Tip Toes.* Hulburt was a singer and dancer whom Rodgers described as an "ebullient Englishman with a half-moon smile." Courtneidge was the daughter of Cecil Courtneidge, a well-known London producer. The couple hoped to become producers and wanted to enlist an American team. They had a book adapted by Harry Ruby and Bert Kalmar, and they approached Rodgers and Hart to do an original score. (The book was later rewritten by Ronald Jeans.)

Lorenz Hart wrote that Hulburt and Courtneidge agreed that musical comedy had become an American monopoly, whereas the English forte was the revue. "The English composer," Hart wrote, "strives to imitate American jazz, and, because his feet do not touch American soil, he falls just short. . . . English comedies are too light. The music is too feathery."

The story offered to Rodgers and Hart concerned a beautiful tennis champion, known as the Lido Lady, also the title of the show. Her father is determined that she marry an outstanding sportsman; her hopeful suitor tries every sport but fails. In the end, he prevails and wins her. The show's hit song was "Here in My Arms," imported from *Dearest Enemy* and interpolated in the first act. The second act featured a song by Henderson, Brown, and De Sylva, "It All Depends on You." The *Times* of London concluded that the story was "always interesting" and that "the music, by Mr. Richard Rodgers, is always tuneful."

Rodgers and Hart left New York together for London in mid-summer 1925, after Mortimer Rodgers' wedding. They decided to make a grand tour, and because the Lido was to be the stage locale of their prospective show, they included Venice in their itinerary. They sailed on the *Conte Biancomano,* which docked at the Bay of Naples, and from Sorrento they went to Milan and then drove across the Dolomites to Venice. They did in fact go to the Lido, where Rodgers noticed a remarkably beautiful woman. While in Venice they ran into Noel Coward, who took them to Cole Porter's cabana. Porter promptly invited them to dinner.

Porter had decided to stay in Paris after World War I. There he met his future wife, Linda Lee Thomas, the widely heralded beauty who turned out to be the very woman Rodgers had seen on the Lido. With residences in France and Italy, the Porters settled into the high society of Europe. Their circle included royalty from various extinct empires of Europe, some of Porter's friends from Yale, some of Broadway's rising songwriters and performers, and Europe's political and literary elite.

Rodgers and Hart were taken by gondola to Porter's residence, the Palazzo Rezzonico. Rodgers, only vaguely aware of Porter's background and musical abilities, was surprised at dinner by Porter's astute observations on the Broadway scene. Rodgers suggested that Porter try Broadway and was embarrassed to learn that Porter had already written a Broadway revue, *Hitchy-koo of 1919*. Porter then confided to Rodgers that he had learned the secret of writing hits: "I'll write Jewish music."[4] Rodgers later commented that although some of Porter's melodies were eastern Mediterranean (for example, "Night and Day"), he could not help but note that some of Broadway's best "Jewish" music was written by an Episcopalian from Peru, Indiana.

Rodgers and Hart returned to London that summer for *Lido Lady*; for some still unexplained reason, they found Jack Hulburt quite cool toward them. Rodgers was dissatisfied with the production as well as the personal treatment he received. Hart gave an interview to the *New York Times* in which he said that they had five weeks to familiarize themselves with their surroundings and to find out what London audiences wanted to see. Their task was facilitated by the fact that "London is mad about American music of the lighter sort." Hart was impressed with the different atmosphere. There was no mad rushing through work, and there were stops for tea. But the "vibrating energy" of opening might was missing, perhaps because the tryouts were long, sometimes running up to nine weeks. On the whole, the show was proving to be frustrating.

Rodgers became bored and announced that he was leaving early, a decision that turned out to be more important than anything connected with *Lido Lady*. Rodgers and Hart sailed on the *Majestic* in late September. Coming on board in Cherbourg were Benjamin Feiner, Sr., his wife, and their daughter, Dorothy. Rodgers had seen Dorothy from time to time, but now a shipboard romance developed. She was then seventeen and returning to America to enroll at Wellesley.[5]

Back in New York, the romance continued with a few nights of dining and dancing before Dorothy left for Boston. A correspondence then began, and through it Rodgers revealed some of the pleasures and frustrations of his profession as he prepared for two new shows. During the Christmas holidays Dorothy returned to New York, where she was escorted by the composer himself to the opening of a new Rodgers and Hart musical. She returned to college shortly thereafter, and Rodgers and Hart made a second trip to London, where *Lido Lady* had become an unexpected success.

Dorothy Feiner had fallen in love. Her brother, in whom she had confided and who had grown up with the Rodgers brothers, assured her that she would get over him, as many others had done. Indeed, Rodgers was a highly eligible young bachelor who was attracted to women, just as they were to him. In New York and London he enjoyed an active social life, though no flaming love affairs or passionate romances had claimed him. His devotion to Dorothy Feiner grew stronger and created a new dimension in his life.

6

PEGGY-ANN

When Richard Rodgers was eight, the great comedian Marie Dressler scored a triumph in a musical called *Tillie's Nightmare*, playing Tillie Blobbs, a maid in a boardinghouse. Tillie's badgering mother prevents her from attending a vaudeville performance with her boyfriend. After others from the boardinghouse leave for the theater, Tillie dreams a series of bizarre and hilarious adventures. She is awakened by the returning crowd, at which point her martinet mother screams, "Tillie!" and the curtain comes down. The show, produced by Lew Fields in 1910, was a tour de force for the formidable Dressler, a master of all forms of comedy.

Fifteen years later Herbert Fields decided that a revival of *Tillie's Nightmare* might make a good musical comedy, and he set to work adapting the original. He made extensive revisions while sticking to the basic plot of the dream sequence. Tillie became Peggy Barnes, and several characters were added. As the partner of Rodgers and Hart, Fields naturally provided for songs aplenty. Lew Fields was intrigued and agreed to produce the show. When Rodgers and Hart returned from London in September 1926, they faced the challenge of turning Fields' script into a musical score.

They resuscitated two songs and wrote sixteen new ones, some of which died before the opening. Because the show, titled *Peggy*, later retitled *Peggy-Ann*, was a combination of music, comedy, fantasy, and burlesque, Rodgers had to stretch for various types of melodies—the usual love songs, a parody or two, pseudo-operatic airs, and even a touch of Gilbert and Sullivan. Hart's sardonic wit was evident throughout, and he outdid himself in the parodies, such as the takeoff on the nightclub hostess Texas Guinan in the song "Peggy":

> Give this little girl a hand!
> Ain't she pretty, ain't she sweet?
> Biggest eyes in all the land.
> Ain't she got the cutest feet?

In the first scene Peggy sings a risqué parody, "A Little Birdie Told Me So," as she dreams she is on sophisticated Fifth Avenue. The melody was very much in the mainstream of the 1920s, lively and syncopated, and again Rodgers used scales as its building blocks. In the prologue, Peggy and her boyfriend, Guy, sing the melody of what was intended to be the musical's major song, "A Tree in the Park." Rodgers created an operatic flavor for the song, and its refrain was similar to that of "Bye and Bye," from *Dearest Enemy*. But regardless of the writers' intention or hopes, it did not survive as the centerpiece.

That honor fell to "Where's That Rainbow?" sung when Peggy (in her dream) finds herself in a department store (where Guy is employed in real life). Originally titled "Where's That Lining?" the song began as a parody of "Look for the Silver Lining":

> Where's that lining you hear about?
> Where's that rainbow they cheer about?

In the final version the two lines were reversed. The refrain is marked "slowly (with tender expression)," and in the published sheet music the melody is written an octave higher, with elaborate arpeggios and other devices that give it a dramatic quality. The idea was to enhance the caustic lyrics with an ironically sweeping melody. The music is not particularly inventive, except for the bridge, where the melody descends chromatically, stepwise, a rather unusual turn for

Rodgers, and a foreshadowing of the approach that Cole Porter would use so effectively in his more famous bridge to "You Do Something to Me" ("do-do, that voo-doo," etc.). "Where's That Rainbow?"—which was meant to be a plaintive lament of Peggy's disillusionment—did not become one of Rodgers and Hart's standards. In the years that followed, various performers increased its tempo. In the film biography of Rodgers and Hart, *Words and Music*, Ann Sothern re-created it as a swinging dance and thereby reminded listeners that it was, in fact, one of the team's better efforts. Another good melody, "Come and Tell Me," was dropped from *Peggy-Ann* but salvaged for a later show.

The female lead is critical in this type of show, and the group had trouble casting the part. Rodgers complained that he had spent one day "trying to squeeze a glimmer of intelligence from the latest applicant." He thought that they had landed Ona Munson, who had appeared in *No, No, Nanette*, but somehow they let her get away. Finally they found that Helen Ford, for whom the show originally was written, would be available when the road company of *Dearest Enemy* closed. She agreed to star, along with the humorous Lulu McConnell (she had played in the road company of *Snapshots*, with Rodgers conducting in the pit). Many of the other featured roles were given to players from the The *Garrick Gaieties*: Edith Meiser played Peggy's mean half sister, Dolores; Lester Cole was Guy; and Betty Starbuck played Lulu McConnell's daughter, Alice Frost, who accompanies Peggy on some of her adventures.

By early November, Rodgers had finished everything but the opening and the finale of *Peggy-Ann*. He reported that he was still working on manuscripts and that it took him about two hours to translate each lead sheet into a piano arrangement. His method involved writing the melody line, with numerical notations for the harmony. Later he transcribed these versions into a fuller treatment for the piano, which in turn was given to the orchestrator to translate into a full orchestral arrangement. Examples of Rodgers' piano arrangements show him to be meticulous and precise, though he confessed that he hated this particular chore. Many composers turned the task over to assistants. In November he spent hours at the piano, sometimes working into the early morning. He took time out to see the Gershwins' new musical *Oh, Kay!* and found the score "absolutely wonderful." By December the full score for *Peggy-Ann* was finished.

Composers rarely had a chance to hear their work performed by an orchestra until quite late in rehearsal, because hiring an orchestra simply to stand by was very expensive. Consequently, cast members learned their songs with piano accompaniment only. This could be disconcerting to newcomers who, having carefully rehearsed with a piano, were suddenly confronted with a conductor and full orchestra. Rodgers did not hear the orchestra for *Peggy-Ann* until December 13, two days before the show opened for its tryout in Philadelphia. As Rodgers listened to the orchestra play on the stage, he was disappointed by what he heard. He ended up working all that night with the conductor, his old friend Roy Webb, and several other arrangers. The next day, with the orchestra now in the pit, he noted a tremendous difference.[1]

Lew Fields reworked the show extensively during its Philadelphia run. One problem was the ending. There was a humorous climax in the original—the mother jolting her daughter back to reality—but in the musical a softer ending was desired. The idea of a final rousing chorus number by the returning crowd was rejected as unrealistic. Finally, the decision was made to end the show in semidarkness with Peggy dancing with Guy to "A Tree in the Park," delicately played on a solo violin. It was blocked out on the day of the opening and used at Lew Fields' insistence. The audience liked it.

Peggy-Ann opened in New York on December 27, 1926, at the Vanderbilt Theatre, to some favorable notices. Percy Hammond of the *New York Herald Tribune* found the music "soft and airy," and *Variety* (January 7, 1927) summed up the show neatly: "Another musical hit." The *New York Times* (December 28, 1926) declared that the trio of Rodgers, Hart, and Fields had "brought freshness and ideas to the musical comedy field, and in the new piece at the Vanderbilt they travel a little further along their road. . . . Mr Rodgers's score contains at least one number, 'Where's That Rainbow?', that lingered after the curtain fell."

The show was transferred to London the following summer and ran for almost four months, with Dorothy Dickson in the role of Peggy. The *Times* grudgingly conceded that it contained at least three "very pleasant tunes."

Rodgers was being harassed by another producer during the time he worked on *Peggy-Ann*. He and Hart had made a major mistake: they had agreed in November to write a show concurrently for the Great Glorifier, Florenz Ziegfeld. No doubt they were dazzled by the chance to be part of a Ziegfeld production, which was a virtual guarantee of success in that era. They were negotiating for two Ziegfeld shows, but contract difficulties led them to settle for one, a book musical titled *Betsy*, written by Irving Caesar and David Freedman. The show was about a single woman named Betsy from the Lower East Side whose mother has decreed that until she has married, none of her brothers or sisters can do so. This of course leads to frantic schemes and plots to marry off Betsy. The part of Betsy's younger sister, Ruth, was to be played by the vaudeville star Belle Baker. Ziegfeld had heard her and was impressed, even though her entire career had been in vaudeville and she had no experience in musical comedy. A tiny woman with a large voice, she opened her act with the song "I'm a Baker," then proceeded to several rowdy but humorous songs, interspersed with some patter. One of her popular numbers was "Put It On, Take It Off, Wrap It Up, Take It Home."

According to the projected schedule, *Betsy* was to open at about the same time as *Peggy-Ann*. Rodgers and Hart had signed contracts on November 3, 1926, and begun work. But, like many of their predecessors, they soon ran into trouble with Ziegfeld, who regretted his decision to do the show, which he had not liked from the beginning. Moreover, he was having difficulties of his own. He had wanted to use the cast of his *Follies* to open a show in Palm Beach, but his financial backers had objected to using the show for an out-of-town theater. He was also building his own new theater, the Ziegfeld, but work was going slowly, and he had to juggle shows for the opening of the new building. In the midst of all of this he was negotiating with Jerome Kern and Oscar Hammerstein to produce a show based on the Edna Ferber novel *Show Boat*.

Rodgers came to have a very poor opinion of the Great Master: "He was awful. There was no relationship at all, except, oh, disagreeable encounters. Ziegfeld, as far as I know, was only good to the girls in his shows. He was very generous to them and very decent to them. But as far as I know, not with anyone else — certainly not with Larry and me."[2] While the show was in preparation, Rodgers wrote Dorothy that Ziegfeld had been "neglectful and not exactly proper in his dealings with me, and complications have arisen." Ziegfeld had a terrific talent for all the mechanics of the theater except for music, and he was adding new numbers "endlessly." His solution, regardless of the composer, was to ask for more songs. The inevitable blowup finally occurred. Ziegfeld said "some rotten things," and Rodgers quit, declaring he was "through with this lousy show." Perhaps he was emboldened to defy the Great Glorifier by a cable that he received from London announcing that his show, *Lido Lady*, was a "sure hit."

His troubles with Ziegfeld blew over, and a few days later he and Ziegfeld were walking around the rehearsal with their arms around each other's waist. Rodgers finished the last of his songs for *Betsy* less than ten days before the opening but then had to try to play the score for the principal performers, "to straighten them out." Throughout all of this he was frantically putting the final touches on *Peggy-Ann*. Despite all the hurly-burly, he wrote, "I still love it!"[3]

At the last minute Irving Caesar wanted to interpolate some of his own songs in *Betsy*, an idea that Rodgers and Hart stoutly resisted. Rodgers finally concluded that there was nothing left to do but pray. *Betsy* previewed in Washington, D.C., shortly before Christmas. Rodgers saw the show and wrote that although it would probably be a big success, he took "no joy in it." He thought that the book was terrible, and the score had been such an extreme annoyance that he was eager to be done with it.

This was in sharp contrast with his warm feelings for *Peggy-Ann*. The score was "light but pleasant, and there is an attractive number called 'A Tree in the Park,'" he wrote. "I have a very fond and friendly feeling for the show as a whole, so I suppose it'll last about two weeks." On the other hand, because the Washington critics were kind to *Betsy*, it was likely to be a hit, Rodgers noted, chagrined by the irony.

Betsy opened at the New Amsterdam on December 28, the night after *Peggy-Ann* opened. In addition to Belle Baker, the cast included the veteran vaudevillian Al Shean as Stonewall Moskovitz. As a measure of the depth of the show, Borrah Minevitch and his Harmonica Symphony performed a version of "Rhapsody in Blue." The reaction of the critics was best summed up by Charles Brackett in the *New Yorker*, who found it all a "mess." Rodgers and Hart were facing their first failure. To add insult to injury, in the middle of the second act Baker sang a new Irving Berlin song, "Blue Skies." Fearing that the show would fail and that she would be humiliated, she had appealed to Berlin, an old friend, for a new song. Although he had nothing available except the beginning of an older melody, Berlin worked out "Blue Skies" with the help of Baker and her husband, also a songwriter. Ziegfeld agreed to let Baker interpolate the song, provided that she not tell Rodgers and Hart.

The song was a sensation on opening night, and Rodgers and Hart were surprised and outraged. Baker was called back for bow after bow, until finally Berlin, who was in the audience, had to stand. Ellin Barrett, Berlin's daughter, suggests that there was more to this story than Baker or Berlin would admit: possibly their scheme was not a last-minute collaboration.[4] Given the orchestration that had to be written, this explanation seems likely. Berlin's presence in the audience that night is also suspicious. What's more, it seems improbable that Rodgers and Hart could have escaped learning about this minor conspiracy, though their disdain for the show and their preoccupation with *Peggy-Ann* may explain their ignorance.

Brooks Atkinson, in his *New York Times* review, noted that Belle Baker made Rodgers and Hart's tunes and lyrics "more than a little heavy and ponderous." It was "not a highly successful evening for Messrs. Rodgers and Hart. . . . Their contributions for the most part were not up to standard."

Freedman and Caesar sued Ziegfeld, claiming that they had not received their share of the gross box office receipts. They asserted that receipts had amounted to $165,000 but that they had received an advance royalty of only $1,000. Countering their charges, Ziegfeld contended that Caesar had absented himself at a crucial moment, forcing him to call in Anthony Maguire to doctor the book. Moreover, he argued that Caesar and Freedman had failed to give him a suitable manuscript within a reasonable time, and that in light of their refusal to cooperate with the stage directors and composers, they had not even earned the advance. The court supported Ziegfeld, who maintained that he had lost $100,000.

The score was not high-quality Rodgers and Hart, and with the exception of one or two songs that were salvaged for other shows, this work faded away. Oddly enough, more than twenty-five years later one of the songs written for Belle Baker, "This Funny World," was revived by the vocalist Matt Dennis and became a standard much admired by musicians. It was nevertheless an uncharacteristic song for Rodgers: The verse has a string of dissonances, and the refrain seems awkward and contrived. Its harmony is unusual, which explains some of its modern attraction. It is so different from the remainder of the score, and from Rodgers' previous work, that it raises a question of what he was trying to achieve. Even though the song was inappropriate for Baker's style, it was assigned to her character. Perhaps Rodgers had perversely decided to write a difficult song for her to sing. In any case, it was not nearly good enough to save Betsy, which closed after thirty-nine performances.

Even before the show closed Rodgers and Hart had booked passage for England on the Aquatania, departing in January. With the two shows behind him, Rodgers could relax. "Once again do I sleep like a babe," Rodgers wrote. "I eat my food with understanding, I snap not at my parents, and I feel a lovely glow of health as I waken toward noon." Peggy-Ann was doing great business, and for a brief time it seemed that even Betsy might succeed. Rodgers wrote to Dorothy that "Mr. Z, big a bastard that he is, is a great showman at heart," but he complained that Ziegfeld was filling the theater with the "scum of the Bronx and the Lower East Side."[5] In London he and Hart settled into their favorite haunt, 29 St. James Street. Betsy closed in New York shortly after they arrived, but their London show, Lido Lady, was breaking "all records." In one of his letters Rodgers claimed that no one could decide whether Lido Lady or Kern and Hammerstein's Sunny was the biggest hit in London.

To compare Lido Lady with Sunny was a flight of ego, however. Sunny was a fine show, and Lido Lady was soon forgotten. Furthermore, Lido Lady was too "English" to cross the Atlantic to Broadway. Nevertheless, it was a mark of Rodgers' newfound status that his work was being talked about in the same breath as that of the exalted Kern, a great favorite in the West End, especially when one considers that only a few years earlier Rodgers had been haunting theater balconies listening to Kern's melodies.

Sunny's popularity in London was no accident. By the mid-1920s British musicals had been overtaken by American imports, though there was no pattern of success: *The Student Prince,* one of Broadway's sensations, failed badly, but the lighter *No, No, Nanette* became popular in the West End. British audiences apparently found old Heidelberg passé, whereas the American Jazz Age was intriguing. This explains why the Gershwins' *Lady Be Good* and *Tip Toes* had settled in for respectable runs.

The success of *Lido Lady* surprised the songwriters, who were not really attuned to the preferences of British audiences or the differences in the performers' styles. A recording of the hit "Here in My Arms" by the two British principals, Jack Hulburt and Phyllis Dare, reveals a more operatic style than the American version. Even though the American versions seem more authentic, the British renditions were presumably more pleasing to English theatergoers.

A year earlier, on their first visit to London, Rodgers and Hart were relatively unknown. But the success of *Lido Lady* changed everything. "You can imagine what fun it is," Rodgers wrote, "to be in London when the biggest hit is yours and is just at the peak of its popularity." They received various offers from British producers, including one from Charles B. Cochran, one of Britain's most successful impresarios, who proposed that they write the score for his next musical revue. Given Cochran's reputation—and because he was "too big to turn down"—Rodgers and Hart agreed, and for the largest royalty they had ever received. The Cochran show was scheduled for May, and both *The Girl Friend* and *Peggy-Ann* were expected to open in London that summer, so Rodgers and Hart thought that they would have four shows running at the same time. As a consequence, they had to prolong their stay by several months, which left the boys from Columbia time to enjoy London and take another tour of the Continent.

They were ebullient. From London Rodgers wrote to his future wife that he "actually loved this country." They had spent a Sunday "tramping across the fields and hills soaking with rain." (Strange as it may seem, he found this a "great joy.") They were being handsomely entertained and in turn were entertaining others at their service flat on St. James. All in all they were feeling "slightly dizzy" as they left London for Paris, where they continued to have "a helluva good time. . . . We tore the old place wide open in a nice way with no ill effects." Then "in a fit of madness" they decided to drive for four days through the French countryside to Cannes.

Rodgers was not taken with the casinos, the gambling, or the "rich bums," and he and Hart were happy to leave Cannes—Rodgers found both the food and the people "too rich." They stopped in Vienna for a few days and then were on to Budapest, which they found to be out of a "fairy-story book." Rodgers wrote, "Whoopee! this is a city!" In Budapest Rodgers and Hart made an important acquaintance: the Hungarian musicologist Dr. Albert Sirmay. Shortly thereafter Sirmay immigrated to America, where he became senior music editor for Harms. In that position he became the musical confidant, mentor, and friend of the Gershwins, Rodgers and Hart, and Cole Porter, among others. Many of the popular songs written by these luminaries owe something to the editing hand of Sirmay.

After Budapest they set out for Berlin, enticed by offers to produce *Dearest Enemy* in German (they fortunately came to naught). Rodgers and Hart found Berlin wonderful and had a "wild time of it," though in a "decent way," Rodgers hastened to add in a letter to Dorothy, who must have read such accounts with dismay. Indeed, one can only wonder at his insensitivity as he wrote these reports to a young woman obviously in love with him. Perhaps it was the insouciance of youth. In any case, he concluded that the whole trip had been "absolute perfection—a hundred times better than last summer."

By the Ides of March the "fun was over," and the pair was back in London preparing for some welcome "mental activity." Hart moved to an adjoining flat, no longer spoiling Rodgers' sleep with his heavy snoring. The two found that Cochran was making life easy for them. Rodgers described his routine: "I am back in London at work, which consists of getting up late, going to rehearsal and making a few pithy suggestions, having dinner somewhere or other and going 'out.' I'm full of sympathy for myself and don't see how I can stand it."[6]

They had already written for Cochran's revue the song that was to be one of their most successful ever, "My Heart Stood Still," reportedly inspired by an incident in a Paris taxi. Rodgers and Hart were being shown the sights by two young women from New York when the taxi had a near-accident. One of the women exclaimed, "Oh, my heart stood still!" Supposedly Hart latched onto the comment as a song title, and Rodgers wrote it down in his little music notebook. Back in London Rodgers came across his notation and decided to write a melody. When he informed Hart that he had finished the song, Hart, who had forgotten the incident, was puzzled but nevertheless wrote the lyric. Although Rodgers' notebook does contain the original draft of the melody, it omits any notation of a title, and the melody line shows significant differences from the final song. But Rodgers swore that the anecdote was true.

Cochran ran a loose production, granting his stars considerable liberty, so initially he had no particular plan for the new song. He had hired the new young star Jessie Matthews, who was only seventeen but already had established herself as Gertrude Lawrence's understudy in *Charlot's Revue*. Matthews, a pert brunette, was a vivacious dancer with a modest singing voice. Rodgers described her as a "very young, bright eyed and toothy doll."

During the first rehearsal Cochran had Rodgers play through the new song, and he then directed Matthews to try it. Cochran was delighted but complained that there was no verse. Hart, who was sitting in the stalls with his hat on the back of his head and chomping on his ever-present cigar, jumped up and ran down the aisle onto the stage. "You wanna verse?" he asked. With that, he pulled out his trusty pencil and envelope and scribbled on the back. He handed it to Matthews, asking, "How d'ya like this, babe? Think you can read my writing?" The verse was about the young English schoolgirl's aversion to the "boys at Harrow" (later changed for the American version). "Jolly good!" Cochran exclaimed.[7]

Matthews' recording of the song, made at about this time, is presumably the same as her stage version. Although she was not an impressive singer, she had a certain charm, much in the manner of Gertrude Lawrence. Her voice had a shaky tremolo, popular in that era, her sense of rhythm was good, and she enunciated clearly.

The show opened May 19, 1927, under the title *One Dam Thing after Another*. The prince of Wales (later Edward VIII), by then a friend of Rodgers', attended opening night, but his presence so unnerved the cast and audience that the performance suffered. Rodgers found the opening "rough" but noted that the audience liked the show and that the notices were "splendid." In fact, the reviews were mixed: "a little disappointing," commented the *Times* in a two-paragraph review that never mentioned Rodgers or Hart. One reviewer identified the music as "ragtime, of course." Several others praised Jessie Matthews and picked out "My Heart Stood Still" as the "good" song.

After this uncertain reception, Cochran considered closing the show. It began to gain an audience, though, as "My Heart Stood Still" became popular—in part because the prince of Wales had declared it his favorite foxtrot and requested it at a social gathering. When the orchestra leader professed ignorance of the melody, the prince taught it to the musicians. The incident was well publicized, and the show ran until early December.

"My Heart Stood Still," one of Rodgers' very best songs, was originally a 1920s-style song, as recorded by such artists as the pianist Edythe Baker. The later, more familiar and smoother renditions of this song were the result of the changing styles of the 1930s and after. Again Rodgers employed a three-note theme, repeated three times, and at different intervals, in the first eight bars and again in the second eight. Toward the end of the final eight bars there is a variant. Like many popular songs of the era it verged on becoming boring and repetitive, but it was helped by Rodgers' clever harmonies, especially in the verse and the release. Of course the melody rested on some memorable lyrics.

The song's popularity in England generated several offers from America, including one from Ziegfeld, who wanted it for the *Follies*. Beatrice Lillie, who was preparing for a new Rodgers and Hart show, also wanted it. As was the custom, the rights to "My Heart Stood Still" belonged to the producer, Charles Cochran. Fearing that Lillie would turn the song into a comic number, Rodgers and Hart bought the rights from Cochran, allegedly for ten thousand dollars, and decided to use it in their next American show. Apparently no money changed hands; Rodgers and Hart simply gave up the royalties Cochran owed them.

All in all, Rodgers enjoyed his stay in London. He and Fred Astaire saw *Desert Song* (the Romberg and Hammerstein musical) at the Royale Theatre, Drury Lane. They hated it but predicted a long run because "this is London," where everything American was popular. Rodgers loved working for Cochran and enjoyed his hospitality. During this visit Hart found his "own group," as Rodgers put it, one of the first indications that they were beginning to drift apart. Rodgers took a quick side trip to Paris to enlist Robert Russell Bennett to do the orchestrations for their British show. Bennett agreed, and thus began a lifelong association.

Rodgers had been invited to the English countryside a few times and counted as new friends Mrs. Lowell Guinness, of the famous brewery family, Lord Delaware, and Lady Port-Arlington. In his letters to Dorothy he insisted that his titled friends were not patronizing. He found them natural and cordial, and he liked the attention. But the name-dropping in his letters embarrassed him; he complained that if you get a couple of shows produced "you're immediately conceited," and if you stay in London a couple of months, you're immediately saddled with a broad accent and a lifted chin. He had not changed, he reassured Dorothy. He did become quite close to the family of Baron d'Erlanger, especially the daughter-in-law, Myrtle, who had introduced him to the prince of Wales. Many years later Richard and Dorothy Rodgers gave refuge to Myrtle's daughter during the World War II blitz of London.

The Richard Rodgers who returned home from London was more sophisticated and self-assured. He also returned a better songwriter, as he soon demonstrated on Broadway.

Rodgers and Hart sailed on May 28, 1927, for New York, where they found that things were "terribly mixed up." The show they had expected to start for

Arthur Hammerstein, then titled *Polly*, had been put off and finally died. Lew Fields, their usual producer, was about to depart for London, and they all were frantically trying to agree on a new show for the fall. One old idea kept coming up, especially from Hart—a story about a Yankee from Hartford, Connecticut, who awakens to find himself in the court of King Arthur.

7

A CONNECTICUT YANKEE

"Dream of being a knight errant in armor in the middle ages." Thus began the notes made by Mark Twain when he conceived his classic satire *A Connecticut Yankee in King Arthur's Court*. He went on to list certain nineteenth-century amenities unavailable to ironclad knights of the fabled court of Camelot: "No pockets in the armor. Can't scratch. Cold in the head—can't blow—can't get at handkerchief, can't use iron sleeve. . . . Can't dress or undress myself. Always getting struck by lightning. Fall down and can't get up." The comedic possibilities were obvious.[1]

Twain began his novel in January 1886 and worked on it for four years. When it finally appeared it was no longer just a humorous romp in King Arthur's court but a biting attack on Twain's own times. His hero, Hank Morgan, transforms Camelot into a modern industrial society only to have that world end in a furious war, with the old traditions and superstitions triumphant.

In 1921, Richard Rodgers and Herbert Fields wandered into the Capitol Theater in New York to see a silent film version of Twain's novel, and they concluded that the idea was perfect for a musical. For a young man to awaken in A.D. 528 armed with knowledge of the 1880s was an intriguing premise. That he would be taken for an alien, arrested, tried, and condemned to the stake, only to save himself by predicting a solar eclipse—this was the stuff of theatrical comedy, especially if one were to add a love affair with a maiden at court. Lorenz Hart agreed, and with the audacity of youth Rodgers negotiated with the lawyers of the Twain estate for a six-month option on the novel. But that was before Rodgers and Hart were names to contend with, and no one showed any interest in their idea.

By the summer of 1927 everything had changed: Rodgers and Hart (and Fields) could write their own ticket. Largely at Hart's insistence, they decided to revive their option with the Twain estate, though this time they had to pay for the privilege—such was the price of fame. Lew Fields was not impressed with Twain's book, as the story becomes increasingly political and ends sadly. So Herbert Fields, displaying an agile ingenuity, reworked the story, preserving the amusing and fun parts, and when his father read through this version he was enthusiastic.

Of course Twain's plot had to be altered for a musical. A prologue was invented to establish the modern characters—Martin, the Yankee (renamed for some reason); Fay Morgan, his shrewish fiancée; and the pretty young Alice Carter, Martin's former girlfriend. During a party in the opening sequence Martin and Alice sing the show's hit love song, "My Heart Stood Still," appropriated from *One Dam Thing after Another*. When Fay discovers Martin flirting with Alice she crowns him with a bottle. He sinks into unconsciousness, to awake in Camelot. In the dream, Martin is apprehended by the pompous and foolish Sir Kay and is taken on the road to Camelot, where he meets Alice, now known as the Demoiselle Alisande Le Carterloise, who becomes simply Sandy. Together they sing "Thou Swell," in which modern slang is contrasted with couplets of Arthurian thees and thous.

The production was extravagant, beginning with a cast of forty-two and a nineteen-piece orchestra. The settings were a stunning reproduction of the pageantry of Camelot, and the eclipse was a mechanical marvel for the time. Roy Webb and Robert Russell Bennett did the orchestrations, and the promising newcomer Busby Berkeley created flamboyant costumed dances.

According to some critics, dance numbers in Broadway musicals were predictable, often simply tacked on to the plot as diversions for the audience. But

Richard Rodgers and Lorenz Hart sailing for Europe on board the *Berengaria* in 1927, the year they wrote the musical version of Mark Twain's *Connecticut Yankee in King Arthur's Court*. They often traveled to London, where many of their successful Broadway shows were transplanted.

Berkeley tried to weave the dances into the story, mainly by building on the jazz rhythms of the score. He exploited the songs, thereby earning a reputation as an innovator. He did not dispense entirely with acrobatics or other "bits of external cleverness"; according to one critic, what he presented was a "substantial type of novelty which depends not upon the inventiveness of one man but grows as well out of the creative work of his collaborators."

Rodgers and Hart's expansive score did not escape cuts by Lew Fields during tryouts. Rodgers lost five songs before rebelling at Fields' proposal to cut "Thou Swell." The song's reception in Philadelphia had been cool, but Fields agreed to keep it in through the New York opening. The Philadelphia critics, noting that Rodgers had written an "appropriate score," mentioned two numbers, "My Heart Stood Still" and "I Feel at Home with You," but not "Thou Swell." The show itself, however, delighted Philadelphians. The *Public Ledger* wrote: "All the glittering pageantry and pomp of King Arthur's court was reproduced in sump-tuous costume and rich setting, as the Knights of the Round Table and their ladies made merry to the tilt of jazz in a strange hybrid of Broadway patois and the stately language of the Crusader days."

Rodgers was enthusiastic: "It's a grand show," he concluded. But how would New York react? On opening night, November 3, 1927, at the Vanderbilt Theatre, Rodgers conducted in place of his friend Roy Webb. Within a few minutes, two of Rodgers and Hart's greatest songs were introduced. Much to Rodgers' sur-prise, the opening-night audience was not overly enthusiastic about "My Heart Stood Still," perhaps because it was no longer new. But when they heard "Thou Swell," Rodgers could feel the response: "Billy [Gaxton] wasn't more than eight bars into the refrain when I began to feel that something on the back of my neck. It wasn't the steady, growing sensation I'd felt during the first *Garrick Gai-eties*, nor was it the more subdued, all-is-well feeling I had during *Dearest Enemy*. This time the audience reaction was so strong that it was like an actual blow. Though there were no audible sounds, I could feel the people loving Gaxton, adoring [Connie] Carpenter and going wild over the song. The applause at the end of the number was deafening, and Billy and Connie returned to give sev-eral encores. That did it; from then on, the show was in. Nothing, I knew, could stop if from being a smash."[2] Little wonder that it was a smash, given Twain's imaginative story and these songs—"Twain plus modern pep," as Lew Fields de-scribed it. *A Connecticut Yankee* became the team's most successful production of the 1920s, running for 418 performances.

The outcome was probably never really in doubt: Rodgers and Hart had writ-ten three hit shows and two outstanding revues. But the competition had been growing tougher and sharper. In the mid-1920s New York erupted with stage plays and musicals. The Gershwins' *Funny Face* opened on Broadway a few days after *A Connecticut Yankee*. Rodgers had seen it in previews in Philadelphia and commented that the score was a "terrible disappointment, but the book [was] unspeakable." It would take a "miracle to fix." Fred Astaire, the star of *Funny Face*, must have agreed with Rodgers, because the book was in fact rewritten, and the show was a success.

The quality of the competition was evident in the durability of many of the shows. Although Rodgers and Hart had been pleased with a run of two hundred to three hundred performances for their shows, *Show Boat*, *Good News*, and *Sunny* each ran for more than five hundred. *A Connecticut Yankee* ranked seventh, behind *Rio Rita* and *Desert Song*, in the 1920s. Given the wealth of musical theater, the public was awash in popular songs. *Sunny* had yielded "Who?" and one could also hear Richard Whiting's "Sleepy Time Gal" and "Birth of the Blues," by De Sylva, Brown, and Henderson; for the more romantically inclined there were George Gershwin's "Someone to Watch over Me" and Kalmar and Ruby's "Thinking of You." Eddie Cantor sang "If You Knew Susie, Like I Know Susie" while the Jazz Age flappers were singing Ray Henderson's "Five Foot Two, Eyes of Blue" and "Yes Sir, That's My Baby," by Gus Kahn and Walter Donaldson.

Audiences were often fickle, and even the critics took note of their unpredictability. But Rodgers' new show was a triumph. "To put it quickly, I think we have a hit," he wrote to Dorothy. The reviews were a torrent of praise, and nearly every reviewer made a point of commending his effort. "The loveliest musical comedy song in recent years is 'My Heart Stood Still,'" wrote Robert Benchley for *Life*. The astute Brooks Atkinson, in the *New York Times* (November 4, 1927), went beyond enthusiasm for the musical to note Rodgers' progress as a composer: "Mr. Rodgers has now graduated from the class of beginners. In his unhackneyed score for the current piece he composes with genuine feeling and versatility. There are many fine passages in his score, all the way from the sincerity of hymn motives through the warmth of romances to the crash of jazz. Once he comes perilously close to oratorio."

One can only imagine the outcome had "My Heart Stood Still" not been transferred from London and had Lew Fields talked Rodgers out of keeping "Thou Swell." Two secondary songs were also worthy of attention. "On a Desert Island with You," a love song between Sir Galahad and Evelyn, served as a complement to "Thou Swell." "I Feel at Home with You," also sung by Evelyn and Galahad, was not as inventive as "My Heart Stood Still" or "Thou Swell" but was very much in the Broadway tradition of Jerome Kern songs.

Another team might have been content to rest a while on its laurels after such a success, and that might have been good advice. But Rodgers, Hart, and Fields seem to have been driven to produce—perhaps by the memory of their earlier years, when they had received little recognition.

They had signed a contract for a new musical to be produced by Charles Dillingham, tentatively entitled *That's My Baby*, with rehearsals scheduled to start when *A Connecticut Yankee* opened. Rodgers later admitted that taking on the show was a mistake, but at the time they were awed by the towering reputation of Dillingham, a regal, elegantly dressed impresario of the old school. He had produced the fabulous *Sunny*, and his shows seemed to be guaranteed success. Once he had arranged for the show, however, he proved elusive. In contrast with Ziegfeld, who was constantly interfering, Dillingham rarely appeared or took much interest.

Dillingham's new show was to star the incomparable British comedian Beatrice Lillie. Although previous Rodgers and Hart shows had had strong casts, they were not built around a particular star. Lillie's prominence meant that Rodgers had to tailor the score to her talents. Unfortunately, he became ill with the flu and the producers became impatient. Hart wanted to give up the whole project, but Rodgers was reluctant, and after a rough start, the show got back on track. Rodgers wrote that the show, called *She's My Baby*, "looked fine" before its tryout in Washington, D.C.

The cast included Clifton Webb, Irene Dunne, and Jack Whiting. The book was by Guy Bolton, Harry Ruby, and Bert Kalmar, whose own show, *Five O'Clock Girl*, had just succeeded on Broadway. The orchestrations were by Robert Russell Bennett as well as Hans Spialek, who went on to orchestrate many of Rodgers and Hart's later shows. The plot was scarcely novel: A young man (Whiting) wants to put on a show starring his girlfriend (Dunne). He must convince his financial backers that he is married with a child. Lillie, the maid, assumes the role of his wife. "Dreary rubbish," wrote Alexander Woollcott in the *New York World* after the show opened on December 26, 1927. Even the music received mixed reviews, and Hart's lyrics were panned for the first time. But Lillie was "perfect," according to one reviewer. Robert Benchley decided that Lillie had been forced into single-handed combat to overcome the deficiencies of the book. She was resorting to her old tricks, but "to complain of Beatrice Lillie's old tricks would be like complaining of the same old pay envelope coming around every Saturday." Despite Lillie's mugging, the show folded after seventy-one performances.[3]

The score was an odd one, and its deficiencies are perhaps explained by Rodgers' illness. Many of the songs were transplants from Rodgers and Hart's

London shows or rejects from other shows. What might have become the best song, "How Was I to Know?" was dropped before the opening, to reappear two years later as "Why Do You Suppose?" Hart provided Lillie with lyrics that gave her clowning full rein. "When I Go on the Stage" contains a couplet that needles the "French" star of Cole Porter's *Paris*:

> I'll make Irene Bordoni
> Look like a poor baloney.

In the interest of serving Lillie's peculiar comic talents, however, Rodgers and Hart wrote nothing memorable.

Shortly after the show opened, Rodgers fled New York for a cruise to Europe with his parents. It was his first show of 1928, a frustrating year for him. By the time he left, his relationship with Dorothy Feiner had begun to cool. She sensed that Rodgers was not yet serious enough to contemplate marriage, and they agreed to stop seeing each other for a time. Dorothy was miserable. She left Wellesley at the end of the fall term and sailed with her parents for Europe. Her outbound ship passed Rodgers' inbound ship, and they exchanged curt cablegrams. Dorothy stayed in Paris to study sculpture, but the two continued to correspond. Rodgers' letters to her during this time reveal that he was an increasingly perplexed and frustrated young man.

Moreover, his trip to Europe with his parents had not gone well. They experienced foul weather everywhere, and when they docked in New York, ice was floating in the Hudson. Rodgers found Paris disappointing this time: "I'll sell my share for two bits. Even the street walkers aren't funny anymore." While still abroad, he wrote a revealing letter to Dorothy: "I wish I could talk to you. Three times now since I left home I've experienced something I've never known before, and tonight is the third. I have an active and intense feeling of depression which is absolutely impossible to shake off. And I can't find a definite enough reason for it."[4] These occasional references to depression portended his troubles in the years ahead.

As Rodgers was getting ready to come home Herbert Fields cabled him that the libretto for a new show was ready. In the wake of the failure of *She's My Baby*, Hart and Rodgers had decided to return to safer ground with a show by the reliable Herbert and Lew Fields. While Rodgers and Hart had been detoured in Dillingham's show, the Fieldses had produced a success, *Hit the Deck*, with music by Vincent Youmans. Herbert Fields was inspired to believe that he could repeat this success simply by transferring the action from the Navy to the Marines. Indeed, two of the leads from *Hit the Deck* were hired.

When Rodgers returned to "rushing" New York in late February 1928, *She's My Baby* was preparing to leave for Chicago, where it was moderately successful because of Lillie's clowning. Rehearsals were to start for the new Fields show, *Present Arms*. Rodgers had read the book and found it fine. Casting was complete except for a leading lady, and Rodgers had finished four numbers. It is a reflection on Rodgers' preoccupation with his music that he never seemed to complain about the book; nor did Hart. During this period they seemed to gravitate toward whatever was offered—by Dillingham, Ziegfeld, or the Fieldses. It was obvious that the faltering shows were those with a poor book or unfortunate casting; even the Gershwins, Youmans, and Kern suffered the misfortune of working with a poor book. Rodgers and Hart later became more particular to the point of developing their own concepts and even trying to write their own scripts (without great success).

Most of the numbers for *Present Arms* were inscribed in Rodgers' musical sketchbook, which Jean and Roy Webb gave to Rodgers when he left for Europe with his parents. Although there are no dates on the individual songs, it is obvious that the first entry (still untitled) was the chorus of "You Took Advantage of Me." The verse, also untitled, was written in the same sketchbook, as were the melodic lines of seven other songs. It is a vivid testimony to Rodgers' talent that these melodic lines, meticulously written and bearing virtually no deletions or erasures, emerged in final form almost exactly as they were created.[5]

During that difficult year of 1928, his grandfather suffered a stroke in Rodgers' presence and died shortly thereafter. Moreover, *Present Arms* was not going well. With just three weeks to go before opening there was still no leading lady (imagine a current Broadway show— *Phantom of the Opera*, say—without a leading lady so close to opening!). And as late as one week before tryouts in Wilmington, Rodgers still had not heard the full orchestra. One of the pleasant surprises, however, was that Busby Berkeley had cast a role for himself. Flora Le Breton was finally chosen as leading lady.

The previews in Wilmington and Atlantic City went smoothly, and *Present Arms* opened in New York at Lew Fields' newly acquired Mansfield Theatre on April 26, 1928. Rodgers was encouraged by the reception but later admitted that "it wasn't a terribly good show." On balance, the critics agreed, but they were not overly harsh, and the show lasted the season. *Present Arms* inevitably invited comparison with *Hit the Deck*, but there was a limit to audiences' fondness for shows about sailors and marines.

This fickleness was evident in the public's reaction to the songs. Rodgers had expected "Do I Hear You Saying 'I Love You'?" to be the hit of the production, and it was plugged three times. But the show's high point was a seemingly minor dance number for Berkeley and Joyce Barbour, "You Took Advantage of Me." With its strong rhythmic beat, the song survived well into the swing era of the 1930s and became a standard.

Hart's lyrics maintained the emphasis on rhythm by repeating the phrase "'cause you took advantage of me" with the repetition of the same musical phrase at the end of each eight bars. This was an effective Hart device: he would pick out the part of the music that seemed to give the melody impetus, search for a word or phrase to fit it, and then construct the entire lyric.

The bridge section of "You Took Advantage of Me" reflects Rodgers' growing complexity as a composer. Like the second eight bars in "Thou Swell," it moves through a downward chromatic passage that is obviously constructed for effect. His sketches and notes indicate that even early in his career he conceived melodies as a whole rather than as phrases to be developed. The chromatic bass for "The Girl Friend," for example, was written on the side of his melodic sketch, apparently as a reminder of how the entire song should be arranged. Because of Rodgers' ability to write a complete piano-vocal version of his songs (a technique he learned as a teenager), a Rodgers song emerged from a show almost exactly as he wanted it presented in the sheet music. Oscar Hammerstein later called Rodgers a "builder and a planner," characteristics that were already evident when he was in his twenties.

The show ran only 155 performances, and after the opening Rodgers headed for Colorado Springs, vacationing at the expansive Broadmoor Hotel (escapes following an opening seemed to be a pattern for Rodgers). There, joined by Dorothy Fields and her brother, Herbert, he savored the mountain air, learned to play golf, and went horseback riding. His mental state was in turmoil, however. On June 10, 1928, he wrote a provocative and perplexing letter to Dorothy: "Dot, there are changes to be made. It's going to take all summer to figure out one or two problems, but there'll be a difference. You're concerned more than you think."[6]

Rodgers was reluctantly beginning to confront the obvious: that he was in love and should get married. He was twenty-six years old and enjoyed an active social life—attending parties in the Hamptons and hobnobbing with New York society through his connection with Cartier's executive Jules Glaenzer, who was obsessed with musical comedy and had co-opted Rodgers. Rodgers was also an occasional member of the lively coterie that gathered at the New York studio of illustrator Neysa McMein, whose apartment became an important literary and show business salon. Among her guests were members of the Algonquin circle and George Gershwin and Irving Berlin. Rodgers relished his celebrity status, often playing piano at these parties.

Rodgers' self-doubts were about to be compounded. While still in Colorado he was bombarded by messages from Herbert Fields, who was back in New York, and from Hart extolling an idea for a new show based on the novel *The Son of the Grand Eunuch*, by Charles Petit. In the story, the son of the Grand Eunuch is chosen to succeed his father. The son panics at the prospect and, assisted by his wife, Chee-Chee, goes to great lengths to avoid castration. Rodgers was appalled by the idea and resisted the blandishments of his comrades. But after returning to New York he gave in, admitting that it would be unique—or, as he later put it, "eunuch."

Rodgers and Hart prided themselves on trying new ideas. Because *Present Arms* had been so conventional, perhaps a radical change was in order. Hart and Fields said that they were determined to make the music an integral part of the story, so Rodgers suggested that they reduce the number of full-blown songs and write eight-bar phrases to be inserted as part of the dialogue. The printed program rather pompously announced that listing all of the numbers would be confusing because they were so "interwoven with the story."

By September 1928 the book and score were complete. The show was titled *Chee-Chee*. The eunuch's son in the story has difficulty escaping his predicament, and Chee-Chee repeatedly intervenes to save him. When her husband is about to be castrated, she persuades the physician to pretend that he has done the deed. He agrees, and Chee-Chee and her husband are reunited in an ambiguous ending.

Rodgers was increasingly impressed by his score and by the show in general. After hearing the orchestra he decided that the music sounded marvelous. He had not realized how "far he had come" musically, even worrying that he had gone too far in his innovations. Helen Ford had reluctantly agreed to play Chee-Chee, but only temporarily. At first Rodgers was sure that he and his collaborators had "done something fine." Ford was giving a delightful performance in the Philadelphia tryouts. But then something went wrong: the conductor, Rodgers' mentor Roy Webb, "sort of fell apart on us." Rodgers took over in the pit, despite the objections of Hart, who wanted Rodgers to participate in the final cutting and polishing. Ford became irritable, a "bitch of the first water," according to Rodgers. She later asserted that Rodgers had claimed to have rewritten the orchestrations in her key when he had done no such thing. She became so incensed that she threw a hairbrush at him (and hit him, according to her account). Their earlier romance was obviously over.[7]

Oddly, Rodgers was still convinced that *Chee-Chee* was the "best musical he had ever seen." Even though audiences were staying away in increasing numbers, he believed that everything would be fine once he got a New York orchestra. Meanwhile, the show's subject matter was proving increasingly controversial. Some Philadelphia critics found the show repellent; others thought that it heralded a new era in musicals.

After the opening on September 25, 1928, the New York critics gave it no better than a yellow light. *Variety* found it "well nigh boresome"; those who disliked it were vehement. There were rumors that the show would be padlocked by the police for indecency. Charles Brackett, writing in the *New Yorker* (October 6, 1928), noted that even before the show opened, "anticipatory lip-smacking was loud in the land." His review concluded that while Rodgers' music was good, the plot reminded him of "those things you have to wade through in Lit IV to learn the stumbling early stages of the novel. Picaresque is the term, I believe." He wished that Rodgers and Hart could be "psyched out of their Gilbert and Sullivan complex." Brackett's criticism of Hart's lyrics was caustic. Quoting from "Moon of My Delight," he wrote: "I want Mr. Hart, who is responsible, to go and stand in a corner and think it over for a while."

Box office receipts were better than average at first, but after two weeks sales dropped dramatically, forcing Lew Fields to close the show after thirty-one performances. It was the worst failure of Rodgers' career. The problem obviously was the book and its exotic subject: there were many long, humorless stretches, and in dealing with such a sensitive topic, humor was essential.

The music was well received, however. Despite Rodgers' injunction against using standard-length songs, those were the offerings that impressed critics and audiences. *Variety* wrote that Rodgers never before had displayed a more "tuneful" collection; "I Must Love You" and "Singing a Love Song" were above-average melodies. Robert Benchley called the score "some of the loveliest work [Rodgers] has done." Rodgers commented that rather than try to create Chinese music he gave his own melodies an occasional Asian inflection. In this he was successful, though he did lapse into some clichés in "Moon of My Delight" (which his sketchbook suggests may have been written for *Betsy*). But the show's failure doomed the songs to obscurity.

Chee-Chee was the end of a long collaboration between the Fields family and Rodgers and Hart. Although some said that *Chee-Chee's* failure led to the breakup, Rodgers stoutly denied the rumor, and they did in fact work together again on Broadway and in Hollywood. But Rodgers decided to join forces with the hugely successful Alex Aarons and Vinton Freedley, who had made their reputation producing shows by the Gershwins. A chance to work with them was enticing, and Rodgers and Hart, minus Fields, were off again, this time on a show entitled *Spring Is Here*.

The show opened in March 1929 but ran only about one hundred performances. (The great song "Spring Is Here" was written much later, for a different show.) The show closed with a "noiseless bang," Rodgers wrote in a letter, and "many were the drooping chins about the Alvin [Theatre]," but the usual post-mortems brought forth no remedies.[8]

The reviews were good, but there was criticism: "As entertainment it is spotty," wrote *Variety*. Again Rodgers' score was singled out for praise, especially "With a Song in My Heart," which the keyed-up Rodgers had written after his first ride in a private airplane, from the Hamptons to Manhattan. "With a Song in My Heart" falls into the same category of dramatic songs as Jerome Kern's "The Song Is You" and Sigmund Romberg's "Lover Come Back to Me." It repeats a two-bar musical phrase for eight bars, lowering it one step in the second eight bars. Its dramatic quality is created by a quarter-note rest on the first beat, allowing accompanying pianos, orchestra, or whatever to strike a hard tonic chord, thus launching the melody. (Jerome Kern employed the same effect in "Why Was I Born?" written at about this time.)

All the while, Dorothy Feiner was studying sculpture in Paris and carrying a torch for Rodgers. When she heard "With a Song in My Heart" on the radio, she burst into tears. Her father had warned her that it would be a mistake to marry Rodgers: he was basking in the glow of success, sought after and flattered by people of note, and "adored by the ladies," as she put it. Although she was prepared to accept her competition from the ladies, she was more uncertain of how to deal with the fringe benefits that Rodgers would have to sacrifice as a married man. No longer would he be available as the extra man for glamorous parties or be free for spur-of-the-moment trips to France. After the opening of *Spring Is Here*, Rodgers did in fact sail for Europe to attend a party in Paris — citing the event as an example of the lifestyle he had come to know.

In 1928, Rodgers had moved into a terrace apartment in the Lombardy Hotel, where one of his neighbors was Edna Ferber. She was incensed to learn that management had rented to a songwriter, but Rodgers placated her with a huge bouquet of flowers, and the two became lifelong friends. His social life included parties given by Cole Porter, who was back in New York; one party, he reported, turned out to be especially fun because Porter got "pie-eyed."

That summer Rodgers became good friends with the conductor Alfred Newman and his producer, Alex Aarons. Newman was a fine musician who later migrated to Hollywood as a conductor and then composer of background music, and his scores eventually won him several Academy Awards (for *Alexander's Ragtime Band*, *Tin Pan Alley*, and *The Song of Bernadette*). Rodgers gave parties for the society set and the Broadway crowd, hired a valet, and began toying with the idea of movies and dickering with new producers.

"This is going to be quite a year," he accurately predicted in mid-July 1929. However, his next show for Freedley and Aarons, tentatively titled *Me for You*, had turned into a mess; after long rewrites and trials it was withdrawn and overhauled to open for a tryout just as the stock market crashed. Despite the omens from Wall Street, Richard Rodgers and Dorothy Feiner became engaged in early December 1929.

8

SIMPLE SIMON

Rodgers was involved in two more shows before he and Dorothy married. The first was for the reliable Alex Aarons and Vinton Freedley, and the second was for their nemesis, Florenz Ziegfeld.

The Aarons and Freedley show finally opened on Armistice Day 1929, but only after long travail. The idea for this show, eventually called *Heads Up*, began with the Aarons and Freedley success *Hold Everything*, a musical by De Sylva, Brown, and Henderson that opened in fall 1928 and ran for a year. Buoyed by their success, the producers signed some of the cast members for their next show. They hired the Pulitzer Prize–winning playwright Owen Davis to do the libretto, and enlisted Rodgers and Hart. Davis, working in California, produced a comedy, originally titled *Me for You*, about rum-running off the coast of Long Island. Rodgers and Hart completed a tentative score. The cast included Ray Bolger, Betty Starbuck, Victor Moore, Lulu McConnell, and Jack Whiting. The Philadelphia tryout had to be canceled because of a strike in that city, and the show was rescheduled for Detroit.

As rehearsals began, Rodgers wrote, "I need a hit as I need food, what with a bad summer and an ap't to pay for." At first he thought the show would be fun, but after the score was finished and as the company moved to Detroit, he noted that the book needed "plenty of fixing." But he was satisfied with his own work, noting that the "score looks marvelous (song hits!)."[1] In fact there were no hits, much of the score was junked, and the one major song that remained was "A Ship Without a Sail," one of the team's most inventive compositions ever. The melancholy melody was enhanced by Hart's lonely lyrics:

> All alone, all at sea!
> Why does nobody care for me?

The first notices were favorable, and ticket sales in Detroit were good, but after two weeks the producers decided to close the show. Rodgers wrote later that the audiences were not responding to the idea of the lovable Moore cast as a smuggler, or to the ending, in which the heroine marries a lawbreaker. In spite of the Detroit closing, Aarons and Freedley did not give up on the show. They had gone through a similar experience with the Gershwins' *Funny Face*, which survived after receiving a great deal of remedial care. Paul Gerard Smith and Jack McGowan were called in to rewrite the play, now called *Heads Up*, and Rodgers and Hart redid their score. "A Ship Without a Sail" was retained, but the most important song of the rewritten show was "Why Do You Suppose?"

The story behind the new song was publicized by Hart in one of his rare newspaper articles. Late one evening after a rehearsal of the revived show in Philadelphia, he and Rodgers stayed behind to write one more song, which had been requested by the producers. Rodgers decided to reuse a melody from *She's My Baby*, titled "How Was I to Know?" Hart's idea for a new lyric was disdainfully rejected by Rodgers. Hart asked, "Why do you suppose we need another song?" Rodgers leaped on Hart's question: that's it! Hart began his lyric, and the whole exercise took no more than half an hour. An orchestration was written overnight, and that evening, in place of the overture, the orchestra played through "Why Do You Suppose?" then performed it a few minutes later without a hitch (an enchanting story, though perhaps too pat and somewhat exaggerated for publication).[2] The song's lively melody and hopeful message contrasted considerably with those of the mournful "Ship Without a Sail."

Despite the stock market collapse in October 1929, *Heads Up* opened on Broadway in November. The musical director was Alfred Newman, orchestrations were by Robert Russell Bennett, and the cast was, for the most part, carried over from the first version. This time the story involved a man who was duped into rum-running; thus, Victor Moore was cast in a more congenial role. Rodgers' score was praised, and Frank Sullivan, writing for the *New York World*, went so far as to assert that "A Ship Without a Sail" was the best song since "Ol' Man River." One critic noted that Hart's lyrics for this show were less sophisticated than his earlier ones and suggested that he had conceded to Tin Pan Alley. The show ran a barely respectable 144 performances.[3]

From the heights of *A Connecticut Yankee*, Rodgers and Hart had descended to a level of more modest accomplishments. Like many Broadway songwriters, they were victims of mediocre books. It may well have been this disappointment with *Heads Up* that led them to sign again with Ziegfeld. Another possible show in London had been postponed, thus opening the door to Ziegfeld's offer.

Once again Ziegfeld wanted to build a show around a star. For Belle Baker he had produced the fiasco *Betsy*. Now he wanted a show for Ed Wynn, known as "The Perfect Fool," who was a much safer box office bet than Baker. Ziegfeld had approached Rodgers and Hart in the summer, before the collapse of *Me for You*. Rodgers credited their decision to do the show to Ed Wynn, whom he found delightful.

The story, appropriately named *Simple Simon*, centers on a dream fantasy that dissolves into the land of Mother Goose fairy tales, providing the vehicle for Wynn's various sketches and characters. The songs obviously had to be tailored to his style. In fact, Wynn often wrote his own comic songs.

The reunion with Ziegfeld was not a happy one for Rodgers and Hart—and they probably should have known better than to attempt it. Ziegfeld, Rodgers once said, should have been a Hollywood producer: he was ignorant of music yet insisted on butting into the songwriting. Proof of Rodgers' contention came when Ziegfeld insisted on cutting "Dancing on the Ceiling." The exasperated Ziegfeld complained that Rodgers and Hart wrote only complicated songs: Why couldn't they write something straightforward and simple? They complied, and the result was "Ten Cents a Dance."

The show was a field day for Wynn, but the critics were not enthralled. Rodgers' score was not exactly panned, but neither was it lavishly praised. It was, however, laden with solid achievements: "Send for Me" was the same melody as "I Must Love You," from *Chee-Chee*. "He Was Too Good for Me" was an unusual melody and therefore likely to have irritated Ziegfeld. "Don't Tell Your Folks" was a highly amusing number with a strong rhythm.

The hit song, of course, was "Ten Cents a Dance," and Ruth Etting's performance of it was singled out for praise. Etting had become a success in the Ziegfeld Follies of 1927 with "Shaking the Blues Away," which Irving Berlin had written for her. She had been appearing in Nine-Fifteen Revue, singing Harold Arlen's "Get Happy." But the night that show closed Ziegfeld called to offer her a role in Simple Simon, which was then still in Boston. She replaced Lee Morse, whom Ziegfeld had fired. Although Rodgers claimed that Etting went on cold on opening night, Etting remembers that she arrived in Boston to find Simple Simon in disarray. Her song, "Ten Cents a Dance," had too great a range for her, so Rodgers and Hart obligingly rewrote parts of it (though Rodgers had no memory of this).

When the show opened in New York a few days later, Etting was a hit. One reviewer called her "letter perfect."[4] Her light voice, good intonation, and sense of rhythm made for a welcome relief from the semioperatic performers in some Broadway shows. She became one of the top vocalists of the 1930s, in part because of her lucky association with major songs. She sang "Ten Cents a Dance" sitting atop a piano, which was mounted on bicycle wheels so that it could be pumped around the stage by Wynn. Despite this dubious device, the song quickly became a hit (Etting recorded it as well) and has endured through the decades. After the opening Ziegfeld dropped "I Still Believe in You" and substituted "Happy Days and Lonely Nights," by Fred Fisher and Billy Rose. Ziegfeld also interpolated an earlier hit by Etting, "Love Me or Leave Me," and he mercifully dropped the mobile piano and allowed her to sing "Ten Cents a Dance" alone.

Jerome Kern enthusiastically pointed out to Rodgers that "Ten Cents" told a story in itself. The lament of a taxi dancer, was, according to Kern, the "best character sketch since Camille."[5] Indeed, it was the "best song that [Rodgers and Hart] had done." The lyrics were poignant, and the melody of the chorus was suitably sad.

Simple Simon ran for only 135 performances, despite Ziegfeld's usual lavish publicity. He took half-page advertisements in the New York Times that proclaimed: "Critics Go Into Ecstasies to Describe Simple Simon" and, in even bolder and larger type, "You can now see the GREATEST of ZIEGFELD SHOWS at reduction of $1 from previous Ziegfeld prices." Wynn took the show on a long tour and eventually returned for two weeks on Broadway. By then the cast had changed and new songs by others writers had been added, though it was still advertised as a Rodgers and Hart show. By the time Wynn returned to Broadway, Rodgers had married, traveled to London and Hollywood, become the father of a baby girl, and written another Broadway show.

Before his marriage in March 1930, a week after the opening of Simple Simon,

Rodgers had agreed to write three scores for First National Pictures, the precursor of Warner Brothers. His motive was simple—money. Rodgers was to receive fifty thousand dollars for his work. The stock market collapse had not hurt Rodgers badly, but it had hurt. Moreover, he now had a wife to support, and, as Dorothy wrote, he was a sybarite, spoiled by her and his parents, and reluctant to give up the comforts of his celebrity. But he was also intrigued by the new medium. In early 1930 he and Hart had written some songs for the Paramount picture Follow Through (later renamed Follow Thru), an early Technicolor movie about golf that starred Buddy Rogers. None of Rodgers and Hart's songs were used; the hit song from the film was "Button Up Your Overcoat," by De Sylva, Brown, and Henderson.

Their show Spring Is Here had been made into a movie, but many of their songs were omitted and songs by other composers added. It did feature "With a Song in My Heart," from the original show. According to the modern-day critic Richard Barrios, the song was performed by Lawrence Gray, whose "skimpily nasal tenor" did the melody no favors, but it was reprised by others at the end of the film.[6] The screen credit read: "Music by Richard Rogers" [sic]. The film was a "light frappe," one critic noted, and it lost money.

Cole Porter and Jerome Kern suffered the same fate in their early films. Men in the Sky was intended to feature a score by Kern, but it was turned into a melodrama, and his music disappeared altogether. Porter's Fifty Million Frenchmen was turned into a comedy for the zany team of Olsen and Johnson, and his score was relegated to background music. Much the same happened to George Gershwin in his first Hollywood outing, Delicious. Ira Gershwin's delightful "Blah, Blah, Blah" did survive, however.

In 1929, Rodgers and Hart themselves had a brief excursion into films, appearing in a short subject called Makers [or Masters] of Melody. They reenacted the writing of several of their songs, beginning with "Manhattan." It was fictitious, of course, and Barrios found their performance "abashed and numbingly self-conscious."[7] The movie nevertheless brought them publicity. They were featured in newspaper articles, and each wrote a supposedly humorous article about the other. Hart, according to Rodgers, liked tall chorus girls, "preferably over six feet," whereas Hart claimed that Rodgers was partial to blonde chorus girls who were "very innocent looking. Brains not essential." Such high jinks were about to end.

Richard Rodgers and Dorothy Feiner were married by a rabbi on March 5, 1930, in a ceremony in her parents' apartment, attended only by the family, with Hart and Fields as ushers.[8] Out of deference to her family, the couple had already held a lavish engagement party. They honeymooned in Italy, Cannes, Paris, and finally London, where work awaited Rodgers. The impact of married life was immediately apparent. During their trips to London, Rodgers and Hart had usually stayed at a service flat in St. James's; when Dorothy Rodgers saw it, she was appalled by its run-down condition. Rodgers sheepishly agreed with her, and they rented a home in Regent's Park. What Dorothy Rodgers had not counted on was that the newlyweds would be joined by Hart! The house was large enough to accommodate Hart (and his various guests), but his unshaven presence at breakfast, together with his ever-present cigar, was more than the new bride could tolerate. For a decade Rodgers and Hart had worked together, occasionally shared an apartment, and collaborated almost daily. After Rodgers married, that began to change. In London, and later in Hollywood, Hart took his own accommodations. But given Hart's reckless lifestyle, this separation from Rodgers compounded the problems of collaboration. Hart was absent without leave more and more frequently, and was difficult to corral for work.

The new trio—Dick, Dorothy, and Larry—was in London for another show by C. B. Cochran, again featuring Jessie Matthews. By then Matthews had become a full-fledged star and would soon marry another well-known British musical performer, Sonnie Hale. She had gained a certain notoriety for being named a corespondent in a divorce action filed by Hale's wife, Evelyn Laye, also a musical comedy star. Rodgers wrote that "her naive charm, gossamer dancing and liquid voice won praise, even adoration." In the new show, Ever Green, she played a young lady who, hoping to break into show business, claims to be her sixty-year-old mother, Harriet Green, who had been a star before moving to Australia.

The score that Rodgers and Hart composed in London included a song rejected by Ziegfeld, "Dancing on the Ceiling," which Cochran gave to Jessie Matthews. The song has some dissonant harmony, uncommon for Rodgers, and clever lyrics—a pleasant surprise, since Hart often paid less attention to the verse.

Rodgers had composed the music first, as usual, and when Hart heard it, he had a feeling of "weightlessness and elevation," the notion of lovers dancing on a ceiling, hence the line "He dances overhead." Rodgers pointed out that the notes ascended in a straight line in the first two bars, descended in the third bar, but then leaped up by a seventh, from D to C. Rodgers cited these musical leaps when he was accused of relying too heavily on scales. Matthews was more a dancer than a singer, but her version of the song was straightforward and, for that era, quite good. The song did not find its success right away, however.

While Rodgers and Hart completed their score, the new couple indulged in the pleasures of the Mayfair set. In this social circle Dorothy, then only twenty, met Rodgers' titled friends and acquaintances, including the prince of Wales (the future Edward VIII) and the duke of Kent. Dorothy ingenuously passed up an invitation from Sir Philip Sassoon to a weekend party for the prince of Wales, to the mortification of her English hosts. This early interlude in their marriage apparently was thoroughly enjoyable. The full force of the Depression had not yet hit, and, as Dorothy wrote, "You could get anything you wanted—if you could afford to pay for it."

The Rodgerses eventually had to give up this "delightful but unrealistic" life to return to New York. Despite her husband's status in London, Dorothy did not become an Anglophile: she found the lax morals of London society unsettling and was deeply disturbed by the barely concealed anti-Americanism and anti-Semitism she found there. While still in London, Dorothy confirmed that she was pregnant. Neither she nor her husband rejoiced at this unexpected news. As a practical matter, it meant giving up Richard's bachelor apartment at the Lombardy, with one year left on the lease, and finding new accommodations.

Beyond that, pregnancy placed physical limitations on her. After returning to New York she was advised by her obstetrician and brother-in-law, Mortimer Rodgers, that she could not risk a rough ocean voyage in October, when Rodgers and Hart were scheduled put the finishing touches on *Ever Green*. This injunction made her "childishly resentful" of her pregnancy, which turned out to be quite difficult.[9]

In June 1930, Rodgers left Dorothy behind and embarked for California to fulfill part of his contract with First National Pictures. Dorothy would join him in July. Hart and Herbert Fields had arrived ahead of Rodgers to work on a picture written by Fields and tentatively titled *The Hot Heiress*. Rodgers immediately found Hollywood exciting. He and Hart had chauffeurs, a suite of offices, and the encouragement of Jack Warner—at least at first. The day after arriving Rodgers and Hart had already written a new song, "Like Ordinary People," which turned out to be the only song of value for that picture. They worked easily in the new atmosphere. Rodgers reported faithfully to his bride, writing that he and Hart had no trouble "tearing off" new songs. Whether it was the climate, the atmosphere, or the novelty of it all, what he and Hart were tearing off was second-rate.

Rodgers did not realize that studios heads, unlike Broadway producers, were in no great hurry. There were no out-of-town deadlines or theaters booked in advance. Often the producers had no idea how a picture would develop. The existence of songs—even good ones—was therefore an embarrassment to the producers. Rodgers and Hart were urged by the studio to take some time off, to enjoy themselves. This was fine with Hart, who found Hollywood alluring, though Rodgers reported to his wife that "Larry is less crazy than usual, and is working like the devil." It must be the air, Rodgers concluded.[10]

Rodgers had finished the score before Dorothy arrived, though nothing had been recorded. The leading players were Ben Lyon and Ona Munson, who had almost been recruited for *Peggy-Ann*. Munson never became a star, but she did play the notorious Belle Watling in *Gone with the Wind*. In the supporting cast of *Hot Heiress* were the future stars Walter Pidgeon and Thelma Todd, neither of whom sang in the film.

Nevertheless, Rodgers was pleased by the handling of his songs; they were given good orchestrations and recorded by fine professionals. Talk around the studio was that the picture would be great. But when *Hot Heiress* was released eight months later it flopped.

Contrary to her husband's prediction, Dorothy Rodgers did not like Hollywood. She found it a lonely, synthetic place. In stark contrast to London, there were no museums and no theater; there was nothing to do but read. The young couple knew few people and had no real social life. Hart, as usual, was involved in his own circle. Finally, in August, feeling deflated and discouraged, they willingly said good-bye. Dorothy wrote: "To say that Hollywood didn't welcome us is a gigantic understatement. We weren't even noticed; we weren't snubbed, just ignored. . . . There was little friendliness among the natives toward people from the theatre. There was, in fact, a good deal of hostility directed toward the likes of us and, indeed, Easterners in general."[11]

Rodgers left Hollywood feeling that although *Hot Heiress* was puerile, at least his songs had been well integrated. And even if he hadn't learned much about writing for films, the process of moviemaking had been fascinating. Years later he recalled the experience as "awful," but that judgment probably was colored by his subsequent misfortunes there.

In late August, Rodgers left for London. Dorothy remained in New York, as advised. Preparations for *Ever Green* were dragging on longer than expected. Cochran had decided to use a revolving stage, and the mechanical difficulties added to the out-of-town problems. In spite of being there without his wife, Rodgers pursued an active social calendar, reporting on the various parties and weekends in his letters. He was friendly with Noel Coward, who was then starring with Gertrude Lawrence in his own new play, *Private Lives*. In the middle of that play Coward sat down at the piano and played eight bars of "Dancing on the Ceiling," to Rodgers' immense satisfaction. For a time his parents, his brother, and his in-laws were also in London. One of their companions was Joyce Barbour, the diminutive dancer who had appeared with Busby Berkeley in *Present*

Arms. She was "quite attractive" and "safe," according to Rodgers, because she was soon to be married. She took him to the dress rehearsal of the latest version of *Charlot's Revue,* starring Beatrice Lillie, which he did not like because of the poor material.

Ever Green went well, but Rodgers called it the strangest show he had ever worked on because writing for it got easier rather than harder. Jessie Matthews' version of "Dancing on the Ceiling" was being done "just as it should be," which was a "rare experience for me these days." Later he complained about the orchestrations, which he thought sounded "square." His life was eased by his decision not to live with Hart. "He's worse than ever," Rodgers wrote, "and if he doesn't go completely mad soon, I will!" He also reported that although Hart was working hard, staging numbers was simple "if Larry isn't there." Rodgers convinced Cochran that he had completed his work and should be allowed to leave London before the opening. He left for New York in late October 1930.[12]

Ever Green, which was more a revue than a book musical, drew praise for its spectacular sets and costumes and the rapid change of scenes via the revolving stage. Rodgers' score shared in the good reviews. The film version of the show—its title telescoped to *Evergreen*—was a popular vehicle for Matthews, though much of the score was changed and most of the songs by Rodgers and Hart were dropped.

Before leaving Great Britain, Rodgers had received a new libretto by Herbert Fields. It was a story about Hollywood, but neither Rodgers nor Hart liked it—Hollywood had been roasted too much to warrant another show about it. Achieving success today, Rodgers wrote, "was too difficult to allow us to do anything that isn't at least fresh in its inception."[13] The plot concerned a young singer, who becomes popular in silent films, and her boyfriend, who does not; when talkies arrive their roles are reversed. Much of the show was a satire on moviemaking—probably Fields' revenge for the unkind treatment his script received in *Hot Heiress.*

Rodgers still had a contract for two more movies, but Warner Brothers officials in New York were stalling, urging him to see Jack Warner. What Rodgers had not comprehended was that musical films were no longer popular and that Warner Brothers was in deep financial trouble. The movie industry was about to experience its worst year. Rodgers went to California, where Warner offered to settle the contract for five thousand dollars. Rodgers was furious but had little choice, so he made a settlement and returned to New York. Times were such that even though Rodgers disliked Fields' script, he agreed to do the show, to be called *America's Sweetheart,* a swipe at Mary Pickford.

The Depression was deepening, and for the first time, Rodgers' telephone was not jangling with offers from producers. In fact, Rodgers, Hart, and Fields had trouble finding a producer, because the easy money of the 1920s was drying up. Finally, they took their show to Lawrence Schwab and Frank Mandel, who had compiled a fine record with *Desert Song*, *New Moon*, and *Good News*. Schwab agreed to produce the show but insisted that one of his discoveries, a young singer and dancer named Harriet Lake, be cast in it. Lake was given the one outstanding song, "I've Got Five Dollars," and she became a hit. (She eventually went to Hollywood, where her name was changed to Ann Sothern.) She found Rodgers a "very, very stern man," an opinion shared by Jessie Matthews. Rodgers' personality apparently was taking on sharper edges.

Rodgers' daughter, Mary, was born on January 11, 1931. Shortly after her birth Rodgers went to Pittsburgh for the tryouts of *America's Sweetheart*. The press proclaimed it a "large, compact and merry jamboree." At this early date, "I've Got Five Dollars" was singled out for special notice, as was Lake. But in New York, in early February, the verdict was different: "The wit is clumsy, much of the humor is foul and the book goes to a great deal of trouble to make both ends meet." The reviewer, Brooks Atkinson, found that there was a "rush" about the music and a "mocking touch" in the lyrics that made the score more "deftly satirical than the production."

Although the score was not one of the team's most durable, it included the fine but forgotten "We'll Be the Same," a lively, sentimental melody with lyrics to match. It is in the same general category as "Why Do You Suppose?" but that type of song was beginning to fade. Rodgers thought that it would be a hit, but as the Depression worsened such airily optimistic songs were becoming difficult for the public to accept—except for those that were purposely ludicrous, such as Harry Warren's "The Gold Diggers' Song (We're in the Money)."

Dorothy Parker, who was substituting for Robert Benchley at the *New Yorker*, wrote a memorable review of *America's Sweetheart* (February 21, 1931). She noted that the new show was by Fields, Rodgers, and Hart—"two of whom seem to me extraordinarily over-rated young men." This barb wasn't aimed at Rodgers, however: "Mr. Hart has donated lyrics the rhymes for which are less internal than colonic; they have a peculiar, even for Broadway, nastiness of flavor. What, by the way, has ever become of that little thing called taste? And Mr. Rodgers has contributed a truly charming score, each number of which gets better each time you hear it." This was the review that ended with the unforgettable line: "Personal: Robert Benchley, please come home. Nothing is forgiven."

Richard Rodgers seated at the piano with his two-
year-old daughter Mary (1933), the future composer
of *Once Upon a Mattress*.

Rodgers and Hart had lampooned the movies in general and talking pictures in particular, but they nonetheless found themselves again headed for Hollywood. Although their shows had not fared well on film—*Spring Is Here* had failed at the box office, and *Heads Up* and *Present Arms* (renamed *Leathernecking*) were undistinguished—the team accepted an offer from Paramount to do a picture for Maurice Chevalier and Jeanette MacDonald. *America's Sweetheart* was their last Broadway show for almost five years.

Again Rodgers' motive for the move was money, but this time he was more hard-pressed. The Depression had begun to take its toll as the cost of a new family grew. Rodgers and his wife had left the Lombardy for a more expensive apartment and furnishings. Dorothy's father had killed himself in October after a long illness that included bouts of depression, and the Rodgerses decided that they could not leave Dorothy's mother alone in New York. So in November 1931, Dick, Dorothy, baby Mary and her nurse, a housemaid, Dorothy's mother—and Larry Hart—left for California, a move that "change[d] . . . the direction of our lives," Dorothy wrote. They had planned to stay only three months, but they did not return to New York to live for almost three years.

9

HOLLYWOOD

Rodgers and Hart were not alone in turning to Hollywood. Given the city's irresistible lure, most of the major songwriters of the 1920s made the same trek. At first, the new film capital was overly eager for musicals. The *New York Times* reported (June 9, 1929) that "scouts were sent to every cabaret in New York and to every night club in a mad search for song writers and lyricists." Irving Berlin supposedly was "snatched" from New York and hustled to California in the belief that "the climate would stimulate his genius."

In fact, Berlin did write some early movies, but he resisted the temptation to leave New York. Gershwin and Kern finally made the move, and Porter shuttled between the coasts. In the early days of talking pictures the songwriters often congregated at the Brown Derby restaurant. One evening a newspaper columnist noted those in attendance: Jack Yellen, the lyricist for "Ain't She Sweet"; Walter Donaldson, composer of "Yes Sir, That's My Baby"; Harry Akst, who wrote "Baby Face"; and Bert Kalmar and Harry Ruby, then writing both movie scripts and songs such as "Three Little Words."

The major studios were interested in having hit songs in their productions, but the musical knowledge of the producers and many of the directors was limited. The studios therefore put together rudimentary staffs of resident songwriters, musical arrangers, and conductors. The cumbersome system did not necessarily stimulate creativity, but eventually it produced a body of good music. Nevertheless, even the established composers lost control over whether and how their songs would be used. The final film might contain only snatches of a song.

The contrast between Hollywood's new energy and the doleful state of Broadway grew increasingly obvious. The total investment in the film industry was reported at about $2.5 billion in 1929–30, and another $500 million was scheduled for investment in sound. In 1931 more than 22,000 picture houses existed. Weekly attendance at the movies grew from about 40 million in 1922 to 115 million in 1930. Performers who had been virtually unknown were exposed to huge audiences. Maurice Chevalier, a star in Paris in the 1920s, became world famous after appearing in several Hollywood films. It was pointed out that more people watched Chevalier perform during a one-week film run at a movie house than during six weeks of personal appearances in Paris.

The music received the same exposure. In a large Broadway house the audience might number up to one thousand for a performance, which meant a weekly total of perhaps seven thousand. But this attendance was easily matched by handful of movie parlors in any large city. The ratios were compelling. The undeniable fact was that a composer could make far more money in Hollywood with minimal effort. A few songs for a movie, written over two or three months, could yield more than even a highly successful Broadway show, which might take months to produce and then run for less than a year.

The popularity of movie musicals began to fall off, reflected in a sharp decline in box office receipts. In 1932 only twelve genuine new film musicals were produced. One of them was the new movie assigned by Paramount to Rodgers and Hart when they arrived in Hollywood. The film, a romantic comedy set in Paris and the French countryside, was the third in a series of innovative musicals produced by Paramount. The first, The Love Parade (1929), starring Maurice Chevalier and Jeanette MacDonald, was a masterpiece of integrated song and story. The director, Ernst Lubitsch, who had acted and studied under Max Reinhardt in Germany, had a refined feel for how music should be woven into the action by means of unusual cinematography. The second movie, *Monte Carlo* (1930), also was directed by Lubitsch and starred MacDonald, though Chevalier's role was given to the British star Jack Buchanan. This duo proved slightly less successful at the box office, so Paramount decided to reunite Chevalier and MacDonald for a third picture, *Love Me Tonight*.

The Paramount series was very much in the operatic tradition, with European settings, European-sounding songs for Chevalier, and arias for MacDonald, so it was somewhat surprising that Rodgers and Hart were chosen to write the score. Sigmund Romberg, Rudolf Friml, or even Jerome Kern would have seemed more logical choices. Hart's boyhood friend Mel Shauer probably was responsible for their receiving the assignment. Shauer was an assistant to Paramount executive Jesse Lasky, and he reminded Lasky of *Makers of Melody*, Rodgers and Hart's successful short subject. Lubitsch was not available to direct this time, so Rouben Mamoulian was hired. This was a major break for Rodgers and Hart. Mamoulian was a skilled musician with a sensitive feel for music and film, and a strong but not dictatorial hand. He would later direct the stage version of Gershwin's *Porgy and Bess,* and in the 1940s he would participate in some of Rodgers' greatest shows.

As soon as they arrived in Hollywood, Rodgers and Hart went to work with Mamoulian — not on the soundstage but in the cutting room, where they studied film techniques. They wrote music to be cut into the production at crucial moments. Hart insisted that there was no easy transfer from Broadway to Hollywood, because the movies were a visual medium that required almost constant action. Although this may have been true, Rodgers' music was not affected. His score was well tailored to the story line, and the action had a European aura. Moreover, most of the movie's popular songs could easily have been adapted to a Broadway score.

In *Love Me Tonight,* Chevalier plays a Parisian tailor who pursues a deadbeat customer, a titled aristocrat, to a nobleman's castle. To avoid embarrassing his customer the tailor poses as a baron. He meets Jeanette MacDonald on his way to the castle, and, naturally, they fall in love. Chevalier's identity is finally exposed: "The son of a gun is nothing but a tailor" was Hart's lyric. The couple are finally reconciled as MacDonald, on horseback, overtakes the train carrying Chevalier back to Paris. The picture received good reviews and became something of a classic.

What distinguished the film was not the pseudo–fairy tale but the sensitive use of the camera. The synergy of Rodgers, Hart, and Mamoulian was evident in the opening scenes of the rooftops of Paris, the Eiffel Tower, and the streets below, where early-morning Paris is stirring, all to the accompaniment of Rodgers' music, which gradually absorbs and replaces the street sounds. The technique was effective in establishing the locale and the ambience of the story (Mamoulian used the same technique to depict Catfish Row in *Porgy and Bess*).

The camera then focuses on Chevalier in his shop singing "Isn't It Romantic?" At first the lyrics express the romance of tailoring for a customer planning marriage. The song is picked up by the customer, who leaves the shop and gets into a taxi, whose driver then continues the melody. A long-haired composer takes it up while strolling along the street; soldiers on a train take over the song and then march through the countryside singing, passing the tune to a Gypsy. Finally, the scene dissolves to Jeanette MacDonald, who, listening to the Gypsies from her castle window, sings the refrain. The music and lyrics foreshadow the story that will follow and even set up MacDonald's premise that a "hero might appear." Not only did this become the main song of the film, but it was one of Rodgers' best to date: "A perfect song . . . superb writing" was the verdict of musicologist Alec Wilder.[1]

After working through most of the score, Rodgers and Hart played it for Chevalier. He sat through their performance stone-faced and then left. They were stunned—this had never happened to them. The next day they learned that Chevalier had been ecstatic but was afraid to let on lest they grow complacent and stop working. Rodgers and Hart had done their jobs well: they had written several very good songs, including a spirited pseudo-French music-hall song for Chevalier, "Mimi," which would forever after be his musical emblem. Few other singers dared try it because it was so closely associated with Chevalier, though several of the characters in the movie reprised it, including Myrna Loy (whose risqué chorus was cut by censors).

The score also included the lovely waltz "Lover," sung by MacDonald when she encounters her soon-to-be suitor. The lyrics for the movie differ from those in the published version, which Hart altered to allow the song to be sung outside of the film's context. The song endured, and in the early 1950s it was revived as a swing version, popularized by the vocalist Peggy Lee, who gave it a hyper, if not weird, treatment against a very fast rhythm. When asked for his reaction to this version, Rodgers caustically commented, "After all, it's a waltz." The title song, "Love Me Tonight," also gained a quick popularity. The entire score is easily one of Rodgers and Hart's best, well above the standard of their more recent Broadway shows.

The boys from New York were off to a solid start. The picture was released in August 1932, and *Variety* called it a "gem of a class production": "Musical numbers are as amusing for once in their lyrics as they are attractive in their melodies."

It soon became apparent that this film was a high point for Rodgers and Hart in Hollywood. Things began going downhill almost immediately, according to Rodgers. The partners, in a new office of their own, were assigned to *Phantom President*, starring George M. Cohan. What should have been a rare opportunity to work with the legendary Broadway showman turned out to be a disagreeable experience. Cohan treated everyone with disdain, and the studio treated him badly in turn. The film was his debut in talking pictures, but he did not engender the respect his reputation called for. He wrote one song and danced a little, but in the end there was no Rodgers and Hart score to speak of (except for "Give Her a Kiss," a solid song). The picture, released in late 1932, shortly after *Love Me Tonight* and just before the presidential elections, did not do well. Even Hoover was more popular, Rodgers commented. Cohan, noted one reviewer, belonged to another era.

For his part, Cohan remarked that he would rather do a term in Leavenworth than return to Hollywood. Rodgers later noted that Cohan was an introvert and a loner; he also speculated that because Cohan himself was a songwriter, he resented having songs written for him. In any case, "he was unpleasant and not a very nice man."[2]

Rodgers and Hart, who had a number of offers from other studios, switched from Paramount to United Artists to write for a picture with Al Jolson, eventually titled *Hallelujah, I'm a Bum*. When Rodgers and Hart entered the production the film had already been made and previewed. But it had not gone over well, and the studio chief, Joseph Schenk, decided that it had to be completely redone, including new music to replace the songs by Irving Caesar. Ben Hecht and S. N. Behrman were called in as the new writers. The chance to work with and write for Jolson was the main incentive for Rodgers and Hart. Almost any good song rendered by Jolson was sure to be successful, and he was a great favorite of Lorenz Hart's. Rodgers liked him, too: "The archetype extrovert, which you knew by listening to him sing, by seeing him and watching him perform. And he was that way in a room. He was that way making a picture. . . . He was delightful to work with, very appreciative, liked things — even liked things that weren't very good. He was fine."[3]

Rodgers and Hart began work on October 18 and finished on November 7, 1932. The story, inspired by the Depression, was a new subject for the movies. A homeless man named Bumper (Jolson) lives in Central Park and leads a community of down-and-outers. Bumper's various sidekicks include a radical socialist, played by the silent film comedian Harry Langdon, who calls the police "Hoover's Cossacks." The mayor of New York, played by Frank Morgan, is a

James Walker type who spends a great deal of time in the park philosophizing with Bumper. Hart supplied some of the dialogue, written in rhyming couplets. Rodgers appeared briefly in the film as a photographer, and Hart as a banker.

The picture was a heavy-handed social and political commentary and satire, and the effort to use the music "rhythmically," as Hart put it, was less than effective. In addition, the story did not quite ring true. At the last minute Rodgers and Hart composed one of their best songs, "You Are Too Beautiful," which was not really compatible with Jolson's style, as his recording of it makes clear. One of the other songs for Jolson was titled "I Gotta Get Back to New York," but that message was not to be for Rodgers and Hart. While final work was under way on *Hallelujah, I'm a Bum*, Rodgers and Hart, through their agent, Phil Berg, began negotiations with MGM and its resident genius, Irving Thalberg.

They signed on with MGM in 1932, and the studio gave them a choice of stories. Rodgers and Hart decided on a romantic comedy about a man who marries an angel. The writer assigned to the book was Moss Hart, then celebrated for *Once in a Lifetime*, his satire on Hollywood. Some of the score for the new film (tentatively titled *I Married an Angel*) was written in February 1933. (The title song became a hit five years later.) But that spring or summer the head of the studio, Louis B. Mayer, decided that the projected story of a man who sleeps with an angel was morally questionable—religious groups reportedly had protested. Later the Breen office would denounce the script as vulgar and profane. The entire project was canceled, and Moss Hart returned to Manhattan to work with Irving Berlin on *As Thousands Cheer*.

Rodgers and Hart nevertheless decided to stay for one more year, especially after they surveyed the dismal prospects of Depression-ridden Broadway. They made a big mistake by signing another contract with MGM that put them at the beck and call of the studio—they received sizable weekly paychecks but no freedom to choose their assignments. Rodgers also began to realize that abandoning Hollywood and returning to New York would not be easy, and this depressing realization began to affect his work.

Rodgers and Hart were soon mired in a mishmash of stories, directors, and writers, including David Selznick, Rodgers' old camp mate. Selznick responded to one song by asking Rodgers whether he could improve it. The pair were told that they should try to sound more like Mack Gordon and Harry Revel, the two Hollywood writers who had composed "Did You Ever See a Dream Walking?"

Their next project was an inchoate revue called *Hollywood Party*, or *Hollywood Revue*, which was to feature a bevy of stars, led by Jimmy Durante, doing an impersonation of Tarzan. Each star would perform a specially written song. So during the summer of 1933, Rodgers and Hart wrote for performers they did not know or had never heard, such as Marlene Dietrich and Jean Harlow. (The Rodgerses eventually met Harlow on the train back to New York. They found her friendly and a lot of fun. She even taught Dorothy Rodgers how to shoot craps.)

Rodgers and Hart wrote about twenty songs for the project, although other songwriters were also assigned to the picture. While working on the revue Rodgers and Hart became caught up in a studio quarrel. On one side were the producers of *Hollywood Party*, who were sponsored by Thalberg, the studio's head. On the other side was Thalberg's rival, Selznick, who was producing *Dancing Lady*, starring Joan Crawford and Clark Gable. Rodgers and Hart were ordered to write songs for Selznick's production, which already had music by Herb Brown and Arthur Freed. Although they balked at the idea of inserting their work into another team's score, they had to comply, and in August, while still working on *Hollywood Party*, they wrote a song requested by Selznick, titled, at his suggestion, "That's the Rhythm of the Day." The original performer died, and the tune was finally performed by a newcomer named Nelson Eddy. (Both the song and the performance ranked with the worst these talents had to offer.) The title song reminded Rodgers of "Ten Cents a Dance," but Selznick did not like it, and it was not used in the picture. They also wrote a song for another MGM picture, *Peg o' My Heart*, titled "When You're Falling in Love with the Irish," which mercifully was dropped.

The team was heading toward rock bottom. One of their producers for *Hollywood Party* (the title kept changing) was the songwriter-lyricist and MGM publicist Howard Dietz. Hart decided that Dietz was out to get him, which did not inspire Hart to produce. Rodgers wrote that Hart's persecution mania was getting worse and making him bitter about everything. Rodgers consulted friends, including Herb Fields, about Hart's mood, but no one was able to help. Rodgers was drinking more during this period, and he reported to Dorothy, who was back in New York briefly, that he had gotten the drunkest he had been in five years. Nevertheless, he kept claiming in his letters that everyone was raving about their music. Joan Crawford "squealed with delight" when she heard one song.

As the popularity of their songs from *Love Me Tonight* grew, other studios began to inquire about borrowing Rodgers and Hart from MGM. They wrote "That's Love" for the Samuel Goldwyn picture *Nana*, starring Ana Sten. According to Rodgers, Goldwyn "yelled and screamed" when he heard it and told Sten that it was the best song ever written. At one point they were told that they were to do the entire score for *Dancing Lady*, but that idea died, along with their songs, including one for Crawford called "Black Diamond," which she was to perform in blackface. The lyric for the verse began, "I've ruby lips and iv'ry teeth and ebony cheeks." Rodgers, Hart, and Crawford must have been relieved that it did not make the movie.

They continued to work on *Hollywood Party*, and in mid-June, Rodgers informed Dorothy that he was exhausted from having written so intensely. He even admitted that he had turned out a song that was pretty bad. Among the many songs written for this disastrous film, and then dropped, was "Fly Away to Ioway," a clever satire on Harry Warren's "Shuffle Off to Buffalo." Another, an amusing number entitled "Reincarnation" and written for Jimmy Durante, survived the cuts and was the only song published from the film.

Out of this rubble came one gem, a song tentatively called "Prayer" because of the opening lyric: "Oh, Lord, if you're not busy up there." Harlow was to sing it in *Hollywood Party*, but it was dropped. Rodgers and Hart rewrote it slightly; it now began:

Oh, Lord!
What is the matter with me?

This version, however, was destined for the gangster movie *Manhattan Melody*, starring Clark Gable, William Powell, and Myrna Loy. Shirley Ross, cast as the vocalist for a band in the Cotton Club, sang the new version and also recorded it. Powell and Loy talked through much of the song, which was limited to one chorus. The song languished. Finally, prodded by the music publisher Jack Robbins, who wanted a commercial lyric, Hart redid it one last time: "Blue moon, you saw me standing alone." "Blue Moon" (published in December 1934) assumed its place as one of Rodgers and Hart's finest songs, and one of the only songs not written for a specific production.

Increasingly frustrated, Rodgers and Hart resigned from MGM, though their differences with the studio were quickly patched up. A casual encounter with Vincent Youmans, who talked about the terrible state of Broadway, convinced them that staying in Hollywood was the right choice. Their next major assignment was to redo the lyrics and some of the background music for an MGM production of *The Merry Widow*. Rodgers wrote some original melodies, but none were used. The screen credits read only "Additional Words and Music by Lorenz Hart and Richard Rodgers."

For Rodgers, matters came to a head when he read a column by the syndicated Broadway writer O. O. MacIntyre, who asked: "Whatever happened to Rodgers and Hart?" Rodgers candidly summed up his recent accomplishments: he had produced one score that was not used at all because the film was never made; one score that was largely unused; one song for Goldwyn; and one song for Selznick. He and Hart decided to return to New York as soon as their contract expired in the spring of 1934. Before leaving, Rodgers felt obligated to say good-bye to Thalberg, who had hired them. He was ushered into the inner sanctum, where Thalberg was conducting a staff meeting. Thalberg's "glassy stare" made it obvious that he had no idea who Rodgers was. Years later, in his autobiography, Rodgers wrote: "To Thalberg we were all faceless, anonymous cogs. Whenever we were needed, all he had to do was press a button and we'd hop over to help turn the company's wheels. . . . What a waste of money, time and talent. . . . I found it impossible to adjust to this unpressured, indolent existence."[4]

There is no doubt that his experience in Hollywood caused a personal and professional crisis for Rodgers. He was apparently so despondent that he sought the advice of a friend and physician, who concluded that his mental troubles were the result of frustrations over his work. Rodgers also discussed his de-pression with Dorothy. If there was a low point in his career after the original *Garrick Gaieties*, this was it. The final eighteen months in Hollywood had com-pletely eroded his confidence.

At first his return to New York did not help his state of mind. Their con-tacts were diminished, and he and Hart found no work on Broadway. Aarons and Freedley had broken up, as had Schwab and Mandel, and Lew Fields was no longer producing. Rodgers had gone increasingly into debt; he was maintain-ing a large household, and another child was expected. In the early summer of 1934, Rodgers and Hart were offered a strictly defined six-week contract from Paramount for one picture, to be produced by Arthur Hornblow, Jr., who had befriended them in their earlier stay in California. Despite his distrust of Holly-wood, he and Hart agreed to return to write the score for *Mississippi*, starring W. C. Fields and the singer Lanny Ross. This time Rodgers' incentive was not only money; his ulterior motive was revenge.

He was determined to prove that the recent dismal period in Hollywood was a fluke. He and Hart wrote quickly, and a solid love song, "Soon," emerged, intended for Ross. Although he had doubts about Ross's ability, Rodgers was satisfied with his own work. He wrote Dorothy from California that he was be-coming more and more comfortable and was no longer nervous, and by the end of his stay he had begun to regain his confidence. He was more excited about his music than he had been in the past seven years: ideas were pouring out, and he felt as though the world was "my particular pie." The contract fulfilled, he returned to New York a "better man." He was especially grateful to Dorothy for being so understanding during his times of unhappiness.[5]

That fall he and Hart received an urgent appeal from the studio for one more song. Ross was being replaced by Bing Crosby, who did not like the score. While remaining in New York, Rodgers and Hart wrote the major song of the film, "It's Easy to Remember," which Crosby recorded and which became a hit when the picture was released in 1935. In the first broadcast of the Hit Parade in the spring of 1935, "Soon" was number one and "It's Easy to Remember" was number ten—both helped by Crosby's recordings.

Rodgers had his revenge for *Dancing Lady* and *Hollywood Party*.

10

ON YOUR TOES

Rodgers and Hart returned to a Broadway that had been significantly damaged by the Depression. The theater was surviving on "half rations": only half of the theaters in New York were in use, fewer than half the actors were employed, and virtually all bankrolls were "hiding." The pundits concluded that the day of five-dollar theater tickets was about over; the average ticket would have to sell for a more modest price, and that would mean lower royalties and salaries.[1]

Only a few successful musicals had been produced on Broadway while Rodgers and Hart were away. Kern had *Music in the Air*, then he bowed out of Broadway (until 1939) with *Roberta* in November 1933. Irving Berlin and Moss Hart scored with *As Thousands Cheer*. The Gershwins had written the Pulitzer Prize–winning *Of Thee I Sing* but failed with *Let 'Em Eat Cake* and *Pardon My English*. In 1935 came George Gershwin's great *Porgy and Bess*. Rodgers saw the show and liked it, though he thought that the long recitatives should have been trimmed. He much preferred the pared-down version produced by Cheryl Crawford in 1942. Perhaps the most notable change was the arrival of Cole Porter as the new king of the Great White Way. When his revue *Paris* opened in 1929 critics wrote that Porter would someday give Broadway an entire musical, and "when he does, the Messrs. Rodgers and Hart had best look to their laurels." His biggest hit was *Anything Goes* of 1934, which Brooks Atkinson called a "thundering good musical show."[2]

The problem for Rodgers and Hart, however, was not the new competition, which never seemed to bother them, but the more practical problem of obtaining financial backing. RKO was looking for another vehicle for Fred Astaire, and Rodgers and Hart developed a story about a relationship between a vaudeville hoofer and a ballet dancer. The man responsible for producing the Astaire-Rogers pictures, Pandro Berman, liked the idea, but his associates supposedly turned it down for some reason.

Generating support for their idea back in New York did not go well either, until they ran into Lee Shubert and Harry Kaufman, who were looking for a story to showcase Ray Bolger. Hart and Rodgers explained their idea, and according to Rodgers the four men struck a deal while standing on the corner of 45th and Broadway. Later, while Rodgers was playing some of the score for Shubert, Hart kept singing louder and louder, until Rodgers turned to see what the problem was: Lee Shubert had fallen asleep! In the time that had passed since the deal was made, the Shuberts had decided to produce a new musical revue, *At Home Abroad*, with Beatrice Lillie. Although they were not ready to go ahead with the Rodgers and Hart show, they refused to relinquish their option.

Rodgers had no choice but to wait out the Shuberts, even though he had generated other interest in his idea. Fortunately, in the late spring of 1935 the super showman Billy Rose made an enticing offer to Rodgers and Hart. Rose, and old friend of Hart's, had married Fanny Brice in 1929 and was constantly chafing under the mantle of his famous wife. He was determined to become famous in his own right. His latest idea was to mount an extravaganza about a circus: it would be set in a big top and feature a live elephant named Jumbo, after the famous Barnum elephant. (The elephant was in fact named Rosie, but after a week's rehearsal she would answer only to Jumbo.) Only the massive Hippodrome on 44th Street could accommodate the ambitious show. Rose hired Ben Hecht and Charles MacArthur as writers and Jimmy Durante as one of the stars.

Rodgers regarded Rose as a "very mixed up" man. He was "very enthusiastic, very bright" as well, and most helpful to Rodgers and Hart.[3] But, Rodgers reported, Rose didn't like to pay his bills and was usually late paying out royalties. It was rumored that the show had been offered to other songwriters, but Rodgers and Hart nevertheless eagerly agreed to do the music. When asked why he had chosen Rodgers and Hart, who had not appeared on Broadway for some time, Rose responded that they were the tops, which must have been gratifying to his new songwriters. This show was also the beginning of Rodgers and Hart's long association with the director, producer, and playwright George Abbott. *Jumbo* also reunited them with John Murray Anderson, who had staged *Dearest Enemy*. Anderson had his hands full trying to manage dozens of animals and performers in complicated scenes.

Rehearsals for *Jumbo* ran almost six months, during which time Rose and his resourceful press agents created an enormous ballyhoo. The Hippodrome had to be refurbished. The elephant was rented from Coney Island, and a white horse used in the show cost six hundred dollars per week because it could pound its hooves on command. Sawdust could not be used because of it would damage the costumes, so an artificial floor was created; sachets of sawdust were sprinkled around the theater for effect. Paul Whiteman and his orchestra were hired at six thousand dollars a week. Rose tried to hire Babe Ruth to appear, but to no avail. He talked Actors Equity out of requiring the usual rehearsal pay by declaring that his show was classified as a circus. Occasionally the elephant would be paraded up Sixth Avenue, wearing a huge sign that read "Sh-h-h . . . Jumbo's rehearsing." The principal investor was the wealthy socialite Jock Whitney, and the extraordinarily high costs prompted the quip that *Jumbo* would either make Billy Rose or break Jock Whitney.

For this strange conglomeration of circus, vaudeville, and musical comedy Rodgers and Hart turned out one their best scores; it included "Little Girl Blue," "The Most Beautiful Girl in the World," "My Romance," and "There's a Small Hotel," which was cut from the show. Not only had they kept their touch, but the music that Rodgers wrote after returning to New York had a new depth— in its harmonic and melodic techniques, as well as in its sense of warmth. The brittleness of the earlier period was fading, and even Hart's lyrics lost some of their edge. In fact, Rodgers thought that the lyrics Hart wrote after leaving Hollywood were "of a higher degree of excellence."

"The Most Beautiful Girl in the World" was one of several waltzes that revealed Rodgers' particular talent in the idiom. He took over the basic form, softened the heavy oompah-pah rhythm, and added exotic harmonies. Hart outdid himself. Drawing on his recent Hollywood experience, he wrote:

> The most beautiful star in the world
> Isn't Garbo, isn't Dietrich,
> It's the sweet trick . . .

"My Romance" was a conventional love song along the lines of "Isn't It Romantic?" The hit of the show was first-act closer "Little Girl Blue," in which the heroine dreamed of the glittering circus she knew as a child. With the strains of this lovely melody as background, the arena was bathed in a blue light as the circus performers worked their magic. The musical structure was unusual: the refrain, in 4/4 time, was followed by a trio in waltz time, which was a song unto itself. Although the chorus was somewhat melancholy, the waltz created an optimistic air; the contrast was perfect.

For this show Rose decreed that there would be no overture—only the composer's mother came to hear the overture, he claimed. Instead, in the preliminary scenes the circus performers came on stage, changed into their costumes, and practiced their acts; the background music to this prelude was another waltz, "Over and Over." The show then officially opened with a sharp fanfare, and in from the wings rode bandleader Paul Whiteman on a white stallion, followed by his orchestra in blue-and-gold uniforms, to "The Circus Is on Parade." Girls were shot out of cannons, high-wire acts flew through the air, and Jumbo charmed everyone.

The show opened to more white ties and sables than had assembled in one place "since the coronation of late Czar of Russia," wrote one magazine. The tiniest showman in New York had somehow produced the biggest show in town, and Jumbo boasted a "calliope of good tunes," wrote Brooks Atkinson. Some of the songs took a while to catch on because Rose insisted that they not be played outside the theater, lest audiences lose interest. It was an odd decree, since theatergoers had for weeks been dropping in on Jumbo's late-night rehearsals after the other shows closed.

The gaudy production itself was the star attraction, but Durante provided the high point of the show. In one scene Durante was leading the elephant across the stage when a police officer accosted him and asked accusingly, "Where are you going with that elephant?" Durante answered, in his inimitable gravelly voice, "What elephant?"

In the end, Jumbo lost a great deal of money, but it was a grand vehicle for Rodgers and Hart's return to Broadway. Thus began a five-year stretch of hit shows; at one point the team had three shows running simultaneously.[4]

After Jumbo, Rodgers and Hart had no trouble interesting backers in their idea for a show built around the world of ballet. For this show, titled On Your Toes, Rodgers and Hart decided to write the book themselves. In fact, their two-page synopsis, written while they were in Hollywood, had sold the Shuberts on the idea in the first place. Once free of the Shubert option they completed the book for their new producer, Dwight Deere Wiman, with whom they were to have a long association. But Rodgers and Hart were not as impressed with their own script as they had hoped to be, so they turned to George Abbott, their director, who did a draft of his own. After the usual delays in production, Abbott became frustrated, quit the show, and left for Florida. On Your Toes was then massaged by others, including a new director. After a one-week run in Boston, Rodgers wrote that the performance was "just impossible"; the cast was terrible and the audience was worse. So Rodgers and Wiman appealed to Abbott to return to the production. He agreed but found that the story line had been destroyed by the rewrites and that the cast was "out of hand." Abbott behaved "ruthlessly," quelling the competition among cast members for solos and restoring the book to his original version.

Ray Bolger was still the star, and the show featured two mini-ballets: "Princess Zenobia," a spoof of serious ballet that poked fun at Scheherazade, and "Slaughter on Tenth Avenue," a so-called jazz ballet that was in many ways Rodgers' most notable composition ever. The story is of a young vaudeville dancer, played by Bolger, who leaves his family's act and becomes a teacher at "Knickerbocker University, W.P.A. extension." There he falls in love with a young songwriter, played by Doris Carson; he also meets a composer who has written a ballet. The three of them try to interest a Russian ballet company in the work. The company's director was played by Monty Woolley, and the prima ballerina by Tamara Geva, who shows more interest in the young teacher than in the ballet. Bolger's character is persuaded to take a part in "Princess Zenobia," and he creates havoc on stage. The ballet was performed with mock seriousness, with all of the movements and parts exaggerated; Bolger's part bordered on slapstick.

Rodgers' score for this segment was a collection of pseudo-Russian themes delightfully orchestrated by Hans Spialek, an important addition to the Rodgers and Hart team. Spialek, working with a twenty-five-piece orchestra, wrote the orchestral scores for the two quite different ballets; for a standard song and dance number, "On Your Toes"; for a fast vaudeville opening, "Two a Day for Keith's"; and for the love songs. He also integrated two pianos into the score, an approach that the Gershwins had used to good effect. Rodgers praised Spialek's "uniformly excellent" work.

The show ends with the ballet "Slaughter on Tenth Avenue," danced by Geva and Bolger. Rodgers' fast opening theme captures the tensions of the tough area around Tenth Avenue just as Gershwin's "American in Paris" evokes the French capital in a few bars. The slow theme represents the sights and sounds of the West Side of Manhattan in the mid-1930s. It also has its humorous moments, such as a quote from "Three Blind Mice." Rodgers even simulated pistol shots by quoting the musical cliché "shave and a haircut—two bits," with pistol shots replacing the "two bits."

On the suggestion of Hart, On Your Toes was choreographed by George Balanchine, who had been married to Geva. At a party celebrating Russian Easter shortly after the opening, he met his future wife, Vera Zorina, who was to star in the London production of the show. Zorina, who had just seen the show on Broadway, remarked to Balanchine that ballet fans had howled at the "Princess Zenobia" parody of ballet conventions. According to Balanchine, the original idea was Hart's. Balanchine and Hart had become friends shortly after Balanchine had arrived in America in 1934. They met through a notorious friend of Hart's, Milton "Doc" Bender, a sometime dentist who became Hart's "manager" and who was generally regarded as unsavory. Hart never learned to drive (which Dorothy Rodgers believed saved his life many times), so Balanchine drove Hart around in a Cadillac. Hart, Balanchine wrote, always appeared "happy and laughing."

After writing some of the ballet music for On Your Toes, Rodgers was uncertain how to proceed. He asked the advice of Balanchine, who replied, "You write. I put on."[5] Rodgers wrote to his wife that he first played his ballet score for "Slaughter on Tenth Avenue" for Wiman and Balanchine in early February 1936. Although Rodgers had been apprehensive about Balanchine's reaction, the choreographer liked it and complimented Rodgers.

Some critics realized that the prominence of the choreography in On Your Toes anticipated an innovation in the American musical theater. Theater Arts magazine (June 1936), for example, noted that "we may have come unknowingly upon a successor to the old musical form, a musical show that is not a comedian's holiday, but a dancer's." Rodgers carried forward the idea of special dance sequences in other shows written with Hart, and even more effectively in shows with Oscar Hammerstein. For Rodgers, Jumbo had not created the feel of "real theater" because it was too large. But On Your Toes gave him the "taste of the old show business for the first time."[6]

This show also introduced the romantic ballad "There's a Small Hotel," which had been cut from Jumbo. It became one of Rodgers and Hart's most durable standards. The plot for On Your Toes called for a song that expressed the desire of the two principals (Ray Bolger and Doris Carson) to be left by themselves. Rodgers credited Hart with the inspiration for the title and lyric. Though a city boy, Hart captured the essence of the bucolic life. Others suggest that Hart had to be bludgeoned into writing the lyrics and in fact did not like the song. Nevertheless, as Alec Wilder commented, it is a "simple, direct, perfectly disciplined song."[7]

The reviews were good. In Boston, one critic noted that the show began on time, catching first-nighters off-guard, and predicted that it would be one of Rodgers and Hart's most successful shows. Following its opening on April 11, 1936, at the Imperial Theatre, Brooks Atkinson was lavish: "If the word 'sophisticated' is not too un-palatable, let it serve as a description of the mocking book, the songs and the performances. . . . Mr. Rodgers has written a jaunty score that entitles him to honors at the general final exam, and Mr. Hart has put words to it that are crisp, impish and gayly ingenious." Writing for Life, even George Jean Nathan was captivated: "Rodgers' tunes and Hart's lyrics are in happy key with the general lark. . . . Nathan says Yes!"[8]

The praise received by the score—it was called jaunty, cheerful, lilting, hummable, singable—reflected Rodgers' newfound confidence. He no longer needed to press for hits; they came naturally. Although the show included songs that did not enjoy the fame of "There's a Small Hotel," such unusual compositions as "Quiet Night" and "Glad to Be Unhappy" strongly advanced Rodgers' art. The music for "Glad to Be Unhappy" is marked to be played "reflectively," and the harmony is oddly disquieting. Hart's gloomy lyrics seem to fit the uneasy melody perfectly:

> Fools rush in, so here I am
> Very glad to be unhappy.

Closer to old-style Broadway songs, however, was "It's Got to Be Love." The melody trips along in a lively manner, and the words are one of Hart's tributes to the agony of true love:

> It's got to be love!
> It couldn't be tonsillitis;
> It feels like neuritis,
> But nevertheless, it's love.

In London, where On Your Toes opened in February 1937, even the stuffy Times noted that "the tunes are numerous, catchy and cheerful, though of a familiar pattern."

The "Slaughter" ballet sequence endured and prompted several revivals of the show. Rodgers in particular defended these revivals as worthwhile nostalgia, and he extolled the virtues of the 1954 version, again directed by George Abbott and choreographed by Balanchine but this time danced by Vera Zorina. Although the book for On Your Toes was criticized as too dated, "Slaughter on Tenth Avenue" was singled out for another round of praise: "Vera Zorina moves with spidery grace through a raucous, still stimulating rendition of the historic Slaughter ballet." [9] Oddly enough, "You Took Advantage of Me" was added and sung in a slow, provocative jazz mode by Elaine Stritch. A more successful revival was staged in 1983, again directed by Abbott; the choreography was by Balanchine with additional sequences by Peter Martins. Spialek's original orchestrations were restored, and the ballerina role was danced by Natalia Makarova. This score was recorded.

Zorina played the ballerina in the movie version (1939), but Bolger was replaced by Eddie Albert and the story was radically changed. "There's a Small Hotel" was used as background music, and only snatches of "Quiet Night" survived. In 1948 the "Slaughter" ballet was re-created for Words and Music, the motion picture biography of Rodgers and Hart. It was given new orchestration, and Gene Kelly danced to his own choreography—and to very favorable reviews.

Jumbo and On Your Toes gave Rodgers and Hart the financial and professional security to do the "kind of creative work that had long been our goal." Until their last show, in 1942, he and Hart would enjoy a string of Broadway successes: "We got off to a very good start when we came back. . . . From then on until Larry's death, we never had a failure. Everything worked from there on. I don't know whether we got better or smarter, or it was just the relief of being back in the theatre, but we had some very big shows." [10]

Fall 1936 brought an odd interlude in Rodgers' professional life. He and Hart wrote a symphonic sketch for Paul Whiteman entitled "All Points West." Whiteman's interest in a Rodgers piece probably grew out of his involvement with Rodgers and Hart in Jumbo. After conferring with Hart, who was to do the lyrics, Rodgers decided to base the symphonic narrative on a stationmaster's public announcement of departing trains.

In this narrative piece, an announcer chants the itinerary, ending with "all points west," and then describes the passengers about to embark, followed by a song about each. Having announced "all points south," the announcer spies a senator about to entrain for Washington, D.C., followed by a song. Then comes a salesman saying good-bye to his family. Next comes a mother saying farewell to her son, who is heading west. Several doughboys arrive to a lively dance rhythm, then a group of college girls, some cops with a prisoner in tow and, finally, a honeymoon couple. When the prisoner tries to escape the police pursue him, shooting the announcer by mistake. After longing for faraway places, the announcer finally goes "west."

Rodgers' themes for each sequence are curiously mundane and seem forced. Perhaps he was too impressed by the prospect of having his work conducted by Whiteman and performed by the Philadelphia Orchestra. The music linking the episodes is also quite ordinary. The piece opens with the musical simulation of an engine huffing and puffing. Each song was performed with lyrics only once, and in the finale there is a great crescendo leading to the gunshots, followed by a sad andante theme as the announcer dies.

Their first outing beyond Broadway and Hollywood was a disappointment. The piece was buried in the Whiteman concert, which also featured *Rhapsody in Blue*. One critic described Rodgers' work—the "first novelty" of the evening— as a "tear-stained monologue-recitative-arioso" but offered no judgment on the value of the music. Nevertheless, Rodgers was satisfied with the work. He told one interviewer that he had wanted to do something that allowed him more freedom than the usual Broadway songs did, and he described the piece as a "faltering step in a basically right direction." This was a perplexing comment for the composer of the brilliant "Slaughter on Tenth Avenue." "All Points West" premiered in Philadelphia on November 27 and 28, 1936, at the Academy of Music, with narration by Ray Middleton and orchestration by Adolph Deutsch (who became a well-known Hollywood composer). A few days later Whiteman conducted the piece again, times time with his own orchestra, in a performance that was broadcast from the Hippodrome. Rudy Vallee even featured it in his floor show on the Astor Roof.

When it was performed in Hollywood in spring 1937, Rodgers was in the audience, but he found the poor performance shocking. Thank goodness movie people don't like music, he commented later—practically none of them heard the performance. A better performance was broadcast a few days later, eliciting compliments on his work.

This symphonic try was just a diversion for Rodgers and Hart, who had already decided on another Broadway show, *Babes in Arms*. The story was their own idea, and they wrote the first version of the book, reportedly inspired by overhearing children making up rules for their games. The plot concerns a group of teenagers left behind in Seaport, Long Island, while their vaudevillian parents are on tour. The sheriff threatens to send the youngsters to a work farm, so to save themselves the teenagers decide to put on a musical revue. The sheriff grants them a reprieve, and the gang is off and running. The book was not par- ticularly new or exciting, and by the second act the story was largely submerged in song and dance. But it may well be the Rodgers and Hart score with the most hit songs: "Where or When," "Babes in Arms," "My Funny Valentine," "Johnny One Note," and "The Lady Is a Tramp" were performed outside the context of the show for decades. Two other fine songs, however, have faded away: "Imagine" and "All At Once" both glitter with an old-fashioned clarity.

Dwight Wiman was again the producer, Balanchine the choreographer, and Hans Spialek the orchestrator. The young stars were Mitzi Green and Ray Heatherton. Rodgers' reports on the preparation of this show reflect the tribulations of staging a hit, as well as his care and concern for detail. After completing the score he worked on the individual performances of his songs. And after a run-through of the entire production he returned to the theater after dinner to "repair the damages done by the run-through." (He was pleased, incidentally, with "The Lady Is a Tramp." Mitzi Green's performance was "like a house on fire!") A few days later, however, he was up until three in the morning after another run-through in which they discovered "a million more things that needed fixing." He complained that there was no time to repair the book and musical numbers and the "nasty little bits that should be cleaned up before we open." [11]

The show opened on April 14, 1937. Again Brooks Atkinson was enthusiastic: "one of the most contagious scores Rodgers and Hart have written." Other critics were impressed by the talents of the young cast, especially the mimicry of Green, the singing of Heatherton, and the dancing of the Nicholas brothers. *Variety* noted, however, that "no nudity, no show girls, no plush or gold plate may mean no sale." *Time* waxed poetic in praising Rodgers: "The Rodgers melodies are fresh as a May wind, artful and surprising as the flight of a barn swallow." Robert Benchley called the show "one of their nicest scores." But he objected to the ending: "I was frankly at sea during the last fifteen minutes, and thought that I had got back into the wrong theater." [12]

In spite of good reviews the show almost collapsed. Mitzi Green, whom the critics described as the spark plug of the show, was out for a time because of illness. Business fell off and ticket prices were reduced, and the show continued to lose money. Then, in the summer, after several other shows closed, *Babes in Arms* was suddenly the only musical on Broadway. Audiences responded, and the show ran through December 1937, a total of 289 performances.

Babes in Arms was a natural for Hollywood, which wanted to exploit its own young stars, Judy Garland and Mickey Rooney. Produced in 1939 by Arthur Freed for MGM, with dance direction by Busby Berkeley, the movie version set a record for a smorgasbord of music. It retained only two songs, "Babes in Arms" and "Where or When." The Hollywood moguls interpolated "I'm Just Wild about Harry," by Eubie Blake; "Ida, Sweet as Apple Cider," by Eddie Leonard; "God's Country," by Harold Arlen and Yip Harburg; and two of Freed's own songs, "You Are My Lucky Star" and "I Cried for You" (Freed and Gus Arnheim), sung by Judy Garland. The movie was running at the Capitol at the same time that the film version of On Your Toes was playing at the Strand.

"The Lady Is a Tramp" became something of a classic, especially as later performed by Lena Horne. Hart's strong, self-deprecating lyrics were well suited to a female performer. Hart took some pleasure, one suspects, in his dig at Hollywood: "Hate California / It's cold and it's damp." The melody was a departure for Rodgers. It was meant to be a swinging song, with the familiar quarter-note rest appearing in the first beat to kick the melodic line. But the melody is surprising because of the flatted seventh in the second bar, which Hart seizes to emphasize each of his couplets.

In "Where or When," a love ballad sung early in the first scene, Rodgers was in a completely different mood, making use of repeated notes.[13] Perhaps the stunning score obscured the delightful but less known "I Wish I Were in Love Again." Again Hart exploited the agony of true love in his sardonic verse:

> You don't know that I felt good
> When we up and parted.

The melody is suitably lively, and the eighth-note pickup before the refrain gives the line impetus. In Words and Music this number is performed by Garland and Rooney (playing Hart). The song was a compelling romp, intended to compensate in part for its having been dropped from the movie version of Babes in Arms.

Before the next Broadway show came along there was another brief interlude in Hollywood. It was for an abortive project called Food for Scandal, a Warner Brothers comedy produced and directed by Mervyn LeRoy and starring Carole Lombard. Rodgers arrived in Hollywood shortly after Babes in Arms opened and was repeatedly complimented on that show. Noel Coward thought it was his best, and F. Scott Fitzgerald declared it the best musical he had ever seen. Rodgers stayed for more than three months yet wrote just a few songs, and only one was used in the picture. While there he made the usual social rounds, and he was much in demand by other studios and producers—he relished this attention as a sort of revenge for his bad old days in Hollywood. He saw Shall We Dance, the Gershwins' picture for Fred Astaire and Ginger Rogers. Although the film was generally admired, Rodgers noted that "the dam fools" did not like Gershwin's score; Rodgers himself thought the tunes were swell. He even found himself at a party with George Gershwin, during which "a record was broken": Gershwin did not approach the piano, because for once Rodgers played most of the evening.

What Rodgers did not know, of course, was that Gershwin was ill and getting worse. He had completed a second picture for Fred Astaire, without Ginger Rogers, *A Damsel in Distress*, and had begun to work on another film for Samuel Goldwyn. In early July 1937, Rodgers wrote Dorothy that Gershwin had had a "mental breakdown" and was too ill to be moved to a sanatorium in the East; the next day he informed her that George had died after an operation for a brain tumor. "The town is in a daze and nobody talks about anything but George's death. It's just awful." [14] Rodgers spent several hours with Ira and Lee Gershwin and wrote Dorothy about the details of the fatal operation. Had Gershwin lived, Rodgers said, he would have been an invalid. Rodgers attended the funeral, at which Oscar Hammerstein spoke "beautifully." Gershwin's last Hollywood assignment, *The Goldwyn Follies*, was to feature a ballet by Balanchine, inspired by his success in *On Your Toes*. The featured ballerina was Vera Zorina. A Gershwin ballet would have been an interesting comparison with "Slaughter on Tenth Avenue."

Soon after Rodgers and Hart arrived in Hollywood the playwrights George Kaufman and Moss Hart approached them with the idea for a Broadway musical spoofing the administration of Franklin Roosevelt. The prospect of working with Kaufman and Hart, who had just won a Pulitzer Prize for *You Can't Take It with You*, was exciting. They had no book, but while Rodgers finished his work on *Food for Scandal*, Kaufman and Hart finished the outline for one act and were searching for a personage, as Moss Hart put it, to play the lead. Someone mentioned that they needed some old-fashioned songs of the George M. Cohan variety, a remark that inspired the Kaufman and Hart to try to recruit Cohan himself. Rodgers and Hart, however, had not forgotten their encounter with Cohan while working on *Phantom President*, and when they heard of Cohan's prospective involvement, they tried to beg off. On the other hand, in a letter informing his wife that Cohan had no objections to the idea, Rodgers noted that "we're relieved as that was our one big fear." Moss Hart entreated them to stay on the project, explaining that Cohan had resented Hollywood, not their music. Moreover, the play was being produced by Cohan's old partner, Sam Harris, who would keep him in line. And Cohan had just appeared in the Theatre Guild's production of *Ah! Wilderness*, without causing trouble. Rodgers and Hart reluctantly agreed to proceed. Cohan shrewdly agreed to the part, having seen only an outline of the play and heard none of the music. Cohan's version was that they all had implored him to do the part and that after hesitating he finally agreed.

Rodgers and Hart's acquiescence proved to be a mistake. Cohan treated them with "thinly veiled patronizing contempt," calling them America's Gilbert and Sullivan. They played the score for him at a specially arranged sitting at the apartment of Rodgers' friend Jules Glaenzer, the Cartier executive. Cohan remained silent, his "eyes half-closed, his mouth drooping." As they finished each song Cohan's expression remained unchanged. Finally, he got up, and as he passed Rodgers on his way out he patted him on the shoulder and said, "Don't take any wooden nickels." [15]

Rodgers and Hart were shocked and depressed. Even if one hated something, Rodgers said, under those circumstances one might "simply nod." Their troubles continued throughout the show. Unfortunately, Cohan was half right: it was a modest score. One of the better melodies, "Everybody Loves You," was cut at Cohan's insistence.

The show, the title of which was changed from *Hooray for Our Side* to *I'd Rather Be Right* (the final title, from the famous remark by Henry Clay, was Dorothy Rodgers' contribution), was a thin political satire-cum-fantasy that named names, unlike the Gershwins' burlesques of fictional politics. It poked fun at Franklin Roosevelt's fireside chats, the Supreme Court, the politico James Farley, as well as the Cabinet secretaries Frances Perkins and Henry Morgenthau. Brooks Atkinson concluded that Roosevelt ought to feel happy about his portrayal by Cohan, who knew how to charm an audience. Moreover, the playwrights showed tender concern for the president while making fun of his administration. One critic pointed out that it was a matter of pride that Americans were free to spoof the president as darkness was descending over Europe. At one point Cohan ad-libbed a political plug for his friend Al Smith, to the chagrin of Kaufman and Moss Hart.

Kaufman's behavior was not much better than Cohan's, as far as Rodgers was concerned; he found Kaufman "extremely difficult, bitter and quite sarcastic." Kaufman had the arrogance to tell Rodgers that he was out to prove that the book was more important than the music. The two engaged in some spirited arguments, which Kaufman won, according to Rodgers, because Kaufman was bigger and richer. The show opened in November 1937 at the Alvin Theatre and ran for 290 performances. It was a tour de force for Cohan, who earned a laudable *New York Times* editorial, but a more modest success for Rodgers and Hart. Brooks Atkinson summed it up: "All Rodgers and Hart's political ditties are keen."

One fine song did become a standard: "Have You Met Miss Jones?" introduced by Cohan, who sings about his secretarial assistant. There is nothing striking about the song's structure, a pleasant stepwise melody with Rodgers'

The group that created *I'd Rather Be Right* (1937), a Broadway musical that spoofed politics: from left, Sam Harris, Lorenz Hart, Richard Rodgers, Moss Hart, George S. Kaufman, and George M. Cohan. Rodgers found Cohan and Kaufman difficult to work with.

ever-present scale linking the themes. The bridge, however, is a departure. In it Rodgers manipulated harmonies and even an enharmonic change leading back to the main refrain. This is solid songwriting from a man well on his way to becoming a master of his art.

While Rodgers and Hart were still in Hollywood their agent, Phil Berg, and the producer Dwight Wiman began negotiations with MGM for rights to the half-finished script for *I Married an Angel*, which had been worked on by Moss Hart but dropped by the studio. After lengthy negotiations MGM agreed to give up all rights in return for a cost-free option to make the story into a motion picture (which the studio did in 1942). The stage was set for the Broadway version of *I Married an Angel*.

The basic idea, taken from a Hungarian play, was that a certain playboy, Count Palaffi (played by Dennis King), vows never to marry unless he is able to wed a genuine angel. That angel turns out to be Vera Zorina (who in real life was a Norwegian named Brigitta Hartwig, a name she changed to accommodate the

Ballets Russes). She had met Rodgers in Hollywood during the filming of the *Goldwyn Follies.* Wiman had urged Rodgers to consider her for a small part. After meeting her, Rodgers wired Wiman: "Small Part, Hell. I've Just Found Angel." Zorina, like many of the performers in Rodgers and Hart's shows, found Lorenz Hart charming: "tiny, affectionate, with a sad look in his eyes." Despite the thirty years' difference in their ages, she felt protective toward him. She was "a bit in awe" of Rodgers, whom she found aloof.[16]

Rodgers and Hart began by writing most of the book themselves, until George Abbott once again rescued them. The director was Joshua Logan, who was working with the team for the first time; Vivienne Segal and Walter Slezak were in the cast. The show opened with the count and others singing the rollicking "Did You Ever Get Stung?" The major songs were "I Married an Angel" and "Spring Is Here," and Zorina danced to Balanchine's "Honeymoon Ballet."

The show opened May 11, 1938, at the Shubert and ran for 338 performances. It was, according to a critic, "one of the best musical comedies of many seasons." Such praise surprised Rodgers, who had concluded, following tryouts and opening night, that the show was a failure. It succeeded in part because of the superior ballet sequences crafted by Balanchine.

The show was not without the usual humorous mishaps. At one point in the play the angel loses her wings because she has sacrificed her status by marrying the count. While offstage, Zorina was reminded not to forget to take her wings off; she did so and made her entrance, only to realize that she was one scene too early. She played the scene without wings, though the dialogue made little sense. In the next scene she awakens in her bed wailing, "My wings! My wings are gone!" The audience howled. Nevertheless, Zorina was a sensation, and the critics heaped praise on Balanchine, dubbing him the First Choreographer of Broadway.

As for the score, Alec Wilder commented in his analysis, "Truly, these men are fantastically talented." [17] The title song, the melody for which had been written four years earlier, is in many ways one of Rodgers' best. The lyrics start with a question: "Have you heard?" (two bars), followed by a quarter-note rest, followed by the answer, "I married an angel" — a fine synthesis of words and music. "Spring Is Here" was one of Rodgers' more surprising songs, in that he used a succession of diminished chords that created a melancholy tone for Hart's pensive lyrics.

The unfortunate film version reunited Nelson Eddy and Jeanette MacDonald. "Spring Is Here" and "I Married an Angel" were not at all suited to the style or voices of the stars. The bounce and wit of the original was lost: it "vigorously rubs the bloom from the wings of the brisk, fresh, imaginative musical that ran on Broadway." [18]

That imaginative musical confirmed the talents of Rodgers and Hart. It was the "patrician successor" to their springtime hits On Your Toes and Babes in Arms, cut from the same beguiling pattern of gaiety and imagination.

II

THE BOYS FROM SYRACUSE

Rodgers and Hart had five solid successes behind them, all written and produced within three years. In fall 1938 they were featured on the cover of *Time* magazine (September 26), along with the caption "The Boys from Columbia," an allusion to their forthcoming musical, *The Boys from Syracuse*. The accompanying story noted that *I Married an Angel* had grossed more than $28,000 in its fifth month and was averaging eighty standees a performance (in fact, it was grossing about $20,000 each week, not each month). The story also noted that "their tunes are whistled in the street, clunked out by hurdy gurdies on the curb. . . . Good taste and an unquenchably romantic point of view are the common denominators of most of the 1,000 songs Rodgers & Hart have written together." According to *Time*, a Rodgers and Hart song "usually has the power of a single musical expression, which not even such a pair of individual talents as P. G. Wodehouse & Jerome Kern could ever quite pull off." On a more mundane note, *Time* wrote that the pair received 6 percent of the gross, which usually meant about $750 per week. To date, their biggest moneymaker had been *The Girl Friend*, which had played all over the world. In addition, they were each getting about $18,000 year from their annual ASCAP earnings. At the time, Rodgers and his family had a duplex on the "swanky east side," and Hart lived on Central Park West with his mother—a "sweet, menacing old lady," in Hart's words.

Rodgers and Hart were also the subjects of a two-part profile in the *New Yorker* (May and June 1938). In it Rodgers and Hart defended themselves against various charges of stealing melodies (accusations that "Where or When," for example, came from *La Bohème*). They told of assigning a number to each note in the scale and then constructing a melody from a telephone number. Their latest invention, a waltz, was supposedly based on the number of police headquarters.

The price of fame was evident in another anecdote. Rodgers and Hart were supposedly in a hotel lobby, where Hart was "fiercely" denouncing the manager, who was trying—with outstretched hands—to explain why he could not obtain a copy of *Variety*. The hotel was in Khartoum. Rodgers and Hart had never been in Sudan, of course, but the story made the point about Hart's obsession with show business. The real Rodgers and Hart were being subsumed by these colorful portraits, which repeated the same anecdotes and asserted how closely the two worked together, each providing inspiration for the other.

A more realistic portrait of this period appears in the memoirs of Joshua Logan, who directed *I Married an Angel*. Logan and Rodgers first met at the Trocadero nightclub in California, where Logan had gotten hopelessly drunk on martinis and was sitting on the floor. As Dick and Dorothy Rodgers danced by, Rodgers introduced himself. Later, when Logan was hired by Rodgers to begin work on *I Married an Angel*, the composer expressed concern about his partner, who was then in Atlantic City and apparently not working on the show. Rodgers urged Logan to join Hart to work on the show's second act. This was Logan's first meeting with Hart, and the two got along well, playing cards and carousing together for a week. Years later Logan recalled: "Oh, my God, he was nice and sweet and funny and bitter. Oh, he hated Dick Rodgers so, because Dick Rodgers always made him work, you see." Hart had, in fact, begun to make caustic references to Rodgers, but it is unlikely that he hated him then or ever.[1]

It was not until the day that Hart and Logan had to return to New York that Hart started to work, scribbling frantically on a pad of paper. They turned these pages over to Rodgers, who rejected them with disgust. Even though there was no second act, rehearsals started. Shortly thereafter Rodgers took Logan to Hart's apartment, where they finished the dialogue in one night. The next evening they wrote the songs and lyrics.

The show included a wild dance sequence, "At the Roxy Music Hall," which had absolutely nothing to do with the plot. Logan questioned whether it belonged, but Hart insisted that the audience would love it for this very reason. In a ballet sequence Balanchine depicted aspects of surrealism, anticipating the much-heralded arrival of Salvador Dalí in America. When Logan was again puzzled by the relationship between surrealism and the so-called Roxy Music Hall, Hart admitted that they had nothing in common. Then why the ballet? "So Zorina can dance and Balanchine can fry Dalí's ass," replied Hart. Logan remained skeptical until he read the opening-night reviews, which praised in particular the ballet sequence and "At the Roxy Music Hall."

Their next show, *The Boys from Syracuse*, arrived on Broadway, as *Time* had promised, and if it was not their best show, it was their most novel. While still working on *I Married an Angel*, Hart and Rodgers had discussed the puzzling fact that Shakespeare's work was not used for musical librettos. Hart had an inspiration: he envisaged his own brother, the actor Teddy Hart, as one of the twins in *A Comedy of Errors*, and the comedian Jimmy Savo, who looked remarkably like Teddy, as the other twin. Before Rodgers and Hart could write much, George Abbott had completed a libretto that avoided Shakespeare's language but used his basic plot about two sets of twins. One line from Shakespeare was retained, and when it was spoken, one of the characters turned to the audience and announced, "*That* was Shakespeare." Indeed, the show opened with the narrator saying: "This is drama of ancient Greece. It is a story of mistaken identity. If it's good enough for Shakespeare, it's good enough for us."

The setting is Ephesus, where the citizens are preparing to execute a man for the crime of coming from Syracuse. In the opening the crowd sings:

> Hurrah! Hurroo!
> There'll be an execution.
> It serves him right.
> The law makes retribution.

Another Syracusan appears and sings the praises of his hometown to a Rodgers song that is a rollicking reminder of vaudeville, especially in the music for the phrase "I want to go back, go back, to dear old Syracuse." After complaining that "this is a terrible city, the people are cattle and swine," he explains why he is so fond of Syracuse:

It is no metropolis,
It has no big Acropolis,
And yet there is a quorum
Of cuties in the forum.

The comedy proceeds with mixups between both sets of twins. The score included Rodgers and Hart's tribute to love in a style that only Hart could master:

This can't be love
Because I feel so well—
No sobs, no sorrows, no sighs.

Hart used Rodgers' sweeping and beautiful waltz "Falling in Love with Love" to remind his listeners of the show's skeptical tone:

Falling in love with love
Is falling for make-believe.
Falling in love with love
Is playing the fool.

Hart continued in this caustic vein in "Ladies of the Evening" and "He and She," both testimonies to his genius in converting obvious subjects to witty but melancholy comments on the human condition.

The Boys from Syracuse prompted an amusing complaint. A patron complained to the New York Times that she had seen I Married an Angel from a seat in "Shubert heaven." From there she "saw" Dennis King and Vivienne Segal go through a lot of "lip movement," but what she heard were brasses, reeds, and strings. "Pianissimo," she begged. Rodgers responded to her letter and agreed, noting that he had conveyed her thoughts to his conductor. He assured the writer that he had gone to the balcony to listen to the songs for The Boys from Syracuse, which were quite audible.

The Boys from Syracuse, which opened November 1938 at the Alvin Theatre, ran for 235 performances. Robert Benchley summed up Rodgers and Hart's work on the show: "the best score that Rodgers and Hart have given us for some time, in fact, for a longer time than that." The show also weathered better than most. It was revived off-Broadway twenty-five years later to another round of favorable reviews. Rodgers described the revival as "bright, fast moving, but in its own wacky way very much in the bawdy Shakespearean tradition." The reviewers noted that the lyrics and music had remained fresh: "Has Richard Rodgers (or anybody) ever written more delightful music?" asked the New Yorker in April 1963.

The critic Walter Kerr went even further: "I don't know that anyone has written more melodic surprise into what was meant to be a conventional musical comedy than Mr. Rodgers did for The Boys from Syracuse, and to hear the unexpected modulation of the 'Shortest Day of the Year,' or 'You Have Cast Your Shadow on the Sea' is, today as twenty-five years ago, a shocker. Mr. Rodgers never did live along Tin Pan Alley; he was lost at sea as a boy and, when rescued, kept hearing inappropriate sounds. They remain inappropriately perfect."[2]

Although his music would always have a trace of Jerome Kern, Rodgers had a versatility that embraced a jazzy ballet like "Slaughter" and thrilling waltzes like "The Most Beautiful Girl in the World" and "Falling in Love" without sacrificing such clever songs as "This Can't Be Love" or "Johnny One Note," to say nothing of such ballads as "Spring Is Here" or "My Funny Valentine." Hart had meanwhile molded his lyrics to his bittersweet philosophy.

With the success of the original Boys from Syracuse, Rodgers and Hart had become the masters of Broadway. Gershwin was dead, and Kern and Berlin were usually in Hollywood. Their only sustained competition was from Cole Porter. Porter as well as Rodgers and Hart was still operating within the bounds of Broadway convention. Despite the seriousness of some of the early satires of the 1930s, it was more comfortable to stay with the book musicals with strong comedic elements or those that were little more than revues. Money was still critical, and a show had to have some preproduction guarantee of success, making the choice of stars even more important. Porter relied on Ethel Merman, just as Rodgers and Hart did on Ray Bolger and Vera Zorina.

One problem was becoming more serious: the deterioration of Lorenz Hart. George Abbott noticed that Hart was drinking heavily and was absent for two or three days at a time during rehearsals for The Boys from Syracuse. When he was needed in Boston for rewrites he couldn't be found, and Rodgers had to redo both the music and lyrics. Yet Abbott was amazed at Hart's abilities: when they needed a verse for "Falling in Love with Love," Hart quickly scratched it out on a piece of old paper. Hart was so ill with pneumonia that he had to miss not only rehearsals for The Boys from Syracuse but also the opening. His doctor ordered him to Florida to recuperate, and in his next show, Too Many Girls, Hart took a crack at the state:

> I will take a trip to Florida
> Where the weather's even horrida.
> I'll eat salami
> Down in Miami.

His sister-in-law, Dorothy Hart, speculated that Larry Hart had begun to lose interest in the routine of writing musicals. His drinking was so out of control that, at his family's urging, he confined himself on occasion to Doctors Hospital in New York, though his stays seemed to have no lasting effect.[3]

Rodgers' own apprehensions about Hart's condition were growing, and Abbott agreed with Rodgers that major trouble lay ahead. Rodgers' worries may have been aggravated by events in his personal life, notably the death of his mother in 1940 and the terrible impact of that loss on his father. The war in Europe had begun, and the Rodgerses' close friend Myrtle d'Erlanger asked whether her daughter, Zoe, and her nurse could live with the Rodgerses in the United States for the duration. They agreed. A year later they learned that Myrtle d'Erlanger had been killed in the blitz and that Zoe's uncle wanted his niece to return to Scotland. About this time the Rodgers family moved from New York to a country home in Fairfield, Connecticut, which became their permanent residence. In effect, they abandoned Manhattan, which may well have added to the estrangement between Rodgers and Hart.

Whether because of Hart's deteriorating condition or for some other reason, their pace was slowing down. *Too Many Girls* did not open until October 1939, a full year after *The Boys from Syracuse* had opened. George Abbott suggested the show, which was about life at a college out West. They were back in familiar "Babes in Arms country," Rodgers said. One reviewer found that the plot was sprinkled with "piquant wise-cracks" and that the score boasted some "delightfully humorous and tuneful moments." Another called the show a "fine comedy," with one of Rodgers and Hart's "pleasantest" scores. The show was not nearly as impressive as its predecessors, however, and it may be best remembered for one of its secondary leads, a young Cuban named Desi Arnaz. He was also recruited for the Hollywood film version, which also included Lucille Ball.

Too Many Girls produced only one lasting song, "I Didn't Know What Time It Was." Its innovative harmonies and oddly constructed melodic line made it one of those songs appreciated by sophisticated listeners. A new ballad written for the film version of *Too Many Girls*, "You're Nearer," was not first-rate Rodgers. One other song from the original is worth remembering, if only for its title: "I Like to Recognize the Tune," with a lyric that asks, "Must you bury the tune?" Rodgers and Hart were not jazz fans, and the various swing versions of their songs left them cold. Hart's lyric complains:

> A guy called Krupa plays the drums like thunder,
> But the melody is six feet under.

Jazz was not the only target of the Rodgers and Hart score. The sardonic "Give It Back to the Indians" was carried more by Hart's skewering lyrics than by Rodgers' melody:

> Broadway's turning into Coney,
> Champagne Charlie's drinking gin,
> Old New York is new and phony—
> Give it back to the Indians.

Rodgers admitted that he would on occasion give the melody from one of his songs to a favored orchestra or performer in advance of publication in the hope that their version would prevail. His distaste for swing renditions of his songs reflected the more serious side of Rodgers' musicianship. His original manuscripts, usually written in pencil for his Broadway shows, demonstrate that he was a careful composer, intent on writing full versions of his songs, as well as background music, overtures, and whatever other pieces were required. In late 1939, Rodgers was tempted into writing a ballet for the Ballet Russe de Monte Carlo, titled *Ghost Town*. Gerald Murphy, a patron of the ballet and friend of Cole Porter's (together they had written a ballet, *Within the Quota* in 1926), suggested the idea of a ballet set in the American West during the mining days. This change in musical form was a welcome relief for Rodgers, and Hans Spialek took over the orchestration. For Spialek, however, Rodgers had written a full piano score, an impressive but laborious undertaking. The ballet premiered in November 1939 at the Metropolitan Opera House, then went on tour; another single performance took place in March 1940 in New York.

Ghost Town drew mixed reviews because of the score, which was criticized as fragmentary. According to the music critic Irving Kolodin, it was hardly suited to ballet. The *New Yorker*, on the other hand, while acknowledging that the score needed "pointing," deemed it a useful basis for the ballet and, as usual, found Rodgers' melodies attractive. *Variety* was more flippant: "Rodgers' New Monte Carlo Ballet Suite Draws Broadway Mob," read the headline. The reviewer called Rodgers' first real attempt at highbrow composition a "trifle light."

Nor were the dance critics kind: they noted that although Rodgers was one of the most gifted composers on Broadway, asking him to make the transition to ballet was "demanding a good deal." John Martin, writing in the *New York Times*, doubted whether even the most experienced choreographer could make a ballet out of Rodgers' score.

A complete ballet was indeed a major undertaking. The songwriter Vernon

Duke, who under his real name, Vladimir Dukelsky, had written larger serious works, commented on the difficulty of the transition for a Broadway song-writer.[4] Broadway ballets, even those for Balanchine, usually required no more than ten minutes of music, he pointed out. Classical ballets required perhaps forty minutes. Consequently, the composer had little time to develop musical themes. Moreover, the Broadway pit orchestras were limited in the music they could produce—there were usually no French horns, for example—and the musicians were often only moderately competent. The composer was therefore compelled to write to the level that could be easily performed in New York and, especially, on the road. Duke admitted that he had great difficulty coping with these limitations, so it is no surprise that Rodgers had difficulty moving from Broadway to the Metropolitan. Nevertheless, Rodgers seemed proud of his accomplishment, if only because he conducted the Metropolitan Orchestra for a performance attended by his parents and other family members. The experience also offered a respite from the "Larry problem."

In spring 1940 another Rodgers and Hart show opened, *Higher and Higher*, starring Jack Haley. It was close to an outright failure (running only 108 performances). A song from the show, "It Never Entered My Mind," was inexplicably dropped from the production but nevertheless caught on. The show's original idea, by Irwin Pincus, involves a conspiracy by the household staff of a wealthy family to pass off one of the maids as a debutante while the family is away, with the hope of finding her a rich society husband. The plot thickens when the family returns, and, of course, the maid (Marta Eggart) falls in love with the butler (Jack Haley). The show may have been doomed from the beginning; at every turn something went wrong. Joshua Logan was the director as well as one of the authors, but Hart opposed a second writer, Gladys Hurlburt, who was called in to fix the show (her major contribution was to recruit a trained seal named Sharkey). Eventually Hart simply lost interest in the show. Logan was ill for part of the time, but when he was able to return, he too lost interest. Up to the last minute Rodgers was trying to fix the musical numbers.

The casting was unfortunate. One of the maids was Shirley Ross, who sang "It Never Entered My Mind" but whose voice was too sweet and commercial for the more raucous songs ("A Barking Dog Never Bites"). Consequently, major changes were constantly being made. One clever song that did survive was "I'm Afraid," which included these lines by Hart:

> I'm afraid of rats and mice
> I'm afraid of Fanny Brice.

In Boston, Elliot Norton was enthusiastic in his review. After the opening in New York, some reviews emphasized Rodgers' "sweet and lively" tunes. The *New York Times* reviewer found Rodgers' music "workmanlike" and gave it only a "passing grade." The *New Yorker* concluded that it was not a terribly good musical, but "it is not such a bad one, either." Haley commanded most of the praise. But John Mason Brown wrote that when Haley had to play the stooge to Sharkey the seal, something was seriously wrong. *Higher and Higher* closed for the summer, but after reopening briefly in August it was forced to close permanently, grossing about $320,000.

Hollywood adopted the show, largely because of Jack Haley. The film version included Frank Sinatra playing himself, but the Rodgers and Hart score was virtually abandoned. The veteran Hollywood writers Jimmy McHugh and Harold Adamson wrote most of the score, including "I Couldn't Sleep a Wink Last Night" for Sinatra.

Spring 1940 marked Rodgers and Hart's twentieth year of working together. But rumors were cropping up that they would soon part company. They denied it, of course, but Rodgers did write publicly about their partnership. He claimed that they were held together by three common bonds: congeniality of spirit, a deep-rooted fear of formula, and the urge to approach each problem as a distinctive challenge. In fact, the article would have supported speculations on their differences more than claims of their similarities. Rodgers wrote, for example (presumably in jest): "We're congenial, but not very. We rarely see the same people; I can't stand his cigars; he thinks I'm a sissy because my limit is four highballs; we don't dress alike, look alike, or think alike, except on a few special subjects. . . . We definitely do agree, and always have agreed, about the theatre." Rodgers went on to note that Hart might drive him crazy by coming to work two hours late, and he, Rodgers, irritated Hart by insisting on working in the daytime rather than the late evening, when "civilized people do their thinking."[5] But all things considered, Rodgers concluded that their mutual respect, mutual responsibility, and mutual aims had kept them together and would probably continue to do so.

A challenge came along to put that view to the test. While Rodgers and Hart were in Boston for the tryouts of *Higher and Higher*, Rodgers received a letter from the writer John O'Hara, whom he knew slightly. O'Hara suggested that some of his recent short stories for the *New Yorker* might be suitable for a musical. The stories were entitled *Pal Joey*.

12

PAL JOEY

In 1938, John O'Hara needed money. In between writing novels and occasional screenplays, the tough-talking author of *Appointment in Samarra* supported himself by writing short stories, mainly for the *New Yorker*. His writing was popular, but from time to time the editor, Harold Ross, would swear that he would never publish another O'Hara story he did not understand. Hoping to find a haven where he could write, O'Hara planned a trip to Philadelphia for a few days. Before leaving New York he stopped at the bar in the Hotel Pierre, where, after a few drinks, he decided to take a room. Two days later, coming off a titanic bender, he began to write a story about a sleazy master of ceremonies in a cheap nightclub. It took the form of a letter from Joey Evans to a friend, a successful bandleader named Ted. The letters, which became a series, were signed "Pal Joey." In these stories Joey emerged as a disreputable hustler, womanizer, braggart, and liar, but not as someone shrewd enough to be truly evil. He was a composite of a number of men O'Hara had encountered in his career as a journalist. He commented that "the more I wrote about the slob the more I got to like him." Ross was also pleased.

A friend in Hollywood suggested to O'Hara that his series would make a good play. For a time he paid no attention to the idea, but in late 1939 or early 1940 he decided there might be a musical in his tales of Pal Joey. O'Hara was a fan of popular music, and his stories and novels were laced with references to songs, songwriters, and jazzmen. "Christ, I knew Bix," wrote Pal Joey to his friend. Gershwin was O'Hara's favorite, but he had been dead for more than two years (it was O'Hara who wrote the most memorable line about Gershwin: "George died on July 11, 1937, but I don't have to believe that if I don't want to."). The natural candidates for his musical were Rodgers and Hart. Hammerstein and Kern were inappropriate, and Porter inhabited a world far removed from O'Hara's. So O'Hara wrote to Rodgers: "I got the idea that the [New Yorker] pieces, or at least the character and the life in general could be made into a book show, and I wonder if you and Larry would be interested in working on it with me."

Rodgers was intrigued. Such a show could open possibilities for a more "realistic view of life than theatergoers were accustomed to." Later Rodgers wrote that "not only would the show be totally different from anything we had ever done before, it would be different from anything anyone else had ever tried. This alone was reason enough for us to want to do it. . . . It seemed time to us that musical comedy get out of its cradle and start standing on its own feet. Looking at the facts of life. The facts of life in this particular case were to be learned in and around a nightclub on Chicago's south side." [1]

O'Hara decided to write a new story, drawing on several incidents in his New Yorker pieces. He came to New York from Hollywood in May 1940 and began collaborating with Rodgers and Hart. George Abbott would direct. O'Hara's new story was about Joey's affair with Vera Simpson, a tough and sophisticated society matron who sees through Joey's posturing but still is bewitched by him. She sponsors him and his nightclub, Chez Joey, but she finally tires of his style and drops him.

The male lead for the story was crucial. Rodgers' candidate was a young dancer named Gene Kelly. Rodgers had seen Kelly in William Saroyan's play The Time of Your Life, in which he played a dancer. Kelly's friend and sometime dancing mentor Robert Alton urged Rodgers to consider him, and Kelly was hired after being auditioned for his singing. He chose "I Didn't Know What Time It

Was" for his audition, which, a friend informed him, was a mistake—Rodgers did not like to hear his own songs at auditions. In fact, Rodgers liked it. For Vera they again chose Hart's favorite, Vivienne Segal. For the lesser but colorful female part of Gladys, the chorus girl, they cast June Havoc, Gypsy Rose Lee's sister (immortalized many years later in *Gypsy* as "Baby June").

The new story had one advantage for a stage musical: much of it was set in a nightclub, allowing for some musical and dance numbers to leaven a drama that had no comic features. These raucous nightclub scenes proved to be great fun for Rodgers and Hart, who tried to make O'Hara's disreputable characters "sing." The broad ambience of the show was created in a routine in which June Havoc and a seedy chorus sing and dance a genuine bump-and-grind number, "That Terrific Rainbow." After a honky-tonk verse Havoc launches the chorus: "I'm a red-hot mama./But I'm blue for you." These numbers turned out to be important in tying together the show.

O'Hara was late with his script, and when it did arrive, it was, according to Abbott, a "disorganized set of scenes without a good story line." A great deal of rewriting was required. Matthew Bruccoli, one of O'Hara's biographers (*The O'Hara Concern*), notes that O'Hara did in fact rewrite his first version because he considered it too sentimental. There was a general air of pessimism about the show. The dance director, Robert Alton, believed that the show was hopeless and wanted to withdraw. Rodgers talked him out of it. The well-known scenic designer Jo Mielziner apparently had more faith in the show. When stumped for a first-act closer he conceived of a finale set in the elaborate (and costly) nightclub that Vera was preparing for Joey. It was the background for a major production number featuring Kelly.

As the show developed, Havoc's part expanded. Naturally, dance sequences starring Kelly occurred throughout. Kelly's friend and future collaborator Stanley Donen was in the cast, as was Van Johnson, who had a song-and-dance routine that helped launch his Hollywood career.

The treatment of Joey, however, was the major challenge: How could O'Hara's realism be preserved without making Joey so odious that the audience would stay away? They succeeded, in some measure because of Kelly's ability to charm the audience at the right moment. His superlative dancing helped, of course. Rodgers offered his own interpretation: "Joey is a disreputable character, and Larry understood and liked disreputable characters. He knew what John O'Hara knew—that Joey was not disreputable because he was mean, but because he had too much imagination to behave himself, and because he was a little weak. If you don't understand this about Joey, you'll probably find him hard to take. If you do understand it, you'll be able to chuckle at him and understand him in more than a superficial sense."[2]

After O'Hara reworked his script and the show went into out-of-town try-outs, he virtually disappeared. (He explained later that he did not want to become a nuisance.) O'Hara did not get along with Rodgers, whom he came to dislike, but it was Rodgers' determination that kept the show together, observed Donen. With O'Hara gone, the rewriting was left to Abbott, who could not capture O'Hara's style. Finally, according to O'Hara, Hart appealed to him, telling him that he was "hurting George Abbott's feelings," which O'Hara found hard to believe.[3] He did return, however, and he remained on the scene. Nevertheless, Abbott thought that he was curiously indifferent toward the show. The truth was that O'Hara desperately wanted a success, so much so that he asked the writer Budd Schulberg to come from California to be with him during the tryouts.

Pal Joey did not lend itself to love songs, but two superb ballads emerged nonetheless. The first, "I Could Write a Book," was sung early in the show by Joey when he attempts to ingratiate himself to a young woman named Linda. The melody is warm, simple, and straightforward, and the lyric seemingly sincere. Although the audience suspects that Joey is a phony, the song prevents them from knowing how bad he is. In the second love song, "Bewitched," Vera contemplates a relationship with Joey and describes her weakness for him. The second couplet of the verse defines her dilemma:

> Men are not a new sensation;
> I've done pretty well, I think.
> But this half-pint imitation
> Put me on the blink.

Then comes the famous chorus:

> I'm wild again,
> Beguiled again,
> A simpering, whimpering child again.

When the song became a hit the lyrics had to be cleaned up.

Rodgers and Hart were able to musically define both Joey and Vera. Aware that she is inviting trouble, in "What Is a Man?" Vera sings:

> There are so many, so many fish in the sea.
> Must I want the one who's not for me?

On the eve of his nightclub opening, Joey sings his philosophy: "What do I care for a dame?" Then, in top hat and cane, he dances a pseudo-ballet to the strains of "Bewitched," in which he foresees his glittering future with the gentry at his club.

The second act has a hilarious showstopper. Joey is interviewed by Melba, a hard-bitten reporter who recognizes him as a phony when he refers to "Dartmouth University" and "Mount Holy Oak." She ruminates on her various interviews and decides that her favorite subject was not the "great Stravinsky" but the star who "worked for Minsky." This burlesque queen, an obvious takeoff on Gypsy Rose Lee, was quite an intellectual. Hart's lyrics describing the stripper's interview in her dressing room are exquisite:

> Zip! Walter Lippmann wasn't brilliant today.
> Zip! Will Saroyan ever write a great play?
> Zip! I was reading Schopenhauer last night.
> Zip! And I think Schopenhauer was right.

All this was done to rim shots from the drummer, plunger growls from the trumpet, and the occasional tom-tom of striptease music. "Zip" brought down the house—and forced Hart to write more choruses. (In the 1952 revival the song was performed by Elaine Stritch, with the same response.)

There was also a risqué duet between Joey and Vera in Joey's apartment, their "Den of Iniquity." According to O'Hara, Rodgers and Hart had furious arguments over the lyrics for the entire show. Rodgers maintained that they were offensive, but Hart refused to compromise. Considering what is acceptable today, such a dispute may sound a trifle exaggerated, but in 1940 Hart's lyrics were as far as one could go on Broadway.

When Vera finally dismisses Joey, Linda offers to withdraw from the competition. "Take Him," she sings. Vera, who has the same idea, answers:

> His thoughts are seldom consecutive
> He just can't write.
> I know a movie executive
> Who's twice as bright.

Joey is outraged at Vera's rejection but finally leaves, and Vera reprises "Bewitched," this time with relief:

> Romance—finis.
> Your chance—finis.

Those ants that invaded my pants—finis.

Bewitched, bothered and bewildered no more.

In the final scene Joey is standing in front of the pet-shop window, just as he was in the scene that opens the show. Linda enters and invites him to dinner, but he declines because he is on his way to New York for a big audition. As she leaves, Joey watches her. Another girl enters and crosses in front of Joey; obviously tempted, he looks first toward Linda but then he changes his mind and heads in the direction of the new girl, singing the refrain from "I Could Write a Book." It is a marvelous bit of theater. The first time Joey sings the song, it suggests that he may have some redeeming virtues, but this time it proves that he has learned nothing and does not intend to change his ways.

The show, which opened on Christmas 1940, provoked an immediate controversy. Donen thought that the cast could sense the audience's discomfort with Joey's unscrupulous character. The critics were divided: some thought it was a major innovation; others thought it vile. The former included Richard Watts, of the *New York Herald Tribune* (December 26, 1940): "Brilliant, sardonic, strikingly original . . . some scabrous lyrics to one of Rodgers' most haunting tunes—'Bewitched.' . . . A hard boiled delight." And Wolcott Gibbs in the *New Yorker* wrote, "Musical comedy took a long step toward maturity." Among the dissenters was Abel Green of *Variety*: "What might broadly pass for 'sophistication' makes for a quite unpleasant evening in the theatre." The key review came from Brooks Atkinson, a fervent supporter of Rodgers and Hart who found himself repelled by the book and its principal characters: "If it is possible to make an entertaining musical comedy out of an odious story, *Pal Joey* is it. The situation is put tentatively here because the ugly topic that is up for discussion stands between this theatregoer and real enjoyment of a well-staged show. . . . If Joey must be acted, Mr. Kelly can do it. . . . Although *Pal Joey* is expertly done, can you draw sweet water from a foul well?"

This review was read aloud to a group that included Hart, and Atkinson's harsh words brought lyricist to tears. He retreated to his room and refused to come out. But the show was a success—indeed, it became their longest-running show to date! Rodgers was always a little irritated by the myth that Atkinson's review, so widely quoted, forced the show to close. It ran out the season, closed for the summer, reopened in September and ran until November, and then toured through April 1942.

Although the excellent music for *Pal Joey* was integral to the spirit of the play, for once Rodgers was overshadowed by the characters, the lyrics, and the play itself. Because of the harsh and realistic story and the biting lyrics, the show became a landmark, acquiring a historical significance that no one had anticipated. It came to be regarded as a milestone in the liberation of the musical from the stale forms of the 1920s and 1930s. This realization, however, did not come for some years. Walter Kerr wrote in the *Herald Tribune* (January 4, 1952) that the show had "one of the shrewdest, toughest and in a way most literate books ever written for musical comedy. It has Richard Rodgers' enchanting score, a perfect blending of witty musical infection and honest melody."

In 1950, Goddard Lieberson, who had pioneered the recording of Broadway cast albums, decided to record *Pal Joey* with a studio cast, including Vivienne Segal. The long-playing recording became popular, and the show had a summer revival on Long Island, with Bob Fosse playing Joey. The recording and revival convinced the composer Jule Styne to produce it for Broadway. Rodgers was skeptical, but Styne persisted. He recruited Vivienne Segal to re-create Vera but chose Harold Lang rather than Fosse to play Joey. This version opened on January 3, 1952, at the Broadhurst Theater and ran for 542 performances, a new Rodgers and Hart record. Before the revival opened, Rodgers wrote that *Pal Joey* mirrored Hart's lifestyle: "Hart understood and liked disreputable characters."[4]

Everyone was waiting for Atkinson's review of the revival. In effect, he recanted. Acknowledging that he had been in a minority in 1940, he recognized that *Pal Joey* was a "pioneer in the moving back of musical frontiers, for it tells an integrated story with a knowing point of view." Noting that Rodgers and Hammerstein were then (in 1952) moving into folk opera, he nonetheless found "something refreshing about the return of musical comedy in an unhackneyed rendering."[5] The revival earned several awards and was a vindication of sorts.

Hart had suffered far more emotionally than Rodgers from the original rebuff of *Pal Joey*, and Rodgers was increasingly insensitive to Hart's feelings. In late August 1941, Rodgers sent Hart's sister-in-law a telegram asking for an urgent meeting. He proposed that they have Hart committed for psychiatric treatment, but Dorothy Hart refused. Hart resented the idea of therapy, and during one stay at Doctors Hospital he was outraged by a doctor who believed that a low temperature that had kept him confined for several weeks was, in fact, psychosomatic. Rodgers even sent over his own psychiatrist, but Hart rejected him with contempt.[6]

Hart's sister-in-law believed that Hart drank because he could not stand to be alone. By the 1940s his drinking had become a serious problem, one that she felt even Rodgers did not fully recognize.

In an effort to protect Hart from himself and to safeguard some of his earnings, Rodgers virtually forced him to take on a financial adviser. Hart's family resented the adviser, Willy Kron. In the meantime, Hart had become increasingly irritated with Rodgers, and at one point he mentioned to Dorothy Hart his grievances against Rodgers: his lack of sympathy and understanding. When Dorothy defended Rodgers, Hart grabbed her by the shoulders and shook her "angrily, roughly and violently."[7]

One result of the team's growing estrangement was an inability to agree on a new show. In 1941, for the first time in five years, Rodgers and Hart had no production under way. There was a brief, odd interlude of writing for a terrible RKO movie, *They Met in Argentina*.

Rodgers had a few ideas for new shows, including a musical version of Edna Ferber's new novel *Saratoga Trunk*. He and Ferber wanted Oscar Hammerstein to do the book and offered it to him in mid-1941. Hart apparently agreed but probably resented the decision to enlist Hammerstein, who might want to do some of the lyrics as well. The project collapsed because of bickering over screen rights. But the correspondence between Hammerstein and Rodgers is revealing. Rodgers wrote: "Even if nothing further comes of this difficult matter it will at least have allowed us to approach each other professionally. Specifically, you feel that I should have a book with 'substance' to write to. Will you think seriously about doing such a book? Let us correspond and when you come east perhaps you and Dorothy will come up here for a week-end."[8]

Rodgers and Hart discussed another show, based on the novel *Hotel Splendide*, but they could not come to a decision about it. Rodgers, perhaps unfairly, blamed the impasse on Hart's condition. There were rumors in the press that the team was breaking up.

By this time, Rodgers had been living outside of New York for several years and had entered the new field of producing. He became a silent partner in the production of the musical *Best Foot Forward*, directed by George Abbott (Rodgers claimed that his participation was silent because of the "Hart problem"), but surely everyone knew of his involvement. The songwriters, Ralph Blane and Hugh Martin, had been writing the show while working as rehearsal pianists for *Pal Joey*. Moreover, Rodgers went to Philadelphia for the tryouts.

Rodgers sensed that his partnership with Hart was coming to an end. In September 1941, during the tryouts, he again discussed the situation with Abbott, who was pessimistic about Hart's condition. Rodgers decided to take the short trip to Doylestown, Pennsylvania, where Oscar Hammerstein had a farm. He confided to Hammerstein that his partnership with Hart was probably over, explaining his difficulties in getting Hart to concentrate on a new show.

Hammerstein suggested that Rodgers continue working with Hart as long as Hart could function, but if the time came when Hart could no longer work, Hammerstein would be there. Moreover, should Hart falter in the middle of a production, Hammerstein said that he would fill in. Although they had no formal agreement, Rodgers must have been encouraged that Hammerstein was interested in joining him. There were also stories that Rodgers had considered Ira Gershwin as a potential partner. Although Rodgers never asked Gershwin outright whether he would like to be a partner, Ira and Lee Gershwin later concluded that Rodgers was looking for a signal that Ira wanted to join forces, but Ira was determined to return to California. Rodgers never mentioned this encounter.

Rodgers and Hart finally agreed on an idea, based on a play from the early 1930s called *The Warrior's Husband*, which had starred Katharine Hepburn in one of her first Broadway roles. The story was about Amazon women and their wimpish husbands. The society is invaded by Greeks, who seek the magic powers of the women warriors and then turn the tables. Rodgers and Hart, after negotiating for the rights, decided to write the story themselves and were lucky enough to enlist Ray Bolger to play the effeminate husband of the Amazonian queen, Hippolyta, the role taken by Benay Venuta. Rodgers decided to produce the show as well, though for insurance he brought on Dwight Wiman as coproducer. The director was Joshua Logan, the conductor was Johnny Green, of "Body and Soul" fame, and the orchestrations were by Don Walker, who gave the show a swing sound.

Work on *The Warrior's Husband* was interrupted by the bombing of Pearl Harbor. Rodgers tried to arrange an army commission, but after passing his physical he was frozen out because of a new order limiting civilian commissions. It is difficult to believe he could not have found a way to serve—after all, he was well connected to the Roosevelts. His failure to gain a commission became a source of emotional distress for him, and he wrote Joshua Logan that he was "desperately unhappy." He felt guilty about sitting comfortably at home, on his "plush behind," while others were "wallowing in mud." He was particularly upset that he had experienced Broadway success during the war. He even claimed that Hammerstein had said that until the war was over, he could not think about the success of *Oklahoma!* and *Carousel* without feeling like a "son-of-a bitch."[9]

Rodgers and his wife supported the war effort in various ways (Red Cross, Writers War Board, USO). He and Hart wrote a theme song for air force bombardiers and a song that Ray Bolger used in the film *Stage Door Canteen*. By the summer following Pearl Harbor, Rodgers was forty years old and well into his next show.

Preparing that show, eventually titled *By Jupiter*, was a nightmare. Rodgers described it in an oral interview many years later:

> [Hart] just wasn't functioning at all. . . . For the last score [*By Jupiter*]
> Larry was in the hospital, and I took a guest room in the hospital. . . .
> In a couple of days he was dried out and able to write. But they
> wouldn't let him out, and he used to come down to this guest room
> every morning, in his bathrobe, and I got Steinway to send up an
> upright piano, and a great part of the score of *By Jupiter* was written
> in Doctors Hospital—which is pretty rough going. It isn't much fun
> writing a musical comedy with that hospital smell of ether. But I did
> it. And by the time I got finished with it, and a lot of other circum-
> stances that were very unpleasant, I was in pretty bad shape myself.[10]

Once released, Hart disappeared for a time, and Rodgers had to redo the lyrics. Dwight Wiman, it turned out, was also elusive and often unavailable, so Rodgers had triple duties—producer and fund raiser, composer, and lyricist. Under these circumstances it is remarkable that Rodgers and Hart could write a score at all, let along one that included "Ev'rything I've Got" and the enchanting waltz "Wait Till You See Her." Hart had been impressed by Venuta's brash voice and style and promised to write a "smash hit" for her. Revising "Ev'ry Thing I've Got" as a duet for Venuta and Bolger, he kept that promise, mainly because of his acidic lyrics:

> I have eyes for you to give you dirty looks.
> I have words that do not come from children's books.
> There's a trick with a knife I'm learning to do,
> And ev'rything I've got belongs to you.

"Wait Till You See Her" came too late in the show and was therefore cut after opening night. This sacrifice was a remarkable example of Rodgers' willingness to surrender his music for the sake of the show itself. Nevertheless, it is one of Rodgers' best waltzes and one of his finest songs. The structure is unusual: after the first eight bars Rodgers repeats the line, but in a minor key in order to transit to the bridge, which is an inverted version of the main theme. Traditionally, the last eight bars of a song are a routine reprise of the first eight, but here Rodgers masterfully inserted eight new bars of descending notes to get to the end.

The hit song of the show was supposed to be "Nobody's Heart," a lament introduced by the sometime movie actress Constance Moore and reprised by

Bolger. It is notable mainly for being one of Hart's last songs, with an almost prophetic forlorn epitaph: "Nobody's heart belongs to me." The song did not become a Rodgers and Hart staple, however. The melody was appropriately sad but not exceptional.

By Jupiter finally opened at the Shubert Theatre on June 3, 1942. The reviews were favorable, with Bolger garnering most of the laurels. The show ran longer than any other Rodgers and Hart show to that date—perhaps fittingly so, since it was their last full-blown collaboration. Yet it was below the musical standards of their previous hits. Wolcott Gibbs commented that although the score was not as memorable as some they had produced, "they still have a comfortable lead over the field."

Shortly before Joshua Logan left for military service, in the summer of 1942, Rodgers told him that he had decided to end his relationship with Hart and join Oscar Hammerstein. The breaking point came in late June 1942 as a result of Rodgers' insistence on starting a new show for the Theatre Guild based on a play from the early 1930s called Green Grow the Lilacs. Hart doubted its value as a musical and refused to begin work. He was determined to go on vacation in Mexico. Rodgers persisted, even threatening to turn to another lyricist.

Why Rodgers pressed matters this far is perplexing. Experience indicated that Hart would sooner or later have come around, either to Rodgers' proposal or to something else. Perhaps having to write By Jupiter in Doctors Hospital was the final straw for Rodgers. And maybe Rodgers, doubting that Hart would ever reform, simply wanted to move on with his career. Hart may have wanted to end the relationship as well, or at least take a long break from Rodgers.

When Hart asked who he had in mind for a new lyricist, Rodgers named Hammerstein. Even this explicit threat did not cause Hart to yield, and they parted, Rodgers in tears. After more than twenty years, the partnership was over. The names Rodgers and Hart never again appeared on the marquee for an original musical.

13

OKLAHOMA!

Oscar Hammerstein needed no persuading from Rodgers to do *Green Grow the Lilacs*, which the team eventually renamed *Oklahoma!* Although Hammerstein found the plot lacking, he was attracted by its "well-defined American characters," and he perceived in the play a "dramatic vitality under a surface gentleness." In May 1942 he had discussed it with Jerome Kern, but Kern turned it down cold. Westerns meant certain death in the theater, Kern argued. His evaluation was the same as Lorenz Hart's: *Green Grow the Lilacs* would not make a good musical.[1]

It is interesting to speculate about a Kern-Hammerstein version of *Oklahoma!* — or, for that matter, a Rodgers and Hart version. Kern and Hammerstein could have done it, although Kern later found that Rodgers' music for *Oklahoma!* was "condescending." A Rodgers and Hart version seems problematical. "Oh, what a beautiful morning" was definitely not Hart's philosophy.

There was another important difference in the new partnership: Hammerstein proposed writing the lyrics first. Kern would not have tolerated this, but Rodgers accommodated Hammerstein, and the result benefited both. This novel arrangement allowed Hammerstein to shape the overall concept of the musical, and his lyrics grew in intellectual breadth and emotional impact. In turn, Rodgers matured as a composer, as he demonstrated again and again in his seventeen-year partnership with Hammerstein.

Oklahoma! was a revolution in American musical theater. Rodgers and Hammerstein perfected a new synthesis of music, libretto, lyrics, dancing, and staging. It was no longer merely a musical but a musical play. Rodgers and Hammerstein continued to perfect this new genre, but, equally important, they eased the way for their followers.

The initial idea for *Oklahoma!* came from Theresa Helburn, a codirector of the Theatre Guild. She had known and admired Richard Rodgers since 1925, when the guild produced the first *Garrick Gaieties*. And in the late 1930s she and her codirector, Lawrence Langner, had approached Rodgers with a proposal for a musical based on Aristophanes' *Lysistrata*. They argued that Rodgers owed it to posterity to produce something of lasting value. Rodgers replied that he had a family to support.

In July 1940 there was a revival of Lynn Riggs' *Green Grow the Lilacs* at the Westport Country Playhouse, in Westport, Connecticut. The original 1931 production by the guild had not fared well, but after the Westport revival Helburn began to promote the idea of a musical based on the play. The guild was again in financial straits, and Langner promptly labeled the proposal "Helburn's folly." Nevertheless, the idea interested Richard Rodgers. Whether he had seen the revival in Westport is not clear—some writers claim that he did, but Rodgers does not mention it in his account of the origins of *Oklahoma!*[2]

Rodgers supposedly discussed the play with Hart after the opening of *By Jupiter*, which would have been in June 1942. But Theatre Guild documents suggest that Rodgers was already discussing it with the guild by March 1942. On July 23, 1942, the *New York Times* reported that the guild was planning a new production, *Green Grow the Lilacs*, with book by Oscar Hammerstein and lyrics and music by Rodgers and Hart. It was a natural mistake. There had been no announcement of the break between Rodgers and Hart, and many considered it only temporary. Rodgers and Hammerstein, however, had begun meeting once or twice a week in New York to dissect the play and reconstruct it as a musical. "Put the right components together and an explosion takes place," Rodgers said. "Oscar and I hit it off from the day we began discussing the show." It may well be that their success was a result of complementary personalities. Langner recalled Hammerstein at that time as a "big, slow-moving man" but a quick thinker, and Rodgers as "quick and volatile, a practical man of the theatre."[3]

After *Oklahoma!* became a success, Hammerstein graciously gave major credit to the original play by Lynn Riggs. In an article for the *New York Times* (May 23, 1943) shortly after the opening, Hammerstein wrote: "Give credit where credit is due. . . . Mr. Riggs' play is the well spring of almost all that is good in *Oklahoma!*" Although the Riggs play remained the core of the new production, Hammerstein significantly improved it. The play was set in the area where Riggs was born and raised, the Indian Territory of Oklahoma, in 1900. It was a love story between two innocents: Laurey, who lived on a farm with her guardian, Aunt Eller, and Curly, who describes himself as a "cowpuncher by trade and profession. I break broncs, mean uns. I bull-dog steers. I ain't never been licked and I ain't never been shot." Both Curly and Laurey are either too shy or too stubborn to declare their affection for each other. To spite Curly, Laurey accepts a ride to a social from the farm's lustful hired hand, Jeeter Fry, a man she actually fears.

Jeeter and Laurey clash at the party, and Jeeter leaves. Soon thereafter Laurey and Curly are married. On the night of their wedding they are subjected to an old-fashioned shivaree, and when Jeeter suddenly appears, he and Curly fight. Jeeter dies accidentally when he falls on his own knife. Curly is arrested, but Aunt Eller talks the authorities into letting him spend one night with his bride before going to jail. Western folk songs are sung throughout.

Curly was played by the future movie actor Franchot Tone; June Walker was Laurey; Helen Westley, the guild's stalwart performer, took the part of Aunt Eller; and Lee Strasberg, artistic director of the Actors Studio, supplied the humor as Ali Hakim, the peddler who courts the unattractive and foolish Ado Annie. In the introduction to the published version of his play Riggs wrote, "The intent has been solely to recapture in a kind of nostalgic glow (but in dramatic dialogue more than in songs) the great range of mood which characterized the old folk songs and ballads I used to hear in my Oklahoma childhood—their quaintness, their sadness, their robustness, their simplicity, their hearty or bawdy humor, their sentimentalities, their melodrama, their touching sweetness."[4] *Green Grow the Lilacs* opened on January 26, 1931, at the Guild Theatre, on 52nd Street, where *Oklahoma!* rehearsed twelve years later. The reviews were mixed. One reviewer found it "full of rich free humor, salty poetry, and some reckless tenderness that was America's before she was tamed and civilized by fences and mortgages."[5] It ran for only sixty-four performances.

Hammerstein and Rodgers agreed that they would allow the play to direct their work, but this plan presented problems. For example, everyone seemed to agree that the shivaree would make a great musical sequence, but Hammerstein found it rough and smirky. Even if they kept it, what about the killing? After some debate they decided to keep both but to make the raucous shivaree more friendly and good-natured. It did not become a musical sequence, however. Rodgers insisted that they go to the final curtain as soon as possible after the killing. But Hammerstein devised a new, happier ending: Aunt Eller would stage a quick mock trial, and Curly would be exonerated. The newlyweds would then ride off while the ensemble sang the finale. Afterward, Hammerstein wrote, "It has been proved again and again that if the background is bright, and gayety surrounds the story, the events of the story can be as dramatic or tragic as anything found in a play without music."[6]

Even before confronting the vexing problems of the ending the team turned to the opening scene. At first Rodgers and Hammerstein searched for a way to bring on the "girls" as soon as possible, perhaps during a strawberry festival or a barn dance. Eventually they returned to the setting of the play itself: the curtain rises to reveal a solitary old woman churning butter. Offstage Curly is heard singing the opening line, "There's a bright golden haze on the meadow."

This song, "Oh, What a Beautiful Mornin'," was Hammerstein's contribution. It took him three weeks to write the lyric, and he spent an entire week fussing over whether to include "Oh." In the end, it was the play itself that provided Hammerstein's inspiration. Riggs' prose set the scene in the original: "It is a radiant summer morning several years ago, the kind of morning which, enveloping the shapes of earth—men, cattle in a meadow, blades of young corn, streams— makes them seem to exist for the first time, their image giving off a visible golden emanation that is partly true and partly a trick of imagination focussing to keep alive a loveliness that may pass away." Throughout, Hammerstein used the Oklahoma dialect, which Riggs described as "lazy, drawling, not Southern, not 'hick,' but rich, half-conscious of its rhythms, its picturesque imagery." This allowed Hammerstein to rhyme "header" with "meader" (meadow) in "The Surrey with the Fringe on Top."

Hammerstein took the lyric for "Oh, What a Beautiful Mornin' " to Rodgers, who was at his home in Connecticut. To Hammerstein's chagrin it took him about ten minutes to write the music. It was almost a reflex, Rodgers said—his musical thoughts were so conditioned by the words that it took about "as long to compose it as to play it."

The melody was a superb creation, and "Oh, What a Beautiful Mornin'" became one of the most famous of Rodgers' songs. The music for the verse and the refrain are organically linked: they are of similar structure, and the last four bars of the verse are repeated notes that naturally lead up to the glorious refrain. The refrain itself is a simple melodic line, but Rodgers introduced an innovation in the third bar that subtly shifts the song from a pleasant waltz to a more radiant one by introducing unexpected dissonant harmonies. Many songwriters might have composed this refrain along conventional lines; it was the nuances that distinguished it as quintessential Richard Rodgers, giving it what Jule Styne called the "Rodgers sound."

Because they had just the right opening, Rodgers and Hammerstein could establish the time, place, and period while introducing Curly as a "guileless, romantic" young cowhand. The critics were enchanted by the simplicity and directness of the opening. During their discussion and writing of the opening song Hammerstein conceived the idea for the trial, which would be funny but also "reasonably just and fair, and common-sensible."

By the end of August the team had a beginning and an ending, and Hammerstein thereafter quickly completed the book. "I had a good time with this script," he said. "It's a long time since any musical has had such an American flavor as this one. That kind of show is my pet," he told interviewers.[7]

They had agreed not to use any of Riggs' cowboy interpolations or to try to write "second hand hillbilly ballads." Rodgers relied on instinct to create the proper Western atmosphere, which he did brilliantly, especially in the second-act song and dance, "The Farmer and the Cowman." Rodgers found compatible the new method of creating music to fit the words. He said that there was "an almost inevitable musical pathway leading from the words." Many years later Rodgers said that having the words at hand gave him an "extra push."

When Rodgers composed at the piano he always whistled the melody as he played the accompaniment with both hands. The "only inspiration," he said, "comes from the plot and the lyrics, and occasionally from a member of the cast, whose personality may suggest an added development to a character." Rodgers' work sheets for Oklahoma! contain the original melodic line to "Oh, What a Beautiful Mornin'," with only slight differences from the finished version. Not every musical idea worked. These work sheets also include a few bars of melodies that were never used.[8] In rehearsals he presented his score on two pianos, the second played by Margot Hopkins, his assistant.

For the second song in the play, Rodgers' melody was again inspired by the lyrics. The scene is the first meeting between Laurey and Curly. Curly hopes to take Laurey to the box social and is determined to impress her. Hammerstein again turned to the original plot for Curly's song, "The Surrey with the Fringe on Top," and even incorporated some of Riggs' prose into the lyrics. The song describes a ride in a grand, imaginary surrey with isinglass curtains and a fringed top, which Curly claims to have hired. Laurey is skeptical, so Curly sets out to describe the surrey in detail. The words included the phrase "clip, clop," the peg for Rodgers' music: his melody suggests the clip-clop of horses through the repetition of the same quarter note; intervals where the melody bounces up imply the scurrying of ducks and geese.

Early typescript drafts of the libretto show that few lyrics had been written beyond the opening, and that the song cues differ from the final score in several places.[9] For example, two songs, "She Likes You Quite a Lot," probably to be sung by Aunt Eller, and "I'll Be at Your Elbow," were never written. There was also an indication of a love song, tentatively titled "Someone Will Teach You," which began:

Someone will teach you
and clearly explain
How really important you are.

It was intended as the first love song in the show but did not survive; it probably was replaced by "People Will Say We're in Love." Finally, Rodgers and Hammerstein wrote "When I Go Out Walking with My Baby." This was not used either, though the melody and lyrics survived. Had Rodgers and Hammerstein settled for an early version of *Oklahoma!* the songs "The Surrey with the Fringe on Top," "People Will Say We're in Love," and "Kansas City" would never have been written.

Hammerstein's incomparable ability to remold a play was evident in his willingness to introduce new characters. He invented the cowboy Will Parker (mentioned only in passing in the play and first called "Bud" by Hammerstein). He wanted to create a subplot, a comedic triangle of the newly minted Will Parker, Ado Annie (now more attractive than in the original), and Ali Hakim. In Hammerstein's new scene Parker has just returned from Kansas City and is eager to describe his adventures to the crowd gathered at Aunt Eller's. In the first draft of the libretto Hammerstein merely noted the general idea, that Kansas City has everything—except Ado Annie. The final song, "Kansas City," picks up this idea in the lyric: "Ev'rythin's up to date in Kansas City"; the song then leads into the first dance.

In spite of the late appearance of the dancers, Agnes de Mille's choreography was one of the stunning innovations of the musical. De Mille had written to apply for the job, and in order to acquaint Rodgers and Hammerstein with her work, Theresa Helburn had taken them to see de Mille's ballet set for Aaron Copland's "Rodeo" (in fact, she wrote the scenario and outlined the choreography, and Copland then set it to music). Rodgers was skeptical that she could make the transition from modern ballet to musical comedy, but he gave in. She became a major addition, but her quarrelsome temperament was a constant problem. Her dancers, featuring the newcomers Bambi Linn and Joan McCracken, were show-stoppers, especially in the striking dream ballet at the end of the first act. But she insisted on hiring dancers for their abilities, causing Rodgers and others to complain — half jokingly — that she went out of her way to pick female dancers who were unattractive or had "ugly legs."

The role of director was originally offered to Joshua Logan even before Rodgers started work with Hammerstein, but Logan was about to be inducted into the army. Helburn approached Elia Kazan in November, but Kazan felt that he didn't click with the play. Finally, Helburn recruited Rouben Mamoulian, who had worked with Rodgers and Hart as well as Hammerstein and Kern in Hollywood. Hammerstein tried to enlist Charlotte Greenwood to play Aunt Eller, but she had other commitments (though she did play the part in the movie version). Helburn wanted Groucho Marx for the peddler and Shirley Temple as Laurey (it's mind-boggling to think of this classic musical with these two stars). But Rodgers and Hammerstein insisted on legitimate Broadway performers, and, in any case, they had to economize. Alfred Drake, who had a minor role in *Babes in Arms*, was hired for Curly.

Rodgers and Hammerstein had first tried to tempt Mary Martin to play Laurey, but she, too, had another show, which happened to try out in Boston at the same time as *Oklahoma!* (her show, *Dancing in the Streets*, closed out of town). Joan Roberts, from Hammerstein's last fiasco, *Sunny River*, played Laurey. She had a strong voice but little acting experience. Audiences thought she was the perfect all-American girl. When asked to read from the original play she did so, but she suggested that the bawdy dialogue be changed because it offended her religious beliefs. Hammerstein reassured her that his version would not embarrass her.

Howard Da Silva played Jeeter, whose name was now Jud, because Jeeter was already a character in *Tobacco Road*. Aunt Eller was played by Betty Garde, a Theatre Guild veteran. Ado Annie's part was taken by Celeste Holm, who until then had no musical comedy experience and was performing in a Broadway play. Her friends thought she was foolish to throw away her career on a Western musical. Akim the peddler was played by Joseph Buloff, a star from the Yiddish theater and the best known performer in the cast (his picture ran alongside the *New York Times* review of the opening).

Hammerstein originally called his adaptation of the play *Oklahoma*, but this was rejected for fear that audiences might confuse it with "Oakies" in *The Grapes of Wrath*. Lawrence Langner's wife, Armina Marshall, who was from Oklahoma, suggested *Cherokee Strip*, which was also rejected lest it evoke images of a burlesque show. Helburn suggested *Away We Go* (a phrase used in calling square dances), which became the working title. No one liked it, however, and during rehearsals the production was referred to as *Green Grow*.

Rodgers and Hammerstein would discuss a blueprint of the show and meet periodically but then go their separate ways to do their work. This was probably a relief for Rodgers, who for years was closeted with Hart for hours and sometimes even days at a time. He was stunned that Hammerstein turned in his lyrics on time and that they were a finished product.

Rodgers had the reputation of being a fast writer, and indeed he was. He could work rapidly, he explained somewhat defensively, because he had discussed the songs extensively beforehand. He thought the result was better when the melody was finished in a rush. "It ain't luck," he once said. Commenting on Rodgers many decades later, Jule Styne, one of the great American songwriters, wrote: "No one ever wrote a piece of music to already written words better than Rodgers. He always made it sound as though the music was composed first. Words motivated him, quite like an actor is inspired by a script. I had the feeling from my many discussions with Dick, that he didn't have to use the piano to write his songs, that he had the melody pretty much in mind before he sat down."[10] Another Rodgers characteristic, Styne added, was to rehearse and conduct the orchestra while standing on stage. In this way he heard the music as the performers heard it and could make changes that maximized the performance. "It taught me a lot," Styne wrote.

Although the team generally wrote the words before the music, Rodgers wrote the melody first for "People Will Say We're in Love." Rodgers later claimed that it was days before he was satisfied with the first eight bars. Originally, the song was not to be introduced until the second act. Hammerstein's early libretto indicated that at that point Laurey and Curly would sing "what will be the best song in the show—when it is written." When the song was transferred to the first act, the lyrics presented a problem, because at that moment Laurey and Curly were bickering. Hammerstein then wrote a classic "list" song, using a list of negatives, such as "don't throw bouquets at me." When the song was reprised in the second act the authors turned the sentiment around, and the list of don'ts became a list of dos: "Let people say we're in love."

Hammerstein wanted to end the first act with a dream ballet centered around a circus, in which Curly might be the ringmaster and Laurey a bareback rider. Agnes de Mille protested that the scenario had nothing to do with the play, and she persuaded him to use a fantasized ballet to illustrate the potential consequences of Laurey's foolish decision to accompany Jud to the box social. The dancers would take the parts of Laurey, Curly, and Jud. Laurey would be torn between the men and would imagine what life would be like with each. Claiming that the play had no sex appeal, de Mille insisted on some silk stockings and bosoms in a dance-hall scene with Jud. The dancers were dressed in scanty costumes, as the innocent Laurey might conceive them. In the ballet Curly and Jud struggle over Laurey, and the fight ends with Curly being murdered by Jud. As the ballet sequence fades and the dream ends, the real Jud appears and takes Laurey off to the party. As de Mille pointed out, the first act could have ended with an ordinary musical comedy finale but instead ended with a stark murder. "The audience was caught on the suspense of the girl's terror." [11]

Rehearsals began in February 1943 at the Guild Theatre. De Mille and Mamoulian immediately clashed. She explained that Mamoulian was accustomed to unquestioned authority and total obedience. As a choreographer, she was accustomed to the same respect; but now she was no longer "Madame the choreographer" but only "the dance director in the basement," where "I see sunlight only twenty minutes a day," wrote de Mille. [12]

Rodgers worked with the dancers for three straight days, causing a great deal of nervousness; finally he indicated his satisfaction by smiling and patting de Mille on the shoulder. Nevertheless, before leaving for tryouts in New Haven, she anguished that the show was being "wrecked, wrecked, wrecked."

Hammerstein and Rodgers kept calm. Of Rodgers, de Mille wrote, "There was only one man who rode the froth quietly and failed to turn a hair." Around midnight at a tense rehearsal, Rodgers stood at center stage, looked out and said: "Do you know what I think is wrong? Almost nothing. Now why don't you all quiet down." De Mille wrote that Rodgers later became one of the "most nervous rehearsers in the business," but in 1943, even with a great deal at stake, he was "blithely sanguine." Dorothy Rodgers explained that he had a "kind of sixth sense" and seemed to know what audiences were ready to accept. Similar praise came from de Mille: "Rodgers is not only a very great songwriter, he is one of the most astute theater men in the world. He concerns himself zestfully and relentlessly with every detail of production. Nothing escapes his attention and he takes vigorous and instant action. This might be interfering if he were not sensitive, sensible and greatly experienced. He knows also when to keep his hands off." [13]

There was an air of pessimism surrounding this show. Hammerstein had not scored a hit in many seasons, and the Rodgers-Hammerstein partnership was untested. After the show succeeded Rodgers and Hammerstein invented a game in which each would elaborate why the show should have failed. In their favorite version they noted: the chorus girls did not appear until after forty minutes into the show; one of the best songs was sung in the first three minutes, while the audience was still being seated; the first act was about a girl who could not decide which man would take her to a box social; there was no other plot to speak of; and in the second act there was only one important song. "This show," they would gleefully conclude, "had to fail."

The tryout opened on Thursday, March 11, 1943, in New Haven. The day before de Mille had written, "There's hell ahead and unless we pull the show up very quick we're sunk." Half the audience for this particular opening night was from New York; some viewers left early to report that "on the whole definitely not a success." Kurt Weill saw the show and didn't think that it was very good. And the producer Max Gordon, who had invested in the show, loudly proclaimed backstage that they should bring on girls sooner in the first act. But *Variety* reported that it "seemed to ring a bell with first nighters."

After New Haven, two scenes were cut and a love duet in the second act, "Boys and Girls Like You and Me," was replaced with a reprise of "People Will Say We're in Love." A further important change was the insertion of the title song. At some point Helburn had suggested to Hammerstein that he and Rodgers write a song about the land—at least that was her version. Mamoulian also claimed to be the inspiration of this song. Within a few days Hammerstein had the lyric for "Oklahoma," which was originally given to Laurey and Curly as a duet. After the tryout in New Haven the song was transformed into a major number for the ensemble and became a high point of the show.

In an interview with Aljean Harmetz years later, Mamoulian claimed that "for the last two weeks before we opened *Oklahoma!* on Broadway, no one even spoke to me. Rodgers thought I was destroying his music. He couldn't accept the singers having their backs to the audience. Everyone wanted me to restage it as an ordinary musical comedy. I refused, and they didn't even invite me to the opening night party." [14]

In Boston on March 15 at the Colonial Theatre, the audience was enthusiastic. The dean of Boston critics, Elliot Norton, wrote: "In that [opening] scene and song, American musical comedy took a new turn away from stilted nonsense towards something like truth and beauty. And Alfred Drake, because he got all that into his manner, his bearing and his exuberant natural singing voice, became in effect the herald of a new age." However, the reviewer for the *Christian Science Monitor* wrote that although Rodgers had been careful to make his songs simple, "unfortunately their simplicity, in common or waltz time, becomes tiresome as the first scene drags on." This reviewer also commented on the murder in the last act. The reviewer closed by saying that the title was to be changed to *Oklahoma*, and "that will help too."

The title was reluctantly changed, first to *Oklahoma*, Hammerstein's original suggestion, and then to *Oklahoma!* The inspiration for using the exclamation point is disputed. Even after the title was changed, however, the advertising in Boston, some of the sheet music, and all the prepublicity continued to use *Away We Go*. Over the years, Theresa Helburn was always quaintly amused when she saw the sets used in revivals, with *Away We Go* painted on the back.

Before the New York opening Oscar Hammerstein wrote to his son: "In one night we suddenly took on the aura of a hit. . . . I now believe that here is the nearest approach to *Show Boat* that the theatre has attained. I don't believe that it has as sound a story or that it will be as great a success. But it is comparable in quality. . . . I *know* that this is a good show. . . . There my neck is out." [15] His neck was indeed out. A few hours before the opening, walking with his wife in Doylestown, he said, "I don't know what to do if they don't like this. I don't know what to do because this is the only kind of show I can write." Dorothy Rodgers, after listening to a full run-through, left the theater and pinned a note on her husband's pillow: "This is the best thing I've ever seen in my life."

The opening-night performance on March 31, 1943, at the St. James Theatre, on 44th Street, was not sold out, perhaps because of unfriendly rumors, perhaps because it was sleeting in the late afternoon, or perhaps because theatergoers had tickets to see Ethel Merman in Cole Porter's *Something for the Boys* or Gertrude Lawrence in *Lady in the Dark* or even Ray Bolger and Nanette Fabray in Rodgers and Hart's *By Jupiter*.

One person who did attend the opening was Lorenz Hart. Some accounts claim that he also saw the tryout in New Haven and that he sat next to Billy Rose, whispering, "It's a flop isn't it?" This seems implausible. Hart did, in fact, attend the New York opening with his mother; from his box he was "applauding, howling with laughter and yelling bravos." But friends like Joshua Logan thought that it must have been painful for him to watch a revolutionary development in American theater that his partner had brought about without him. After the curtain, at the party at Sardi's, Hart burst through the crowd, hugged Rodgers, proclaimed that the new show would run longer than the operetta *Blossom Time*, and quickly left. His friends believed that success of *Oklahoma!* was the final traumatic blow to Hart.

The critics agreed with Hart. Wolcott Gibbs, in the *New Yorker* of April 10, 1943, wrote, "A completely enchanting performance — gay, stylish, imaginative, and equipped with some of the best music and dancing in a long time. [Rodgers and Hammerstein have] heightened rather than diminished their material. . . . I feel nothing but the deepest affection for everybody in it. To the Theatre Guild which made all of these joys available, my gratitude is practically boundless." *Oklahoma!* had found its place in history and legend.

Rodgers must have been particularly gratified by the success of his first effort without Hart. He modestly cited technical reasons for the triumph: all the songs and lyrics were tied into the plot, and all the melodies were related. In truth, the songs themselves were a major contribution. When asked about the time it took to compose the score for *Oklahoma!* Rodgers answered, "Flying time or elapsed time?" What he meant was that composing the songs took about five hours, but the elapsed time covered months of planning and thinking. No melodies were running around in his head, he said: "A song almost never occurs to me spontaneously. What I have to say is essentially musical, but it isn't simply melody for melody's sake." Nevertheless, Rodgers' melodic sketches for various shows, including *Oklahoma!* indicate that he experimented with different melodies.

Beginning with *Oklahoma!* his melodies became more sober or somber. He lost some of the zest inspired by his collaboration with Hart. Because Hammerstein was writing the lyrics first, and because the plays had become more serious, Rodgers' style was bound to be affected. More mature and pristine melodies emerged, beginning with "People Will Say We're in Love." This simple melodic line is not radically different from "I Could Write a Book," written three years earlier, or "Wait Till You See Her," which was dropped from *By Jupiter*. But the change would become more noticeable in subsequent shows. Rodgers resented speculation about a change in his work, insisting that his music was, as always, written to fit the text for a show.

This was the key to Richard Rodgers: he was first and last a showman. He wrote for a specific character and a specific slot in the show, with the purpose of establishing a personality, a time, or a place. His genius was that he wrote sterling music even within these confines.

Oklahoma! was awarded a special Pulitzer Prize the following year. Its record run of five years and nine months on Broadway was unbroken until *My Fair Lady* in 1956. Between 1943 and 1953, ten million people would see the show in New York or on the road. The London show set another record. *Oklahoma!* brought great financial reward to its backers and enduring fame to Rodgers and Hammerstein.

Given the ultimate enormous success of *Oklahoma!* it is ironic how much trouble the team had raising money and getting the production to Broadway. Money was scarce, partly because of the war but also because few had faith in a musical about farmhands, as one wealthy matron put it, much less one in which a murder takes place. The guild needed almost ninety thousand dollars to put the show on Broadway, and the funds were found in small increments. Rodgers and Hammerstein even had to resort to performing in Park Avenue penthouses for potential donors: Rodgers played the piano, and Hammerstein took the roles of Jud and Aunt Eller.

The movie moguls were obviously expecting a flop from this underfinanced show with no stars. MGM, which owned the rights to *Green Grow the Lilacs*, turned down the guild's pleas for money but sold Rodgers and Hammerstein an option to buy all the movie rights for forty thousand dollars, an option that had to be exercised within a few weeks of the Broadway opening. They did so in less than a week, and their purchase eventually earned them several million dollars.

What accounts for the success this show? Obviously, the words and music were critical. The story, timing, and circumstances of the show were also important. The critic Stanley Green believed that *Oklahoma!* gave wartime audiences a chance to feel pride in their country's history and implied hope for the future. Brooks Atkinson, returning from World War II, commented on the verse of "Oh, What a Beautiful Mornin' ": "After a verse like that, sung to a buoyant melody, the banalities of the old musical stage became intolerable."

Rodgers was determined to pursue his new partnership, but Hammerstein had another commitment. He was transforming Bizet's *Carmen* into a Broadway show with an all-black cast, to be called *Carmen Jones*.

So Rodgers decided, after a discussion with his old friend and collaborator Herbert Fields, to try to do something for Hart. The lyricist had been toying with a new operetta to be based on a book by the sportswriter and novelist Paul Gallico, with music by Emmerich Kalman. Hart wrote some lyrics, but nothing came of the project. It was a bitter experience for Kalman, because Hart was again drinking too much. Shortly after *Oklahoma!* opened Hart's mother died, which added to his depression. What Rodgers and Fields had in mind for Hart was a revival and reworking of *A Connecticut Yankee*. Fortunately for Hart,

Richard Rodgers in 1953, beneath a painting of a scene from *Oklahoma!* by Doris Lee.

he would not have to do an entirely new set of lyrics and he would be working with people he knew. Hart not only agreed but made a major effort to stay
sober and to work according to schedule. Rodgers, acting as producer, publicly
announced the project on June 30, 1943. He said that there would be a few new
songs and some tinkering with the book.

Some of the songwriting was done at Rodgers' home. The plot was revised,
changing Martin, the Hartford mechanic, into a naval officer. Six new songs
were written, though not all were used. The cast included Dick Foran and Julie
Warren as the principals, along with Vivienne Segal as Morgan Le Fay. Playing
Lady Evelyn was the future movie star Vera-Ellen. One of the new songs in the
first act included "To Keep My Love Alive," which became a hit. It was a caustic
and witty recitation of the various reasons a woman did away with her lovers.
It is believed to have been Hart's last lyric.

The show received reasonably good reviews, though it did not run very long.
Howard Barnes concluded that it was a "good show." Lewis Nichols thought
that it was "pretty to look at [and] agreeable to hear." As for the music, Wolcott
Gibbs wrote that with the exception of "To Keep My Love Alive," the new material was "nothing much."

After the show opened in late October for its Philadelphia tryout, Hart
plunged back into his old habits. He was apparently disconcerted by the fact
that Oscar Hammerstein was also in Philadelphia previewing *Carmen Jones*. The
contrast between the self-assured Hammerstein and the disheveled Hart was too
obvious. Hart contracted pneumonia and returned to New York, where he was
hospitalized briefly. By the time *Connecticut Yankee* opened on Broadway he was
desperately ill, though none of his friends or relations seem to have realized it.
He insisted on attending opening night, but his companions lost track of him.
As the curtain opened, Dorothy Rodgers, in her usual seat in the last row, felt
something brush her hair. She looked up and saw Lorenz Hart in his accustomed
place in the theater gangway.

He made something of a noisy scene later in the performance and was hustled
out of the theater. That night Dorothy Hart took her brother-in-law home with
her. He disappeared briefly, then was discovered at his apartment, critically ill.
He was rushed to the hospital, where he remained unconscious until the evening of November 22, 1943. He died during a brief wartime blackout. According
to a nurse, his last words were, "What have I lived for?" [16]

Hart had composed his own epitaph several years earlier, for a song called
"Glad to Be Unhappy." In the refrain Hart told the story of his own life:

Fools rush in, so here I am,
Very glad to be unhappy.
I can't win, but here I am.
More than glad to be unhappy.
Unrequited love's a bore
And I've got it pretty bad.

Rodgers, however, usually went out of his way to dispute the notion that Hart was in fact "glad" to be unhappy.

The preceding June, Hart had made a new will, apparently on the advice of his financial adviser, Willy Kron. The will named Rodgers as one of the executors. But Hart's brother, Teddy, contested the will, particularly a legacy to Kron. Teddy Hart claimed that his brother had been in no condition to make sound judgments and had been unduly influenced by Kron. Rodgers, who was asked to testify concerning Hart's condition, insisted that Hart had done some of his best work in his last months and was not only competent but a "little sharper" than Rodgers had ever seen him. "He knew exactly what he was doing every minute," Rodgers said. "His mind was clicking properly." [17] This decisive testimony left Teddy Hart and his wife bitter about Rodgers. Perhaps Rodgers was reluctant to testify to Hart's deterioration. He had, after all, tolerated a great deal over the years without any public comment, and to strike a blow against Hart after he was dead was probably more than Rodgers could do. And, of course, Hart had done some good work on the revival up to the tryout.

Hart's death and the success of *Oklahoma!* constituted an important turning point for Richard Rodgers. What might have been an interlude, had Hart recovered, became a permanent change. Had *Oklahoma!* failed, Rodgers and Hammerstein might have gone their separate ways. Instead, the partnership was solidified, and they began a long process of probing the frontiers of the musical theater.

The new team became the dominant force on Broadway and eventually transformed themselves into an institution. For the next two decades the voice of Broadway, and the musical language of America, would be that of Rodgers and Hammerstein.

14

CAROUSEL

Cementing the new partnership was more important to Rodgers than to Hammerstein. Rodgers had worked with one man exclusively for more than twenty years, whereas Hammerstein had collaborated with several composers. The thought of careening from one lyricist to another must have been disturbing for a man of Rodgers' temperament. Hammerstein was methodical, meticulous, and reliable, if sometimes slow, characteristics that made him an ideal complement to Rodgers. Although Rodgers sometimes grew impatient with his partner's measured gait, he found that the partners gave each other a sense of certainty.

Hammerstein's willingness to write the book as well as the lyrics meant that Rodgers no longer had to worry about where the next script would come from or who would write it. And it gave him an opportunity to help shape their productions in the early phases. Hammerstein's preferences in both lyrics and story lines could not help but affect the music Rodgers was expected to supply. By allowing Hammerstein to write the lyrics first, Rodgers gave up the autonomy he had enjoyed with Hart. But Rodgers was flexible, and he obviously wanted more order in his life than he had in the final years with Hart. At age forty-one he was still a young man, and he had broken with Hart in part because he felt he had many years of creative work ahead. Moreover, Rodgers had become more ambitious. He had already involved himself in producing (with George Abbott), and Hammerstein also was interested in trying his hand at producing.

For a time it was not clear that their partnership would continue. The success of *Oklahoma!* meant that Hammerstein's lean years were over, and offers of work began pouring in—there were rumors that he was negotiating with Jerome Kern for a new musical. Rodgers decided to press Hammerstein on the idea of their partnership; Hammerstein agreed, though no written contract was ever executed. The production company they formed would produce their own shows as well as works by others. And they had already wisely decided to publish their own music, beginning with the songs from *Oklahoma!* in a partnership with Chappell Music that they named Williamson Music, Inc. Gradually, almost imperceptibly, "R&H" was coming into existence.

Still, there was one enormous problem: how to follow *Oklahoma!* They chose not to accept Samuel Goldwyn's caustic advice for an encore: "Shoot yourself." They knew that their next show would not be easy, if only because they were determined not to write a sequel. They also knew that whatever they wrote would immediately be compared with *Oklahoma!*—and no doubt unfavorably. Rodgers once commented that with the opening of every Rodgers and Hammerstein show, *Oklahoma!* gained a new round of good reviews. Harold Arlen and Yip Harburg's *Bloomer Girl*, which opened the following season, was hailed as another *Oklahoma!* even before it reached Broadway.

For most of 1943 Hammerstein was preoccupied with *Carmen Jones*, which opened to strong reviews in December. Rodgers was caught up with the revival of *A Connecticut Yankee* in November and with Hart's death shortly thereafter.

One of the offers following *Oklahoma!* came from Darryl Zanuck, head of 20th Century–Fox. Hollywood concluded that if *Oklahoma!* was such a hit, it should be copied. Filming the show itself was out of the question, because a long stage run seemed probable. But *Oklahoma!* prompted a rash of new musicals, including *Centennial Summer*, with music by Jerome Kern, and *Meet Me in St. Louis*. Zanuck's idea was to remake the popular 1933 movie *State Fair*, which had starred

Will Rogers and Janet Gaynor. Rodgers and Hammerstein agreed to write the score, but only if they could work in New York. Zanuck consented, and Hammerstein began a draft of a screenplay in January 1944, relying heavily on the original movie script. In early April the studio announced that the script and score were supposedly halfway completed. The producer, William Perlberg, had visited Rodgers and Hammerstein in New York, and on returning to Hollywood he proclaimed that the remake promised to be "another *Oklahoma!*" The studio had already budgeted two million dollars for *State Fair*; the story, of an Iowa farm family's adventures, would not be radically different from the Will Rogers version, except for the music. Perlberg said that even the grunts of the famous prize pig would be set to music (which must have been a surprise to Rodgers).

Although Zanuck had agreed that Rodgers and Hammerstein could work in New York, he insisted that they come to Hollywood to oversee the early rehearsals. Rodgers arrived to discover that Zanuck mainly wanted to demonstrate that he was the one in charge. (Hammerstein was ill and could not make the trip.) Nevertheless, when the complete score was submitted, Rodgers gleefully remarked that not a note was touched — such was their newfound authority.

The movie was even billed as "Rodgers and Hammerstein's *State Fair*." (The partnership was never Hammerstein and Rodgers; it could have been, on the grounds of seniority or even alphabetical listing.) In some respects this film, with its rural setting and charming, uncomplicated family, turned out to be the musical sequel to *Oklahoma!* Dick Haymes, "Fox's answer to Frank Sinatra," was to play Wayne Frakes, the romantic lead. Wayne's love interest was Vivian Blaine (not yet the Adelaide of *Guys and Dolls*). Jeanne Crain, as the starry-eyed daughter Margy, played opposite Dana Andrews.

The musical director was Alfred Newman, Rodgers' longtime friend; Newman's involvement may explain the effective use of the songs. Rodgers and Hammerstein had hoped to use the music and lyrics to assist in the plot and move the story forward. They were partly successful: most of the songs seemed to fit the characters or to illuminate the atmosphere. Much of the music was reminiscent of *Oklahoma!* In fact, "Our State Fair" and "It's a Grand Night for Singing" would have readily worked in the Broadway version of that show.

The most enduring hit proved to be "It Might as Well Be Spring," sung first by Crain (whose voice was dubbed), reprised by others, and used throughout as a theme song. The song originated while Hammerstein was musing about the uneasiness of the female lead. He told Rodgers that even though state fairs were never held in the spring, Margy's mood was such that it might as well be spring. Rodgers immediately recognized a song title. (Hammerstein liked to tell this story to illustrate the complementary character of their partnership.) Hammerstein had marked that song for late in the plot, when Margy is mooning over her romance after the fair, but it was moved to the opening to establish her restless mood before the fair.[1]

Rodgers experimented with a melodic line, this time with what he called the graphic contours of music—that is, the way the line of notes looked on paper. For "The Surrey with the Fringe on the Top," he had used repeated notes, the contour of which was flat and straight, like a road. In "It Might as Well Be Spring," Rodgers' melodic line, like the young girl, was jumpy, or as he described it, "nervous and insecure." Thus, the phrase in the fourth bar ended with what Rodgers called a "tentative, slightly worried F-natural" rather than a more positive-sounding F sharp. The feeling of hesitation in this phrase is also created by the use of sixteenth and eighth notes rather than the steady eighth notes. (Most singers ignored this fine distinction, unfortunately.) The song won an Academy Award, the first for Rodgers and the second for Hammerstein, who had scored with "The Last Time I Saw Paris." According to Rodgers, Newman slowed the tempo of "It Might as Well Be Spring." Rodgers complained, but when he heard this rendition he conceded that Newman was right. Perhaps because of the style of Haymes and Blaine, the songs that did survive seem more deliberately pop than was usual for Rodgers.

Before releasing the picture in August 1945 the producer had the score played for Kurt Weill and Ira Gershwin. Weill thought that it was "very weak," and Gershwin told Perlberg he didn't like it. Critics were charmed, however. *Variety* found the tunes "whammo." Another review invoked the inevitable comparison: "It is to movie musicals what *Oklahoma!* is to stage musicals." The movie itself got mixed reviews: "no more than an average screen musical," wrote Bosley Crowther, of the *New York Times*. Zanuck was pleased with the film and held it up as example to his colleagues. But in one of his famous memoranda he noted that using the lyrics and music to advance the story had not really worked and that they had had to shoot extra scenes to explain the action (though these sections do not stand out in the film).

Rodgers wrote Josh Logan that he was satisfied with the film but that its production was a typical Hollywood ordeal. He cited the endless quarreling and the questionable taste: "This, for instance, is symptomatic of the whole job: the little girl from the farm is dressed in very fancy dirndl clothes and the [production] boys have proceeded on the theory that if the woman's bosom is attractive to an audience, she will be ten times as attractive if her bosom is ten times as big. They've taken a cute little kid [Jeanne Crain] and stuffed her out so that she follows her chest across the screen all evening. But don't get me wrong—I hate Hollywood."[2]

As work on *State Fair* wound down Rodgers and Hammerstein launched their first commercial venture as producers of a nonmusical. Dorothy Rodgers had read a collection of stories by Kathryn Anderson Forbes entitled *Mama's Bank Account* and thought they would make a good play. Her husband and Hammerstein agreed and commissioned John Van Druten to write it. Van Druten already had a hit, *Voice of the Turtle*, and was beginning a long and successful career as a dramatist (he later wrote *I Am a Camera*, based on Christopher Isherwood's *Berlin Stories*, and *Bell, Book and Candle*). He transformed Forbes' stories into a series of scenes dramatizing the life of a large Norwegian family living in San Francisco at the turn of the century. The show, now titled *I Remember Mama*, opened in October 1944 and was immediately hailed. It had a long run, became a motion picture, and was turned into a television series.

This production interrupted what was to be the new partners' next Broadway hit, *Carousel*. The inspiration for *Carousel*—like that of *Oklahoma!*—came from Theresa Helburn and Lawrence Langner of the Theatre Guild. In January 1944, over lunch at Sardi's, they suggested to Rodgers and Hammerstein that they adapt Ferenc Molnár's play *Liliom* for a musical. The Theatre Guild had produced the American debut of the play in 1921 and revived it in 1940 with Burgess Meredith and Ingrid Bergman; both Rodgers and Hammerstein had seen this production. *Liliom*, set in pre–World War I Budapest, is a dour tale of ill-fated love. Rodgers and Hammerstein firmly rejected the idea of a musical with a Hungarian backdrop. Helburn later suggested transferring the story to America, perhaps New Orleans. Hammerstein looked into the idea of using a Creole dialect but again rejected the project.

In spite of their objections, both men kept returning to the idea: they were obviously intrigued, possibly because it was so different from the average Broadway story. Or perhaps they felt they owed the guild something for having faith in *Oklahoma!* (a debt that was handsomely repaid). Finally, Rodgers suggested using New England as the locale, on the rather dubious grounds that because he had a home in Connecticut he could imagine a New England setting. Hammerstein grew enthusiastic; a coastal town could be used to bring in the sea, whalers, sailors, hornpipe dances, and the like, and New England, with its mill workers, might be a credible background for an ensemble.

These conversations took place over several months, and in October the guild obtained the rights from Molnár, who had immigrated to the United States. Years earlier he had reportedly rejected Puccini's effort to turn his play into an opera, remarking that he wanted his play to be remembered as Molnár's Liliom, not Puccini's. Molnár was a musician, and in Europe he had been a fan of Viennese operettas. In 1937 he also turned down Kurt Weill's offer to make a musical of Liliom, so it was surprising that he agreed to a Rodgers and Hammerstein version. Perhaps he was grateful to the Theatre Guild, or maybe he had seen a performance of Oklahoma! A more likely reason, however, was that he was given 1 percent of the gross and a flat twenty-five hundred dollars for "personal services." Thus, the musical version of Liliom became Carousel.

Rodgers and Hammerstein signed contracts with the guild in August 1944, but rehearsals did not begin until the next January. The story was a far greater challenge than had Riggs' Green Grow the Lilacs. The Riggs play was known to theater aficionados but not to the general public. Liliom, on the other hand, was familiar throughout the United States and Europe. Although Hammerstein had preserved Green Grow the Lilacs in the main, Liliom presented more formidable problems. Molnár's play was about the underside of Budapest before the collapse of the Dual Monarchy. It protested the class rigidities of that society and the hopelessness created by social oppression. The writing was encumbered with political asides, including a dose of anti-Semitism, was loaded with symbolism, and combined realism and fantasy. Liliom was a romance of sorts, though robbery, suicide, and wife beating figured in the story.

In Oklahoma! the two leads were sympathetic, if a trifle naive. The principal characters in Liliom were not. The dominant male, a reprehensible roughneck nicknamed Liliom (Hungarian slang for a "lily," that is, a tough guy), was rechristened Billy Bigelow by Hammerstein and made a carnival barker with an unsavory reputation as a womanizer and petty criminal. Liliom falls in love with the servant girl Julie Jordan (she's a mill worker in the musical), who repeatedly excuses his faults. They begin living together (they marry in the musical), and she becomes pregnant. His worries about supporting a child drive him to take part in a robbery, which goes awry. Liliom/Billy then commits suicide. In heaven he is judged but promised a chance to redeem himself. But when he returns to help his daughter he botches the encounter, defeated by his own flaws and his inability to cope with life. Not exactly the stuff of musical comedy.

Hammerstein tried to use both the story and lyrics to explain more sympathetically the circumstances and motivation of the lovers. He said that he and Rodgers wanted to create a musical play based on Liliom, not Liliom with a few songs added. As in Oklahoma! he built up the parts of two secondary characters, Julie's friend, Carrie Pepperidge, and her prim and proper beau, Enoch Snow (called Wolf Berkowitz in the original). In Molnár's play Marie (Carrie) is almost incidental.

Hammerstein wanted to create a counterpoint between Julie's doomed romance and the middle-class success of Carrie and Mr. Snow. His treatment suggested that Julie's love involved deeper emotion than did Carrie's prosperous marriage. He used Carrie to elucidate Julie early in the musical, with the song "You're a Queer One, Julie Jordan."

> You're a queer one, Julie Jordan.
> You won't even tell a body what you think.
> You're as tight-lipped as an oyster,
> And as silent as an old Saharia Spink.

Carrie's mispronunciation of "Sphinx" is corrected by Julie, a subtle touch that distinguishes each woman. The song and the dialogue between Julie and Carrie are a prelude to the first long encounter between Billy and Julie. The two warily test each other around a park bench: Billy alleges that she has been out with men before, but Julie denies it; she must worry about her reputation, because she intends never to marry.

They are interrupted by the mill owner and a policeman, who warn her that she must return to the mill's boardinghouse. The policeman describes Billy: "A pretty fly gazaybo. Come up from Coney Island. . . . He works on carousels, makes a specialty of young things, like this'n." But Julie stays with Billy, who is impressed but puzzled. He sings his own chorus:

> You're a queer one, Julie Jordan.
> Ain't you sorry you didn't run away?

She sings that she doesn't have any money for him to steal, but that if she did, she would give it to him. Billy asks whether she would marry anyone like him. She answers, "Yes, I would, if I loved you."

Hammerstein used this exchange, borrowed from Molnár, to lead into the extended version of the show's great duet, "If I Loved You." Finally, blossoms float down from the acacia trees, the lovers kiss, the lights dim, and the curtains close. It is one of the American musical's finest romantic scenes. The song was critical because it had to make a dramatic impact but not seem too sophisticated for the characters' mundane background; above all, it had to be singable by both of the principals. No matter what happened afterward, the audience was bound to be sympathetic to Billy and Julie.

Hammerstein then lightened the story with the rousing "June Is Bustin' Out All Over" and the famous "Soliloquy," in which Billy imagines how he will treat his new son, "My boy Bill." In the second act this light air slowly disintegrates. In "What's the Use of Wond'rin'," Julie asks:

> What's the use of wond'rin'
> If he's good or if he's bad.

When she pleads with Billy not to join in the robbery he brushes her aside.

This leads into the second great moment in the musical: as Julie lingers over Billy's body, he tries to explain why—"I couldn't see anything ahead." Julie says to Billy: "Sleep—sleep peacefully. One thing I never told you . . . I love you." Encouraged by Aunt Nettie, Julie sings "You'll Never Walk Alone." And when she breaks down, Nettie finishes one chorus of the melody. This is surely Rodgers and Hammerstein's most dramatic song, though it has been sung so many times that its impact has been lost in maudlin revivals. The melody is lovely, but the lyrics carry it to great heights.

In Molnár's play the remorseless Liliom is indicted before a court of imperious judges and sentenced to sixteen years in the "crimson fire," but the judges promise that after that time he will be allowed to return earth to do a good deed for his child. Liliom trivializes this solemn pronouncement by asking for a cigarette.

Hammerstein altered this considerably. Billy was rough, but not a villain. Hammerstein substituted for the judges a stern but kindly "Starkeeper," who explains Billy's opportunity now that sixteen years have passed.

In a long ballet, Billy's daughter, Louise, dances to the melody of "If I Loved You." When Billy witnesses Mr. Snow's son taunting Louise he makes himself visible and tries to console her. She flinches and wards him off with her arm, and Billy impulsively slaps her hand away. She flees into the house. Louise brings Julie into the yard, but there is no one there. When she wonders how she could have been struck yet felt not pain, Julie explains that it is quite possible for someone to hit you—and hit you hard—and not to hurt at all.

At this point Molnár's play ends. But Hammerstein continued: "Failure!" shouts Billy's heavenly friend. "You struck out blindly again." Hammerstein then devised a new ending. At Louise's graduation, the town's minister urges the graduates to go out and find happiness for themselves. Regardless of what their parents have done, "You just stand on your own two feet." The ensemble begins to sing "You'll Never Walk Alone." Billy, still invisible, whispers to Louise, "Listen to him. Believe him." She seems startled. Billy then whispers to Julie, "I loved you, Julie." Her face lights up and she joins in the singing. The girl next to Louise puts her arm around her (this gesture was Rodgers' idea). The heavenly friend beckons to Billy. They leave as all sing "You'll Never Walk Alone." Curtain.

Carousel opened on April 19, 1945, at the Majestic Theatre, diagonally across the street from the St. James, where *Oklahoma!* was still going strong. It was another triumph for Rodgers and Hammerstein but also for the stars, John Raitt and Jan Clayton; for Rouben Mamoulian, the director; and for Agnes de Mille, the choreographer—Bambi Linn, dancing Louise's long ballet, stopped the show on opening night. A new member of the production team, recruited by de Mille, was Trude Rittmann, a German refugee and a highly trained classical musician who had been writing dance arrangements for the New York City Ballet. She arranged the dance music for *Carousel*. Rittmann claimed that Rodgers distrusted women musicians, and she found him difficult to work with. But as she proved her worth, Rodgers began to rely on her. She continued her association with his shows into the 1970s.[3]

Rodgers attended the opening on a stretcher, having wrenched his back a few days earlier. He was so groggy from sedatives that he thought the show was failing. The show came to be Rodgers' favorite, probably because there were thirty-one musical episodes, compared with about twelve for most musicals.

Once again Rodgers had abolished the overture, explaining that the audience could hear only the brasses. There was a more germane reason, however. Molnár's opening scene was a panorama of the carnival grounds and the carousel. Crowds were milling about with with the jugglers, fire-eaters, and other performers. For this prologue, which Hammerstein retained in pantomime, Rodgers composed an extended waltz that underscored the opening six minutes of the pantomime. It is during this interval that Billy first encounters Julie.

One of the musical themes of the "Carousel Waltz" was written in 1932, in sketches for the movie *Hallelujah, I'm a Bum*. The finished composition creates the flavor of a carousel and hurdy-gurdy without resorting to sound effects. The Boston Symphony later performed the waltz as a concert piece, to Rodgers' great delight. He even drove to Boston to hear it.

Rodgers also contributed the famous "Soliloquy"; he played a dummy melody to give Hammerstein the idea for the lyric. It was the discussion of how to handle this episode that finally convinced them that they could turn *Liliom* into a musical. The soliloquy offered a persuasive motivation for Billy's desperation in participating in the robbery.

Indeed, Rodgers' reputation for fast work was garnished with new anecdotes, at Hammerstein's expense. It took two weeks for Hammerstein to work out the lyrics for the soliloquy, but only two hours for Rodgers to set the words to music. For *State Fair*, Hammerstein worked out a lyric, gave it to Rodgers at their New York office, and went down the hall to visit someone. A few minutes later, Rodgers emerged, inquired where Hammerstein had gone, and then returned to his desk. Hammerstein stopped back at Rodgers' secretary's desk and mockingly exclaimed, "Not finished yet?" The secretary answered: "Finished? He's been out looking for you." The song was "It's a Grand Night for Singing."

Carousel has proved a hardy perennial. There have been several notable revivals and recordings of the score, in addition to the original cast recording. There have been innumerable versions and revivals of the show, but Raitt's reading of Billy is the strongest. Rodgers and Hammerstein were still earning significant royalties—on the order of twenty thousand dollars a year—from revivals ten years after the show opened on Broadway. In 1956, *Carousel* was made into a film starring Gordon MacRae and Shirley Jones. A controversial revival directed by Nicholas Hytner was staged in London in December 1992. It traveled to New York, where it was hailed as a *Carousel* for the 1990s because it was darker than the original. A "defining *Carousel*—hard-edged, imaginative and exciting," wrote Clive Barnes for the *New York Post*. The opening was changed to show an assembly line of women working beneath a giant clock. It emphasized the class consciousness of the story in other respects as well.

Some critics found that a "grittiness" had been restored. The singing, according to the critic David Richards, mattered less than the "proletarian authenticity of the characters." This was an ironic commentary, since Marxists had attacked the original play for its lack of genuine class consciousness, inherent in Liliom's plight. Other reviewers found the score corny and the book stale; still others concluded that it was Rodgers at his "most tuneful."[4]

In 1945, however, there was scarcely any dissent.[5] Even Molnár thought that the show was beautiful, especially the ending. His only complaint about the production was that Mamoulian smoked too much. Molnár became an American citizen in 1947 and died in 1952. On his tombstone was engraved Julie's epitaph for her lover: "Sleep Liliom, my boy, sleep."

For seasons to come *Carousel* symbolized a radical advance in both subject matter and the treatment of music, dialogue, and plot. Despite their success, Rodgers and Hammerstein decided against immediately launching another venture of their own. They turned again to producing.

15

ALLEGRO

Rodgers and Hammerstein said that they wanted to become producers because of the "great satisfactions that go with a sense of accomplishment and progress in our recently chosen field." However
lofty their aims, they ended up making a small fortune as producers
of their own musicals and other plays. In the fall of 1945 they were
contemplating an idea thrown at them by their old friend Dorothy
Fields: a show with Ethel Merman as Annie Oakley. It did not take
long for them to encourage Fields to write it. Although they did not
intend to write the music and lyrics themselves, few other songwriters could do justice to a Rodgers and Hammerstein production.
Hammerstein suggested enlisting his old partner Jerome Kern, who
was languishing in Hollywood. (Some people thought Kern was jealous over Hammerstein's triumph in *Oklahoma!* but the men were still
close.)

In August, Hammerstein was on the West Coast to discuss a revival of *Show Boat* with Kern and to interest him in the Annie Oakley show. Kern resisted because he did not want to endure another failure like the 1939 show *Very Warm for May*, the last show he and Hammerstein had done. Kern blamed the failure on the producer, Max Gordon. To reassure him, Rodgers invited Kern to write the show: "It would be one of the greatest honors in my life if you would consent to write the music for this show." Kern's acceptance was "enthusiastic," according to Rodgers.[1]

Kern may have been encouraged by the thought of working with Hammerstein once again. Hammerstein was helping him with the lyrics for "All Through the Day," which Kern was writing for the movie *Centennial Summer*. He and Hammerstein also had written a new song for *Show Boat*, "Nobody Else but Me," to replace the comedy routine Norma Terris had performed in the original. Kern visited New York that fall to work on the *Show Boat* revival and to discuss the Annie Oakley show. On that visit he suffered a heart attack and collapsed; he died a few days later, on November 11, 1945, at the age of sixty. One wonders how Kern would have fared with the score for Dorothy Fields' show, *Annie Get Your Gun*. It would have been fascinating to observe the interaction between Rodgers and his boyhood idol.

Rodgers and Hammerstein needed a new songwriter, but, once again, who could do their production justice? Rodgers had an inspiration—Irving Berlin! Rodgers' colleagues were highly skeptical, because Berlin always dominated his shows. Why would he subordinate himself to other producers? Hammerstein suggested that they at least ask him; the worst Berlin could do would be to turn them down. Rodgers approached Berlin, who hesitated. Would it be billed as Irving Berlin's *Annie Get Your Gun*? Rodgers and Hammerstein said no, which is an interesting comment on their approach to producing. Despite their lofty sentiments about serving the best interests of the theater, they were hardheaded businessmen, jealously guarding their prerogatives. But had Berlin backed out over the question of billing, it would have been a major loss. In the end they all agreed that Berlin's name would be set in the same size type as the others. The final result, however, was that the billing read:

ETHEL MERMAN
In the Richard Rodgers–Oscar Hammerstein II production
ANNIE GET YOUR GUN
Music and Lyrics by IRVING BERLIN

Forty-five years later, a new recording of the original score was advertised as Irving Berlin's *Annie Get Your Gun*, and the names Rodgers and Hammerstein had disappeared altogether. And appropriately so; the show was, above all, Berlin's.

Berlin professed doubts about writing the score—expectations would naturally be high. Why, Berlin asked, didn't Hammerstein and Rodgers write the show themselves? This was not their kind of show, he was told, a comment that did little to allay Berlin's fears. Berlin hesitated and Rodgers became impatient, asking him to read some of the script. Berlin did and in one weekend wrote several songs. His friends believe that he wanted to prove to Rodgers that he still had it in him. Rodgers was thrilled with the result, and an agreement was signed.[2]

That *Annie Get Your Gun* was not "their kind of show" was a provocative comment, for it was not all that far from *Oklahoma!* And it was no lighter or merrier than a dozen Rodgers and Hart shows or, for that matter, many of Hammerstein's shows with Kern. What they meant, apparently, was that they intended to pursue more serious endeavors. *Annie* turned out to be a sensation, and one wonders whether Rodgers and Hammerstein could have infused the show with the humor, vigor, and boisterous musical aura imparted by Berlin, who wrote both the words and the music.

As a rule, neither Rodgers nor Hammerstein interfered with their nonmusical productions unless it was absolutely necessary. They were deeply involved in the planning, attended rehearsals and auditions, and had some influence on the casting. For Berlin's show, however, after a small group listened to a run-through of the score by Berlin, Rodgers noted that Berlin had dropped one song. Rodgers asked why, and Berlin explained that the look on their faces suggested they did not like that particular song. They all protested, and "There's No Business Like Show Business" was back in. Later, during another session, Rodgers and the show's director, Joshua Logan, whispered that they needed another song for Annie and Frank Butler, her boyfriend and a competitive sharpshooter. Berlin, overhearing them, asked what kind of song they wanted. Since the two characters were still feuding at that point, a love song would be out of order. Rodgers suggested a "challenge" song. Berlin was inspired, and during a taxi ride to his apartment wrote "Anything You Can Do, I Can Do Better."

Rodgers also intervened during the out-of-town tryout. As was the custom, the entire orchestra was not called in until late in the rehearsals. But when the orchestra performed Berlin's score for the first time, there was trouble. Fields sensed it as soon as she heard the music. Berlin and Rodgers agreed that the tone of the orchestrations (by Phil Lang) was not right. They wired for emergency

Ethel Merman, Richard Rodgers, and Irving Berlin during rehearsals for *Annie Get Your Gun* (1946), the first musical produced by Rodgers and Hammerstein. Berlin wrote both music and lyrics for this hit.

help from Robert Russell Bennett, who redid most of the score to the satisfaction of both Berlin and Rodgers.

On opening night on Broadway (May 16, 1946), the audience was at first strangely cool. New Yorkers had expected a sophisticated, complex Rodgers and Hammerstein show, but they were confronted by Ethel Merman giving them an old-fashioned musical comedy. But by the first-act curtain they understood *Annie* and liked it. The critics agreed. It would become the second longest-running show after *Oklahoma!* In its first three years the show grossed more than $4 million, a handsome profit for R&H productions.

The following autumn Rodgers and Hammerstein produced another success, *Happy Birthday*, written by Anita Loos and starring Helen Hayes. This, too, made money—over $1.5 million. They now had two productions running in addition to *Oklahoma!* and *Carousel.* One unintended by-product of their achievements was that it put increasing pressure on them to succeed in their future projects. But success also gave them considerable freedom to decide how to proceed. Oscar Hammerstein had always hoped to write a serious drama that would address the problems of life confronting the ordinary mortal. He was inspired by Thorton Wilder's *Our Town* to consider an idea of his own.

In March 1946, while *Annie Get Your Gun* was still in rehearsals, he tried out an idea on Rodgers: a musical with two men as the principal characters rather than the usual boy and girl. As the two discussed it over the weeks that followed, the idea changed to the life story of one man, a doctor. This appealed to Rodgers, whose father and brother were doctors. By September they had settled on a basic story about the doctor's effort to make his way in the world without compromising his principles.

Hammerstein wrote a few pages of the book, now called *Allegro*, before he and his wife sailed for Australia to visit her mother. On the ship he finished more of the text, and on arrival in Brisbane he mailed it to Rodgers. As might have been expected, Rodgers sat down and wrote three songs. This was not a usual assignment, even for a Rodgers and Hammerstein show. Although *Carousel* had serious themes, it was lively entertainment as well. This new show would be radically different.

To adequately cover one person's entire life, the action would have had to be spread over a very large canvas—too large, as it turned out. So they settled on a story that moved from birth through adolescence and on to maturity in two acts. They decided to exploit every theatrical device available—including fluid movement on stage, novel settings, imaginative light and sound mixtures, and, of course, music and lyrics—to convey the progress of the main character, Joseph Taylor, Jr., from his birth in 1905 to age thirty-five. To help with the development, a so-called Greek chorus would comment on the story, explain it to the audience, and offer advice to the players.

In the first scene, the mother is in bed with her newborn son, and the chorus solemnly announces, to music, that she is the wife of Doctor Taylor and that except for her wedding day, "this is the happiest day of her life." This chanting sets the musical mood for the show. The baby's father appears but must leave to attend another patient who is having a baby (that baby is Jenny Brinker, future sweetheart of the Taylors' baby). His grandmother holds little Joe and sings the show's second song, "It Can Happen Again," forecasting his promising life. After a mélange by the chorus and disembodied voices, as might be heard by the young child, the chorus sings the chantlike "One Foot, Other Foot" as the boy learns to walk.

This was obviously not a typical Broadway musical, and the music and lyrics had to be even more integral to the story than they had been in *Carousel*. Hammerstein finished the first act by July. In it Joe grows up, goes to high school, and falls in love with Jenny. His father works hard, hoping for a small hospital some day. He predicts that Joe will become a doctor and assist him. At this point the parents sing a song that seemed made for a more traditional musical, the Rodgers-style love song "A Fellow Needs a Girl." It seems jarringly out of place compared with the music that precedes and follows it. Perhaps it was a bow to convention, but more likely it was intended to show that the older couple embodied some of the old-fashioned virtues. In this sense it fit.

Joe goes to college but moons for Jenny, who is sowing some wild oats. He is persuaded to go on a blind date with Beulah, who sings, "So Far," a strong Rodgers melody with puzzling lyrics. There is no love interest between Joe and Beulah, who disappears from the show; her plaintive words, "we have nothing to remember so far," are never resolved, because they never do have anything to remember. In the show the song had an operatic quality, but later it was given a more conventional and more satisfying treatment by popular singers, Sylvia Sims in particular.

Reunited with Jenny, Joe sings, "You Are Never Away," a strong, sweeping melody that includes an interlude in a different key, before returning to the refrain, and a novel sixteen-bar ending. It was necessary to make a strong statement of Joe's devotion to Jenny, who begins to emerge as a questionable personality. His mother believes that Jenny's crass ambitions will be bad for Joe, and after a confrontation with Jenny she has a heart attack and dies. In the final scene of the first act, Joe and Jenny are married. The chorus intones throughout, and the ghosts of his grandmother and mother appear. Various characters give voice to their inner thoughts, and dancers perform intricate choreography by Agnes de Mille, who was also the director of the show.

De Mille had been hired to direct because Rodgers and Hammerstein wanted to use almost constant movement on stage and a rhythmic dialogue throughout.[3] They also employed the great scenic designer Jo Mielziner, who used a number of innovations. There was no scenery as such, and the set was little more than a bare stage. The imaginative lighting included lantern slides and projections. In keeping with this spartan approach, it was anticipated that the cast would also be lean. In the end, however, because of the chorus and the large dance corps, the production became ponderous. Joshua Logan, when asked his opinion, was impressed but also quite critical, even of some of the music.

In the second act Joe becomes a doctor and helps his father in his practice. His wife is frustrated; the Great Depression has intervened, and she is reduced to living as an ordinary housewife. She and her friends sing the cynical and biting "Money Isn't Everything."

> Money isn't everything!
> What can money buy?
> An automobile so you won't get wet,
> Champagne so you won't get dry!

For Jenny, money is everything, and she seduces Joe into joining a large hospital in Chicago. He is successful, but along the way he becomes vain and superficial, beguiled by high society and the perquisites of wealth and station. The title song expresses the fast tempo of their corrupt lifestyle. In the end, Jenny's infidelity shocks Joe into facing reality. He is saved by the love of his nurse, Emily, who sings "The Gentleman Is a Dope." His mother's ghost reappears and sings "Come Home."

> Come home, come home,
> Where the brown birds fly
> Through a pale, blue sky,
> To a tall green tree,
> There is no finer sight for a man to see—
> Come home, Joe, come home!

This song probably was meant to be analogous to "You'll Never Walk Alone." Unfortunately, not only are the lyrics trite, but the melody fails. Joe does go home, of course, accompanied by Emily, and everyone sings a brief reprise of "One Foot, Other Foot."

The show opened on October 10, 1947, and if there was ever a show that received mixed reviews, it was *Allegro*. Brooks Atkinson wrote in the *New York Times* that the first act had the "lyric rapture of a musical masterpiece." Not surprisingly, many critics noted that the trouble was in the second act. Some thought that *Allegro* "made history," but others attacked it. One could choose between those who found it a "vast disappointment" or a "distinguished musical play," too "slow" or too "tumultuous." Some were bored by the countless platitudes, while others discovered a masterpiece. Part of the problem lay in the great expectations that preceded the show: it had enormous advance sales ($750,000, at roughly $6 per ticket). It could not possibly rank with *Oklahoma!* or *Carousel*, critically or commercially. Defending *Allegro* was Robert Coleman, of the *New York Daily Mirror*: "Perfection is a thrilling thing, be it a Sid Luckman pass, a Ken Strong kick, a Joe DiMaggio catch of an outfield drive, a Cushing brain operation, a

Richard Rodgers and Oscar Hammerstein II in Boston for the tryout of *Allegro* (1947). The show failed critically and financially but became a cult phenomenon because of its many theatrical innovations.

Rembrandt painting, a Whistler etching, a Markova-Dolin *Giselle*, or *Allegro*, the great new musical by Richard Rodgers and Oscar Hammerstein. Perfection and great are not words to be lightly used. They have become commonplace through misuse. But *Allegro* is perfection, great."[4]

The hostile reviews singled out the plot as the primary culprit. George Jean Nathan wrote, "*Allegro* is as pretentious as artificial jewelry, and just about as valuable." The *New Yorker* review by Wolcott Gibbs (October 18, 1947) concluded that Hammerstein had turned out a "radio script, and a very bad one." On the other hand, John Mason Brown decided that for sheer craftsmanship, *Allegro* was the equal of *Carousel* and *Oklahoma!* but that it grievously lacked a book of their inspiration.[5]

The direction received a split verdict. The dance critics liked de Mille's use of movement throughout, but some of the drama critics found her contributions "either irritating or meaningless." De Mille herself thought that some of her choreography was "strained," but she also blamed Rodgers for hobbling her direction. Rodgers had been her champion in preparing for *Oklahoma!* but in this show he was antagonistic.

For the first time, Rodgers' music did not escape criticism. Although there was praise for the score, the venerable Cecil Smith attacked Rodgers head-on: "There is no evading the uncomfortable fact that Mr. Rodgers has already stubbed his toe on two earlier occasions, with the ballet score for *Ghost Town* and the second half of *Carousel*. In *Allegro* he has not merely stubbed his toe; he has taken a headlong spill. It seems that the minute he leaves the metier of conventional musical comedy, in which he excels, and ventures into a more exacting area of theatre music he passes outside the limits of his technique and his ideas alike." Smith concluded that too many of the songs were affected with a "Salvation Army soddenness" and that the instrumental passages accompanying the dramatic scenes were "really terrible," leaning on "empty build-ups as written by Russell Bennett for twenty years." The score, he wrote, was "not very good Broadway" and did not "satisfy the minimal requirements of the lyric theater."[6]

Twenty years earlier, in spite of the dismal flop of *Chee-Chee*, Rodgers had been acclaimed. Even some of the mediocre Rodgers and Hart shows were usually acknowledged for their bright scores. Rodgers seemed unaffected by Smith's criticism, however, or at least he adopted that pose. But he did not defend *Allegro*. Thirty years later he noted only that the show was "probably too preachy" but was his favorite candidate for a show that should be seen again.

Allegro was also a failure financially, and investors did not get their money back. Unfortunately, Rodgers and Hammerstein had formed their own company to participate in the financing. The play lost about sixty-five thousand dollars.

Hammerstein was devastated and outraged by the criticism. He was no stranger to failures on Broadway, but this time he took it personally. He was particularly irritated by the critics who took him to task for praising small-town doctors and small-town virtues while attacking big-city practices. He denied that this was his intention and pointed out that in his play the small-town girl, Jenny, is "crass and vicious baggage," and her father, a small-town businessman, a "smug Babbitt."

Defenders of Hammerstein also explained that if the last act seemed forced, it was because he ran out of time while writing it. Hammerstein virtually admitted this to de Mille when she criticized him for not having written the play he had described to her. Indeed, he had become like his main character, surrounded by numerous duties—producing, working on various charities, serving on boards. Yet even in his impassioned defense of his work (written in January 1948 as a preface to the published play), he offered a strange philosophical observation: "It is a law of our civilization that as soon as a man proves he can contribute to the well-being of the world, there be created an immediate conspiracy to destroy his usefulness, a conspiracy in which he is usually a willing collaborator. Sometimes he awakens to his danger and does something about it."[7]

To those critics who denigrated the show as too familiar, Hammerstein said that he was trying to make the point: "If men continue to squander their time and usefulness for the wrong things [it] would seem important to point this out to them. That is the simple reason why *Allegro* was written. If you don't like that reason, you won't like *Allegro*."[8] The show ran longer than many of the Rodgers and Hart shows but was nevertheless considered a failure. In listings of works by Rodgers and Hammerstein, *Allegro* is often quietly passed over. Some of the songs, including "A Fellow Needs a Girl" and "So Far," achieved a brief popularity, but there were almost no revivals and no movie version. Years later, when Hammerstein died, it was said that he was working on a revision. In a large collection of Rodgers' songs, published in 1990, none were from *Allegro*.

The show is difficult to evaluate from a distance of several decades. The innovative staging, choreography, settings, lighting, and direction were clearly important—much more so than in most Broadway outings. It came to be something of a cult phenomenon, pointing toward the concept shows of Stephen Sondheim. The young Sondheim, in fact, worked as an assistant to Hammerstein during *Allegro* and witnessed the frustrations and ordeal of putting such a show together. Sondheim took a roughly similar approach in *Merrily We Roll Along*, which suffered an initial failure.

The critics may have been right: as theater, the play seems leaden and the lyrics repetitive, mawkish, and irritating. Rodgers obviously encountered more difficulties than usual in composing this score. There are, for example, many different melodic sketches for scenes and songs that were either never used or later replaced. Even some that survived were reworked, which was uncommon for Rodgers.

The original cast recording suggests that Bennett's orchestration was one problem: the tone is that of *Oklahoma!* which seems out of place in this show. "Joseph Taylor Jr." even contains some clip-clopping rhythm. "One Foot, Other Foot" has a sort of marchlike persistence that becomes grating. For most of the play Rodgers was writing to Hammerstein's involved lyrics, narratives that did not lend themselves to the traditional song forms of Broadway. Where Rodgers was freer to compose—in the love songs, for example—he wrote melodies comparable to those in *Oklahoma!* or *Carousel*. "A Fellow Needs a Girl" is vintage

Rodgers, perhaps only a cut or two below "People Will Say We're in Love" or "If I Loved You." In "So Far" and "You Were Never Away," Rodgers adheres to his basic formula of simple lines but interesting harmonies. Moreover, it is worth remembering that during this show Rodgers wrote the melody to a song that was not finished but would become "Younger Than Springtime."

A critic, writing several weeks after the opening, noted another problem with the music: songs that were integral to the play sounded wrong outside of the theater. On the other hand, songs that became popular did not seem to fit the serious message of the play.

In the late 1960s Rodgers summed up his reaction to *Allegro*: it was "nothing to be ashamed of, certainly," but he also tended to blame de Mille's direction.[9] Angry about the whole experience, Rodgers and Hammerstein were determined to outdo themselves the next time. When they met James Michener, the author of their next show, he commented that they were so fired up they could have written a hit musical from the Bronx telephone book. That show, of course, was more than the phone book. It was *South Pacific*.

16

SOUTH PACIFIC

Allegro was a valley between towering twin peaks. On one side stood *Oklahoma!* and *Carousel*, and on the other side would stand *South Pacific* and *The King and I*. In the history of the American musical theater there has never been a stretch of eight years marked by greater artistic and commercial success for a team of songwriters. If one includes *State Fair*, Richard Rodgers wrote about one hundred songs during this period. These represent his best work with Hammerstein and are comparable to, if not better than, the songs he wrote during his last seven years with Lorenz Hart. From *Jumbo* in 1935 through the spring of 1951, after the premiere of *The King and I*, Rodgers achieved an unparalleled record. The lifetime output of Irving Berlin or Jerome Kern may well rival that of Rodgers, but their careers stretched over longer periods and their works were often buried in less memorable shows and films. In his monumental study of the American popular song, Alec Wilder concluded, "Rodgers' songs have, over the years, revealed a higher degree of consistent excellence, inventiveness, and sophistication than those of any other writer I have studied."[1]

In light of this unalloyed praise, Hammerstein's defenders have put forward an extraordinary claim: namely, that after *Allegro*, Hammerstein's potential for writing weightier works was hobbled by Rodgers' music. Some argue that Hammerstein could have achieved a true revolution in the American theater with a composer less wedded to commercial success and more interested in creating a profound art form.

Hammerstein was undoubtedly brilliant. He not only wrote lyrics but created some of America's greatest musicals, including *Show Boat* and *Oklahoma!* Both, however, were adapted from the work of others, as were *Carousel*, *South Pacific*, and *The King and I*. Hammerstein's own creations were less impressive, suggesting that he could not in fact have produced a revolution in theater. The reality was that Hammerstein preferred the comfort of a known collaboration over the excitement of inventing new theatrical forms. He and Rodgers settled down to refine the style they had originated, and they took it as far as they could.

In spite of the failure of *Allegro* there was never any thought that Rodgers and Hammerstein would go their separate ways. Instead, they were seriously looking for a new vehicle. On Broadway, *Carousel* closed in May 1947, *Oklahoma!* in May 1948, and *Allegro* in July 1948. *Oklahoma!* closed quietly; it was not possible to heap any further acclaim on a musical that had become a legend. On closing night reporters noted that the halls backstage were littered with baggage as the cast prepared to leave for another national tour. That evening, in a gauche gesture typical of the commercial demands of Broadway, the *Oklahoma!* poster was plastered over with the announcement of the next show, *Sleepy Hollow*, which ran one week.

Rodgers went to Hollywood, not to write another film but to consult on his film biography. The talented lyric writer Arthur Freed, MGM's resident musical genius (of *Singin' in the Rain* fame), had recognized that biographies of composers offered a chance to reprise a dozen famous songs performed by various stars without having to be overly true to real-life details. He had already produced a largely fictional version of Jerome Kern's life story, *Till the Clouds Roll By*, and decided that Rodgers and Hart would be his next subjects. Rodgers opposed the idea until his lawyers persuaded him to cooperate—they believed that Hart's estate could make a claim against him if he refused.

Rodgers commented that the 1948 film, called *Words and Music*, "impinged on the truth, but not very often."[2] Although it was not as fictitious as Kern's story,

A scene from *Words and Music* (1948), an MGM film biography that starred Tom Drake (left) as Rodgers and Mickey Rooney as Hart. Marshall Thompson (right) played a character based on Herbert Fields. Showcasing a dozen or more of Rodgers and Hart's best songs, the movie testified to the impact of their music on American culture.

it did embellish on an early romance: Rodgers was supposedly rejected by a well-known Broadway star, played by Ann Sothern in the movie. Sothern had, in fact, made her debut on Broadway in *America's Sweetheart*, but there was never any romance; presumably the film refers to Helen Ford. Similarly, in the movie Lorenz Hart is rejected by his lifelong love (played by Betty Garrett) and then turns to drink. The script was written by Guy Bolton, Kern's librettist from the Princess Theatre days.

The casting pleased Rodgers—he was played by Tom Drake, and his wife by Janet Leigh—though he questioned being portrayed by the actor with the least prominence. Mickey Rooney was the obvious choice to play Hart. Judy Garland, playing herself, and Rooney turned in a boisterous "I Wish I Were in Love Again." The other performances were also legendary: Lena Horne captured "The Lady Is a Tramp" as well as "Where or When"; June Allyson sang and danced to "Thou Swell"; Ann Sothern revived "Where's That Rainbow?"; Perry Como sang

"Mountain Greenery"; and Gene Kelly re-created his version of "Slaughter on Tenth Avenue." The movie was a reminder of how deeply the words and music of Rodgers and Hart had become embedded in popular culture. Rodgers professed to enjoy the entire experience. Years later, however, when asked for an endorsement of Freed for use in a book about him, Rodgers replied that he had little contact with him. This was a strange comment, considering that Rodgers undoubtedly encountered Freed in New York and Hollywood in the 1930s. Obviously, Rodgers was not as content with the movie as he professed.[3]

The nostalgia created by the film may have further encouraged Rodgers to get to work on his next project with Hammerstein. They had decided to transform a collection of short stories by James Michener into a full-blown musical about sailors and Seabees in the South Pacific.

The old cliché that success has many fathers certainly applied to *South Pacific*. Joshua Logan claimed credit for discovering James Michener's *Tales of the South Pacific* and for recognizing in one story, "Fo' Dolla' " (Four Dollars), the basis for a musical. Michener had written the stories during and just after his service in the Pacific as a naval lieutenant. They were published in 1947 by Macmillan, where he had worked as an editor. At that time Logan was directing and writing the play *Mister Roberts*, based on Thomas Heggan's book, which was also set in the South Pacific. In early December 1947, at the suggestion of a colleague, Logan read Michener's book to get the flavor of the wartime Pacific.

Logan was impressed and mentioned the book to Leland Hayward, the producer of *Mister Roberts*. Hayward also read the stories, and the men decided to secure the stage rights. Hayward thought that the stories might make an opera, but Logan saw in them a production for Rodgers and Hammerstein. He and Hayward pledged secrecy while they negotiated with Michener for the rights. But at a party Logan blurted out his idea to Rodgers, who made a note, "Fo' Dolla'," which he later found incomprehensible.

Meanwhile, *Mister Roberts* was in Philadelphia for tryouts in February 1948, and Hammerstein saw the show. On Logan's invitation, he offered some suggestions and then asked whether Logan had any ideas for Rodgers and him. Surprised, Logan asked whether Rodgers had mentioned *Tales of the South Pacific*. Hammerstein called Rodgers, who then remembered. (According to other accounts Logan called Rodgers to remind him.) Hammerstein and Rodgers thought that Logan owned the theatrical rights to the stories, but in fact Hayward had not yet persuaded Michener to sell them. Rodgers and Hammerstein proposed a partnership. Hayward was incensed, recognizing that Rodgers and Hammerstein would simply take over the project. He was right: they demanded 51 percent and ultimate control. Logan, however, would direct, and Hayward would be coproducer.

Hayward had contacted Michener—who lived only a few minutes from Hammerstein's farm in Doylestown—and tried to sign him for an advance of five hundred dollars. Michener refused, preferring a percentage. Rodgers and Hammerstein took over negotiations at this point, playing down the chance that his disparate tales would result in a success. They reminded Michener that Lynn Riggs had written a successful play as the basis for *Oklahoma!* and had settled for a small percentage of the gross, whereas Michener had written only some stories. Michener knew that Riggs had received 1.5 percent, so he settled for 1 percent.

His bargaining leverage would have been stronger had he known that he would receive the Pulitzer Prize, a distinct achievement for a collection of stories. Michener played no role in the production of the musical but was delighted with the book created by Hammerstein and Logan. Of course, his percentage earned him a great deal of money. The supposedly hard-hearted business team of Rodgers and Hammerstein turned soft at the last minute. Realizing that they had a hit, they offered Michener a chance to buy a second share for forty-five hundred dollars. He had to decline, he said, because he did not even have one thousand dollars. Rodgers and Hammerstein lent him the money, which was paid back out of his handsome royalties. This generous gesture gave Michener lifelong financial independence, enabling him to work full-time as a writer.

Comparing Michener's stories unfavorably with Riggs' play may have been a negotiating ploy, but Rodgers and Hammerstein had a point. Weaving a coherent libretto from Michener's tales would not be easy. "Fo' Dolla'," the story that Logan had pitched, was the love story between Marine Lieutenant Joe Cable and a Polynesian (or Tonkinese in the Michener version) named Liat. Her repulsive mother, "Bloody Mary," sells grass skirts, shrunken heads, and boars' teeth to the GIs. Cable falls in love with Liat but refuses to marry her, knowing he cannot take her home to Philadelphia. At the end of Michener's story he is ordered into combat, seen off by Bloody Mary's vile denunciation. His fate is not spelled out by Michener.

Rodgers and Hammerstein felt that this story was too close to *Madame Butterfly* (subsequent reviewers of the show also pointed out this similarity). But both were intrigued by "Our Heroine," a love story about Nellie Forbush, a nurse from Little Rock, and Emile de Becque, a local French planter. They too fall in love, but Nellie recoils after learning that he has six children by three different women. She vows to break off the affair, but in the end she is reconciled.

Rodgers and Hammerstein decided to keep the two love stories, which share the theme of racial prejudice. They also kept Bloody Mary, whose character was lightened and they borrowed from another story the comic character of Luther Billis, a Seabee who is a master manipulator.

The show was publicly announced on February 18, 1948. Hammerstein immediately ran into trouble with his script. As he readily admitted, he loathed the military to the point that he was unable to write about it. Rodgers was becoming exasperated with Hammerstein's lack of progress and urged Joshua Logan to assist Hammerstein, who eagerly accepted. Logan had served in the Air Force during the war and had just finished his rewrite of *Mister Roberts*.

When Logan arrived at Hammerstein's farm he found that Hammerstein had not gotten beyond the opening scene between Emile and Nellie. He had written an informal narrative of the show, but without any dramatization, dialogue, or musical scenes. The only lyrics he had produced were for Nellie's opening song, "A Wonderful Guy." Logan began to write the dialogue for Nellie and for the various GIs, and then he dictated a script. In ten days they finished a script that Logan said was close to the one that went into rehearsals. They dedicated the final book to "patient Dorothy and Nedda, who liked it even when all the parts were sung and acted by us."

Logan was so convinced that the show would be a hit that he asked for a co-author credit. Hammerstein agreed and Rodgers apparently concurred. But they refused to share the copyright, because it was against "company policy." Sharing the copyright would have meant not only partaking of earnings from all future subsidiary rights—movies, revivals, and so forth—but also acquiring a veto. They also turned down his request to transfer his director's royalties to author's royalties, which would have the same financial effect as participating in the copyright. Finally, they insisted that he sign his director's contract within hours or be dismissed. Logan did not know of this ultimatum, however, because his lawyer signed the contract for him. When he later found out he blamed Rodgers, and he was probably right to do so. This issue festered for almost forty years; from time to time Logan brought it up, insisting on some compensation. Logan included his version of the story in his memoirs, *Josh*, a version that Rodgers disputed.

Well before the libretto was finished, Rodgers and Hammerstein had rashly decided to hire Ezio Pinza, the basso from the Metropolitan Opera who had no experience in musicals. He had left the Met ostensibly to play in a Broadway show, but when the project collapsed a shrewd public relations agent from Hollywood called Rodgers about him. Rodgers decided that Pinza would be perfect for the part of Emile de Becque, and they bought up his contract in late June 1948. Then they hired Mary Martin. Rodgers and Hammerstein, who usually tried to enlist new performers, now had two stars on their hands—and no script.

Martin was already working for Rodgers and Hammerstein in the road company of *Annie Get Your Gun*. She had desperately wanted to play the part of Annie, and one weekend at Rodgers' country house she had stunned Rodgers and Hammerstein with a rousing rendition of songs from the show. She was given the first road company of the show, and Rodgers and Hammerstein saw her opening in Los Angeles while they were musing about *South Pacific*. Apparently they discussed their new show with her husband, Richard Halliday, and he in turn mentioned it to her.

Martin was uncertain about the idea. After all, the thought of singing alongside Pinza was daunting. But Rodgers assured her that he would write only duets in which she sang in contrast to Pinza, never against him (a promise that he did not quite keep). She returned to New York in July, and she and her husband, as well as the Logans, the Haywards, and the Hammersteins all gathered at Rodgers' home to hear several of the songs, including "Some Enchanted Evening." She then eagerly agreed to do the part, though she was disappointed that "Some Enchanted Evening" was intended for Pinza (in the show she did in fact sing a chorus).

Rehearsals did not begin until January 1949, one year after Rodgers had learned of Michener's stories. As promised, Logan was the director and Hayward was a coproducer. The orchestrations were to be by the omnipresent Robert Russell Bennett, with dance music arranged by Trude Rittmann and settings by Jo Mielziner. Betta St. John played Liat, Juanita Hall played Bloody Mary, William Tabbert was Lieutenant Cable, and Myron McCormick played Luther Billis.

After the second complete run-through in New Haven, on February 20, Logan's notes to Rodgers and Hammerstein were enthusiastic: "It is in wonderful shape, even if it had to open tomorrow night as it is." Martin was "absolutely marvelous," he wrote. He had some criticism, of course: "I wish the nurses would get off their cans a little bit."[4]

Ironically, some of the music was not working. Three songs were cut and two were replaced with much better ones. The love song that Cable was to sing to Liat was criticized by Logan, much to Rodgers and Hammerstein's dismay. The melody, which exists in Rodgers' handwriting in his collection at the Library of Congress, is scarcely inspired. His second try was also rebuffed, and the miffed Rodgers at first refused to write on "spec" for Logan. But Logan persuaded them to try just once more. Rodgers resurrected a melody from *Allegro* that, according to Rodgers, his daughters remembered fondly and called to his attention. Ham-

From left, Joshua Logan, Richard Rodgers, Oscar Hammerstein II, Mary Martin, and James Michener preparing for *South Pacific*, based on Michener's Pulitzer Prize–winning *Tales of the South Pacific*. In 1949 the musical was considered controversial because of its racial subplot.

merstein rewrote the lyrics, and they returned in two days with "Younger Than Springtime."

The second song rejected by Logan reappeared with new lyrics in *The King and I*, as "Getting to Know You." Its rolling triplets, even at a much slower tempo, do not seem right for that romantic moment in *South Pacific*. Moreover, Hammerstein's lyrics were neither romantic nor inspiring:

> Suddenly lucky
> Suddenly our arms are lucky;
> Suddenly lucky
> Suddenly our lips have kissed.[5]

Perhaps Logan was right. Also cut before the opening in New York was the melancholy "Loneliness of Evening," which threatened to depress the audience. (It reemerged in the second production of the television show *Cinderella*.) Another song that was out of place, and therefore cut, was the plaintive "My Girl Back Home," to be sung by Lieutenant Cable as he debates whether to stay with Liat:

> My girl back home —
> I'd almost forgot!
> A blue-eyed kid —
> I liked her a lot.
>
> How far away!
> Philadelphia, Pa.
> Princeton, N.J.
> From coconut palms
> And banyan trees
> And coral sands
> And Tonkinese!

This song suggested that Cable was resisting his romance with Liat because of his girl, when the point of the episode was supposed to be the problem of racial prejudice. Later the song was resuscitated for the movie version of the show.

Some of Michener's friends had appealed to him to take out the racial subplot and eliminate the song "You've Got To Be Carefully Taught," which was Cable's explanation of racial prejudice to Emile — it was not inborn, as Nellie Forbush had claimed, but taught. Michener refused, and when he related this incident to Hammerstein, the latter replied, "That's what the play is about." Rodgers later said, however, that the racial aspect was not central. Nevertheless, for Hammerstein the show was basically a message musical, much like *Allegro* and *Carousel*, or, for that matter, *Show Boat*. But Rodgers claimed that the song was written only because it was needed for Cable at that point in the show. One suspects that the song could have easily been dropped, without much damage to the story or the musical line. Of course, no one seriously considered doing so.

One of the ongoing problems was Pinza's accent and his limited command of English. In fact, Logan and Hayward wanted to replace him (Logan denied this), but Rodgers and Hammerstein resisted. Pinza later claimed that he was on the verge of quitting, bewildered by the constant changes in dialogue and songs. After all, he had been accustomed to the hallowed traditions of operas. Shifting his songs or forcing him to learn new ones had to be avoided (Martin read music poorly, and Pinza couldn't read it at all).

Pinza's character, De Becque, has an important moment as he and Cable prepare for a combat assignment. They are headed for a remote island to observe the movements of Japanese fleets. De Becque has volunteered for the mission after Nellie has "washed him right out of her hair." Before leaving he reflects on what might have been in his relationship with Nellie. This scene called for a dramatic song, and Rodgers and Hammerstein wrote "Now Is the Time." The melody, in 6/8 time, was strange and not nearly one of Rodgers' best. The lyrics were also odd, insisting that "now is the time of your life." Cable begins:

> Now is the time!
> The time to act!
> No other time will do.

And Emile answers:

> Live and play your part,
> And give away your heart.
> And take what the world gives you!

It was dropped, in part because Logan complained that it was not in Pinza's class and was too hard for the actor playing Cable to sing. Logan wanted something along the lines of the "Soliloquy" in *Carousel*. The song had to be replaced as quickly as possible so that Pinza could learn the new lyrics and melody. Rodgers asked for a lead phrase, and Hammerstein suggested "this nearly was mine," which became the title.

Rodgers' music for this "big, bass" waltz was one of his finest endeavors. "This Nearly Was Mine" was a perfect Rodgers model: only five notes are used in the first four bars, four of them the same note, and the phrase then is repeated beginning on a higher note, with a variation in the seventh and eighth bar. As he had done so many times, he surprised the listener by shifting harmonies to diminished and minor chords. The melody ends an octave higher than the first note, a perfect vehicle for Pinza's great booming voice. The verse following the refrain is in a minor key and sets the mood for a return to the final refrain. It all fits beautifully. "This Nearly Was Mine" is as good a melody as "Some Enchanted Evening," which became far more popular, in part because of its engaging lyrics.

Two of the show's better songs, "Younger Than Springtime" and "This Nearly Was Mine," therefore came about as a result of interaction among Rodgers, Hammerstein, and Logan. Indeed, this show was an outstanding example of professionals working well together. It had every ingredient of a successful musical: two love stories, great performers, comedy relief in both the songs and the characters, the dramatic tension of the war, a conflict over serious issues that was becoming a Rodgers and Hammerstein hallmark—this time racial prejudice, and, above all, finely hewn music.

One of the most famous anecdotes from this show concerns "Bali Ha'i." Before rehearsals began, Logan, Rodgers, and Michener were discussing the play, noting that one major song remained unfinished, the one in which Bloody Mary explains the small, mist-shrouded island of Bali Ha'i, seen in the distance. During a lunch at Logan's apartment, Hammerstein came in with the lyric for "Bali Ha'i." Rodgers immediately wrote out the melody, using "Bali Ha'i" as the first words for his three-note motif. It turned out to be one the show's most poignant melodies. These three notes, the first the audience heard, began Bennett's overture. Rodgers was defensive about this anecdote, which was invariably cited as the prime example of his instant writing.

The story grew in the telling. Some accounts claim that he wrote it in five minutes, sitting at the luncheon table; there is a photograph, supposedly of this occasion, but it is doubtful a photographer was at a working lunch. Others claim that he left the table, went into the next room, and came back for coffee with the completed melody. Rodgers himself noted years later that it probably took about five minutes but that he had brooded over the proper melody for some time—he had known for months that the title would be "Bali Ha'i." And he knew that the music had to be Oriental in flavor and right for a contralto voice. Once the lyrics were in hand he was able to translate them quickly: "If you have your trade, you know how to apply it." In fact, the identical opening three-note phrase appears in a melody that Rodgers wrote many years earlier.[6]

Almost twenty years later, commenting on a revival, the music critic Winthrop Sargeant wrote sarcastically that the song was reported to have been composed in half an hour, and "sounds as if it had." He was certainly in a minority. By mid-June, "Bali Ha'i," "A Wonderful Guy," and "Some Enchanted Evening" were all on the Hit Parade. In New York, the Columbia cast album sold ten thousand copies the first day (Rodgers and Hammerstein received 10 percent of the gross sales).

The most celebrated song from the show was "Some Enchanted Evening." When Rodgers first played it for Pinza, he told him that it would be a hit, but Pinza countered that "A Wonderful Guy" was the more likely hit, which seemed to hurt Rodgers. "Some Enchanted Evening" is a good Rodgers song, reminiscent of "With a Song in My Heart." Pinza's resonant rendition helped greatly on the stage and in the initial recordings (which, incidentally, preceded the show's opening). But it took quite a while for Pinza to stop pronouncing it

"Some Enchanted Evening." Until someone had the courage to correct him, he was puzzled by the obvious discomfort of Rodgers and Hammerstein when he rehearsed it.

One of the most memorable bits of theater was Mary Martin's inspiration to actually wash her hair on stage rather than just sing about it. Her husband warned her not to mention it, because he knew that it would be adopted immediately. She did, of course, and it was eagerly adopted. Rodgers quickly wrote the tune to Hammerstein's words, but because the audience was buzzing when she washed and sang, it was changed so that she sang and then washed her hair and danced around to the orchestra's reprise.

Hammerstein also wanted to use "Happy Talk," a song sung by Bloody Mary, but he doubted that it could be staged. Rodgers suggested it might be a chance for Betta St. John to show her skill as a dancer. Logan insisted on hearing the music and promptly staged it as a sort of pantomime dance by Liat to demonstrate to Cable their life together. It also become one of the many highlights of the show. Another was an old-fashioned vaudeville number featuring Martin. The sailors decide to put on a Thanksgiving show, and Nellie, appearing in a baggy sailor's suit, sings "Honey Bun," a song that could have come from any second-class burlesque house. It was so trite that Hammerstein was embarrassed when he gave the lyric to Martin, who loved it, as did the cast and audience. Not only did "Honey Bun" become a hit, but the picture of Mary Martin in that oversized white sailor's uniform and cap became the show's logo.

The structure of the show was also becoming something of a Rodgers and Hammerstein trademark: a long first act followed by a much shorter second act. The various characters are introduced and their problems delineated in the first act, and everything is rather quickly resolved in the last act. As in *Oklahoma!* and *Carousel*, the first scene ended with a major love song that was then reprised, a conventional but effective Broadway device. In *South Pacific*, however, there was no elaborate choreography. By 1949 the surrealistic dance sequence or ballet productions had been overdone, and Rodgers and Hammerstein, who had inaugurated these concepts, had dropped them. On the other hand, more comic relief was employed ("There Is Nothin' Like a Dame") to balance the serious subject matter.

Even the show's first performance, in New Haven, was heralded: "The new sensation has everything in the way of exciting theatre" was the New Haven verdict. In the audience were Cole Porter, Thornton Wilder, Libby Holman, Theresa Helburn, and Mike Todd. In Boston, Elliot Norton judged it to be more dramatic than *Oklahoma!* more solidly realistic than *Carousel*, and, unlike *Allegro*, free of any burdensome social message.

The show opened in New York on April 7, 1949, at the Majestic Theatre, on the same stage that had hosted *Carousel* four years earlier. *South Pacific* was a hit of legendary proportions. Over the years it was second only to *Oklahoma!* in its Broadway run. Its financial success was truly impressive. It was produced by the Rodgers and Hammerstein corporation Surrey Enterprise, Inc., which allowed them to enjoy their profits at a lower tax rate. The initial financing of $225,000 had been raised from some fifty backers, all of whom were repaid within four months and thereafter sat back to gather their rewards. Among the investors were many of their old friends, as well as Dorothy Rodgers (who bought two shares, worth $9,000) and Mortimer Rodgers. Most of the Hammerstein family invested. Logan even persuaded the Hollywood director William Wyler to invest in a one-half share. Even though he was a coproducer, Leland Hayward invested almost $20,000.

By the time the show opened in New York, it had cost about $163,000, including $65,000 for scenery, props, and equipment, $18,000 for costumes, and $40,000 for rehearsal salaries. The advance sale of tickets ran to $500,000. Each week it was grossing about $50,000, of which royalties of 10 percent were allocated to Rodgers, Hammerstein, Michener, and Logan. The show was making a net profit of about $10,000 each week, half of which went to the producers; of that $5,000 Rodgers and Hammerstein's corporation took 60 percent. Rodgers and Hammerstein were both making a "fantastic amount of money," according to one news story, which did not hazard a guess as to how much. Moreover, the show generated a large number of tie-ins—there were *South Pacific* dolls, music boxes, hair brushes and hair cream, and so forth. A movie, tentatively titled *Wings Over the South Pacific*, was squelched, but only after a personal letter from Hammerstein to Louis B. Mayer.

Tickets were so difficult to obtain that scalpers were getting as much as seventy-five dollars, necessitating an investigation by the New York City district attorney. The main target was the Shubert Organization, which managed the theater. The Rodgers and Hammerstein organization cooperated fully in the investigation and was absolved of any blame. Because of the scandal, there were a few days when the show was threatened with closing.

Mary Martin was on the cover of *Life*, *Look*, and *Newsweek*. On opening night a producer from Hollywood, where Martin had never fared very well, rushed backstage and exclaimed, "Why didn't you tell us you were that good?"

The critical reaction was unanimous. Yip Harburg wired Hammerstein that the show was a "salute to perfection." But perhaps the best review came from Michener himself. After seeing the dress rehearsal, he wrote to a friend, "The whole tenor of the show is superb. . . . The thing that impressed me was the warmth and right-heartedness of the whole damned thing."[7]

After the opening Hammerstein wrote to Logan, who was traveling, that all the news was "better than good," since advance ticket sales were running between $400,000 and $500,000. Pinza, he added, "continues to hover over Mary Martin to everyone's delight and, perhaps, his own private frustration." Rodgers wrote along similar lines that the spirit of the company was "electric," that Martin was the sparkplug, and that Pinza kept all the female actors in a pleasant state of anxiety, since they never knew "what end to protect." Rodgers added that the cast album was the best of its kind and was outselling "Kiss Me Cole," a snide reference to Cole Porter's *Kiss Me Kate*. Hammerstein wrote that the authors of *Kiss Me Kate*, Sam and Bella Spewack, had come backstage to chat with Martin but never once mentioned *South Pacific*.[8]

Everyone was ecstatic, especially when the play received the Pulitzer Prize — and not merely a special Pulitzer, as awarded to *Oklahoma!* And this time — unlike in 1930, when George Gershwin was not recognized as sharing the Pulitzer for *Of Thee I Sing* — the composer Richard Rodgers was included. But the initial announcement of the Pulitzer committee neglected to include Joshua Logan as coauthor, an oversight that added to Logan's bitterness. In his memoirs he exonerates Hammerstein but does not spare Rodgers: "An enormous change had taken place in Dick Rodgers' life that affected our relationship. It came with his gigantic and worldwide success. He became, almost in front of our eyes, a monument. He was so sought after that he had to closet himself in an office and dictate letters daily in order to handle his business affairs and to fend off the many people who wanted to sap his talent. To me, his fun seemed gone — the fun he and I used to have."[9] In the Rodgers and Hart days, when Logan directed their shows, he and Rodgers would sometimes take members of the chorus out for dinner and a "warm evening." But not now: "stratospheric fame" had taken away the fun, Logan decided. Over the years, Logan's attitude toward Rodgers fluctuated, but he always considered him highly intelligent and a brilliant talent with a strong sense of discipline. At one point Logan praised Rodgers effusively for having the courage to hire him after he suffered a mental breakdown, making it possible for Logan to resume his career.

Hugh Fordin, Oscar Hammerstein's biographer (*Getting To Know Him*), more or less concurred with Logan's original conclusion. Hammerstein was thought of as benign — a poet, and a good, kind man. Rodgers was considered almost the opposite. Nevertheless, Rodgers and Hammerstein as an organization had a reputation for ruthlessness. Indeed, Oscar Hammerstein enjoyed the successes and was reluctant to tamper with the formula. There was strain in the relationship: Rodgers seemed determined to be dominant, even though Hammerstein was seven years his senior. Rodgers became increasingly autocratic on the business side, eventually creating a rift. Hammerstein, who had studied law, felt that he was as capable on the business side as Rodgers.

In later years Rodgers conceded that Hammerstein may have even been a better businessman, but that he was averse to office work. Rodgers was not about to neglect that increasingly important aspect of their partnership. Their attorney, Howard Reinheimer, and their managers, Morris Jacobs in New York and Jerry Whyte in London, were strong members of their organization and in some part responsible for their reputation as tough bargainers and coldhearted businessmen. Yet it was Rodgers himself who asked Pinza and Martin to cut their salaries because of budget overruns; surprisingly, they agreed.

The daily routine of business for Rodgers and Hammerstein was growing at an alarming rate. Several times a week they had to deal with problems, minor and major, concerning not only South Pacific but all their other shows. The lawyers peppered them with memorandums about contracts for lighting, salaries, future productions, movie rights, and the like. How far these seemingly petty matters went was illustrated by a memorandum from Rodgers himself explaining the leave policy for Holy Week, including a calculation of losses.

Telegrams, phone messages, and letters poured in from friends and old colleagues who were seeking tickets or even a part in the show. Hammerstein's assistant suggested that her gravestone be inscribed "I'm terribly sorry, but we don't have single seat left for tonight." Difficult as it is to believe, Gertrude Lawrence let them know that she wanted to play Nellie when South Pacific came to London. An investor who represented the Philip Morris Company complained to them that in South Pacific the Seabees were smoking Chesterfields (it turned out that the stage manager had made his own deal).

South Pacific closed on January 16, 1954, after turning a net profit of $7 million. It won all the customary awards and ran for 1,925 performances (compared with 2,212 for Oklahoma!). At one point Rodgers counted forty-nine recordings of South Pacific's songs, an "all-time record in vulgarity," he wrote to Hammerstein. The cast album pleased him, however. According to Hammerstein's assistant at that recording session, Rodgers, "who looks like he's at Rabbi Wise's funeral, even in his happiest moments, didn't find one spot where someone might be accused of breathing incorrectly."

Rodgers' score was duly praised: some noted that it was not his best, but, added Wolcott Gibbs in the New Yorker, it was not far from it. Most of the reviews focused on Martin and Pinza. In the *New Republic*, Harold Clurman wrote that Martin was "our ideal, our dream, our faith. She is fresh, lively, humorous, useful and very, very, very good company." It was clever of Rodgers and Hammerstein, Clurman decided, to have set Pinza down among all that "resplendent American corn." No writer could have asked for more than the opinion of the veteran Ward Morehouse: "It's the best musical show I ever saw and I've been going to the theater with something approximating fanatical zeal since my teen age years." [10]

The film version, released in 1958, starred Rossano Brazzi (whose voice was dubbed) and Mitzi Gaynor. Logan was the director and Alfred Newman the musical director. Despite an advance of $1 million for the film rights, Rodgers strongly disliked the movie: "I thought it was awful." It was overproduced, and the use of color was "atrocious," he said. According to Rodgers, Logan went "wild" in the staging of the scenes. [11] During the original run of the Broadway show Rodgers and Hammerstein had clashed with Logan over his restaging of the show after some cast changes. Hammerstein pointed out to Logan that performances of Gilbert and Sullivan's shows had remained unchanged during their run. How could Hammerstein possibly know that, Logan asked.

Pinza left the original production when his contract expired and after missing many performances because of his health. He was replaced by Ray Middleton. In November 1951, Martin left the New York production to open in London; she was replaced by Janet Blair. Even without Martin and Pinza the show stood up well over the years.

The London version, which ran for eight hundred performances, produced another rift between Rodgers and Logan. Rodgers was upset by changes in the road-company version, and he was appalled at the staging he saw in the London rehearsals, as was Martin. Logan claimed that Martin was playing it "woodenly." The reviews were complimentary, though less so than the New York reviews. Laurence Olivier complained that Logan had slowed the show for the English audience, and the playwright Terence Rattigan kept slapping his knee and whispering, "Get on with it." Even Noel Coward confided to his diary: "Show incredibly slow. Audience wildly hysterical." Indeed, at the opening Mary Martin was forced to appear for dozens of curtain calls and finally had to sing another chorus of "A Wonderful Guy."

By the time of the British opening, Rodgers had behind him yet another great musical, *The King and* I. The two back-to-back shows were the high-water mark for Rodgers and Hammerstein.

17

THE KING AND I

In May 1950, Richard Rodgers marked the twenty-fifth anniversary of his entry on Broadway with *The Garrick Gaieties*. The Theatre Guild threw a party attended by many of the original cast members: Edith Meiser, who was to have done the lyrics until she was replaced by Lorenz Hart; Betty Starbuck, who had sung "April Fool" with Romney Brent; and Sterling Holloway, who sang "Manhattan," as he had done twenty-five years earlier. Performers from his current shows sang many of the tunes from the guild shows. And at the end of a festive evening the guild presented Rodgers with a silver tray inscribed with the titles of all the songs he had written for its shows.

Various other honors were coming his way. There was the Pulitzer Prize for *South Pacific*, which, in October 1950, had the highest weekly gross in history. The National Conference of Christians and Jews awarded Rodgers and Hammerstein special citations for promoting brother-hood; the awards were presented by Nelson Rockefeller at the Waldorf-Astoria Hotel. Rodgers was elected to the board of trustees of the Actors Fund of America, a theatrical charity, and Columbia University gave both Rodgers and Hammerstein the university's Medals of Excellence at commencement cere-monies led by the university's new president, Dwight D. Eisenhower. They were selected by an elite New York group, called the Hundred Years Association, for awards for outstanding cultural achievements in New York City. Previous hon-orees included Cardinal Spellman and Fiorello H. La Guardia.

It seemed that as producers they would continue to prosper. At the beginning of 1950 they produced a nonmusical play, *The Happy Time*. It was a comedy set in Canada in the 1920s and was adapted from a novel and rewritten by Samuel Taylor, a successful radio writer who created the *Aldrich Family* series. One critic called *The Happy Time* a "good show, but not a good play." It was nevertheless a success and enjoyed a run of more than six hundred performances; in 1968 it was turned into a less successful musical by John Kander and Fred Ebb.

Then Rodgers and Hammerstein suffered a setback as producers, when Graham Greene's first play, *The Heart of the Matter*, closed out of town in February 1950. There were problems from the beginning; among other things, it was a victim of Britain's austerity program, which limited the number of pounds that could be exchanged for dollars. Greene wanted to write and supervise the play in New York, but the Royal Treasury turned down his request for per-diem pay in dollars. He therefore wrote his play from England and benefited from no ex-changes during the process. The play was based on his successful novel of the same name, and Greene had just enjoyed a triumph with his screenplay for *The Third Man*. So in fall 1949, Rodgers and Hammerstein had reason to be enthusias-tic about their involvement with this new play.

By the time the play opened for previews in Boston, however, it was a shambles. The direction by Greene's coauthor, Basil Dean, had further damaged an already faulty script. Relations between Dean and Rodgers and Hammerstein had become tense, and they appealed to Greene to come to the United States. Greene himself admitted that it was a bad play, and he worked with Hammer-stein to fix it. Greene wrote in a letter: "Poor Oscar Hammerstein was more fussed than me. I like him enormously. Rodgers less so. Dean has treated both very badly, so that they have welcomed me all the more." [1]

Despite vigorous rewriting, the outlook was dismal. Rodgers and Hammer-stein had dinner with Greene and informed him that they were closing the pro-duction. Greene did not seem to hold the failure against his producers. In closing the show Rodgers and Hammerstein saved face by suggesting that the opening would be deferred until the next season. This was their first failure as producers.

That year another illustrious author signed to a Rodgers and Hammerstein production. John Steinbeck had written what he called a novelette-play titled *Burning Bright*, a heavy drama about the intense relationship between a middle-aged acrobat and his young wife. The various themes—impotence, infidelity, murder—were not normally associated with Rodgers and Hammerstein.

Why they produced it is puzzling, although they were friends with Steinbeck through his wife, Elaine Scott, who had been a stage manager for the Theatre Guild and was stage manager for *Oklahoma!* Steinbeck's reputation seemed to ensure a success. Despite considerable reworking out of town, the play was sharply criticized when it reached Broadway in October. The hostile reviews prompted a lengthy response in the *Saturday Review of Literature* from Steinbeck, who invoked Rodgers' observation that when a theatergoer buys a ticket, he or she enters into a contract to try to leap a gulf of unreality into the greater reality of the play. This time, Steinbeck wrote, the leap was too great. The show had to close, but Steinbeck did not hold it against his producers.

This was Rodgers and Hammerstein's last attempt at producing nonmusicals in the United States, though they continued to do so in London for a time. It was probably a wise decision. They were more and more occupied with the business of managing the many successful shows they had on Broadway or on tour. In fact, matters reached a point at which Rodgers complained that although songwriting was no more difficult for him, finding the time to do it was—this from a man who had the reputation of being a fast writer. It was equally likely that two straight failures convinced them that producing drama was no longer worth the effort.

There were other extracurricular activities as well. Both Rodgers and Hammerstein were political activists, though Hammerstein was the more committed of the two. He was an ardent member of the World Federalists, a liberal internationalist organization born during World War II. It advocated world federalism as an antidote to the virulent nationalism that had spawned the war and as a replacement for the nation-state. Hammerstein's political activity in the 1930s and 1940s caused him some problems. In 1953 he was granted a restricted passport because of his support of left-wing causes (for example, he was a sponsor of the Hollywood League Against Nazism, chaired by Donald Ogden Stewart). Hammerstein was indignant at the vague charges and fought back. His stature, however, put him beyond the reach of McCarthy's blacklist and the anti-Red campaign. Indeed, when casting one of their productions he was told that an actor they had hired was on the blacklist; Hammerstein dismissed the information, saying he was right for the part.

Rodgers' political activities were more sporadic. He helped to found the Committee to Defend the First Amendment, which sponsored the cavalcade of Hollywood stars, led by Humphrey Bogart and Lauren Bacall, that went to Washington to confront the House Un-American Activities Committee in October 1947. Whereas Hammerstein defied the blacklist of actors, writers, and directors, Rodgers seemed less adamant about the threat, or at least he was less vocal about it. In the 1952 election campaign he decided to support Eisenhower, who had become president of Columbia University in 1948. The two became friends while Rodgers was trying to establish an arts center at the university. Eisenhower supported the idea but left before it came to fruition; Rodgers abandoned the effort for lack of financial support.

Initially, Eisenhower had "no more loyal or active partisan" than Rodgers. But after meeting with Adlai Stevenson, Rodgers told reporters that he was switching candidates: he explained that he had wanted General Eisenhower, not Senator Taft; Eisenhower, not McCarthy. Now, he said, "we find that we have lost a general and inherited the other two." His change of heart was publicized, and he became active in supporting Stevenson. Some years later Rodgers and Eisenhower were reconciled at the White House, although Rodgers remained skeptical of Eisenhower's strategy of letting McCarthy do himself in. Later Rodgers said that Stevenson in fact may have been "too bright for the job."

Well before the election Rodgers and Hammerstein's next show, a highly unusual proposal, came to them almost by chance. Gertrude Lawrence and Fanny Holtzmann, Lawrence's lawyer and friend, had been searching for a production that would ensure Lawrence a fairly long run in New York so that she could be near her husband, Richard Aldrich. A long run meant a musical, but she had not appeared in a book musical since the sensational *Lady in the Dark* of 1941, having become more in demand for straight plays. While she was touring in *The Glass Menagerie*, the William Morris Agency pointed her toward the book *Anna and the King of Siam*, by Margaret Landon, which in 1946 had been made into a film starring Rex Harrison and Irene Dunne. The movie was a straight drama that chronicled the remarkable encounters between a British governess, Anna Leonowens, and her employer, King Mongkut of Siam, in the 1860s.

The possibilities for a musical were obvious to Lawrence: she would be Anna, perhaps Noel Coward would play the king, and Cole Porter would compose the score. Lawrence secured the rights to the book, but neither Coward nor Porter was available. A chance encounter between Holtzmann and Dorothy Hammerstein led to an offer for Rodgers and Hammerstein to produce and to write the book, music, and lyrics. Rodgers was skeptical at first, because they had never had to deal with the restrictions of writing for a single star. But after a private viewing of the film they decided to do it: "Here was a project Oscar and I could really believe in, and we notified Fanny that we were ready to go to work."[2]

In fact, they were not ready. They could not promise a production before the spring of 1951. Lawrence agreed to the delay and spent most of the year on Martha's Vineyard at her husband's home. Meanwhile, casting the part of the king was presenting problems. Rodgers wanted Rex Harrison, who begged off (he later noted that if had he played the full run of the *King and I*, he would have missed *My Fair Lady*). Next they turned to Alfred Drake, who since appearing in *Oklahoma!* had become a star. He, too, was busy, though he eventually played the role as a summer replacement.

Discouraged, Rodgers and Hammerstein went to a routine audition and settled into their seats to observe the next candidate, an Asian-looking man who was balding but quite muscular. He glowered at the empty seats, sat down, crossed his legs, thumped a chord on his guitar, and began wailing an unintelligible song. After he spoke a few lines the producers knew that they had found their king — Yul Brynner.

Brynner had been urged to audition by Mary Martin, who had appeared with him in *Lute Song* and who no doubt pleaded his case. At the time, Brynner was a successful director for CBS and was reluctant to plunge into Broadway. Martin and Brynner's wife changed his mind. Rodgers immediately warned him not to read the book, because his character was to be changed significantly. He disobeyed and began to shape the part to suit his own personality.

The role was critical. Even though Anna had the starring part, she played off the personality of the king and the intrigues of the royal court. The king was by no means a sympathetic character. In real life he was Somdetch Phra Paramendr Maha Mongkut, the grandson of Rama I and the son of Rama II, the rulers of Siam (modern-day Thailand). Their dynasty had come to power in the late eighteenth century after the overthrow of Burmese rule in a costly and bloody war. Mongkut, born in 1804, was forty-seven when he assumed the throne. Unlike the dashing stars who would portray him, he suffered a disorder that caused his mouth to droop on one side, and he wore false teeth made of redwood.

By all accounts Mongkut was a tyrant, though a more enlightened one than most Asian rulers. He was determined to modernize his country while preserving its independence. His great fear was that the European powers would swallow up Siam, as they had his neighbors in Indochina and Burma. He concluded that the colonial powers might be held at bay if his kingdom was sufficiently modernized. Reform, however, meant tearing down the old institutions and traditions, and thus threatening the monarchy itself.

He decided that his children should have a British governess. At first he employed the wives of Christian missionaries, but he resented their proselytizing. He then hired Anna Leonowens, a widow who had been born in Wales but had lived in India and, more recently, in Singapore, following the death of her husband, Major Leonowens. Or so she claimed. In fact, she was born in India and raised by grandparents in England, though she did return to India; her husband, Tom Owens, was not an officer but a clerk.

Leonowens arrived in Bangkok in 1862 and stayed for five years. The king's conditions for employment were that she not teach religion and that she live in the palace. Her stormy relationship with the king became the subject of her own writings, and in 1944, Margaret Landon turned her books into a more succinct collection of episodes.

Rodgers and Hammerstein drew on Landon's book as well as on the excellent film. In writing about their production before it opened, they emphasized that they wanted to capture the "remote reality" of Siam while lending that required "glow" to the musical. Anna and the king had to be both genuine and fascinating. The strength of the story lay in the changes that each provoked in the other. As in every Hammerstein script, there was an optimistic message: that love and mutual understanding would conquer all, even racism.[3]

For the first time, however, there were no American characters in their play. Moreover, there was no love interest between the two principals. Anna and the king frequently clashed, and their conflict went beyond personalities to represent the cultural differences between East and West. Hammerstein had to spin a tale that would hold the audience without lapsing into clichés about the inscrutable East.

Similarly, Rodgers had to write a score that was Asian in flavor but not imitative of gongs and cymbals. Bernard Herrmann, the fine composer who had written the film score, offered his research into Siamese music, but Rodgers politely declined. He compared his problems to those of the artist Grant Wood. Suppose that Wood had spent a few weeks in Thailand: the resulting artwork, Rodgers wrote, would look very much like Thailand, but it would also look like Grant Wood. His goal was to draw the audience into the picture and, having done so, make the audience feel the emotional impact of what the picture expressed.[4]

He wrote two distinct sets of songs. The first was occidental in character, and those songs were performed mainly by Gertrude Lawrence. The second set, including some of the dance music, was Asian in flavor and was sung mainly by the king or the members of the court. The confrontational relationship between the central characters also meant that the love songs had to be assigned to the secondary leads, the king's Burmese concubine, Tuptim, and her lover, Lun Tha. Brynner could sing, but he also chose to talk through some of the songs, and quite effectively (four years before Rex Harrison did the same in *My Fair Lady*). Rodgers' problems were compounded by the limited vocal range of Lawrence, who Rodgers thought always sang flat.

Both Rodgers and Hammerstein wanted Joshua Logan to direct, but, still upset over his experiences with *South Pacific*, he turned them down. As late as May 1950, Hammerstein wrote that Logan remained their first choice and that the offer was still open. In June they tried to interest Noel Coward, making him a lucrative offer that would have allowed him to both act and direct: 2 percent of the gross, which was about one thousand dollars a week, plus five thousand dollars down. In September 1950 Rodgers sent him the first act, which Coward found charming, and over lunch Rodgers fought "like a steer," Coward said, to persuade him to direct. Edna Ferber advised him to decline and return to writing. Despite his long friendship with Lawrence he rejected the offer and left for Jamaica to write a new play.[5] The playwright John Van Druten, who had directed his own successful comedy *Bell, Book and Candle*, was hired.

Lawrence was not easy to work with, and many times Brynner had to calm her down and soothe her feelings. The two leads established a good relationship early on. Lawrence's role was arduous, with numerous changes from one heavy hoopskirt to another. Moreover, she had only one respite, during a ballet. A reporter described the scene backstage: "She has nine costume changes which involve six hoop-skirt dresses that weigh thirty-five pounds apiece. . . . She comes zinging off stage, with a maid scuttling along behind holding the hoop-skirts off the ground, darts into the change room (which used to be a prop men's room) and there two more maids have another dress all laid out for her to step into. . . . If she has time, she drags briefly on a cup of tea and then returns to the wings, with the maid following behind to arrange the hoops."[6]

The costumes—both Lawrence's dresses and the exotic Siamese garb—were central to the success of the production. Hollywood designer Irene Sharaff did a brilliant job. The team from *South Pacific* was called on once again: Robert Russell Bennett did the orchestrations; Trude Rittmann the dance music; and Jo Mielziner the sets. Bennett claimed to have worked sixteen hours a day to complete the orchestrations before the opening in New Haven. The day before, however, he had still not written the overture; he finished it that evening, and the following morning professional copyists wrote out the parts for the individual instruments. Bennett rehearsed it at 5:30 that afternoon, and at 8:15 the orchestra played it through for the first-nighters.

Van Druten had difficulty handling the musical numbers, which were turned over to a new choreographer, Jerome Robbins. His first task was to choreograph the initial meeting between Anna and her charges, the charming "March of the Siamese Children." But his major assignment was a ballet in the second act, which was written in as part of the evening's entertainment for visiting British diplomats. The ballet was Hammerstein's idea, but Robbins was perplexed over the treatment of the theme; Rodgers suggested a humorous approach. Having just completed a hilarious Keystone Kops–style dance routine for *High Button Shoes*, Robbins eventually devised "The Small House of Uncle Thomas," an amusing and charming Siamese version of *Uncle Tom's Cabin*. The ballet was popular with audiences, but one critic thought that the authors had gone too far to inject a little humor. The music was stitched together by Trude Rittmann, who at one point proved too inventive for Rodgers' taste. He reminded her that the show was by Rodgers and Hammerstein, not Rittmann and Hammerstein. She said that she never received the proper credit for this creation. Years later Jerome Robbins restaged the ballet for his own show, *Robbins on Broadway*.

All of this—the costumes, scenery, salaries—amounted to their most expensive production ever, costing $360,000, or four times as much as *Oklahoma!* The money was easily raised. Family members and their lawyers contributed healthy sums, and everyone realized profits of more than 100 percent.

Hammerstein's book was a skillful interweaving of the Landon book, the movie script, and his own ideas. The king's character was moderated: he remained an autocrat but displayed greater personal sensitivity than in the book. His family, rebellious in the book, was portrayed as loyal and loving toward him, as in the film. His favorite wife, Lady Thiang, sums him up nicely when she sings:

> This is a man who thinks with his heart.
> His heart is not always wise.
> This is man who stumbles and falls,
> But this is a man who tries.

In the first act, after conversing with his son, the king puzzles over his position and the state of the world:

> When I was a boy
> World was a better spot

What was so was so,
What was not was not.
Now I am a man —
World have changed a lot:
Some things nearly so,
Others nearly not.

Yul Brynner's exclamation "Is a puzzlement!" became one the classic lines of American musicals. Later in this soliloquy by the king, Hammerstein, the one-time World Federalist, took a crack at power politics and the nuclear age:

Shall I join with other nations in alliance?
If allies are weak, am I not best alone?
If allies are strong with power to protect me,
Might they not protect me out of all I own?
Is a danger to be trusting one another,
One will seldom want to do what other wishes . . .
But unless someday somebody trust somebody,
There'll be nothing left on earth excepting fishes!

Anna's role remained dominant, of course, and Lawrence was off the stage only during the "Uncle Thomas" ballet. Like the king, Anna is proud and stubborn. A lady of principle, she rebels at the barbarism of the court, especially the king's arbitrariness. Her final confrontation comes over the king's decision to punish the infidelity of Tuptim, who has fallen in love with Lun Tha. Tuptim was played by Doretta Morrow, a classically trained singer, and Lun Tha by Larry Douglas. Dorothy Sarnoff played the strong role of the king's first wife, Lady Thiang.

Rodgers' score was more closely tied to the action than it had been in *South Pacific*, which had its share of purely entertaining songs. The opening song, for example, "I Whistle a Happy Tune," sung by Anna to her young son on shipboard as they dock at Bangkok, establishes her trepidation over her new employment, but the light-hearted melody and words also convey the stiff upper lip of a woman from a "civilized land called Wales." It was a delightful moment that helped to establish Anna's character.

Her most romantic song occurs in the next scene, in which she is reminded of her husband and sings "Hello, Young Lovers." This is the archetypical Rodgers ballad — simple, with only two chords in the first eight bars, but moving in its directness, a waltz that does not seem to be in waltz time. It is startling how often

Rodgers used plain harmony in his ballads. His strongest melody was "We Kiss in the Shadow," given an Asiatic flavor by his use of a glissando to introduce every other measure. The effect is a tinkling sound made by perhaps a harp or wind chimes. Lun Tha sings "We Kiss in the Shadow," as well as the theme song of the play, "I Have Dreamed," which is reprised as underscoring for the last scene.

Before their final confrontation, Anna and the king dance in celebration of his successful reception for the British dignitaries. "Shall We Dance?" was added late in the tryouts, and it is the only moment when there is a whiff of romance between them. After the show opened Hammerstein disclosed his feelings about the relationship between the Anna and the king (in answer to a letter from a fan, R. J. Kaplan, dated April 9, 1953): "I think that Anna and the King are really in love with each other, but I don't believe that either one or the other knows it. . . . There always seemed to me a suggestion of something more between them." Kaplan questioned whether Anna and the king had slept together, to which Hammerstein replied: "I don't believe she might [have], but I believe that she could have had she not been a Victorian, had he not been an Oriental, and had all the conditions that surrounded their life together been changed. I feel that I am getting obscure, but what I really mean to say is that they felt this attraction but were inhibited not only from expressing it to each other but each to himself. When they dance the polka they come closest to feeling and show this desire."[7] The dance to which Hammerstein referred has the feeling of a waltz, with Anna's hoopskirt billowing around her and the king, but it is, in fact, a polka with exaggerated rhythm.

There was, of course, the usual incidental music, especially "The March of the Siamese Children," which Rodgers gave an Oriental twist by using chromatics, minor chords, and dissonances. The opening passage jumps up an octave and then down one half-step, which is identical to the opening three notes of "Bali Ha'i." The same Asiatic mode is reflected in "My Lord and Master," in which the king's autocratic rule is mocked by Tuptim. Later Anna unloads her own frustrations with Siamese conventions in a biting but humorous complaint:

I do not like polygamy
Or even moderate bigamy.

When the king orders a whipping for Tuptim because of her infidelity, Anna faces him down and humiliates him. She is preparing to leave Siam when the king takes ill. They reconcile as he lies dying, to the strains of "I Have Dreamed." As in all Rodgers and Hammerstein shows, the play ends not with a song but with a gesture. The children bow to their new king, their brother Chulalong-korn, and the music swells. The king dies with Anna at his bedside.

This scene was made from whole cloth by Hammerstein. In reality Anna Leonowens left Siam before the king died. And she did not save Tuptim, who was allegedly burned outside Anna's quarters (historians question the entire incident, because it was out of character for Mongkut and not in keeping with Siamese tradition).

Shortly before rehearsals began in January 1951, Rodgers invited Gertrude Lawrence to hear the entire score sung by Doretta Morrow. He explained that be-cause he and Hammerstein could not sing their way through it, he had enlisted Morrow's help. Lawrence listened calmly and left, but the next day at the first rehearsal she was ice-cold to Rodgers, cutting him dead after warmly greeting Hammerstein. She apparently had assumed that Morrow's preview was intended to point up the limits to her own voice. Rodgers subsequently claimed that she did sing flat and continued to do so throughout the show.[8]

It is also possible that Lawrence had realized that the better songs had been given to Morrow. In any case, she never fully reconciled with Rodgers, who was forced to hire a coach to help her learn the music rather than teach her him-self. She and her friends complained that the score was written in keys that were too high. But this could have been easily remedied, had she asked. In fact, she sang her songs (as recorded in the cast album) in keys lower than those in the published sheet music. The thinness of her voice is obvious in those recordings, especially when compared with her version of "Someone to Watch Over Me," which she had sung thirty years earlier in Gershwin's Oh, Kay! But the recordings should not obscure her dramatic performance. Even Rodgers conceded that her presence on stage was electrifying.

Nevertheless, Rodgers found Lawrence very insecure. Her friends later con-fided that she was terrified to be involved in something that was much more than another comic revue. The King and I bordered on operetta, and the show's suc-cess rested on her role. Her health was also beginning to be a problem, though no one knew quite what was wrong with her. She missed several rehearsals, in-cluding the dress rehearsal in New Haven, as well as several performances in the out-of-town shows.

The show went through the typical scrutiny during its tryouts: it was too long, it needed new material, it was too heavy in the first act, and so forth. Three songs were added and four were dropped, one of which, entitled "Why?" was sung by the king:

Why? Why?

Why? Why? Why?

Why are your people so peculiar?

Why can't your people be like mine?

Why don't your people ever even try?

Two of Anna's songs, "Waiting" and "Now You Leave," were also cut—which meant that Lawrence's part was shrinking. Moreover, Rodgers rewrote "We Kiss in the Shadow," making it into one of the show's finest songs.

To lighten the first act Lawrence suggested that she sing to the Siamese children (recruiting and disciplining the child actors proved a monumental task), out of which came "Getting to Know You." It was a charming song that greatly helped the show and elaborated the relationship between "Mrs. Anna" and her pupils. The melody was salvaged from *South Pacific*, but the song was brighter in its new incarnation.

From the moment the show was mentioned, everyone predicted a major success. This in itself was unusual, because even *South Pacific* had had its doubters. In fact, Rodgers and Hammerstein may have been the only ones with qualms, which they voiced after the first out-of-town previews. Rodgers complained that people did not care whether the show was good or not but whether it was better than *South Pacific*. By the time the show reached New York, Rodgers and Hammerstein professed to be worried. This was a season in which *Kiss Me Kate* was still running, along with Cole Porter's *Out of This World*, not to mention *Guys and Dolls* and *Gentlemen Prefer Blondes*. Across the street at the Majestic was *South Pacific*, and a block away was Irving Berlin's *Call Me Madam*, with Ethel Merman.

Their chief concern was still the reaction of the opening-night audience. "Getting to Know You" had been added in the last week, and Lawrence's absences contributed to an uneasy feeling. Nevertheless, as one observer noted, the name Gertrude Lawrence on the marquee created a sense of excitement. The opening took place on March 29, 1951, at the St. James Theatre, where *Oklahoma!* had opened almost eight years earlier. Unfortunately, Rodgers and Hammerstein could not control the weather that night; 44th Street became a "swashy and drizzily" thoroughfare, and a downpour threatened a few minutes before curtain time. Just as Rodgers and Hammerstein arrived the rain stopped, and limousines and taxis began making the turn from Eighth Avenue. Margaret Truman came, as did Moss Hart and Kitty Carlisle, George Kaufman, Billy Rose and Eleanor Holm, Deems Taylor, Arthur Schwartz, and Herbert Bayard Swope. Mike Todd wore black tie, and Edna Ferber arrived in ermine.

Backstage at the 1952 Tony Awards, five of which went to *The King and* I. From left,
Oscar Hammerstein II, Gertrude Lawrence, Richard Rodgers, Helen Hayes,
Phil Silvers, Judy Garland, and Yul Brynner.

Two things happened that night that could not have been anticipated. First, Yul Brynner was stunning and nearly stole the show. Then Lawrence, sensing that everyone was nervous because of her, came to life, demonstrating why she had been a major star for twenty-five years. John Van Druten described opening night: "She came on the stage with a new and dazzling quality, as though an extra power had been added to the brilliance of her own stage light. She was radiant and wonderful. . . . Gertie's quality was magic. She had a star quality at its best. That is a radiance, indefinable but intensely vivid, that comes from something other than the human or technical talents of the actress." [9]

The critics were overwhelmed: "They have done it again," wrote John Mason Brown. It was "an inspired musical drama," wrote Brooks Atkinson, "a beautiful and lovable musical play." Others declared this Rodgers' best score because it contributed most to the dramatic development. George Jean Nathan complimented Rodgers for breaking out of the compositional "safety" of *Oklahoma!* and *South Pacific.*

Rodgers had tailored his approach more to the story than in previous efforts, but without going too far in trying to sound Siamese. He was becoming a "sub-dued giant" because he was subordinating his songs to the principle of making the story move along "swiftly and coherently." Richard Watts, writing for the *New York Post*, revisited the show late that summer and wrote that on second hearing Rodgers' score was not only as good as he had originally thought but "brilliant and beautiful." Sigmund Romberg's letter to Hammerstein may have been the most gratifying response: "[A] monumental piece of work. I think to be in a position to write what you want to write, when you want to write it, is reaching the highest pinnacle of one's ambition and just puts you, in my estima-tion, in a unique class, leading all other men in your field bar none." [10] Dorothy Fields, Rodgers' old friend and collaborator from amateur-show days, wired, "Above everything else I have seen, I most admire and love 'The King and I.' It is beautiful, touching, charming and funny."

The "team from Siam," as they were described, once again captured the Donaldson and Tony awards for musical, book, and score. The play ran for 1,246 performances. Rodgers and Hammerstein were also becoming richer by the week. They had split an estimated $1.5 million in 1951, in addition to earning royalties for works written before their partnership.

In London *The King and I* ran longer than *South Pacific*; after the opening, in October 1953, Hammerstein wired his office: SHOW A REAL SMASH LOOKS BIGGER THAN SOUTH PACIFIC. Gertrude Lawrence was not there. She had been deter-mined to open in the London version in 1953, the year Elizabeth II was to be crowned. She was ill, however, and her performances in New York had suffered to the point where Rodgers and Hammerstein composed a letter demanding that she quit, though they never mailed it. In 1952 she asked for time off for Holy Week but was turned down. It is not clear why—if they were so worried over her performance, refusing to close the show for a week or to use a replacement seems inexplicable, especially given the profits pouring in.

She finally took off several weeks in the summer of 1952, during which time she was replaced by Celeste Holm. Her letters reassured Hammerstein that she was recovering. And when she returned in late August, rested and seemingly in good form, she was even pleasant to Rodgers. But she soon grew ill again, and this time she entered the hospital. She died soon thereafter, on September 6, 1952. She had been suffering for some time from cancer, which had been misdiag-nosed as hepatitis. Hammerstein spoke at her memorial service and invoked her "magic light." She was buried in the gown she wore in the last act of *The King and I*.

By the time the show finally closed, the king had become the dominant role.

Brynner played the part in a brilliant movie version, with Deborah Kerr as Anna (Marni Nixon's voice was dubbed). The movie version, released in June 1956, was so good that most memories of The King and I reflect the movie, which differed in some ways from the musical. It was easily the best of the Rodgers' musical films, in part because of Kerr's outstanding performance. It was one of the few movie adaptations of their plays that Rodgers enjoyed. An advance of $400,000 may have helped. Nevertheless, Rodgers and Hammerstein had considered making the film in England with Valerie Hobson and Herbert Lom, who played the principal parts in the West End version. Brynner returned to his stage role in 1977; he was, according to Brendan Gill, "if anything, more attractive and compelling than he was in 1951." He continued to play the role until he died in 1985. In 1996, a revival based on new staging by Australian director Christopher Renshaw opened on Broadway to favorable reviews.

With this show Rodgers and Hammerstein had reached the apogee of their careers. They never again achieved the back-to-back success of South Pacific and The King and I, though they would go on to create very good music and lyrics. They had pressed the form that they had created in Oklahoma! to its limits. Perhaps it was an unconscious realization of this turning point that led to a pause in their relationship. It may have actually been a break, but if so, neither man acknowledged it, then or later.

Joshua Logan related that during preparations for The King and I, Oscar Hammerstein had asked him to stop by. As they talked, Hammerstein complained bitterly about Rodgers' diffident reaction to a lyric that had taken Hammerstein a long time to compose ("Hello, Young Lovers"). He began to pour out to Logan some of his frustration with Rodgers—but then checked himself.[11] That incident forms the basis for speculations of a strain in their relationship. For the next year they each found other outlets for their talents and energies.

It is an interesting commentary on the team's continuing concern for their own productions that both looked in on performances of The King and I from time to time and wrote long, sharp critiques for the stage manager. They even asked Van Druten, the original director, to come back and rehearse the cast for a week, which he did.

In late 1951, after The King and I had opened, the composer Jule Styne decided to produce Pal Joey on Broadway, much to Rodgers' surprise. The show opened in February 1952 and was again a success, despite Rodgers' negative predictions (although Noel Coward did find the show "very common"). The favorable reception was a belated recognition of Rodgers' pioneering efforts in the theater.

Other forms of tribute were forthcoming. NBC produced a special evening with Rodgers, and CBS produced a similar show, "The Richard Rodgers Story."

Of greater musical interest to Rodgers was the request from the U.S. Navy to write the background score for a new television documentary series, *Victory at Sea*, scheduled for twenty-six episodes. This challenge differed markedly from a Broadway score. Technically, it was beyond Rodgers' capabilities; writing to film required composing with a stopwatch and providing snatches of melody and orchestral sounds to fit a scene or sequence already on film. Rodgers wisely turned down this offer. He did agree, however, to write some musical themes against a written script describing the scenes on film. The major work of translating the themes into an orchestral score would then be turned over to Robert Russell Bennett. The Navy eagerly agreed to Rodgers' terms, and in 1952 he set to work. He had in hand a collection of "logs," written notes with explanations of various scenes—planes landing on a carrier, for example. The project turned out to be a massive undertaking. Over sixty million feet of film were examined by the producers. The average episode used fifty thousand feet of film, which had to be cut to twenty-three hundred feet for each half-hour segment. The basic script followed the historian Samuel Eliot Morison's account of naval operations. Rodgers commented that writing music with no words was a new experience: "I had to express a mood and even a picture with music. In this way the job has been challenging." [12]

Bennett undertook the "dirty work," as Rodgers put it, of orchestrating the score. He commented that he had to take into account that airplanes flew in F sharp. *Victory at Sea* was narrated by Leonard Graves, who had a part in *The King and I* and replaced Brynner in 1955. It took Rodgers about eight months to finish his score, including the orchestrations. The television series premiered in October 1952 and was a success with both audiences and critics. The *New York Times* called *Victory at Sea* a documentary of "rare power and poetry." The reviewer added that "hardly enough can be said for the score of Mr. Rodgers, running as it does to a total of thirteen hours for the full series. Especially in the portions accompanying the scenes of the sea and the tension of battle, his work has a compelling beauty and vigor that adds incalculably to the emotional intensity of the series. . . . The work is deserving of more than a single hearing." [13]

The NBC Symphony, conducted by Bennett, recorded the score as a collection of historical episodes. Heard without the film, the score loses some of its power. It is episodic, with a large measure of martial music, drum rolls, cymbal crashes, marches, and occasional sound effects. Moreover, there is no attempt to develop the themes musically, as might have been appropriate in a long work of this kind. The opening theme, recapitulated throughout, is a stirring melody that seems to capture the spirit of the entire production. Because the television series was repeated many times, some of Rodgers' themes became better known, or at least more recognizable, than many of his Broadway songs. One of the major melodies, "Beneath the Southern Cross," is a languid tango that was turned into a popular song for a later Rodgers and Hammerstein show. When *Victory at Sea* is heard today, "Beneath the Southern Cross" surprises the listener, who probably recognizes the melody as "No Other Love."

The work must have been satisfying and encouraging for Rodgers. He was awarded the U.S. Navy's Distinguished Service Award in 1953. In fact, Rodgers was sufficiently buoyed that he persuaded Hammerstein to resume work, this time on a favorite idea of Rodgers'—an old-fashioned musical with singing, dancing, and all the backstage ambience of a Broadway show, an arena that both knew so well. They embarked on *Me and Juliet*.

18

R & H

In the summer of 1952, Richard Rodgers turned fifty. Oscar Hammerstein sent congratulations that read: "At the age of fifty you are
Dick Rodgers. I think that is a very good thing to be."

That same year, West 44th Street had become a Rodgers festival.
He had three hits running simultaneously: *South Pacific* at the Majestic
Theatre, *The King and* I across the street at the St. James, and a revival
of *Pal Joey* down the block at the Shubert.

Some critics deplored the success of Rodgers and Hammerstein's
musicals, saying that the shows were driving out serious drama. But
Rodgers maintained that the theater was a place of escape and that
any outlet for the emotions, whether music or drama, was appropriate: "We laugh or cry or we're stimulated to excitement." Although

the number of dramatic plays had fallen off, the theater was benefiting from the more serious musicals, he argued.[1]

The charge against musicals was ironic, considering that only twelve years earlier *Pal Joey* had been attacked for its off-color themes. Now it was receiving praise, even from Brooks Atkinson, one of the harshest critics of this early effort by Rodgers and Hart: "'Pal Joey' is the epitome of Broadway and as exhilarating as though it had just been written. 'South Pacific' and 'The King and I' have bigger themes. Their music has greater depth and loveliness, for Mr. Rodgers has matured not only in years but in talent, and his association with Mr. Hammerstein has widened the horizon. They both accepted a certain sense of responsibility about the world in which they are living."[2]

In the dozen years since *Pal Joey*, Rodgers had changed. He had been happily married to an adoring wife for twenty-two years. He was the father of two daughters: Mary was married and expecting her first child, and Linda was to attend Smith College.

He had long been more than a popular Broadway songwriter—if he ever was only that. He was wealthy and powerful and half of Broadway's most astoundingly successful team. Brooks Atkinson called him the most gifted composer on Broadway. Together and separately Rodgers and Hammerstein had been involved in sixty productions and written more than a thousand songs; as a team they had created five original musicals, which had won them two Pulitzer Prizes and a shelf full of prestigious awards.

Rodgers did not look or act like Broadway's most gifted songwriter, however. He was usually immaculately attired in a pinstripe suit, white shirt, and conservative tie, and reporters frequently noted that he seemed more like a banker or a Wall Street broker than a composer. He did not play golf, bet on the ponies, or play poker with the boys. And unlike many songwriters, he did not frequent Lindy's. He had few close friends, and those he did have were not actors, singers, or songwriters. He did drink, smoke, and admire pretty women, but he stayed away from Broadway bars and New York nightclubs.

By fifty, Rodgers' shock of thick black hair was beginning to thin, and he had grown rather stocky. He had an assertive jaw and often-furrowed brow, and he spoke softly in a clipped New York accent, usually without much emotion. Moments of temper were leavened by a stream of humor that was sharpened by years of theater banter. Agnes de Mille noted that "when considering, he becomes fixed and monolithic like a primitive. His piercing black eyes grow as opaque as an Aztec's, his face expressionless."[3] This concentration created the impression of a stern and foreboding force that was to be respected if not feared. Dorothy felt that these moments of intense preoccupation were misleading and that at rehearsals they were too often mistaken for ill humor. The real Richard Rodgers, she claimed, was lively and funny. On this point, however, de Mille had a more profound insight: "I suspect he feels in some ways cut off, even yearning; the banter is too constant, the quips too quick and sharp to betoken anything but vulnerability. He moves behind verbal machine guns. But just as the greatest quality in his music is a lilting delicious scherzo with overtones of a hovering sweetness, so in his manner and in his eyes (when he is off guard) there is a brooding quiet, a kind of unappeased hunger, a woe."[4] His daughter Mary also wrote that "there's a kind of marvelous, rich emotional quality to what my father wrote that didn't often manifest itself in his personality."[5]

In 1951, Carol Hughes, of *Coronet* magazine, described him as "conservative [and] quite demonstrative, with a concise attitude about living." His devotion to his job was "akin to religion," though he could discuss his work in a "cool undramatic fashion." He worked according to a strict schedule, composing at home each morning for a given period. His brother-in-law described Rodgers' work habits in the late 1940s: "Rodgers works in more conventional fashion, operating at the family piano in the living room. He doesn't bother to shut the doors. His wife, two pretty teen-aged daughters, the cook, the maid and a matronly poodle named Penny wander in and out all day. He frequently stops in the middle of a song to chat with the family."[6] Mary Rodgers also wrote that these morning sessions were a rather public happening. Her father asked only that the family not sing or whistle or otherwise distract him. Then, in the late morning, he took a taxi from his duplex apartment on the Upper East Side to his office on Broadway, attending to business matters until five o'clock. That was the one aspect of the theater that he claimed to dislike. Nevertheless, the organization he created with Oscar Hammerstein grew to more than one hundred employees. Rodgers' private office, decorated in soft greens and yellows, contained a green leather couch and matching chairs; a small, highly polished desk, which was always neat; and numerous photographs of past shows. A large Bechstein concert grand sat by the window, though he rarely composed in the office.

Much of his time was spent at his country homes in Connecticut: first in Fairfield, on Black Rock Turnpike; then in Southport, at "Rockmeadow"; and later nearby in a house designed by Dorothy. In the living room, a black concert grand with "graceful curves and [a] satiny surface" was the only evidence of a musical household. The electronic equipment for playing recorded music was

Dorothy and Richard Rodgers at Rockmeadow, their home in Southport, Connecticut. Dorothy, known for her gracious entertaining, once invited the entire cast of *South Pacific* for a picnic.

carefully hidden by Dorothy's skillful decorating. Moreover, there was music in only one room. Piped music following Rodgers from room to room would have been "pure torture" for him.

Dorothy and Richard filled their homes with high-quality artwork. Initially they bought work by Impressionists and post-Impressionists, but their later tastes came to include more modern artists. Over the years they amassed an impressive collection, including some masterpieces.

Rodgers was gregarious and liked to entertain. Dorothy planned weekends at their country homes carefully, including the choice of house guests. Dorothy, in addition to being a creative interior designer and businesswoman, was a gracious hostess and gave memorable dinner parties, sometimes for close friends, sometimes for business associates, and sometimes for the cast of their shows.[7] For one of her husband's birthdays she organized a surprise party and an all-day picnic for the cast of *South Pacific*. The ingredients for a good party, Dorothy wrote, were a little something to drink and lots of food. Performers did not drink as much as popularly alleged, she noted, but they could "out-eat any crowd in the world." At one such party Rodgers and Hammerstein donned female costumes and performed as Ado Annie and Laurey in *Oklahoma!*

On the opening night of Rodgers' shows he and Dorothy sat in the last row, usually making a break for the exit at intermissions and the end. Dorothy, dressed in a favorite gray dress for luck, occasionally mingled during intermission to catch the small talk of the audience. Opening-night parties, which were sometimes restricted to family, were mandatory as everyone awaited the critics' verdicts. Before *South Pacific* opened, however, Rodgers and Hammerstein were confident enough to plan a party on the roof garden of the St. Regis Hotel, complete with pink tablecloths, champagne, and music.

Among their favorite forays were the occasional weeks in August spent at Sagamore, the lakeside "camp" of Margaret Emerson Vanderbilt, the former wife of Alfred Gwynne Vanderbilt. Dorothy devoted a chapter of her memoirs to this summer retreat in the Adirondacks, where the appointments of a "picnic" included damask linens, crystal, china, and silver flatware, as well as silver platters and wine coolers; the food for these occasions was ferried across the lake to the picnic grounds. Here, the Rodgerses socialized with the elite of New York society, enlivened by such Broadway figures as George Abbott. They might weekend with Averell Harriman, then an industrialist and financier; Herbert Bayard Swope, Jr., the son of the famous newspaper editor; or the socialite William Rhinelander Stewart.

At Sagamore and at Sand Point, Margaret Emerson's estate on Long Island Sound, ferocious croquet tournaments took place, with Rodgers a key player. Although he could write a song in the midst of backstage uproar, the mere rustling of a leaf during these games could unsettle him. Dorothy was one of the few women permitted to play. Accordingly, the Rodgerses had their own croquet lawn installed at Rockmeadow.

After World War II the couple went abroad occasionally, despite Rodgers' growing aversion to travel. The enormous success of his shows, however, left him little choice. Rodgers and Hammerstein worked more closely than any other Broadway team, but their private lives remained separate. The couples sometimes traveled together for business or got together for weekends in Connecticut or in Doylestown. After the success of his shows with Rodgers, however, Hammerstein became even more withdrawn from the tumult of Broadway socializing.

Inevitably, Rodgers and Hammerstein were referred to as America's Gilbert and Sullivan. In 1950, when the team was given a prestigious award by General Eisenhower, their friend Deems Taylor invoked their famous British counterparts: "Dick Rodgers' music is so simple, we often forget how good it is. Oscar Hammerstein has brought to the lyric theater something that Gilbert never did—poetry. He is better than Gilbert. So, I'll lay eight to five that if Gilbert and Sullivan lasted seventy-five years, 'Oklahoma!' will be playing in A.D. 2000." [8]

In fact, they were quite unlike the fabled English team. True, Sir William S. Gilbert wrote the libretto and the lyrics first and then presented them to Arthur Sullivan, who composed the music. But the Rodgers and Hammerstein method was quite different. The duo's first step was to discuss at length the blueprint of the play. They would identify problems, such as the killing scene in Oklahoma! or the suicide in Carousel, and then decide how to deal with them. They would agree on how much of the story was to be told in dialogue and how much in song, attempting to use music as much as possible. They would also agree on where to spot a song and what the burden of the song would be. Rodgers sometimes would have an idea for a lyric, and sometimes Hammerstein would have an idea for a melody. Hammerstein disavowed any gift for melody, but he did believe that he had a feeling for the score and its place in the play's structure.

In spite of all the planning, the early ideas for some of their shows were often far removed from the final versions. The ideas for songs—even the more famous ones—were often little more than a title. When the actual construction of the play began, the details were often changed significantly, especially in the use of music. Hammerstein wrote: "There are few things in life of which I am certain, but I am sure of this one thing, that the song is the servant of the play, that it is wrong to write first what you think is an attractive song and then try to wedge it into a story." [9] On several occasions, however, a song was either wedged in or altered drastically during the out-of-town tryouts. Rodgers and Hammerstein were both practical, vastly experienced composers. "They were like doctors who refused to diagnose until they had personally taken the pulse," wrote de Mille. They realized that the play had to not only please the audience but engage their sympathy and understanding as well. The traditional method of titillating the crowd with a loud, fast opening was not their style: "An ice breaker indicated a lack of integrity in the musical comedy writing of those days," wrote Hammerstein. The success of the famous serene opening of Oklahoma! convinced them to trust their theatrical instincts.

Rodgers had a fairly simple formula for performing music. He believed that the song, if good enough, would carry the performance and reach the audience emotionally. The music had to be presented in as straightforward a manner as possible, allowing, of course, for the particular moment in the play. De Mille commented that Rodgers preferred a direct, proven method for reaching the audience: "He thinks the words of a song should be heard and understood, and the best place for the singer is, therefore, standing on the footlight and facing front, all but motionless, surrounded and framed by perfect quiet. . . . This handicaps directors and gives small scope to movement, and can become monotonous, but Rodgers is not concerned, because if the song is good enough there will be no talk of monotony. And under his care the song is generally good enough." [10]

Rodgers was not obsessed with his music. When de Mille sought advice on a ballet for Oklahoma! she presented him with a detailed scenario, which he promptly stuffed into his pocket, merely commenting that she knew all the songs to use. She and her group then put together the ballet; for Curly's murder by Jud in the dream sequence, she decided to have no music at all. Rodgers liked the result, adding only some timpani during the murder itself and writing a musical coda for the ending. By this point in the production Rodgers had been sternly, silently watching the dancers for days; he finally broke into a broad smile and congratulated de Mille.

Congratulations from Rodgers, however, were rare. He was never extravagant with praise, and "adequate" was considered an accolade. Jan Clayton, his star in the original Carousel, wrote later, "Dick is a fantastic workman . . . stern, you bet, but fair, courteous and exuding confidence. . . . His scoldings could be gentle, too—pointed but gentle. . . . All the artists who worked with Dick were conscious of his desire and demand for the best that could be given. When I think how Dick got better and more work out of us during every rehearsal, followed up by tender loving care the weeks of playing, I also think of what incredible patience he must have had and how sorely tried he must have been constantly by Larry [Hart]." [11]

Hammerstein, too, was careful and meticulous, though more willing to experiment than Rodgers. Hammerstein believed that one of the values of close collaboration was the opportunity to get a quick reaction from one's partner, thus eliminating bad ideas quickly and sustaining the good ones. As an example, he liked to cite "It Might as Well Be Spring," from State Fair, which originated when he was musing that the young girl's mood was akin to spring fever, a phrase that Rodgers immediately urged him to adopt.

Hammerstein liked to compose a melody to accompany his lyrics; these "dummy" melodies were considered awful by all concerned, as were some of his dummy titles. He was often chagrined at how easily Rodgers developed his melodies to support Hammerstein's words. Hammerstein's feel for musical techniques influenced his lyrics; so many beats in a measure, so many measures in a refrain were elements that could not be ignored. "There is a rhythm and a tempo, and its continuity must not be broken." If a song was not singable, he wrote, it was "no song at all." For him, the most important ingredient of a good song was sincerity. Although he admired Hart's "fluidity and humor," Hammerstein refused to try to compete in these terms.

An effective collaboration is never easy. It involves many virtues, including loyalty, respect, and tolerance. These are especially important in the theater, where two people may be not only writing, casting, and directing a show but producing it as well. They are bound to be thrown together to make joint decisions and to face directors, conductors, stars, and bit players with a common front. Any disagreements have to be carefully concealed.

Both men went out of their way to insist on the viability of their partnership. Hammerstein said, "We have fallen into a rhythm of work which suits us both. Our social lives and our personal habits are similar. Our theatrical tastes and standards are as nearly as identical as they could be. . . . Our professional union has been incredibly smooth and happy." [12] During rehearsals they spoke softly, intelligently, and politely, and their manner was courteous and charming. They generally divided their labor, Rodgers taking charge of everything but the writing and reading of lines. He usually could be seen sitting and watching (sometimes scowling) while Hammerstein, more relaxed, was busy with rewrites. Rodgers insisted that a performance be letter perfect, since his songs usually had no diversions or devices as enhancements. Consequently, Rodgers was a scrupulous supervisor during rehearsals. De Mille described him at a typical rehearsal: "Dick is considerate and quiet too, but always noticed. He takes a chair by the director, or by the piano, or he sits chatting in the auditorium with a member of the cast, or he dictates his entire morning mail. But he misses nothing, not an inflection, not a turn of the wrist or a grace note. And none of us ever misses the fact that he is watching. In music rehearsals, of course, he is an active participant; he plays well and frequently takes the piano to give pace and dynamics." [13] He may not have talked much at rehearsals, but he did issue pronouncements. The cast would wait in uneasy anticipation while he contemplated something he had just seen, frozen in concentration. Then would come the verdict, from what de Mille called the "Star Chamber."

Hammerstein and Rodgers shared one trait: a serious concern with details. Rodgers went so far as to correct the breathing of his singers. Hammerstein coached the actors and even served as a part-time director. Both had a keen appreciation for talent and respected the other's judgment. Anyone could audition, and all the cast, even the better-known stars, had to try out. Even after *Oklahoma!* opened, auditions continued to be held every Thursday; if an opening suddenly occurred in the show, they often had seen the right person to fill in. George Abbott said that Rodgers was quick to make up his mind during auditions, as was Abbott himself, but that Rodgers was too courteous to dismiss a performer quickly. This was not always true; he did not like a young actor named Marlon Brando, who auditioned for *I Remember Mama*, and argued against hiring him. The director, John Van Druten, overruled him.

If a performer was sufficiently talented Rodgers and Hammerstein would occasionally put him or her under contract. Shirley Jones was signed in this manner; initially she was made a member of a road company of *South Pacific*, but their ultimate intention was to use her as the lead in the movie version of *Oklahoma!*

Nothing was overlooked. They had the final word, and after each opening Rodgers "policed the theater with a zest and concern extraordinary for someone who had seen so very many shows through long runs." Agnes de Mille summed them up: "Here at last were the aristocrats of the business."

What sustained the partnership of Rodgers and Hammerstein? One of Rodgers' admiring biographers, Stanley Green, asserted that they got along because they had similar outlooks on life, came from similar middle-class backgrounds, had similar habits, kept regular hours, and drank only socially. Others who knew them made roughly the same claim of shared lifestyles and attitudes.[14] Their lives, and especially their backgrounds, were, in fact, quite different. Their outlooks differed, too: Hammerstein was the cock-eyed optimist, whereas Rodgers was often the pessimist. What bonded them was not their personalities—though that link was, of course, critical—but their shared philosophy of the American musical theater. As Hammerstein put it, "We have almost an identical set of ethics."

Their strongest common commitment was to the integrity of the show. Rodgers once said that "my big involvement is with people. Not the actors, but the characters they play. I must know how they feel, and then I can give them a song to express it." Hammerstein expressed a similar view: "We can write words and music best when they are required by a situation or a characterization in a story." The practical effect of these attitudes was that Hammerstein became the dominant creative force, at least at the outset, for he determined the characters and stimulated Rodgers' melodies.

Neither partner exercised a veto right, though it was implicit in their collaboration. Songs dropped from one show were not necessarily abandoned; they might turn up in later shows. Although the songwriters were critical of transferring a song from one scene to another or even from one act to another, they in fact did this many times—and usually to good effect.

As far as the actual performance was concerned, Rodgers particularly liked a reprise of the stronger songs. For example, the famous love song "People Will Say We're in Love" was reprised in Oklahoma! as was "Some Enchanted Evening" in South Pacific. Some playwrights or lyric writers complained of this practice, and before joining with Hammerstein, Rodgers quarreled with directors over whether to reprise one his songs. But Hammerstein never quibbled over it.

Beyond the context of the play, there was an overall philosophy derived largely from Hammerstein: the critics called it "sweetness and light." Hammerstein preferred to call it sincerity. He wrote, "I don't deny the ugly and tragic—but somebody has to keep saying that life's pretty wonderful, too. Because it's true. I guess I just can't write anything without hope in it." Rodgers also defended this viewpoint: "What's wrong with 'sweetness and light'? It's been around quite a while. Even a cliche, you know, has a right to be true."

The charge of excessive sentimentality seems odd when one considers that Oklahoma! featured a killing; Carousel, a suicide, a robbery, and an attempted rape; and Allegro, marital infidelity. What's more, South Pacific denounced racial prejudice, and the protagonist in The King and I was a tyrant who dies at the end. The indictment of sentimentality over the years came less from the content of the show than from the spirit of the songs that endured: "Oh, What a Beautiful Mornin'," "If I Loved You," "You'll Never Walk Alone," "A Fellow Needs a Girl," "Some Enchanted Evening," and "Hello, Young Lovers."

The key to Rodgers and Hammerstein's success was that they could combine their sensibilities with the harsh realities of theater production. Unexpected defense of their emotionalism came from the critic George Jean Nathan. He praised Hammerstein for writing "warmly and simply" of "warm and simple subjects," since one did not go to a musical in the same mood as to a serious drama. As for Rodgers, Nathan wrote that the Newer Criticism, and the "toadies" associated with it, resented the fact that his music was "strongly given to melody"; they wanted a gallon of "butyric acid" poured into the piano. Nathan concluded, somewhat condescendingly, "Rodgers, like Hammerstein, is not writing for the Metropolitan but for the lighter stage. . . . That lighter stage occupies the same position in music that the cocktail does at the dinner table; it whets, or should whet, the appetite for the better things to come; and Rodgers is one of the best cocktails served hereabouts." [15]

Rodgers and Hammerstein compared the complexities of producing a musical not to mixing a cocktail but to the art of war. In military strategy, as in the theater, the numerous components must fit together, but in the theater such combinations are more subtle and tenuous. Thus the pair supervised the casting and nursed the cast during rehearsals. Rodgers paid close attention to the orchestrations, to the point of suggesting voicing as well as choice of instruments, even though his orchestrators were highly experienced and talented. He also watched over the orchestra, listening to it from various angles.

Few musicals went to New Haven, Boston, or Philadelphia and returned to New York unscathed. Rodgers once quipped that he would not open a can of sardines unless he was in Boston. Both men could accommodate changes—even drastic ones—by being ready to write new lyrics and music, and quickly. For example, they wrote three songs for the same spot in *South Pacific* before settling on the best one, which had been composed in one day, out of town.

Indeed, once they reached Boston it was no longer possible to return to the quiet of Doylestown or Rockmeadow. This pressure was more of a problem for Hammerstein, who preferred to work slowly. After all, it was Rodgers who said, "I cannot do without the stimulus of this work." His brother-in-law commented that Rodgers was normally placid but that when he talked about the theater he burst with enthusiasm, happily pacing the floor while describing the problems of his latest production, pausing occasionally to sit in various chairs: "Rodgers is a great chair tester." In her introduction to his republished autobiography, Mary Rodgers also wrote about his encompassing love for the theater: "Theatre, and theatre only, turned him on and cheered him up—all aspects of it, not just the writing. He loved auditions (pretty girls), rehearsals, and out-of-town tryouts especially. New Haven with its miserable Taft Hotel (lumpy beds, lousy room service) and Kasey's (a greasy-spoon theatrical hangout across the street from the Shubert theatre, where the food was so terrible I got sick once just from eating the pickles) was, to Daddy, a joyful excursion." [16]

Most important, both partners knew that the audience counted above all. They were determined to write the kind of musical that satisfied their own ethic but that also drew people into the theaters. In a jointly written article about life in the theater, they used an analogy: "As a man is kept alive by the flow of blood through his circulatory system, so is the theatre kept alive by the flow of audiences through its aisles. The heart that pumps this flow and keeps it constant is that dedicated group of playwrights, composers, producers . . . whose own stage-struck hearts belong to the theatre." [17] Richard Rodgers and Oscar Hammerstein were two such stagestruck hearts.

19

ME AND JULIET

Rodgers and Hammerstein still faced what was becoming their
eternal dilemma: how to create an encore worthy of their most recent success. They had answered the challenge of *South Pacific* with *The
King and I*. But the law of averages was now against them, so that the
chances of a third smash hit were diminishing. They decided that
a change of pace was in order and began work on a contemporary
play set in the heart of what they knew best—the theater.

Me and Juliet turned out to be the Rodgers and Hammerstein hit
with the poorest reviews. It proved, as one critic put it, that one
could write a review-proof musical—provided, of course, that one
had already written *Oklahoma!*, *Carousel*, *South Pacific*, and *The King and I*.

Although a show about the backstage life of a musical was hardly
innovative, few were more familiar with every aspect of that world

than were Rodgers and Hammerstein. In their version they went out of their way to avoid the "trite old formulas": there were no kids putting on a musical in a barn, no grumbling but lovable doorman named Pop, no perky little understudy who goes on for the star, no phony Hollywood idealizations. They wanted to mirror *real* life in the theater, to show the evolution of relationships as a show progresses. They pointed out that at first, during out-of-town tryouts, backstage relationships are usually tentative. But by the end of a long run everyone comes to know everyone else's secrets and loves. "They share loyalties," as Rodgers put it. The authors were particularly determined to put down certain myths, for example, that theater people were "jealous, temperamental goons." To the contrary, Rodgers insisted, chorus girls were expert, accomplished dancers and the men were far from the cliché of effeminate: try that one backstage, Rodgers said, and "you might get your arms broken."

Interwoven with the backstage story line is a "show within the show," originally titled *Juliet and Hercules* but wisely changed to *Me and Juliet*. The story embraces not only the various cast members but also the stagehands, electricians, stage managers, and even the producer. The authors incorporated all the familiar paraphernalia of the theater—lights, sets, costumes—and depicted rehearsals and even a scene in the orchestra pit. There was, for example, an audition in which the disembodied voice of the producer in the empty theater is heard saying "Thank you very much" to one candidate. He asks another, whom he apparently knows rather well, to leave her name and number, even though his female choreographer has turned her down for the part.

There is a romantic triangle: Jeanie, a dancer in the chorus; her boyfriend of the moment, Bob, a stage electrician; and Larry, the assistant stage manager who is smitten with Jeanie. Larry has been too shy to approach Jeanie during the early weeks of rehearsals, whereas the more aggressive Bob has captivated her. As the show solidifies, Jeanie aspires to improve her position and auditions to become an understudy. She also starts to fall in love with Larry, who coaches her audition. Their romance blossoms, but secretly, because Bob is not only a jealous suitor but a sadistic bully. In a dramatic scene at the end of the first act Bob attempts to harm Jeanie by dropping a sandbag from above. In addition, within the hypothetical show, he uses his control of the spotlight to stalk her onstage. The curtain comes down on his shocking acts of violence.

In the second act Bob finally confronts Jeanie and Larry in a scene that becomes a brawl involving several members of the company. Bob hits his head on a radiator and is knocked out. When he awakens, he is informed that Larry and Jeanie are married. He grudgingly acquiesces to this news, which seems to mollify him and satisfy his vanity. He rejoins the company as they start a "rehearsal," during which the final curtain descends to the music of "No Other Love."

Hammerstein created the story from scratch, because there was nothing to adapt or rewrite: as Rodgers explained, there had never been a play about the musical theater. Hammerstein was reportedly not enthusiastic about the project. (On the other hand, he later claimed in public that he had first broached it with Rodgers around Christmas 1952 and discovered that Rodgers had been thinking along the same line.) Rodgers said that for six or seven years he had been toying with ideas for a backstage show in order to get some dance music out of his system. "We felt a desire to change pace," Rodgers said, "to have some fun . . . and also to get into the kind of musical score we haven't had a chance to do together." Having earlier pressed for his own project, *Allegro*, Hammerstein relented and went along with Rodgers' idea.

In spring 1952, in Palm Beach, the writers decided to limit the story to backstage events during the performance of a long-running show. Rodgers wanted no overture until that of the show within a show. In August, Hammerstein began sketching out the plot; by early fall he had a first draft virtually finished, and by the following March the final draft was almost complete. Rehearsals began on March 19, 1953.

The show was billed as a musical comedy—a red alert that it would definitely not be *Carousel* or *South Pacific*. When asked about the billing, Rodgers defended their choice:

> When you say we're going back to musical comedy, it sounds as if we're returning to Schwab and Mandel and "Good News" which [*Me and Juliet*] isn't at all. The old time musical comedy was an artificiality, a convention by which people didn't have to talk like human beings. There was a tenor, a soprano and a baritone and a certain number of lines leading into a song. There was never any attempt at realism, not an overt attack on the emotions. We don't have to apologize for our characters and situations by saying "Oh, well they're musical comedy characters." Our people are, we think, human beings, real people.[1]

George Abbott was the ideal director for a musical about a musical. Jo Mielziner was again recruited, this time to solve the problem of a show within a show using sets that would simultaneously display scenes onstage and backstage. It could be done, he told the authors, but it would be expensive (it cost an additional three hundred thousand dollars). Robert Alton, the dance director, had worked frequently with Rodgers and Hart and had choreographed *Hazel Flagg* before taking on *Me and Juliet*. The leads were Robert Hayes as Larry and Isabel Bigley as Jeanie, and the chorus included Shirley MacLaine. As in most Hammerstein stories, there was a subplot, a love story between the stage manager, played by Ray Walston, and a new dancer, Betty, played by Joan McCracken. To prove his point that their story was about the real theater, Rodgers cited the careers of Joan McCracken and Isabel Bigley, both of whom had started with smaller parts in *Oklahoma!*

Writing the show turned out to be more difficult than anticipated. Hammerstein's early drafts were far removed from the final version. The placement of songs shifted radically, and several songs either were not written or were cut (for example, "Wake Up Little Theater," and "Life in a Long Run Show"). George Abbott did not like the original script but suppressed his criticism, assuming that a team as successful as Rodgers and Hammerstein must know what they were doing. He also expected that some high points would be created by the show within a show.

Hammerstein finally asked Abbott to cut the script himself and to make changes as if it were his own draft. Abbott performed such major surgery that it is surprising Rodgers and Hammerstein did not object; perhaps both instinctively knew that the show was in trouble. Despite his own changes, Abbott still had qualms: in his opinion, the score was below Rodgers' standard and the book was too sentimental. During out-of-town tryouts Hammerstein did a great deal of additional cutting and rewriting. Observers, however, began to remind him of *Allegro* and its failure. He claimed that the fact that *Me and Juliet* was also an original, and not an adaptation, was merely coincidental. Moreover, he bristled to an interviewer that he "liked" *Allegro* and insisted there was no comparison.

This defensive tone was evident in a letter from Hammerstein to John Van Druten: "Me and Juliet looks like a great big hit." Although he was still polishing it, he anticipated criticism in some quarters because it was not as "highfalutin" as their most recent effort. This show was in fact an out-and-out musical comedy. "If this be treason make the most of it," he wrote.[2] After the show opened Hammerstein complained that the critics were "thrown off balance and built up some kind of strange resentment against Dick and me having the right to a 'light moment.'"

It indeed was a light moment, the brightest spots being the songs about show business and the theater. "The Big Black Giant" describes an audience that is at times a "coughing giant" or a "sleeping giant" or a "laughing giant." The second act opens on the fictitious audience discussing the fictitious "Me and Juliet" during intermission. The witty and biting lyrics in this scene, which are worthy of Lorenz Hart, include snatches of the show's real songs, sung badly and incorrectly by members of the fictitious audience. Their chitchat concludes with the refrain "The theater is dying," set to a tongue-in-cheek Rodgers waltz.

Another show-business song occurs at the end of the first act, when the two female leads muse about becoming a star ("It's Me"):

> My picture hangs in Sardi's
> For all the world to see.
> I sit beneath my picture there
> And no one looks at me.
> I sometimes wear dark glasses,
> Concealing who I am,
> Then all at once I take them off—
> And no one gives a damn!
> But when I start to play a part, I play the part okay;
> No longer am I no one when I'm someone in a play.

The music had a jazzy Broadway sound and a touch of Latin (Rodgers borrowed the tango rhythm of "No Other Love" from *Victory at Sea*). He also added more brass to the orchestra pit: four trumpets, four trombones and, for the first time in years, saxophones. The orchestrations were by Don Walker, who was more attuned to a modern swing sound than was Russell Bennett. Some of the songs were performed on stage by the legitimate jazz trio of Barbara Carroll (piano), Milton Shulman (bass), and Herbert Wasserman (drums). The score smacked more of Rodgers and Hart than of Rodgers and Hammerstein.

One of the highlights was "Keep It Gay," a song that passed through several characters and settings, rather as "Isn't It Romantic?" did in *Love Me Tonight*. Despite its bouncy rhythm and lively lyrics, "Keep It Gay" was an ordinary Broadway song. But the staging gave it momentary fame. The song begins with two electricians on a bridge high over the stage, followed by a blackout; the lights then come up on a chorus done by the dancers in the "show within," followed by another blackout; the same dancers, this time in workout clothes, appear to do a final chorus. Hammerstein cited this number as an example of the influence of the book on the music. Although he gave credit for the final concept of this well-received routine to the stage designer, Jo Mielziner, he was careful to note that his script had called for something similar at this point.

The show tried out in Cleveland, where the rehearsals and previews caused a considerable stir. In their customary interviews, both Rodgers and Hammerstein expressed their hope for a success. At the dress rehearsal, however, Hammerstein dictated eight pages of notes. Saul Pett, a traveling reporter, wrote in the *Philadelphia Inquirer* of the tribulations in Cleveland: "Suddenly the whole 'Keep It Gay' number falls shockingly apart. Singers and dancers all mixed up. Whistles blow. Rodgers, Hammerstein, Abbott and Alton race down to the stage, like parents racing after a kid who's riding on his bike. They're more worried about the kid than the bike. They reassure them in gentle whispers."[3] At the first preview, Pett noted that the same performers who had seemed half-dead two hours before the curtain had come "vitally alive." One local critic, however, found "something basically lacking in this musical about young love in the theater. . . . The musical masters not only have written what at this writing appears to be a mediocre score and book, but at times they have gotten strangely off key, for them, in the kind of material around which they have written some of their situations, their lyrics and their songs."[4]

Even before they took the show back to New York, Rodgers and Hammerstein realized they might have a failure on their hands. There were last-minute attempts to save the show: two brief new scenes were written in Boston; two numbers were cut altogether; a new song, "Meat and Potatoes," was written and then withdrawn; another, "We Deserve Each Other," was written and added after Cleveland. Elliot Norton, the venerable Boston critic, was moderately enthusiastic, especially about the music. During an intermission in Boston, however, the authors heard the audience raving about the sets, a reaction that always meant that the show itself was in trouble (the sets were in fact considered a great attraction of this production). Abbott had hoped that the choreography would counteract the slow pace but was unhappy with Bob Alton's staging of the dance numbers. When discreetly asked whether he could fix the dances, Jerome Robbins replied that he could but that he would not, out of respect for Alton.

Large advance sales guaranteed a respectable run (the show grossed fifty-eight thousand dollars a week and paid off by the end of October). As expected, the reviews were lukewarm. The problem, according to most reviewers, was that the shifts between the backstage story and the show within a show did not come off: "Rodgers and Hammerstein have come perilously close to writing a show-without-a-show," wrote Walter Kerr. The show had "just about everything," Brooks Atkinson decided (*New York Times*, May 29, 1953), "except an intelligible story." The reviewers were generally kind regarding Rodgers' work: they called the music "lovely, fresh and charming" and "one of his most melodious scores." Atkinson wrote that the score had "grace, humor, sentiment, and richness."

Rodgers' notes indicate that he did not write his melodic sketches in the order they appear in the show. Presumably, he was writing to the lyrics as Hammerstein completed them. There are, however, some sketches for songs not used and some variations on songs that were finally used. He wrote one song, entitled only "Baby Sequence," that included an interpolation of a part of the "Soliloquy" from *Carousel*, but it was cut.

Abbott later concluded that the show had failed because Rodgers and Hammerstein were too sure of themselves. Moreover, he believed that they craved publicity and were too protective of each other:

> Dick and Oscar worked together with perfect understanding. Each respected the other not only as a person but as a workman, and I think that each made a very conscious effort not to jeopardize the relationship. . . . [Rodgers] in those days had quite a feeling of dependence on his collaborators. I knew he had been inordinately tolerant of Larry Hart's irresponsibility—partly because he was fond of him, but also because he felt that he needed him. Now, having achieved even greater success with Oscar, he cherished him. One day he said to me, "I never want to have another collaborator as long as I live." . . . Dick's work took on a more solid earthy character when he began to work with Hammerstein. The hits Rodgers wrote with Hammerstein were much bigger that those with Hart, and the financial reward was also much bigger. The solid meat is more popular than the souffle.[5]

Abbott found their score for *Me and Juliet* less than their best, however. They were too talented to write a bad score, but this one was not "top drawer."

The show, which opened on May 28, 1953, at the Majestic, ran the entire season and into the next. On opening night, Rodgers and Hammerstein accepted the usual congratulations "glumly." *Me and Juliet* did not "fail violently," as Abbott noted, but "just died gently." A revival of *Oklahoma!* on Broadway, however, meant that the team had four shows running at the same time as *Me and Juliet*. (The others were *South Pacific* and *The King and I*.) This extraordinary concurrence prompted Mayor Vincent Impellitteri to declare the first week in September Rodgers and Hammerstein Week.

The reappearance of *Oklahoma!* was fortuitous. Rodgers and Hammerstein had purchased the rights to the production from the Theatre Guild for more than over $850,000 but had steadfastly refused offers to turn it into a Hollywood picture. The tenth anniversary was marked in March 1953 at a gathering in Washington, D.C., where the show was currently playing. Theresa Helburn, Lawrence

Langner, and some of the original cast members attended, but Rodgers was absent because of illness. When a revival was produced in August 1953 at the City Center in New York, it produced yet another round of praise.

The observance of Rodgers and Hammerstein Week in New York prompted Brooks Atkinson to ruminate on the team's work. He refrained from trying to choose their best and instead noted the differences among the shows. One could not weigh *Oklahoma!* against *The King and I*; the former was a folk opera out of American sources, the latter an earnest study in character. Atkinson stressed the importance of *Oklahoma!* "Nothing will ever impair the affection American audiences have for this earliest of the Rodgers and Hammerstein collaborations."

In the summer of 1954, Rodgers and Hammerstein were ready to move *Oklahoma!* onto the screen. Mike Todd had persuaded them to try his new wide-angle technique, Todd-AO, which they found intriguing. Rodgers grew disgusted with Todd for some reason and walked out of one of their conferences, insisting that he would never do business with him. Nevertheless, Hammerstein and the team's lawyer, Howard Reinheimer, reached an agreement with Todd without further consulting Rodgers. Rodgers was angered by this furtive deal (and even brought it up in his memoirs twenty years later), but rather than allow the issue to cause a rupture with Hammerstein, he swallowed his pride. Rodgers' sensitivity over this incident suggests that he was sincerely concerned about the future of their partnership and wanted to avoid any strain.

Rodgers and Hammerstein produced the film of *Oklahoma!* themselves, but they hired their friend Arthur Hornblow, Jr., as executive producer and Fred Zinnemann as director. Even though Zinnemann had no experience with musicals, he had several major movies to his credit, including the Academy Award–winning *From Here to Eternity*. Hornblow and Zinnemann had a veto on the casting, but Rodgers and Hammerstein made the final decisions. The candidates for Curly were mind-boggling: a young actor named Paul Newman and another named James Dean were up for the part. Zinnemann scheduled an interview with James Dean in New York, at the posh Hotel Pierre. Dean, dressed in cowboy clothes, arrived very late; he explained that the hotel staff had refused him entrance, so he had had to slip onto a freight elevator. Dean tested for the role, but neither he nor Newman could sing. The role of Curly finally went to Gordon MacRae, who had already made a few musicals with Doris Day. Hornblow found Rod Steiger ideal for Jud. Charlotte Greenwood, who had turned down the part of Aunt Eller on Broadway, now agreed to play her. The role of Laurey was given to a Rodgers and Hammerstein protégée, Shirley Jones, whom they had "discovered" during a routine audition and had nurtured with this part in mind.

The problems during filming were formidable. Todd-AO used a special wide-angle camera, but at the time there was only one such camera in existence. For insurance, each scene was therefore shot twice, once in Todd-AO and once in CinemaScope. (It was the CinemaScope version that survived for subsequent generations.) The reliance on the Todd-AO camera also meant that early tests had to be shot in Hollywood and then flown to the laboratory in Buffalo for development and viewing, an expensive and time-consuming process.

The setting for the movie was also a problem, because Rodgers and Hammerstein wanted authenticity, such as real corn as high as an elephant's eye, but in an open area where they could create a farmhouse setting, Jud's shack, and other backdrops. They settled on a valley near Nogales, Arizona, though the crop of corn that was planted had to be stimulated to grow to the desired height. The corn through which Gordon MacRae rides as he sings "Oh, What a Beautiful Mornin'" is genuine, as is the white wood farmhouse that he approaches. But the mountains in the background would have been a surprise to Aunt Eller and her Oklahoma neighbors.

It turned out that Nogales was not ideal. The filming site was on a stretch of desert criss-crossed by arroyos, which flooded and sometimes washed out the old wooden bridges. These six-foot-high "walls of water" came roaring out of nowhere almost every day. Zinnemann described the ordeal: "By 2:00 the entire sky was an ominous shade of black, and then all hell broke loose—sizzling flashes of lightning, rolling thunderclaps sounding like heavy artillery, and solid walls of water coming down. . . . Often the heavy passenger car [shuttling cast members back and forth] was caught crossing an arroyo and was carried for almost fifty yards by the flash flood. That particular ditch was afterwards known as 'Cadillac Gulch.'"[6] Difficult as it is to imagine Richard Rodgers and Oscar Hammerstein in such a setting, they kept a close watch over the production. There are photographs to prove it: in one, Rodgers, looking quite out of place in a Bermuda sport shirt, is surrounded by ersatz Oklahoma cowboys and others in Western garb.

Filming continued on Hollywood soundstages. Rodgers took particular pleasure in occupying the office once used by Irving Thalberg—the very office in which Thalberg had slighted him twenty years earlier. Rodgers and Hammerstein were determined to film the version they had produced on Broadway, not a remake for Hollywood.

Agnes de Mille returned to redo her dances and immediately got into a quarrel with Rodgers. He did not like her new ideas for the dances, now spread over a huge soundstage rather than the tiny stage of the Majestic Theatre. In the end, her choreography was similar to that of the original. As she and the musical director, Jay Blackton, rode back and forth to the set, de Mille dished Rodgers. According to Mary Rodgers, her father came to regard de Mille as a "pain in the ass." She was not hired for the movie version of *Carousel*.[7]

This was the Shirley Jones' first movie. After discovering her, Rodgers and Hammerstein had signed her to a rare personal contract, putting her first in the chorus of *South Pacific* and then in *Me and Juliet*, during its last month. In addition to fitting their image of Laurey, she was extraordinarily attractive and could sing like an angel. Consequently, while still a teenager, she found herself the star of a major motion picture. She subsequently toured with *Oklahoma!* (her costar was Jack Cassidy, her future husband), and she appeared in the film version of *Carousel*.[8]

The film of *Oklahoma!* was in production from July to December 1954 and became the most expensive movie produced to that date (mainly because of being shot in both Todd-AO and CinemaScope). It opened in October 1955 and was very successful, commercially as well as critically. Bosley Crowther, the film critic for the *New York Times*, wrote that the production "magnifies and strengthens all the charm that it had upon the stage." The director had brought forth a full-bodied *Oklahoma!* to "match in vitality, eloquence and melody any musical this reviewer has ever seen."

By this time R&H had already finished their next Broadway production, *Pipe Dream*, based on a new novel by John Steinbeck. Some years earlier Steinbeck had sounded out his publisher and editor on the idea of a musical version of *Cannery Row*. Cy Feuer and Ernest Martin, who had produced *Guys and Dolls*, were interested, especially if Frank Loesser could do the music. As Steinbeck delved into the musical, however, he decided to write a sequel to *Cannery Row*, a short novel that could easily be adapted for the stage. As Steinbeck's pace slowed, Loesser decided to return to writing a show of his own, *Most Happy Fella*. Steinbeck then turned to Rodgers and Hammerstein, who were old friends and had produced his abortive play *Burning Bright*. They were interested in Steinbeck's idea, and in the late summer of 1953 he sent them some of his early drafts of his novel, which at that time was titled *Bear Flag Cafe*. Hammerstein, who took the notes with him to England, liked the idea, but he and Steinbeck still had to sell it to Rodgers.

Rodgers dissented for a time, mainly because the story dealt with a prostitute, but eventually he gave in. They reached an agreement with Steinbeck, as well as with Feuer and Martin, who got 20 percent of the profits in return for giving up all rights. By then Steinbeck had finished his short novel, now entitled

Sweet Thursday, and in due course it was published, to rather tepid reviews. Nevertheless, Rodgers and Hammerstein were off and running.

Rodgers defended their decision to take on the project on the grounds that *Pipe Dream* was deliberately new, in the sense that Rodgers and Hammerstein's audiences had never met such characters in their plays. These people had simple problems, such as how to find a job. Such mundane problems were "stimulating" not only because they differed from the subjects of their earlier shows but because he and Hammerstein found it pleasant not to have to worry about deeper issues. Because they were treating simple people, they wanted to write "along straight and easily understandable lines." This defense sounded much like the rationale for *Me and Juliet* as a new approach to the "real" theater people.

The simple people of *Sweet Thursday* were drawn from the original *Cannery Row*. The main character was the same: Doc, a marine biologist, who had become the first citizen of Cannery Row, a stretch of territory in Monterey that had housed sardine-canning factories before World War II. Doc works sporadically, collecting and examining marine specimens in a makeshift laboratory, but his real occupation is drinking and talking with the denizens of Cannery Row. His friends are two men named Mack and Hazel, both of whom live at the Palace Flophouse, and Dora, madame of the Bear Flag Restaurant and house of ill repute.

In *Sweet Thursday*, Doc returns from World War II to find Cannery Row almost deserted and several of his friends gone: "The street that once roared with trucks was quiet and empty." Dora has died, leaving her cafe to her sister, Flora, who is always called Fauna. Mack (Mac in the musical) and Hazel are still around, but Chong Lee, the proprietor of the grocery store, has left for the South Seas, replaced by Joseph and Mary Rivas (one person).

Doc is vaguely discontented, and his friends diagnose his problem as loneliness—lack of female companionship. They conspire to match him up with the newly arrived Suzy, a vagrant who works as one of Fauna's ladies at the Bear Flag. At first Doc and Suzy do not get along, but Doc finally realizes he needs Suzy, and they enjoy a brief romance. She decides she wants to marry him and proposes, but he is reluctant. To demonstrate her independence and remorse at her behavior, she moves into an old boiler (a large section of pipe) in a vacant lot—hence the name of the musical, *Pipe Dream*.

Doc visits her, but they decide they are wrong for each other; she tells his friends she will not go back to him unless he becomes sick—for example, if he breaks an arm. Doc does in fact suffer a broken arm, secretly administered by Hazel while Doc is asleep, thereby making it necessary for Suzy to come back and care for him. Finally Doc and Suzy decide to go off to La Jolla to collect marine specimens for Doc's experiment. The citizens of Cannery Row sing the title song as Doc and Suzy ride off (an ending reminiscent of *Oklahoma!*).

Rodgers put his finger on the main problem immediately: how to depict a working prostitute and her relationship to Doc. Both Rodgers and Hammerstein were determined to clean up the plot, but as Steinbeck pointed out several times, Suzy's redemption, and Doc's need for her despite her profession, were at the heart of the show. Nevertheless, Steinbeck was at first pleased with the beginning of Hammerstein's script. As rehearsals started, he wrote a friend: "Lord! it's a good show. Fine score and book and wonderful direction and cast."[9] This reaction is somewhat puzzling, because the opening songs and lyrics were syrupy and a trifle silly, which was not the Cannery Row depicted in Steinbeck's novel.

Some years later Steinbeck wrote that he lost heart when he learned that the new title was *Pipe Dream*; to him that indicated that Rodgers and Hammerstein did not believe in the play and would therefore be unable to make audiences believe.

Originally, Steinbeck had hoped that Doc might be played by Henry Fonda and Suzy by Julie Andrews. But neither was available. Among the other candidates were Walter Matthau ("may not sing well enough") and Frank Sinatra! For Suzy, the list included Betty Garrett, Polly Bergen, and Shirley Jones. Eventually Rodgers chose a young woman he had discovered on television, Judy Tyler; William Johnson, a Broadway regular, played Doc. Steinbeck's reputation probably led Rodgers and Hammerstein to enlist Harold Clurman as the director for Steinbeck's first musical. Rodgers had the brainstorm of recruiting the Metropolitan Opera singer Helen Traubel to play Fauna. The decision was a major blunder, though at the time it seemed inspired, much like the casting of Ezio Pinza in *South Pacific*. Her presence also helped sell an enormous number of advance tickets.

This show was a long time maturing. Hammerstein wrote a draft of sorts in late 1953, and he sent Joshua Logan another draft a year later, asking for his critique (Logan thought it could become one of Hammerstein's greatest successes).

Rehearsals began in September 1955, but on an ominous note. On the first day Rodgers assembled the cast and informed them that he was entering the hospital for an operation, reassuring them that everything would be fine. In fact, he had been complaining about a jaw pain for some time. Initially Rodgers' dentist had assured him that there was nothing wrong, but an examination by a surgeon resulted in a diagnosis of cancer and an immediate operation was scheduled. He spent the weekend before his surgery writing one last song and finishing three piano manuscripts for *Pipe Dream*. On Tuesday morning, after speaking to the cast, he left for lunch with his wife, who drove him to the hospital. The operation, which was performed on September 21, 1955, was successful, though some lymph nodes and part of his left jaw and tongue had to be removed. He was in pain for some time and had difficulty speaking, eating, and controlling dripping saliva. Two years later he wrote that his left arm had been "handicapped" because of the surgery.

Rodgers was proud of his appearance, so this operation was a "terrible thing," a "colossal, colossal hurt," according to his casting director, John Fearnley. Nevertheless, ten days after his operation he insisted on returning to the theater, though only as a spectator for some time. While in the hospital, Rodgers had received a humorous letter from Steinbeck urging him not to worry, because Steinbeck's wife, Elaine, had changed his songs and the lyrics, fired three actors, and replaced them with her friends: "But just rest easy."[10]

Rodgers commented that if this episode had conformed to the standard Hollywood formula for musicals, he would have risen from his sickbed just in time to attend the opening of *Pipe Dream*, tearfully acknowledging the thunderous ovation. In reality, he added, if there were tears, it was because *Pipe Dream* was "universally accepted" as their weakest show.

Rodgers' absence as the play floundered was indeed disastrous. Clurman had difficulty with the musical numbers, and Hammerstein had to take over. Traubel was clearly out of character as the madame. Moreover, her voice was not projecting and her singing was inconsistent. She became upset with her songs and role, saying that all of her songs were down songs, while all of Rodgers and Hammerstein's hits were up songs. She sang "Sweet Thursday," which she hated, as well as a Mozartian ensemble song with her "girls." She complained in a detailed letter to Rodgers and Hammerstein, who rebutted her complaints line by line. The real problem, according to Rodgers, was that she had lost her voice and could not be heard. After Rodgers' illness Traubel decided not to make an issue of her problems, but she did note that Steinbeck, too, was discontented.[11]

Indeed, Steinbeck was quite unhappy with the treatment of his characters. He realized that Rodgers and Hammerstein were the wrong choices for his style. During the out-of-town tryouts he bickered with Rodgers and Hammerstein every night after the performance. As a courtesy, Rodgers and Hammerstein accepted Steinbeck's "notes" but made no effort to introduce his changes. Rodgers dismissed his complaints by noting archly that Rodgers and Hammerstein produced family entertainment. As a consequence, Steinbeck's letters to Hammerstein became increasingly shrill and frustrated. He argued that the show equivocated in identifying Suzy's true position at the Bear Flag Cafe: "It's either a whore house or it isn't. Suzy either took a job there or she didn't." In another letter, he wrote that the show "side-steps, hesitates, mish mashes and never faces its theme." Steinbeck claimed that he feared failure less than he did a "pale and half-assed success which to me would be worse than failure." Finally, Steinbeck wrote an eloquent appeal: "What emerges now is a good old-fashioned love story. And that is not good enough to people who have looked forward to this show based on you and me and Dick. When Oklahoma! came out it violated every conventional rule of Musical Comedy. You were out on a limb. They loved it and were for you. South Pacific made a great jump. . . . But Oscar, time has moved. The form has moved. You can't stand still. That's the price you have to pay for being Rodgers and Hammerstein." Exasperated, he accused Hammerstein of turning his Suzy into a "visiting nurse." [12]

He was right. Rodgers and Hammerstein had written a song called "Suzy Is a Good Thing," a maudlin lyric and melody sung by Fauna. In the end Steinbeck concluded that although Rodgers and Hammerstein were attracted to his kind of writing, they were "temperamentally incapable of doing it." In Boston everyone knew they were in real trouble. The show required "drastic work," wrote the critic Elliot Norton.

On November 30, 1955, they brought the play to New York, where the reviews were not all bad. Some were even favorable, and Rodgers' music was again singled out for praise. Walter Kerr wrote that "every bit [of the story], it should be quickly said, is accompanied by light, deft, sometimes wonderfully melodic improvisation by Richard Rodgers." The book, however, was trashed: "dull," wrote one; "RH negative," concluded another. John McClain wrote in the New York Journal-American: "This is a far cry from the exalted talents of the team that produced South Pacific. They must be human after all." It ran for 246 performances, the fewest of any of their shows, and lost a great deal of money (including investments made by Rodgers' family).

Rodgers' music, if judged on its own merits, was quite good, and better than that of Me and Juliet. "All at Once You Love Her," whose unadorned four-note theme is repeated at intervals throughout, is vintage Rodgers. The harmony for the first eight bars is once again conventional, and the middle section is a variant on the main theme, but Rodgers added a final eight bars (probably as required by the lyrics). Though hardly in the same league as the major love songs of his bigger shows, it is nonetheless a romantic theme that plays well without the lyrics.

"Sweet Thursday" is a Rodgers rarity—a cakewalk (at least it is marked "quasi-cakewalk"). It has a jaunty melody and rhythm, but in the show it seems out of place, even though it is meant to be part of the grand party being planned for Cannery Row. As sung by Traubel, it disintegrates; it is totally out of character for her voice. Similarly, "The Next Time It Happens" is a serviceable Rodgers-like melody sung by Doc and Suzy, who explain why their romance will not work; but again, the music seems out of character with the plot. What was needed was a more melancholy melody, to match the sentiment of the lyrics:

> The next time it happens
> I'll be wise enough to know.

The same could be said of Doc's reverie, "The Man I Used to Be," during which he thinks back over his earlier life. The situation seems to call for a lament, but instead the melody has a strong two-beat rhythm marked "light schottisch tempo." Finally, Suzy's first song, "Everybody's Got a Home but Me," which introduces her down-and-out plight, is perhaps overly reminiscent of the melody of "You'll Never Walk Alone." The melody seems much too dramatic, especially at this early moment in the story.

One suspects that the music might have been changed or adapted had Rodgers been in good health throughout production. His illness shifted the musical burden to Hammerstein, who wanted to avoid trouble and controversy. The net result, however, was that a solid score by Rodgers was lost. Brooks Atkinson, in his Sunday column, took note:

> Mr. Rodgers is still writing like a composer out of his own heart and mind—a rare enough circumstance on Broadway to be worth noting. The "Pipe Dream" score retains the melodic richness that characterizes all his work. Particularly when he is writing in a romantic vein, he expresses deep feeling. . . . He is not afraid of emotion. He does not have to dazzle the audience with technical virtuosity to mask an emptiness within. Mr. Rodgers has plenty to say about human beings, and music is his language and the score for "Pipe Dream" is characteristically moody, perceptive and beautiful.[13]

Nevertheless, the show was considered a relative failure. Rodgers said in a later interview that it was the one show he disliked. If you start with a bad idea, he explained, everything becomes infected. Moreover, the characters were not right for Rodgers and Hammerstein: "We shouldn't have been dealing with prostitutes and tramps." In his autobiography, he concluded that the show was more a failure of expectations. Because audiences expected something else from the team, they were cool toward it.

Their chagrin could not have been mitigated by the fact that they had passed up an opportunity to write and produce *Fanny*. Joshua Logan and the producer,

David Merrick, who was then making his New York debut, made the offer in 1953. Hammerstein liked the idea, but for some reason Rodgers refused to collaborate with Merrick. The music and lyrics for *Fanny* were finally written by Harold Rome; Ezio Pinza and Florence Henderson were the leads. The show opened in November 1954, a year before *Pipe Dream*, and ran for two years.

At about this time an eight-week revival of *On Your Toes* prompted an interesting commentary by the respected critic Eric Bentley. He wrote that if asked to pick the one man who could do the most to provide a good musical, "I would reply: Richard Rodgers." Bentley explained that he did not necessarily approve of the trend of Rodgers and Hammerstein's productions; indeed, he feared that Hammerstein's soul was in peril because he was trying to create the "musical-that-is-more-than-a-musical." Bentley believed that there had been a change in public opinion since the 1940s; supposedly people no longer wanted comedy. Bentley deplored this trend and noted that Rodgers' *On Your Toes* provided the "breath of a less stuffy generation." What had been lost in the 1940s and early 1950s was recaptured in the earlier Rodgers show: "namely, a cocky, satirical, devil-may-care philosophy that [was] certainly very attractive and possibly useful." *On Your Toes* was, he concluded, true musical comedy.[14]

Rodgers and Hammerstein would not return to true musical comedy. Nevertheless, on March 15, 1956, three months after *Pipe Dream* opened, Broadway was stunned by *My Fair Lady*. Rodgers and Hammerstein had toyed with the Pygmalion story and given it up, as had many others, but Alan Jay Lerner and Frederick Loewe mastered it. How ironic that the form created and perfected by Rodgers and Hammerstein was brought to its climax by two other writers. The success of the show signaled that the Hammerstein and Rodgers era was fading, though no one would have been so bold as to suggest it. *Pipe Dream* closed in June 1956, and for the first time since the opening of *Oklahoma!* in 1943, there were no Rodgers and Hammerstein productions on Broadway.

20

CINDERELLA

In the mid-1950s, the names Rodgers and Hammerstein still appeared on marquees, but not those at the St. James or the Majestic. Instead, they were in lights at the Paramount or Roxy movie houses, where their great Broadway hits were reemerging on film.

The film version of *Carousel* was produced by 20th Century–Fox and starred Shirley Jones and Gordon MacRae. Frank Sinatra had been signed for the part of Billy, but he dropped out on the day that filming was to begin. It was probably a wise decision on his part, for it is a stretch to imagine him as Billy Bigelow. In any case, the reviews were favorable, noting that the stars remained Rodgers and Hammerstein, whose work was still fresh and appealing. During the preparation for *Carousel*, Rodgers and Hammerstein received complaints from the so-called Breen office, which monitored the morality of films. There were two directives about the script: that Billy Bigelow could not commit suicide and that Billy and Jigger could not plot the cold-blooded murder of Mr. Bascombe (because they were portrayed as sympathetic characters). In both cases the story was adjusted: Billy "falls" on his knife, and Billy and Jigger plan only a robbery. In any case, Rodgers disliked the movie version.

Reviews of their movies were also an occasion for the commentators to praise the original once again. Hollis Alpert, writing for the *Saturday Review of Literature* (March 15, 1956), offered this judgment: "I suspect that when future historians try to decide what constituted native American opera in our time they'll have to give some careful consideration to *Carousel*. In that case this movie version should be very helpful."

In the meantime Rodgers and Hammerstein had moved on to the new frontier, television. In 1954 the General Foods Corporation sponsored a CBS television special featuring the best-known songs of the team. It was to be carried by 256 stations, in the largest commercial hookup ever. According to ballyhoo that preceded the show, the extravaganza cost at least $500,000. The program included Jack Benny, Edgar Bergen and Charlie McCarthy, and Groucho Marx, who played a game on *You Bet Your Life* with Rodgers and Hammerstein as the contestants. Marx professed to believe that Rodgers was really the cowboy Roy Rogers. The ninety-minute show featured Gordon MacRae, singing "Oh, What a Beautiful Mornin'"; John Raitt and Jan Clayton, singing "If I Loved You"; and Mary Martin, singing "It Might as Well Be Spring." In the middle of the show, Martin and Ezio Pinza did "Some Enchanted Evening."

Rodgers was pleased with the program, but reviewers were less than enchanted. Jack Gould called it a "heartbreaking disappointment." The show was too slow and lacked the "gaiety, warmth and light touch vital to exciting theatre." He offered a left-handed tribute to the authors, however, noting that to do only excerpts from Rodgers and Hammerstein's shows might be unfair to the composers. As the "two men who had revitalized the American musical play, their achievements have much more meaning in the whole than in bits and pieces."

In April 1955, Rodgers donated his original handwritten scores to the Library of Congress, where they still reside. The music critic Deems Taylor, who opened an exhibition of the collection, remarked on the charming simplicity of Rodgers' manuscripts and songs—there were never any flourishes or offbeat dissonances. "That's part of Rodgers' secret of success," he said. "He can take one note and build a whole song around it without boring anybody." Taylor was both a friend and an admirer. In his biography of the team, *Some Enchanted Evening: The Story of Rodgers and Hammerstein*, published in 1953, he referred to them as "two talented people of whom I am very fond and whom I admire inordinately." While Rodgers and Hammerstein were on leave from Broadway their work had become an annual feature at the outdoor summer concerts at Lewisohn Stadium, on the Upper West Side of New York. One evening in late July 1956, some eighteen thousand came to hear a selection from their shows.

At one concert, Mrs. Charles Guggenheim, the sponsor of the concerts, made an appeal for "Money. Lots of It." Richard and Dorothy Rodgers were no strangers to philanthropic appeals. In 1956 Dorothy became a trustee of the Federation of Jewish Philanthropies of New York. Richard Rodgers was honored at a fund-raising affair for two institutions of American Reform Judaism: the Union of American Hebrew Congregations and the Hebrew Union College–Jewish Institute of Religion. At the award dinner at the Waldorf-Astoria, Rodgers was honored for his great contribution to the "happiness of the American people."

He was also honored, once again, by his alma mater, Columbia University. Along with Hammerstein he received the Alexander Hamilton Alumni Award, presented at another dinner at the Waldorf. The president of Columbia, Grayson Kirk, was on hand to lend an "academic sanction to the rollicking affair." Naturally he lauded both: "These two men may not realize it, but they know more than many a learned doctor about the cure for the tensions of our time." The dinner menu featured such delicacies as "Carousel of Fresh Tropical Fruits, South Pacific," and "Prime Ribs of State Fair Blue Ribbon Boar," with "fresh Oklahoma mushrooms."

This particular affair produced a long double interview with the honorees, published in the *New York Times* (April 5, 1956) under the headline "The G. & S. of Broadway." The reporter noted that Rodgers had brown eyes that could clearly register anything from "mischief and angelic charm to penetrating shrewdness." He was "impeccable in dress and speech, efficient and smooth in business," and he had the "air of a man long used to success."

Rodgers and Hammerstein may have been honored and acclaimed in New York, but farther south, it was a different story. Two members of the Georgia legislature denounced *South Pacific* as "propaganda" and announced their intention to introduce legislation to prohibit the showing of movies or plays that had an "underlying philosophy inspired by Moscow." The charge of propaganda was provoked by the song "You've Got To Be Carefully Taught," which the legislators believed urged interracial marriage. Hammerstein responded that they were right in thinking that the song was a protest against racial prejudice. He added that he was surprised by the idea that anything kind and humane "must necessarily originate in Moscow." Rodgers had no comment that was recorded.

He was embroiled in a different controversy. Rodgers was a member of the board of the Philharmonic Society of New York, the parent organization of the orchestra. The 1955–56 season was a financial disaster, marking the orchestra's largest gross deficit (over $500,000). That led to a management shake-up, and a new managing director was appointed. The artistic criticism focused on the lack of unity in the orchestra's season. It was a fortuitous collection of guest conductors and soloists, with no underlying theme. In September 1956, Rodgers was appointed to a special committee to study the musical aspects of the organization's problems.

The big news, however, was that Rodgers and Hammerstein were venturing into television. They decided to take the plunge for one simple reason—Julie Andrews. She was Broadway's newest luminescent as the star of My Fair Lady, and her agent wanted to exploit her new status. Television was emerging as a more varied medium, and a live musical seemed a perfect vehicle. The proposed story, "Cinderella," also seemed a perfect match. CBS was interested, especially in light of NBC's success with Mary Martin playing Peter Pan in 1955. The network paid Rodgers and Hammerstein $300,000, gave them the rights to subsequent shows, and turned over the production to the R&H organization.

In September, Hammerstein began writing the book. The team had decided to play the story as a traditional costumed fairy tale; their only changes were to make Cinderella's stepmother and stepsisters more comical. Rodgers and Hammerstein approached the project as if it were a Broadway show, even though it was telecast on only one night. The cast was carefully selected for both acting and singing abilities: Howard Lindsay, the playwright, and his wife, Dorothy Stickney, played the king and queen; they were presented as concerned, slightly befuddled parents who were determined to find a proper wife for their son. Cinderella's sisters were played by Alice Ghostley and Kaye Ballard, who enhanced the comic aspects of their characters, and the stepmother was played by Ilka Chase. The role of the prince was sung by a man with the unfortunate name of Jon Cypher. The fairy godmother was played by Edie Adams. The producer for CBS was Richard Lewine, a cousin of Rodgers', and the director was Ralph Nelson. It was billed:

Tonight at the stroke of 8
the first television production by
America's most famous composer-librettist team

The production schedule was arranged so that a dress rehearsal could be filmed on kinescope, giving the authors, producer, and director the equivalent of a New Haven tryout. The same process was repeated later, which in effect constituted a Boston tryout. Only one number was cut. Hammerstein found writing for television easier than writing for Broadway: entrances and exits did not have to be staged, intimacy could be created by camera angles, and there was no strain to project the lyrics to the last balcony. The orchestra was much larger, as was the number of technicians. Because it was a live production, however, timing was something of a problem.

Rodgers insisted that there was no difference between writing for a mass audience and for the theater. "If you try to write for anybody but yourself you fall flat on your face," Rodgers said before the telecast. "There's no formula. If our taste coincides with the public's you're a success." Even before the show was aired Rodgers speculated that they might do another. "I'm willing to try anything. I wouldn't even be afraid to write a night club show. It would be exciting and different. I once did, in 1926 as a matter of fact. It was lots of fun and a tremendous failure."[1]

Cinderella provides a good example of the process of producing a song. The script called for a love song between the prince and Cinderella ("Do I Love You Because You're Beautiful?"). It was Hammerstein's idea that the prince be perplexed: Did he love her because she was beautiful, or was she beautiful because he loved her? Once Hammerstein set that line, he had to follow it with other couplets, going through dozens of similar variants. An early version was

> Is your smile a stolen sunbeam from the skies,
> or has my heart been throwing mist in my eyes?

Finally he settled on:

> Am I making believe I see in you
> a girl too lovely to be really true?

Hammerstein gave this version to Rodgers, who wrote the music for it.

Still, Hammerstein questioned his own line "Am I making believe" because it seemed too unimportant as an expression of love.[2] He proposed:

> Am I telling my heart I see in you
> A girl too lovely to be really true?

Rodgers replied that the phrase "making believe" worked well. Moreover, "to be really true" sounded too much like a split infinitive. Hammerstein was naturally provoked by the charge of a split infinitive and proposed to drop "really," which required dropping two musical notes. Rodgers wrapped up the episode by proposing that they thrash it out when they met in person (Hammerstein had gone to Australia with his wife). The upshot was that "Am I making believe" stayed in the song, as did the so-called split infinitive. In his autobiography, Rodgers commented that although an outsider might find this exchange hairsplitting, the authors felt that "an inexact note or an imprecise word" ruined the desired effect.

The score was scintillating, and, as one might expect of Rodgers and Hammerstein, carefully integrated into the story line. The opening, "In My Own Little Corner," begins with a melancholy verse establishing Cinderella's plight in the scullery but forecasts the miracle that is to come. "Impossible," a duet between Cinderella and her fairy godmother (Edie Adams), was a second delightful melody. Contrary to the traditional version of the tale, the godmother tries to discourage Cinderella from attending the ball because it is "impossible." But she then concludes that "impossible things are happening every day." Rodgers returned to the waltz form with "Ten Minutes Ago" (one of his better waltzes), sung by the prince. There is also an instrumental waltz played at the royal ball that naturally invited comparison with Lerner and Loewe's in My Fair Lady. "Cinderella's Waltz" was as good as Lerner and Loewe's, perhaps better, and the brief "Gavotte" from Cinderella is only slightly less witty and bouncing than the music for the famous racing scene in My Fair Lady.

One suspects that both Rodgers and Hammerstein were sensitive to comparisons of Julie Andrews in My Fair Lady. James Michener, returning from a extended stay abroad, found that My Fair Lady was being compared to South Pacific and wrote a stout defense of his work and of Rodgers and Hammerstein.

Of course, a ninety-minute television show was not comparable to a full-scale Broadway production, but the music and lyrics were first-rate—which was a distinct improvement over Me and Juliet and Pipe Dream. Aware that the music would be heard only once, Rodgers had arranged to have a recording issued before the telecast. He explained that the music for Oklahoma! or South Pacific would have been "pretty tough" to sell had it been heard on only one evening. Consequently, the music for Cinderella enjoyed some popularity (his favorite was "Do I Love You Because You're Beautiful?"). Rodgers also commented that one had to be "damn careful" with television: "If you're not—it's murder. One mistake and sixty million people see it."

The reviews were not enthusiastic. Television reviewers criticized the changes in the sisters' personalities and in general found the production was thin and slow. The music and theater critics, though irritated by the commercial interruptions, were more impressed. Rodgers received major accolades (helped by the preproduction release of the songs). Irving Kolodin wrote in the *Saturday Review of Literature* that it was "in large part high-grade Rodgers and Hammerstein with such cleverly rhymed lyrics as 'Impossible,' 'Lovely Night' and 'In My Own Little Corner' set to music which attests to Rodgers's continued success in wooing the muse and improving the 'inspirational' elements by many skillful devices." According to *Time* (March 25, 1957), Rodgers was the "hero of the evening" and gave a better imitation of Richard Rodgers than anyone else. Some carped that the lyrics and music were too sugary and should have been punched up as they might have been on Broadway. But as Kaye Ballard commented, "After all, it is *Cinderella*."

One aspect of the show that pleased Rodgers was the large viewing audience, estimated by CBS at more than 100 million. Rodgers calculated that it had taken five years for four million people to see *Oklahoma!* and that *Cinderella* would have to run 107 years for that same 100 million to see it on stage. A version of *Cinderella* did appear briefly in London, and in 1965 the entire show was repeated on television; this time, however, it was put on videotape, which is still available. In that version Rodgers added "Loneliness of Evening" (dropped from *South Pacific*) and "Boys and Girls like You and Me," one of his first songs with Hammerstein (dropped from *Oklahoma!*). In that revival Cinderella was played by Lesley Ann Warren and the queen by Ginger Rogers, who even danced a little.

Subsequent theater productions were often criticized because the show was simply not designed for a large stage. One, the 1993 production by the New York City Opera, was relatively successful, possibly because Steve Allen had rewritten the book. For this, the song "My Best Love," from *Flower Drum Song*, was added. Cinderella, a reviewer noted, was the one character in fairy-tale lore who was a prime Rodgers-and-Hammerstein-style heroine; she was "a cockeyed optimist who climbs every mountain until she finds her dream." A review of another revival at the City Center in November 1995 noted that the evening belonged to Rodgers and Hammerstein: "Rodgers wrote few melodies as waltzingly beautiful as 'Ten Minutes Ago,'" and Hammerstein's lyrics reminded listeners that he was Stephen Sondheim's most important mentor.

As it turned out, the ebullient spirit of *Cinderella* was not a reflection of Rodgers' mood. In spring 1957, Rodgers became aware of a "new and mystifying illness: depression." In his memoirs he wrote: "I began sleeping late, ducking appointments and withdrawing into long periods of silence. I lost all interest in my work and barely spoke either to Dorothy or to my children. I simply didn't give a dam about doing anything or seeing anyone. One of the most disturbing manifestations was that I began to drink."[3] His periods of withdrawal became longer and longer. Rodgers had no idea of the cause, though he was convinced that it was not the failure of *Pipe Dream*. His own diagnosis was that he had returned to work too soon after his jaw surgery. Moreover, he insisted that he did not drink to the point of alcoholism.

Nevertheless, in June 1957 he checked himself into the Payne Whitney Clinic, the foremost psychiatric facility in New York. Located on the grounds of New York Hospital along the East River, Payne Whitney had the look of an elegant hotel; the stylish furniture, marble floors, and elaborate fireplaces were offset, however, by barred windows and soundproof rooms.

Since its founding in 1932, Payne Whitney had treated many celebrities. In *The Group*, the novelist Mary McCarthy, a patient at one time, described the treatment of the elite on the fourth floor, which was more like a college dormitory: "The windows were not barred; the patients were not locked in; [and] they had regular visiting hours; they could turn off their lights when they wanted. . . . The patients were kept pretty busy in the daytime, but in the evening they played bridge until it was time for their hot chocolate or Ovaltine. There was a ping-pong table; twice a week they had movies.[4] The writer Jean Stafford, who was there for a year, wrote that although it was "a high class booby hatch," she could hear the "really disordered patients on the floor above, screaming, beating their heads on the floor." A high grill separated them from the "free world," and "you feel that at any moment passersby will toss us peanuts." She also described a "gruesome dance" in the gymnasium, "where all the crazy men met up with all the crazy women and danced to the music of a sedate four-piece orchestra."[5] Marilyn Monroe, an unwitting patient in 1961, sent by her psychiatrist, wrote, "They put me in a cell (I mean cement blocks and all). . . . I felt I was in some kind of prison."[6]

Whatever the experiences of others, for his part Rodgers found that once in the clinic, free from pressures and problems, he began to feel better. His spirits improved, and he became so well adjusted that he turned into something of a "doctor's helper." He had visitors, including Oscar Hammerstein, but he spent most of his time reading, playing cards, or chatting with other patients confined for similar reasons. His twelve-week stay passed quickly, and he returned home "as if nothing had happened."

Of course, something quite serious had happened, and there may have been signs along the way. It seems likely that Rodgers' operation, the resulting disfigurement of his jaw, and the long wait to discover whether the cancer had been checked created emotional tensions and a sense of crisis. His last two shows had been only moderately successful, there was no new show on the horizon, and the television special had been frustrating. Moreover, he and Hammerstein had apparently experienced a short-lived rift after the closing of *Pipe Dream*. As for drinking, his letters of the 1920s and early 1930s suggest that his fondness for liquor was something of a problem even then; during these years he had also been subject to occasional bouts of depression.

Some felt that his problem was provoked by watching his shows falter while those of other composers prospered—for example, Lerner and Lowe's *My Fair Lady*. Yet Rodgers was always secure in his talent and was never known to be jealous or spiteful. He was, in fact, generous in praising his colleagues.

It is most likely that Rodgers' depression was a hereditary affliction. He noted his own tendency toward hypochondria, which was apparently also a problem for his mother. The uncertainty over whether his cancer would return probably triggered his inherent depression. Creative people try to alleviate their depression by creating—that is, by working or writing or composing. But in the spring of 1957 there was no Rodgers and Hammerstein show on the horizon. His mental reaction was similar to his reaction in the early 1930s in Hollywood, when he found himself with no real assignments from the studio.

After Dorothy Rodgers' death her daughter Mary wrote a revealing introduction to a new edition of her father's memoirs: "When you come right down to it, my father was an extremely complicated man and deeply unhappy much of the time. (Chemically depressed is what we'd call it now; then, we didn't know what to call it, except tough to live with)."[7] The comment that he was deeply unhappy suggests darker psychological roots, perhaps reflecting the unhappiness of his childhood. Mary Rodgers also wrote that the "marvelous, rich emotional quality" of her father's music did not often manifest itself in his personality. He could be "quite sharp-tongued" with his children and sometimes "quite frightening when mad." She added that although he could be affectionate toward his children, after an obligatory "squeeze," the implication was that they should go away and not bother him. This comment is eerily reminiscent of Rodgers' description of his relationship with his mother: on "rare" occasions she would give his hand a gentle squeeze, but displays of affection did not come easily to her. Apparently they did not come easily to her son either.

While Rodgers was hospitalized, the film version of *South Pacific* began shooting on the Hawaiian island of Kauai. It was directed by Joshua Logan and starred

Mitzi Gaynor and Rossano Brazzi. Predictably, the overall result greatly disappointed Rodgers—*The King and I* was the only movie version of his work that he ever liked. During the final stages of the filming of *South Pacific*, Hammerstein encountered an old friend, the screenwriter Joseph Fields, the elder brother of Dorothy and Herbert Fields. At that time he was negotiating for the right to produce a version of a novel entitled *The Flower Drum Song*, by C. Y. Lee. The original story was about the patriarch of an immigrant Chinese family and his rebellious and Americanized son. Hammerstein was intrigued by the title and thought that the story had possibilities as a musical; Rodgers was skeptical but then concurred. Joseph Fields and Hammerstein agreed to collaborate on the book. Hammerstein ended up being the primary author, because Fields became ill.

Hammerstein conducted a correspondence with the author, quizzing him about various Chinese customs. The reworked story, set in San Francisco's Chinatown, departed significantly from Lee's book, which Hammerstein described as a sort of Chinese *Life with Father*. Fields and Hammerstein edged the father into the background and focused more on the story of Mei Li, a Chinese girl illegally brought to the United States. She has been selected as a picture bride by the bridegroom's mother, according to Chinese tradition, and arrived to marry Sammy Fong, a hustler who runs the Celestial Palace, a tawdry nightclub. Sammy has no interest in his picture bride because he has been living for five years with a "thoroughly Americanized" Chinese woman, Linda Low, who performs in his club.

He tries to extricate himself from his mother's marriage contract and offers his bride to the venerable Master Wang Chi-Yang for his son Wang Ta. It turns out, however, that Wang Ta is also infatuated by Linda Low. After some twists and turns, a romance between Mei Li and Wang Ta develops, and in the end they are united, as are Sammy and Linda. Thus, Rodgers and Hammerstein were once again writing about parallel romances. "Every light play has two kinds of women," Rodgers noted.

Casting was difficult, Rodgers said. The producers supposedly scoured the Chinatowns in San Francisco, Los Angeles, New York, and Boston. They found few Chinese-Americans capable of starring in a Broadway musical. In the end they recruited a Japanese-American, Miyoshi Umeki, to play the shy Mei Li, and Pat Suzuki, also Japanese and already a popular recording star, to play the brash Linda. The courtly Master Wang was played by Keye Luke, Charlie Chan's "number one" son. Larry Storch was initially cast as the disreputable Sammy Fong. The real stroke of genius was in choosing Gene Kelly as director; his dance director was Carol Haney.

Rehearsals were temporarily postponed when Hammerstein entered the hospital for surgery on his gall bladder. His absence proved a problem, because Kelly's direction turned out to be uncertain. The score was also ragged: one song did not seem to fit anywhere; one was discarded altogether; another, "Don't Marry Me," was written in one afternoon (disproving the belief that Hammerstein could not work at Rodgers' fast pace).

The overall theme was the confrontation between Far Eastern and American cultures. In this sense it was similar to the conflict in *The King and I*. As Rodgers put it, the story was "told in terms of the conflicts between first and second generation Chinese-Americans in San Francisco." This clash between the Americanized lifestyle of the young Chinese and the traditions of their parents allowed Rodgers to write in both a modern swing style and a pseudo-Chinese tone. Hammerstein spelled out the generational clash in a long, humorous song in which the older and younger generations ridicule each other. In the end the West seems to prevail, at least in the resolution of the story.

One of the major songs was "A Hundred Million Miracles," a so-called flower drum song, initially performed only to the accompaniment of the small Chinese drum traditionally decorated with flowers. Rodgers and Hammerstein agreed early on that the song would probably be "less traditional" than the lyrics in the Lee novel "because it must be made to serve the story more directly." In an early draft Hammerstein put down a reference to "A Hundred Million Miracles," but he did not supply a lyric for some months. The words he eventually wrote convey the idea that there could well be miracles every day—a sort of reprise of the spirit of "Impossible" in *Cinderella*.

The most enduring song was the love ballad "Love, Look Away." Hammerstein had written a rather long verse but found that he did not like Rodgers' music for it. Rather than confront his partner he quietly wrote another two-line verse. This incident was later cited as an example of how the partnership survived for so long; both men were adept at finding subtle ways to transcend their differences. (No doubt they did find such resolutions, but the verse to "Love, Look Away" is in fact ten bars long and has ten lines of lyrics).

There was even a striptease, "Fan Tan Fanny," and a strong swing number, "Grant Avenue." These modern numbers sound much like songs from Rodgers' earlier shows. He was able to re-create his trademark Asian flavor, this time using the semi-chant "a hundred million miracles," which had a Chinese sound when repeated without harmonic accompaniment. The same effect was created for the comical song "Chop Suey," which was performed with a Chinese accent by Juanita Hall, who also performed "Happy Talk" in *South Pacific*.

The show was in bad shape out of town. The cast was exhausted by the endless changes in dialogue and song. Kelly, who had almost given up as director, had to rely on gimmicks to save the show. After the show opened in Boston it was decided that Storch would be replaced because his comic style was not appropriate to the character of Sammy Fong. Rodgers was nominated to fire him. His replacement, Larry Blyden, however, was in the process of divorcing the dance director, Carol Haney. With the addition of Blyden, Hammerstein and Rodgers dropped one song and wrote a new one, "Don't Marry Me."

A reporter who followed the show from its inception wrote that the rehearsals "blended into sustained and absolute fatigue." At one intermission Rodgers rushed backstage complaining: "Terrible! It's slow, slow, slow." During rehearsals, "Rodgers sat stoically for hours admonishing a piercing oboe, or reminding the chorus of their diction during a complicated song. Occasionally he took a cat-nap at the back of the theatre. . . . At 3 a.m., seven hours after it began, the rehearsal was finished, and Rodgers, Hammerstein, Fields and Kelly solemnly retired to the Ritz."[8] The following evening, at the final dress rehearsal, all went well. Rodgers walked "soberly" up the aisle and hugged whoever was handy. Kelly told the cast they had done an "extraordinarily wonderful job," and Hammerstein said that it was a very gratifying evening—though "two days ago I wouldn't have bet on it." The "well-oiled machine" of Rodgers and Hammerstein rolled on, observed the reporter. Rodgers' view was reflected in a letter written after the first preview in Boston: "Things are very rosy this morning because of last night's audience reaction which could not have been better and today's notices which are equally enthusiastic. I think we'll come in with a big success."[9]

Rodgers was right. The show overcame any negative expectations that had arisen during the tryouts. *Flower Drum Song* opened on December 1, 1958, at the St. James Theatre, which had just been renovated, and ran for six hundred performances. Advance ticket sales amounted to $1.2 million, the largest ever for one of their shows. After the opening Hammerstein told his son that he had experienced some well-deserved hits and some unlucky flops, but *Flower Drum Song* was his first "lucky hit."

In spite of the long run on Broadway and a successful movie version, the score for *Flower Drum Song* never approached the popularity or durability of those for *South Pacific* and *The King and I*. One reason was the changing times. Popular music as written by Rodgers and Hammerstein now competed with newer, harsher songs and performers. Even Broadway shows were becoming rougher and tougher (for example, *West Side Story*).

The critics were pleased with *Flower Drum Song*, but they echoed a worrisome theme—that Rodgers and Hammerstein were repeating themselves. *Variety* praised the score but compared it with previous efforts: "Rodgers has written one of his melodious scores, and although the music sounds at moments vaguely reminiscent of some of his memorable past successes, it still has a lush texture and depth that no other contemporary legit composer can match." Even one of their strongest boosters, Brooks Atkinson, made the same observation in the *New York Times* (December 11, 1958): "Having been over similar ground before, Mr. Rodgers seems to have nothing more to contribute in the field of pseudo-Asian music. But he has written some wistful melodies and comic songs that are literate and entertaining." Roughly the same point was made by the *New Yorker* critic Kenneth Tynan: "What I saw before me simply was a stale Broadway confection wrapped up in spurious Chinese trimmings" (December 13, 1958). But Tynan raised another, more painful point about the show's approach to Asian culture: "The authors' attitude toward exotic peoples in general seems to have changed hardly at all since they wrote 'South Pacific' and 'The King and I.' If friendly, the natives have a simple, primitive, childlike sweetness. . . . It seems to have worried neither Mr. Rodgers nor Mr. Hammerstein very much that the behavior of war-torn Pacific islanders and nineteenth-century Siamese might be slightly different from that of Chinese residents of present-day California."

Years later, after the war in Vietnam, some critics even began to speculate whether idealizing the superficiality of the clash between East and West contributed to American errors in Vietnam. One writer claimed that the popularity of Rodgers and Hammerstein's "Oriental" shows rested on a conviction that all people were fundamentally the same, that culture was only skin deep.[10] A similar argument was made when *The King and I* was revived in 1996.

It is true that in all three of their so-called Oriental shows Hammerstein's philosophy was that people did not differ very much. He was dealing with romantic love, however, not intercultural sociology. The notion that East is East and West is West was "nonsense," Rodgers said. Their views reflected the classic liberalism of the 1950s and early 1960s. Moreover, Rodgers and Hammerstein's shows with an Asian story line had little to do with the geopolitical and anticommunist motives that led America into Vietnam. Such a radical political distortion of their musicals would probably have appalled them. Rodgers commented in 1958 that "we wanted to put together an entertaining show and we think we've done it."

For Rodgers, the success of *Flower Drum Song* was a tonic. It proved that he had overcome his breakdown. His only thought, he wrote later, was "to keep on doing what I was doing, and I saw nothing in the future that could stop me."

21

THE SOUND OF MUSIC

Ordinarily Rodgers and Hammerstein allowed two years between shows — one for rest and recuperation and one for the preparation of a new show. But this time they agreed on a new project even
before the opening of *Flower Drum Song*, largely at the urging of Mary
Martin. The project became *The Sound of Music*, their last show together.

After *Flower Drum Song* opened, another Rodgers musical opened
on Broadway, this one by his daughter Mary. *Once Upon a Mattress,* for
which she wrote the music, was based on the fairy tale "The Princess
and the Pea." Although both Mary and Linda Rodgers were musically talented, their father did not encourage them during their early
years; what he heard of Mary's teenage musical output he found
"embarrassing," she said. Later he decided that some of the children's
songs were "not so bad," and from that point on he supported her

efforts. The sisters wrote a mini-revue for children entitled "Three to Make Music," as part of a show starring Mary Martin. For this sketch Mary Rodgers wrote the lyrics and Linda the music.

Dorothy Rodgers was strict with her daughters, and Mary rebelled. In her memoirs Dorothy reports that they had a "very stormy time during her childhood and teenage years." There were the usual disputes over what Mary and Linda wore and the pleas to keep their rooms neat. Dorothy Rodgers later wrote of the difficulties experienced by both children and parents in the family of a famous person. She believed that the children inevitably resent the achievements of the successful parent and end up desperately searching for their own identity. After their children were grown Dorothy wrote that she and her husband did not share their children's lives "very often."

In the 1970s, however, Mary and her mother wrote a joint column for *McCall's* magazine, "Of Two Minds," in which they offered advice to mothers and wives. Dorothy, a classic liberal, emerged as rather conservative, whereas Mary's contributions were witty and pointed—for example, she conferred the Greed Award on one letter writer. In one column Mary Rodgers divided society into "downers" and those who are forced to console them. Her mother found this a "lovely caricature" but too categorical. Mary Rodgers published several successful children's stories, notably *Freaky Friday* (1972) and *A Billion for Boris* (1974).

She studied music at the Mannes School of Music in Manhattan and then decided to enter Wellesley (her mother's alma mater), where she wrote student shows, much as her father had at Columbia. Bored by the academic life, she quit, as her mother had done. She then worked as an assistant to Leonard Bernstein in his Young People's Concerts and went on to write, with Marshall Barer, *Once Upon a Mattress* for the Poconos resort Tamiment. The show, which was performed by professional actors and musicians from New York, attracted the attention of George Abbott, who proposed directing it on Broadway. The Broadway version, starring the newcomer Carol Burnett, opened to good reviews: "Mary Rodgers has written a highly enjoyable score" was Brooks Atkinson's verdict. She was nominated for a Tony and thus was in competition with her father, who assiduously disclaimed any role in promoting his daughter's show, to the point of refusing to pose for a photograph of himself at the piano with Mary listening; he insisted on the reverse.

As *Once Upon a Mattress* opened on Broadway in May 1959, Rodgers and Hammerstein were well into their new show, based on the story of the von Trapp family's escape from Nazi-occupied Austria. Maria von Trapp had written her story some years earlier and was living in Vermont. A friend of Mary Martin's, the director Vincent Donehue, had seen a German film of the story while working for Paramount Pictures. Although Donehue knew that Paramount was considering the story for Audrey Hepburn, he believed that it would be a perfect vehicle for Martin. He reasoned that because the Trapp Singers had gained international fame as a performing group, Martin could use the folk music of the Austrian Alps as background for a dramatic love story between the young Maria and Captain Georg von Trapp.

Martin and her husband, Richard Halliday, embraced the project, and their theatrical lawyer set about the arduous task of securing the rights from Maria von Trapp and her seven stepchildren. Leland Hayward joined as coproducer and recruited Howard Lindsay and Russel Crouse to do the book. They had won the Pulitzer Prize for *State of the Union* and had written *Call Me Madam* for Irving Berlin. At some point Martin suggested to Rodgers that he and Hammerstein supply one or two new songs in addition to the Austrian folk songs. They turned down the offer, commenting that they did not wish to compete with Mozart (the von Trapp villa was near Salzburg).

Meanwhile, Lindsay and Crouse wrote a long outline that was acceptable to Martin. With this outline in hand the group again turned to Rodgers and Hammerstein, who this time suggested that all the music be original. They decided to write the score, but because they could not disentangle themselves from *Flower Drum Song*, everyone agreed to wait for a year.

In spring 1959, Rodgers and Hammerstein began work on the new play, the first show that Hammerstein did not have to write or adapt. He seemed relieved to be spared this chore and remarked that he would have stopped writing the book for musicals long ago had he been able to count on writers as talented as Lindsay and Crouse.

In the story, Maria is a postulant in the abbey of Nonnberg and is having trouble adjusting to the religious life. The abbess directs her to take a leave of absence to serve as governess to the family of Captain Georg von Trapp, a widower with seven children. The captain is a stern disciplinarian who summons his children with a boatswain's whistle, whereas Maria is a free and gentle spirit. Although they initially clash over their differing approaches to the children, they eventually fall in love and are married. The Nazis occupy Austria and demand that von Trapp join the German navy; he refuses and plots the escape of his family, using a singing contest as a ruse.

Using the Lindsay and Crouse synopsis, Rodgers and Hammerstein laid out the songs. Again their tentative list of titles differed from the final version. Early in the first act, for example, they listed two songs, titled simply "Sad Song" and

"Happy Song." As Rodgers and Hammerstein went to work Lindsay and Crouse were diverted to another play of their own, which soon failed. While waiting for the authors to resume work, Hammerstein went to Jamaica, where he had rented a villa. There he wrote the lyrics to the title song and sketched some of the lyrics for "Climb Ev'ry Mountain." He began this song with an explanatory note pointing out that love actually is not blind, and initially he titled it "Face Life." That Hammerstein could conjure the images of these songs in the incongruous setting of Montego Bay is a testimony not only to the artist's craft but to Hammerstein's experience. Perhaps it was not as difficult as it seemed. After all, Jerome Kern had written "Ol' Man River" in Bronxville; Richard Rodgers had written "Bali Ha'i" in a Manhattan apartment; and Hammerstein had supplied lyrics to both without ever seeing the Mississippi or the South Pacific.

The final version of the famous title song emerged more slowly.[1] Hammerstein's original lyric for the refrain was

The hillside is sweet
Today the air is sweet with summer music.

"Summer music" then became the "sound of summer" and, finally, the "sound of music." Even Hammerstein's final version was changed to accommodate the play and the music. Hammerstein had written

The hills fill my heart
with the sound of music.

But the final version as performed read:

The hills are alive
with the sound of music.

Shortly after Hammerstein returned from Jamaica, Lindsay and Crouse started the full libretto. In the process, they turned to Hammerstein for help in expressing the new romantic involvement between Captain von Trapp and Maria, and Rodgers and Hammerstein wrote the duet "An Ordinary Couple." Mary Martin later commented that she liked the lyrics but not the music, because the song went "downhill" (the melody line does descend). The reverse pattern was used in an early song describing Maria's spirited personality. In this instance Hammerstein borrowed some of the dialogue for his lyrics, as he had done with great success in both Oklahoma! and Carousel. On the whole, however, his lyrics for The Sound of Music were original.

As with almost every Rodgers and Hammerstein production, the opening

Richard Rodgers in 1959, about the time
of *The Sound of Music*.

scene is unusual. This show begins with a "preludium" set in the abbey. The
chapel bells ring solemnly as the nuns begin to chant their evening prayers.
While singing, they anxiously await the arrival of Maria, who is habitually late.
Rodgers, in writing the opening music, consulted the nun who headed the
music department at Manhattanville College, in Purchase, New York. She invited
him to services, where he absorbed the atmosphere for the opening preludium.

The next scene reveals Maria on a mountainside, surveying the surrounding
hills from atop a tree. As she sings the title song, the tree sweeps forward on the
stage. Mary Martin was always somewhat uncomfortable with this potentially
dangerous trick, and Leland Hayward warned Rodgers and Hammerstein of the
physical risks of this scene. Two years later, however, when Martin saw her role
performed by Florence Henderson in the touring company, she realized how
dramatic her entrance had been.

When Maria finally returns to the abbey, too late for the evening vespers, she is mildly reprimanded by the Mother Abbess, who has already debated Maria's suitability for the religious life with the other nuns. They sing "How Do You Solve a Problem Like Maria?" in which she is variously described:

> She is gentle,
> She is wild,
> She's a riddle,
> She's a child.

The result is that Maria is temporarily detached from the abbey, but before she leaves, she and the Mother Abbess sing "My Favorite Things." At first Hammerstein experimented with a line that began "These are the things I like." Then he turned to a list song and in the process made several long lists of rhymes: clings, kings, rings, sings, strings, swings, and wings. He composed a similar list for mittens and kittens. It became a delightful song that displayed Hammerstein at his most evocative.[2] The first chorus runs:

> Raindrops on roses and whiskers on kittens,
> Bright copper kettles and warm woolen mittens,
> Brown paper packages tied up with strings —
> These are a few of my favorite things.

Maria arrives at the von Trapp villa to find that the children, neglected by their father, are resentful of yet another governess. They are set to rebel but quickly form a strong attachment to Maria. In "Do-Re-Mi" she gives them their music lesson, and in "Sixteen Going on Seventeen," she advises the oldest daughter, Liesl, who is smitten by a young boy, Rolf. During a thunderstorm Maria comforts the children by singing "The Lonely Goatherd," in which she repeatedly yodels (in the movie version this is replaced by "My Favorite Things," which is more effective).

Maria teaches the children to sing "The Sound of Music" as a group, and when the captain hears them he is deeply touched and joins in. At a party for Captain von Trapp's fiancée, Elsa Schraeder, Maria dances the Laendler, a folk dance, with the captain, and they realize that they are falling in love. Maria flees back to the abbey, where she confesses her plight to the Mother Abbess, who advises her in song to return and face her destiny, to "Climb Ev'ry Mountain."

In the second act, von Trapp's fiancée and his friend Max Detweiler try to persuade him to be ready to accommodate the new Nazi regime ("No Way to Stop It"). Von Trapp is adamantly opposed, and Elsa, recognizing that their differences are too deep, breaks their engagement. Maria returns to the villa, and she and the captain acknowledge their love for each other ("An Ordinary Couple"). After their marriage, Austria is consumed by the *Anschluss*. It turns out that Liesl's boyfriend is a Nazi. Moreover, the German government insists that von Trapp accept a commission in the Nazi navy. He is determined to resist, and with Maria plans an escape. That night, at a singing contest, the family members perform as a group and then exit one by one. They flee to the abbey, where they are discovered by Rolf, who decides to look the other way. They then make their way to the hills, and as the curtain falls they all sing "Climb ev'ry mountain . . . Till you find your dream!"

There were special considerations in dramatizing the story. To begin with, Maria von Trapp was still alive, and Mary Martin was careful to consult her and cultivate her friendship. Mrs. von Trapp was particularly impressed with the kindliness of Oscar Hammerstein. When she read the full libretto she was overwhelmed: it was "one of the highlights of my life," she told Richard Halliday. She did complain that her husband was depicted as too Prussian.

The first few scenes in the abbey also had to be carefully handled. Martin consulted her close friend Sister Gregory, of Rosary College, near Chicago. Sister Gregory assured them that life in the abbey was not as dull and dreary as they might imagine, but she pleaded that they not have the nuns giggle in the early scenes. She encouraged the song "My Favorite Things" and urged Rodgers to write an original chant for the opening and even supplied the Latin words for it. Like Maria von Trapp, she felt that the character of the captain was too cold.

The role of the nuns provided some moments of hilarity. During tryouts in Boston, a few cast members, fully costumed in nuns' habits, went across the street to a restaurant for a drink or two while they awaited their call. Naturally, passersby were horrified. When some real-life nuns appeared backstage as the guests of Mary Martin, they were hustled to the dressing rooms by an unwitting stage manager.

The team also had to avoid turning the story into a Viennese operetta. Lindsay observed, "We're in operetta country with this show. The minute you have a waltz you're sunk."[3] Mary Martin and Theodore Bikel, who played Captain von Trapp, were definitely not Jeanette MacDonald and Nelson Eddy, but some disappointed critics noted that the show had "succumb[ed] to the cliches" of an operetta. The authors and songwriters also tried to avoid overindulging in sentimentality, especially with regard to the children. Again, they were not completely successful, as a number of critics pointed out. Brooks Atkinson, writing for the *New York Times* (November 17, 1959), concluded that without Martin's "bright personality and guileless voice," the story could have become "sticky." In any case, he wrote, after a "joyous" beginning, the play "gradually drifts off into operetta routines."

There was also the problem of the Nazis. In the New Haven and Boston try-outs, the idea of the Nazis pursuing the von Trapps seemed too melodramatic. When pressed on this point, Rodgers argued that having Nazis in the play was not a problem. "After all," he commented, "whom are we going to offend, people who like Nazis?"[4] But they decided to keep the Nazis out of sight, making them even more menacing than they had been onstage, Rodgers said.

This score was a major musical undertaking for Rodgers. There were forty-seven musical episodes, compared with thirty-one for *Carousel* and nineteen for *Pal Joey*. The foreign setting meant that Rodgers again had to create an ambience through the music. To do so, he employed one mountain song, "The Lonely Goatherd," the melody of which was based on a yodel, and an instrumental for the dance, the "Laendler."

"The Sound of Music" and "Climb Ev'ry Mountain" are splendid examples of Rodgers' style and talent. The dramatic mode of "Climb Ev'ry Mountain" is reminiscent of such earlier songs by Rodgers and Hammerstein as "You'll Never Walk Alone"; these songs are inspirational in tone and rise in a final crescendo. The music for "Climb Ev'ry Mountain" is marked "with deep feeling, like a prayer." Accordingly, there is a hymnlike quality to the melody. The solemn style of such music customarily involves basic, open harmonies, but Rodgers intro-duced a chromatic in the melody and harmony. Moreover, he supplied a novel ending: the music swells in volume and is sustained by five strongly emphasized notes—"till you find your dream!"—creating a feeling of triumph.

This was inspired craftsmanship. Listeners appreciate that they are experienc-ing the work of an accomplished professional, one who takes the care to create a melodic statement wedded to the drama of the play and imagery of the lyrics. There was none better at this melding than Richard Rodgers.

As in many Rodgers and Hammerstein plays, the second act had only two new songs. But the final song, "Edelweiss," sung before the reprise of "Climb Ev'ry Mountain," was to be the last ever written by the team of Richard Rodgers and Oscar Hammerstein. Many believed it to be an old folk song, so convincing were the feeling and simplicity of the music. One woman commented to Rodgers that she had known that song all of her life, but in German. The melody was, in fact, original Rodgers. The idea for the song had come about as tryouts progressed in New Haven and Boston. Theodore Bikel was a fine folk singer, but the duets and ensemble numbers that he had been given did not make full use of his talent.

Moreover, the final, tragic scene seemed to call for a political statement, preferably musical, as Captain von Trapp is about to flee his beloved country.

Rodgers devised a simple melody for Bikel to sing, accompanied only by his guitar. "Edelweiss" is a thirty-two-bar waltz with no tricks or innovations. Bikel learned the melody, and Hammerstein wrote the final lyric in Boston. According to Bikel, however, Rodgers and Hammerstein adjourned to a room offstage and wrote the entire song in an hour. Whatever the case, Hammerstein used the mountain flower edelweiss as his theme and ended on a patriotic note: "Bless my homeland forever."

The show required the normal work out of town. Rodgers ended up playing a major role in shaping the performance because Hammerstein was recovering from an operation. Bikel found Rodgers a witty companion to the cast, calling his humor quite impish and at times "raunchy." He found Mary Martin a trifle distant and overly dependent on her husband. Martin "adored the show" and believed in it so much that she was the principal investor in the original production. She called *The Sound of Music* a "triumph of audience over critics."[5]

The show opened in New York on November 16, 1959, at the Lunt-Fontanne Theatre. Some critics were harsh, though not as harsh as both Martin and Bikel later recalled. And a few were positive, hailing Rodgers' score his "freshest" since *The King and* I. The story was judged too sentimental, criticism that Rodgers and Hammerstein brusquely rejected. Walter Kerr wrote: "Before the play is halfway through its promising chores, it becomes not only too sweet for words, but almost too sweet for music." When Noel Coward saw the show much later, he wrote in his diary:

> It was embarrassing at moments, mainly owing to some of the late Oscar's lyrics being sawney and arch, but the music was lovely, the sets superb, the story straightforward and the performance fine. Mary Martin, although much too old to play a roguish young postulant, was wonderful and at moments genuinely moving. There were too many nuns careening about and crossing themselves and singing jaunty little songs, and there *was*, I must admit, a heavy pall of Jewish-Catholic schmaltz enveloping the whole thing, but it was far more professional, melodic and entertaining than any of the other musicals I've seen.[6]

Kenneth Tynan described the show as "Rodgers's and Hammerstein's Great Leap Backward," an allusion to Communist China's Great Leap Forward, which occurred about this time.

The show had run up advance sales of over $2 million and caught the public's fancy despite the mixed reviews. It became a huge success, running for 1,443 performances. Rodgers believed that some shows became hits no matter what the reviews, and in this case *The Sound of Music* succeeded largely by word of mouth. Another reason, Rodgers suggested, was that in the case of hits, the original performers—true stars such as Mary Martin, Ezio Pinza, and Yul Brunner—created an immediate bond with the audiences from which all subsequent performances benefited. Again defending sentimentality, he said that there was nothing in *The Sound of Music* to offend anyone "except a fake intellectual"; only people who struck an "intellectual attitude" couldn't afford to like it. "They are the only dissenters," he told an interviewer as the show settled into its third year. Ironically, it was the film version rather than the theatrical version that is best remembered. The history of the film paralleled the history of the stage show: a dubious reception ballooned into an enormous success.

In 1960 the authors and producers sold the rights to 20th Century–Fox for more than $1.8 million and 10 percent of the gross, but on the condition that the movie could not be released before 1964. The studio soon shut down owing to a financial crisis; it reopened under the leadership of Darryl Zanuck and his son, Richard, who produced the movie version. Robert Wise, an Academy Award winner for *West Side Story*, was the director. Ernest Lehman wrote the script. He talked beforehand with Rodgers, who caustically commented that he assumed they would hire Doris Day. But Lehman replied that only Julie Andrews could play the part; Rodgers just looked at Lehman "with those rich melodic steely eyes" and said, "So what else is new"?[7]

Andrews' performance as Maria was the strongest attraction of the production. The movie, which was filmed partly in Salzburg, cost over $8 million, a great gamble for a studio close to bankruptcy. Two songs were dropped, others were shifted about: Maria sings "My Favorite Things" to the Trapp children rather than with the abbess, as in the original. Rodgers wrote the music and lyrics for two new songs, which were serviceable but not particularly distinguished: Maria sings "I Have Confidence" on her way to the von Trapp villa and "Something Good" to explain her good fortunate in marrying the captain. The melody of the latter is interesting, but Rodgers' lyrics are odd. The opening line, "Perhaps I had a wicked childhood," seems a strange sentiment for the joyous Maria.

The score was reorchestrated by Irwin Kostal, whose lush treatment won him an Academy Award. The film score gained much in grandeur but lost much in charm (for example, the simple but effective treatment of "Edelweiss" in the theater and the overblown version of the film).

Following a preview of the film in Minneapolis, the audience stood and cheered, and Zanuck and Wise realized that they might have a hit. Some of the New York critics were vicious, however. Brendan Gill, in the *New Yorker*, called the movie a "huge, tasteless blowup of the celebrated Rodgers and Hammerstein musical. . . . Even the handful of authentic location shots have a hokey studio sheen." Other such attacks followed. Nevertheless, the film began to draw audiences, and over time it became one of the largest money-makers in film history, ranking second only to *Gone With the Wind* until the 1980s. Rodgers, of course, was delighted with this surprising commercial turn.

The success of the original Broadway show was overshadowed by the dark cloud of Hammerstein's illness. Shortly after rehearsals began, doctors hospitalized him in order to perform surgery on his recently diagnosed stomach cancer. The operation was described as successful. In fact it was not. For a time the truth was concealed even from Hammerstein. Before entering the hospital he had informed the cast of his operation, which caused him to miss the out-of-town tryouts in New Haven and most of the early performances in Boston. When he finally did see the show there, he was deeply touched.

Despite the success of the show, there were grim days ahead. Rodgers and Hammerstein and their wives spent several weeks in London supervising the British version of *Flower Drum Song*. Rodgers kept up a pretense of talking about new shows and other business for the future. They even discussed a new film version of *State Fair*. By the early summer of 1960 Hammerstein began to withdraw from public life. He said his good-byes, and at a final luncheon with Richard Rodgers at the Oak Room of the Plaza Hotel, he talked quietly about his worsening condition. He matter-of-factly reviewed his options and concluded that he would return to his farm to die without any further treatments. They then talked of Rodgers' future. Hammerstein urged him to collaborate with a younger man, someone who could provide new stimulation and whom Rodgers, in turn, could help along the way. They talked over some business details and parted for the last time.

Shortly after midnight of August 23, 1960, Oscar Greeley Clendenning Hammerstein II died. At his funeral service, Howard Lindsay read from the lyric to "Climb Ev'ry Mountain." That evening, along Broadway and in London's West End, the lights of every theater were dimmed for three minutes in tribute.

22

WORDS AND MUSIC

In spite of their long collaboration, Oscar Hammerstein and Richard Rodgers never quite understood each other. Hammerstein said as much shortly before he died. He asked the young Stephen Sondheim, who was a friend of Mary Rodgers', what Rodgers was really like. This question, though probably rhetorical, betrayed Hammerstein's perplexity: "We've worked together all these years and I don't really know him." Rodgers was a man of the theater, but it was his whole life, Hammerstein added, implying that there was more to life than their profession. Hammerstein's remark suggests that Rodgers was uninterested in anything more.[1]

For his part, Rodgers commented in the 1970s that he never really knew whether Hammerstein liked him: "To this day I don't know."

How could two men work so closely and still have such doubts about the other? Hugh Fordin, in his biography of Hammerstein, suggests that each considered the other hidden and unknowable. Hammerstein thought that Rodgers was impersonal, and Rodgers thought that Hammerstein was uncommunicative. According to Fordin's evaluation, for eighteen years they kept a lid on a "potential powder keg."

They did indeed wall off their professional and personal lives. Their work required that they spend weeks together preparing for a show, supervising it out of town, and traveling together. Once the shows were completed they usually went their separate ways. Hammerstein spent more and more time on his farm and rarely visited their business office, whereas Rodgers spent much of his time there. Both men nervously coddled their shows, of course. And while Hammerstein could put a show behind him, the restless Rodgers could never quite let go and seemed obsessed with looking back or ahead.

Shortly before he died Oscar Hammerstein celebrated his sixty-fifth birthday at his farm, surrounded by close friends and family. Richard Rodgers was not there, though he did write a birthday tribute that appeared in the *New York Times*. His article was naturally laudatory, but there was an aloofness to it, as though it had been written by a knowledgeable outsider rather than an intimate partner. By this time he knew that Hammerstein's health was worsening and had to be careful to avoid an epitaph-like tone.

In his autobiography, written fifteen years after Hammerstein's death, Rodgers enumerated his partner's admirable qualities.[2] He was a loving man, but not overtly so; a hard worker, but slow and meticulous; practical and hardheaded, but also an idealist; soft-spoken, but furious over injustice. Rodgers described him as a "genuinely sophisticated, worldly man, yet he will probably be best remembered for his unequaled ability to express the simplest, most frequently overlooked pleasures of life." Rodgers' evaluation reveals something about himself. It was almost exactly what Rodgers wished others thought of him. The partners did share certain traits, but there were also significant differences. Rodgers and Hammerstein were both loving and caring, but Rodgers was far more guarded. Hammerstein was widely liked and admired, whereas Rodgers did not evoke warmth or affection. Cast members usually went to Hammerstein for sympathy and understanding, not to Rodgers. Both men worked intensely, but Rodgers was quicker and more self-confident than Hammerstein. Whereas Hammerstein had suffered bitter defeats and setbacks, Rodgers had, until the late 1960s, experienced few failures and had enjoyed many more professional successes than his partner. Hammerstein had learned to live with failure and to move on. When faced with adversity, Rodgers became depressed. Both were practical, but Rodgers was no idealist.

In one respect they were quite alike: each was capable of fully developing an idea or feeling through his talent. Rodgers praised Hammerstein's ability to express ordinary pleasures in his lyrics, though he, of course, did essentially the same thing through his music, which was ostensibly simple in design but complex in expression. Hammerstein offered this appraisal of Rodgers: "He is essentially a composer for plays. He writes music to depict story and character and is, therefore, a dramatist. He is not an abstractionist in any sense and, as far as I can see, he has no interest in the mere creation of sound, however unusual or ingenious. . . . His melodies are clean and well-defined. His scores are carefully built, logically allied to the stories and characters they describe. No overgrown forests and weed-clogged meadows of music here, but neat rows of tenderly grown flowers on well-kept lawns."[3] This is a reasonable appraisal, but it applied more to the mature Rodgers of the Hammerstein period than to the young partner of Lorenz Hart.

While he and Hart were partners, Rodgers' music assumed a tone that was carefree, lively, and slightly cynical, reflecting his own personality as well as Hart's style. It also mirrored the era in which they wrote, from the Roaring Twenties through the more depressed but still rhythm-conscious 1930s. During that period Rodgers' songs were usually based on the orthodox thirty-two-bar formula and an A-A-B-A structure. Unlike most composers of his generation, he did not employ much syncopation, but he did convey a feeling for jazz through the strong forward impetus of his melodies—"Dancing on the Ceiling" and "Where's That Rainbow?" are good early examples. "Blue Room" is also an example of his tendency toward jazz rhythms: following a long, ascending scale in the first part of the bridge, he inserts a quarter-note rest that emphasizes the next upbeat, much as Gershwin might have done.

Even during the Hart period Rodgers could write intricate music with carefully crafted changes of key, unanticipated modulations, and unexpected harmonic turns, as in "My Funny Valentine." Too often these characteristics were overlooked—that is, until Hammerstein provided a different canvas.[4]

The chief consequence of Rodgers' transition from Hart to Hammerstein was that his melodies assumed a greater depth. Writing with Hart, he often had no more to guide him than a title, a fragment of a lyric, or an idea for a song, set somewhere in a loosely knit plot. Until Hart's lyrics were complete, he had to write pure melodies, relying only on his imagination of the ensuing scene.

Not confined by prepackaged lyrics, he could experiment: "You Took Advantage of Me," for example, was written not only with no lyrics at hand but with no story in front of him. In working with Hammerstein, Rodgers had to mold his melodies to fit not only the words, which were almost always in place first, but the mood as well. "Oh, What a Beautiful Mornin'" is the obvious example. The opening scene, with Aunt Eller alone onstage churning butter and Curly singing offstage, called for the kind of gentle waltz that Rodgers wrote so well. If he had been writing to only a rough idea of a Western set in Oklahoma, he could easily have started with a barn dance.

From the beginning, his fundamental musical instinct was to write simply, and his collaboration with Hammerstein strengthened this tendency. Many of his major songs begin with a tonic chord, alternating only between the dominant or subdominant, sometimes for up to sixteen bars. In addition, his melodies usually begin on one of the notes of the tonic triad, increasing the risk of boredom. In the hands of another composer, this musical style might have been dull. But Rodgers had the savvy, skill, and natural talent to vary the formula, introducing nuances to lift his melodic line at just the right moment. In spite of his early music studies, he had no theory of composition. Stephen Sondheim once spent an hour discussing composition with Rodgers but came away frustrated with Rodgers' explanation. The truth was that he simply heard his melodies and was able to sit down and play them.

Consider, for example, one of his most famous songs, "If I Loved You," the refrain of which begins conventionally over routine harmony. Dozens of popular songs conform to this straightforward pattern. But because the lyrics of "If I Loved You" bordered on the maudlin, Rodgers had to write a love song that was not too syrupy. By manipulating the harmonies, Rodgers changed the entire concept of the song, introducing a slightly sad shading that characterized the relationship between Billy and Julie in *Carousel*. His combination of small surprises in the melody and harmonies intrigued listeners. Psychologists who have studied brain activity with regard to music claim that adults become accustomed to patterns; thus, after hearing ten notes, they are able to anticipate the eleventh. When that note differs from their expectations, they are either pleasantly surprised or irritated. Obviously, Rodgers found the formula to please.[5]

His sense of theater was evident again in the song's ending. Because this was the first love song between the two principals, Rodgers sensed that more than a conventional ending was needed at this dramatic juncture. So he added a four-bar tag to the last eight bars, driving the melody upward toward a much stronger climax. This finale clinched the song's impact on the audience. He used much the same technique fifteen years later for "Climb Ev'ry Mountain." The melody begins as a simple statement, with traditional harmonies, but then soars to a climax. Having carefully established this style in *Carousel*, Rodgers continued to use it in the important love songs in *Allegro*, *South Pacific*, and *The King and I*, with great dramatic effect.

In sum, Rodgers wrote popular songs with Hart; with Hammerstein he wrote theater music. Some critics contend that Rodgers was at his best with Hart, who no doubt needled him to write in a somewhat boisterous style that combined cynicism with humor. Rodgers later fell back on this experience for some Hart-like melodies, such as "There Is Nothing Like a Dame."

After 1935, when Rodgers returned from Hollywood, his music assumed greater complexity. "Little Girl Blue" (1935), "I Didn't Know What Time It Was" (1939), and "It Never Entered My Mind" (1940) all have unusual structures. By the time he joined Hammerstein he was already in a period of transition. As the critic Cecil Smith noted, Rodgers took a long step away from Broadway toward a more "universal and less insular type of light music." With Hammerstein he broadened his scope, using fewer popular rhythms and thirty-two-bar forms and more complex harmonies.

Some admirers thought that his music for Hammerstein's lyrics had gotten better; others found it too predictable. Rodgers and Hart had attacked each show with a certain madcap humor—largely because of Hart's lifestyle. Hammerstein was sometimes exasperatingly slow for Rodgers, but he was dependable, a quality that reassured Rodgers and led both of them into new arenas.

Did success spoil Richard Rodgers or sap his creativity? Some critics claimed that Rodgers and Hammerstein became driven by profits, so much so that when their experiments failed they quickly returned to their proven formulas. In fact, the opposite is more accurate. Although they enjoyed the financial rewards of their success, profit was never the sole motivation of either man. Their financial independence allowed them to experiment and to shape their own productions from inception to completion.

How much of the credit for the success of the Rodgers and Hammerstein style rests with Hammerstein? Over the years the music seems to have survived better than the books. Other songwriters, such as Jerome Kern, Cole Porter, or Harold Arlen, could probably have written one of two of their best shows, but not all of them: not *Oklahoma!* and *Carousel* and *South Pacific* and *The King and I* and *The Sound of Music*. It was Rodgers' particular genius that he could run the gamut from a turn-of-the-century Western to the kingdom of Siam without invoking clichés and imitations.

It was inevitable that Rodgers and Hammerstein developed patterns and formulas: their subjects were semiserious, or at least realistic; there were no outright comedies; and their plots were enlivened by interesting characters, based in part on plays and novels but amplified by Hammerstein. The shows were bound by close links between the dramatic scenes, the lyrics, and the melodies. They earned a reputation for realism and created a new musical art form, without ever sacrificing entertainment, humor, or even a bit of slapstick. There were critics, of course, then and later. The latter-day critics in particular have looked back at their work with a certain condescension. Martin Gottfried, in his book *A Theater Divided*, is quite savage. Hammerstein's plays, he wrote, were "embarrassing and childish," and his ideas "without musical quality—simpleminded stories making simpleminded points."[6]

Nevertheless, Rodgers and Hammerstein have stood the test of time. Their durability can be explained partly because of the nature of their plays, which still interest audiences in the 1990s (for example, the revivals of *Carousel* and *The King and I*), and partly because of the compelling music. Finally, Rodgers and Hammerstein seem to reflect a happier time. Such echoes inevitably were criticized as deceptive or misleading. One recent critic, the playwright A. J. Gurney, has suggested that Rodgers and Hammerstein's penchant for operettas finally ushered in the European invasion of Broadway in the 1980s—a rather long stretch between cause and effect. Ethan Mordden, in his book *Rodgers and Hammerstein*, sums them up best: "Tonight is R&H, this week and next year. Their works survive. . . . R&H are unique and essential American theatre."[7]

In 1960, to critics and admirers alike, it seemed as if Rodgers and Hammerstein shows would go on forever. At the age of fifty-eight, Richard Rodgers had become Broadway's most complete composer—as melodic as Kern, as innovative as Gershwin, as versatile as Berlin, and even as sophisticated as Porter. Then, suddenly, he was alone.

23

NO STRINGS

The death of Oscar Hammerstein was a crushing blow for Richard Rodgers, more so professionally than personally. Naturally he was grieved, but he was also frightened by the grim reminder of his own cancer. He could not imagine spending the rest of his days "reliving past glories," as he put it, so he plunged ahead with his work.[1] He told an interviewer: "I have found there is this terrific drive to survive. Something takes hold of you—a determination not to get killed. I was 58. I was not ready to be turned out to pasture. It's very easy for an upset man to retire. As you get older you get more scared. But what would I do? I'm not a golfer. What would I do after a cruise around the world—live on my memories?"[2]

Any picture of Richard Rodgers relaxing on a world cruise would have been wildly out of focus. No one doubted that he would continue his career, but a new show would have to wait until he fulfilled his commitment to revise and update the score for the 20th Century–Fox remake of *State Fair*. But first Rodgers was obligated to finish the score for an ABC television special entitled *The Valiant Years*, a documentary series on the wartime career of Winston Churchill. Rodgers had begun the project while Hammerstein was still alive. Because the score did not require lyrics, his work on the series had filled a gap as he and Hammerstein continued to talk of new shows that Rodgers knew would never be undertaken. The twenty-six-part series promised to be serious and engaging, and Rodgers had accepted ABC's offer with enthusiasm. Gary Merrill was to narrate, and Richard Burton would read from Churchill's speeches.

Rodgers' task was similar to that in *Victory at Sea*. He supplied themes as indicated in an outline or in response to a request from the producers. One segment, for instance, required a Mediterranean theme—"four more yards of Mediterranean," as he put it—and another was labeled "Jolly Churchill." There were three orchestrators—Hershy Kay and Eddie Sauter, two brilliant young musicians, and Robert Emmett Dolan, also the musical director. They turned Rodgers' "piles of manuscripts" into a score.

For Rodgers the job was basically the same one he had faced for forty years: how to express a particular character or situation in music. He had solved this problem hundreds of times in the theater, but with the help of lyrics. Television offered new challenges and opportunities. Rodgers compared the show to his theater work: "For this program instead of words you've got pictures. You're not confined, as you often are when you're writing for the theatre, to a certain number of bars. But the job is still to say in music what the picture says and what the character says. What you want the music to do is to implement the words and the picture. The basic problem in both media is to express mood, scene, character and situation. But the theatre is a much more circumscribed form. [Television] is more open."[3] The series premiered in late November 1960 and drew strong praise, for both the production and the score, which won Rodgers an Emmy.

By the time the series aired Rodgers had already turned to the *State Fair* project. This commitment was part of an earlier package deal that included the sale of film rights to *The Sound of Music*. The remake was to be his first try at writing his own lyrics.

It was a logical decision. He could not bring himself to become involved with another writer—and selecting a lyricist was not like choosing an umbrella, he said. Furthermore, he doubted that he would be lucky enough to develop another permanent relationship with a lyricist. But writing lyrics was not as novel or formidable a challenge for Rodgers as it might have seemed. He had been forced to supply lyrics during Lorenz Hart's frequent disappearances, and he had often discussed Hart's lyrics with him, line by line. After Hart's death Rodgers sometimes revised the lyrics for a revival of one of their shows. Moreover, some of Hammerstein and Hart's know-how had doubtlessly rubbed off. But Rodgers never minimized the difficulty of writing lyrics. Indeed, he called such work "extremely difficult," and he disagreed with Hammerstein's contention that whereas composition required esoteric creativity, everyone had some facility with words. Thus began what he called the "big experiment." If the experiment worked, he would consider doing both the words and music for a Broadway show of his own.[4]

When he informed the executives at 20th Century–Fox that he would be writing his own lyrics, he told them that if they did not like his work they could certainly find someone else. Of course it is hard to imagine any studio turning down Richard Rodgers, especially on a film he had helped to create.

Unfortunately, Fox executives had decided to move the locale of *State Fair* from Iowa to Texas. In addition, they wanted some new songs. In the remake, Pat Boone and Ann-Margret had the roles originated by Dick Haymes and Vivian Blaine, and Bobby Darin and Pamela Tiffin would re-create the roles played by Dana Andrews and Jeanne Crain. Tiffin's singing was dubbed by Anita Gordon. Tom Ewell played the father, and, in a pleasant surprise, Alice Faye was coaxed out of retirement to play the mother. Rodgers worked at home and sent five new songs.

The charming tale of bucolic summer romance turned into a horrible, glitzy mishmash. Wonderful songs from the first film were interspersed with extremely ordinary songs newly supplied by Rodgers. Faye was given only one number, the new and rather awkward "Never Say No (to a Man)," a mother's advice to her daughter. "Willing and Eager" was a new waltz written in a characteristic Rodgers style for Pat Boone and Ann-Margret. It had a pleasing melody but paled next to "It Might as Well Be Spring" or "That's for Me," from the original. *Variety* commented that the story was as American as apple pie but that "the pie is stale after 17 years in the pantry." Following its release in March 1962, other reviews were somewhat more friendly. The new songs were not exactly "world beaters," Rodgers conceded, but then "neither was the picture." He was right.

Meanwhile, in December 1961 Rodgers received a prestigious award from the Broadway Association, granted "For the Greatest Achievement for the Advancement of Broadway." This occasion prompted a column in the *New York Times* from Brooks Atkinson, who mused about Rodgers' talent:

He is a genius in melody. "Genius" is a big word. But if it applies to Jerome Kern, and it does, it also fits Mr. Rodgers, who has filled America with good music. Like many New Yorkers he lives in the midst of it. A large portion of the melody that drifts through barber shops and sweetens elevators in this town is the work of Mr. Rodgers. During the three quarters of an hour that it takes to get a haircut and shampoo at the Astor barbershop, half the musical accompaniment seems to come from the Rodgers portfolio. It is as comforting as sharp scissors.[5]

Atkinson mentioned that Rodgers was already casting a new show and writing the lyrics. The producer Max Gordon remarked, "They're going to surprise you."

Rodgers' idea for a new show was inspired by television. He was a fan of television, and like millions of ordinary Americans, three or four nights a week he would change into his pajamas and settle down to watch the *Tonight Show*, starring Jack Paar. One evening he saw the black singer and actress Diahann Carroll perform. In her black cocktail dress and bouffant hairstyle, she made such a stunning impression that Rodgers conceived the idea of starring her in a musical. She would play a chic, sophisticated woman of the world, but her character would neither represent a cause nor be a symbol of her race. He believed that such casting would be more effective than "anything strident or preachy in breaking down racial stereotypes that had persisted for too long on Broadway." He explained later that he wanted to take black characters out of the "bandanna and gingham" mode.[6]

He knew Carroll from auditions for *Flower Drum Song*, but trying to make her over as an Asian had proved too awkward. She had subsequently achieved stardom in Harold Arlen's *House of Flowers*. Rodgers called her and invited her for a drink at Gallagher's, the well-known show business pub. Carroll at first thought her caller was playing a practical joke, but then she was pleasantly surprised and agreed to meet Rodgers. Although she was unaware of his idea for the show, she decided to make an impression by wearing an elegant pink suit by Givenchy. Her stylish entrance proved just the right move. Rodgers commented that she looked marvelous—exactly the way he envisioned her on stage. Rodgers asked if she had done any modeling, because his idea involved a young American living in Paris and working as a high-fashion model. Musing about the idea, he acknowledged that a musical about a successful black model would not be plausible if set in the United States but would be believable in Europe.

Carroll was enthusiastic and wondered which writer could deal sympatheti-cally with the struggles of young black woman. They parted with Rodgers' promise to call her after a trip to Europe. Carroll left, doubting that she would hear more. Rodgers did travel to Europe, for the British opening of The Sound of Music. The show enjoyed a record-breaking run in London, but some of the critics were not kind. Rodgers was particularly incensed by attacks on the sen-timentality of the book and lyrics, believing that it was bad form to criticize Hammerstein so soon after his death. He always professed not to be impressed by criticism, but he was in fact quite sensitive to critics' reactions. His wife wrote that even when the criticisms were not personal or savage, they hurt. Self-pity, however, was not among his weaknesses.

Upon his return from Europe, he was ready to pursue the show he had dis-cussed with Carroll. Rodgers had already decided on the writer he wanted: the playwright Samuel Taylor, who had written The Happy Time (which was produced by Rodgers and Hammerstein in 1950), Sabrina Fair, and The Pleasure of His Company. Rodgers felt comfortable with Taylor and regarded him as a "thoughtful, accom-modating, highly skilled craftsman." The two agreed on Paris as the setting in order to make the interracial romance credible. Taylor met with Carroll to ex-plain the story. She was to play an American model living in Paris, where she falls in love with an American expatriate, David Jordan, a Pulitzer Prize–winning novelist who has abandoned serious writing and is sponging off his friends. Car-roll's character, named Barbara Woodruff, restores his confidence. They quarrel only to reunite. Jordan vows to return to writing but realizes that he can write effectively only in his native Maine. She offers to return with him, but they both recognize that it will not work. He leaves and she stays. They part with no strings.

Rodgers offered the part of the American writer to Richard Kiley, who quickly agreed (this was before his great triumph in Man of LaMancha). Events moved rapidly. Rodgers asked Carroll to choose her favorite conductor, and she sug-gested Peter Matz. A month or so later she wrote: "I found myself sitting with Peter in Rodgers' office on Madison Avenue listening to him play his new score for me. I was entranced. The melodies were so beautiful, so appealing. He said this is your love song, and played a few bars of 'The Sweetest Sounds.' " Rodgers said that he was pleased to be composing his own lyrics: "You can't imagine how wonderful it feels," he told Carroll as they were saying good-bye, "to have written this score and not have to search all over the globe for that drunken little fag." In her autobiography Carroll wrote that she was stunned: "The unex-pected cruelty of the remark shook me to my very being." From that moment, she claimed that she never quite trusted Rodgers.[7]

Carroll related this incident twenty years later, after she and Rodgers had a falling out. That Rodgers would so disparage Lorenz Hart in front of a woman he knew only casually is highly implausible, though the comment may well have reflected Rodgers' feelings. Rodgers always avoided discussing Hart's homosexuality. Indeed, it was rumored that he had denied it to his sometime biographer David Ewen. In 1968, Rodgers did address the issue in a interview for Columbia University's Oral History Program. He acknowledged that Hart probably had been a homosexual but that he, Rodgers, had been only dimly aware of it. Rodgers remembered that when someone from a Hollywood scandal sheet had asked Rodgers about it, he had grabbed the questioner by the collar and threatened him if he printed anything of the sort. In the Columbia interview he summed up his feeling with an odd remark: "I guess it's something like marriage anyway: I was probably the last one to know."[8]

Whatever he may have said to Carroll, he was pleased with the prospects for his new show. Early in the summer of 1962 Rodgers and his wife visited Taylor in Maine to discuss details of the story, which they had decided to call No Strings. At that time the interracial romance was a bold undertaking—there was explosive racial tension in the South and the civil rights movement was still in its early phase. The subject would have to be handled tastefully and carefully. In the final published version of the play, there was an introductory author's note: "The part of Barbara Woodruff in No Strings is designed to be played by an American colored girl in her early twenties. It is proposed that she also be beautiful, have style, and wear clothes well; be intelligent, witty, warmly human, and wise. The play itself never refers to her color."[9] Even at end of the play, when it is obvious that the lovers part because of anticipated racial prejudice in the United States, "we were careful to avoid mentioning the issue directly," Rodgers said. He and Taylor seemed to think that this subtlety would be more effective than addressing the racial issue directly.

During the rehearsals, however, Carroll and Kiley both questioned the failure to mention the character's color. Taylor and Rodgers refused to reconsider. As far as Carroll was concerned, the ending was an evasion. After spending the first hour of the play getting the couple together, the writers then permitted them to part in the final few minutes. Carroll and Kiley both argued that their characters should leave for America together, but Taylor insisted that such an ending would be totally unrealistic. He was probably right. Finally, it was decided to compromise and rewrite the ending in a way that implied that the romance might have been a dream. The critics, of course, pounced on this as a cop-out.

With an outline and the basic characters decided, Rodgers began to work on the score. One of the benefits of writing his own lyrics was that "I was always there when I wanted me." As to his method, he explained that he sometimes thought of a title and then wrote the first few bars; he sometimes finished the music and lyrics together; and he sometimes jotted down only a few lines of a lyric that would later suggest a melody. Occasionally this process would be reversed, and he would think of a musical phrase. "Never did I write a complete lyric and then set it to music," an obvious reference to his method with Hammerstein.

Some years later, however, he reversed himself and said that he had written entire lyrics and then set them to music "as though somebody else had written the words." His work style seemed to combine the idiosyncrasies of both Hart and Hammerstein. His manuscripts show scribbling worthy of Hart, but with many careful emendations and amendments worthy of Hammerstein. There is even one lyric on the back of an envelope, which would have amused Hart. The absent Hart might have enjoyed "I Was There," a slightly bawdy song that Rodgers wrote around this time, not for the show but for his own amusement:

> A prince I knew in Venice had libido.
> One night a dame relieved him of his crown.
> They played a game called follow the Lido.
> But I didn't have a thing to write it down.[10]

The first song that Rodgers finished was the opening number, "The Sweetest Sounds"; the second was "No Strings," which was the last in the show, sung just before the final reprise of "The Sweetest Sounds." This order was probably deliberate, for Rodgers understood the importance of defining the play through his music and lyrics, and in these two songs he created the bookends for the show. Altogether he wrote fourteen songs, one of which was cut.

No Strings involved some significant innovations. Rodgers always had been troubled by the chasm between the orchestra in the pit and the performers on stage. Wishing to involve the musicians in this intimate love story, he decided to seat them onstage or in the wings. He worked this out with the director, Joe Layton, who was known primarily as a choreographer but had staged musical numbers in the Sound of Music.

Rodgers also decided that the orchestra should consist entirely of brass, percussion, and woodwinds—that is, no strings. This was not an attempt to capitalize on the title but a musical concept that interested Rodgers. In the end the orchestra had only a flute, clarinet, oboe, bassoon, trumpet, trombone, and drums. The orchestrations were by Ralph Burns, a newcomer to Rodgers' shows.

Choosing Burns was an important decision for this show. In 1942, at the age of nineteen, he had broken into the music world as an arranger for Charlie Barnet's swing band. Burns' major contribution was to translate the modern sounds of the beboppers Dizzy Gillespie and Charlie Parker into full orchestral conceptions for big bands, thereby influencing an entire generation of arrangers. It was Burns who, along with Neal Hefti, provided the exciting new combinations for Woody Herman's Thundering Herd. In 1946 he wrote an extended work, "Summer Sequence," as well as "Early Autumn," which featured Herman's four tenor saxophone players, including Stan Getz.

In No Strings, Burns used the small group to great effect, creating orchestrations that made routine numbers come alive, especially "Eager Beaver" and the swinging ending of "You Don't Tell Me." He even made effective use of the tiny brass section. It was Burns who gave the show a different, modern sound. He later recorded the score with a larger orchestra, including strings, which by contrast pointed up the radical and worthwhile innovation by Rodgers in using the small group. The cast album became popular and stayed on Billboard's chart for several months.

To establish this new musical concept from the outset, there was no overture, in keeping with Rodgers' dislike of them. The curtain of No Strings opens on a darkened stage. A lone flute is heard as a spotlight comes up on Diahann Carroll. Accompanied only by the flute at first, she sings "The Sweetest Sounds" as the orchestra fades in. Then, on the other side of the stage, a clarinet plays an obligato, and Richard Kiley enters and sings his own chorus of the song. Later the same musical technique is used with only a trombone, as the opening accompaniment for the waltz "Love Makes the World Go." At the end of the first act "Nobody Told Me" is performed by a drummer only. The action on stage implies that the two main characters, who are in the bedroom, will make love, but the stage does not go dark; instead, the drummer, spotlighted in blue, plays a furious solo.

All of these novel arrangements, especially the interracial romance, might have deterred a lesser producer, but Rodgers presented his rationale in an interview: "The worst trap that anyone can fall into in the theatre is to play it safe, to think there is a fool-proof formula. I have seen an awful lot of fellows, who thought they had found the secret of success on Broadway, disappear because they tried to repeat what had worked in earlier shows, their own or others'. The public expects you to come up with something new. But even if this were not true, a man owes it to himself to try."[11] The show had a two-month tryout period: first in Detroit, where it was "in trouble," followed by Toronto, Cleveland, and New Haven. Rodgers decided to insert an extra week of tryouts because in Toronto the show had played in a cavernous theater and Alan Jay Lerner had warned Rodgers against going from a large theater to a much smaller one. The extra time was also necessary because of the many technical problems. The mobile sets, for example, were moved about by the cast members. In New York, there was a dispute over which theater to use.

Opening night in Detroit was a fiasco. Joe Layton insisted on including two dance numbers, despite Carroll's protests that she could not dance. On opening night she froze and did neither of the dances. After the show Layton admitted she was no dancer. Perhaps more important was her growing lack of communication with Rodgers: "[He] wasn't exactly intimidating, but there was never any of that easy give and take and sense of camaraderie between composer and company I had experienced with Harold Arlen. . . . Rodgers was much more formal. As time passed I came to the conclusion that he was really incapable of hearing someone else's point of view without regarding that person as a potential adversary, and his frequent insensitivity was appalling." [12]

In Detroit the show provoked some racial protests. Kiley recalled that members of the audience began to walk out. In his memoirs Rodgers did not recall any incidents, but the subsequent road company encountered some protests and closed early.

Shortly before the New York opening an anxious Rodgers had a "sinking feeling" over an insistent question: What will be said of the lyrics, the concept, and the form of "No Strings," with movable scenery and musicians on stage? "I don't look forward to failure any more than I do to a broken hip. But until I know what I've got or what audiences tell me I've got, I'm scared." This sounds like the standard preopening comments. Another writer claimed that Rodgers acted like a man who had just put down a heavy suitcase. Rodgers said that he had a "curious sensation" that he had not had in years: "I feel awfully young. I sleep well, and I have more energy than the kids in the chorus." This sentiment was seconded by his wife, who said that "he's never felt so completely free and independent, so un-held down." [13] Was this whistling in the dark, or a way of proclaiming his liberation from the ghost of his former partner?

The show opened at the 54th Street Theater on March 15, 1962. The first scene, with Carroll and Kiley singing alternate choruses of "The Sweetest Sounds," captured the spirit of the play and captivated the audiences with its originality. The whole story has been foreshadowed. In their song both characters are looking for love but do not expect it. Even after they find it together (the duet), they part. The lyric for their opening song is perhaps the best of Rodgers' own creations:

> The sweetest sounds I'll ever hear
> Are still inside my head.
> The kindest words I'll ever know
> Are waiting to be said.
> The most entrancing sight of all
> Is yet for me to see.
> And the dearest love in all the world
> Is waiting somewhere for me.
> Is waiting somewhere for me.

This is also the strongest melody of the show. It was reprised for the ending with similar staging. It was the singers' way of saying that the entire play may have been in their imagination and that their dearest love was still waiting somewhere.

Another major song was "Look No Further," a plaintive love song written in traditional form. Rodgers used an old Hammerstein device by beginning a line with the last word of the preceding line:

> Don't move an inch away, stay.
> Stay with one who loves you.
> This is the journey's end, friend.
> Friend has turned to lover.

Unfortunately, this song was never very popular and has been largely forgotten. Most of the remainder of the score is less than impressive. "Maine," for example, is an important element in the play, but it is not a good song because of its cumbersome lyrics. Although there is no reference to race, these were the lyrics that were intended to make audiences aware of the differences in the couple's background. David Jordan is from New England and Barbara Woodruff is from the Upper West Side of Manhattan. Kiley begins, singing:

> Let snow come down,
> Before the sun comes up
> Maine is the main thing.

Carroll then answers, singing,

> When the sun goes down
> The kids are up and out
> East of the Hudson.

He sings "mainly I do like Maine," but she rebuts with

> There's a sidewalk symphony
> of song and shout
> Up north of Central Park.

The song becomes a duel, signifying their incompatibility. It is hardly subtle, and even a great melody would not have helped.

Some critics ripped into the book. John Simon wrote in *Theatre Arts* that Taylor's book was a "concoction guaranteed to give ptomaine poisoning the moment one takes in the situation." The show ends, he wrote, "as pretentiously and falsely as it began." On the whole, however, the music and lyrics were applauded. John Chapman, of the *Daily News*, wrote that "Rodgers just can't think of any wrong notes, so his melodies are beguiling—and the lyrics he has written for them are pleasant and graceful." Richard Watts found in *No Strings* a "particularly lovely score. . . . [The] lyrics have a simple and attractive style of their own, and they fit perfectly with the notable beauty of the music." For the *New Yorker*, Edith Oliver wrote, "Though [his lyrics] may not be as good as the best of Hart's and Hammerstein's, they are plenty good enough." Walter Kerr was not especially impressed, however: the lyrics do not "rise into the shadow of that near poetry that makes lyrics lyrical. They seem also, unless I am mistaken, to be using up some of Mr. Rodgers' composing energy without quite tapping his composer's inspiration." Howard Taubman, aware of Rodgers' comments about being nervous, set his mind at ease in the *New York Times*: "Richard Rodgers need not have worried. He is still a magician of the musical theatre."

Rodgers thought that most critics were poorly prepared to review an entire score after one hearing on opening night. Although critics read nonmusical plays in advance, and even studied the text, they refused to listen to music beforehand. This was one reason he occasionally released a recording of a show's songs before the opening. Rodgers believed that Brooks Atkinson of the *New York Times* had tried to study the music more seriously than most critics. He also liked the reviews of Gilbert Gabriel of the old *New York Sun*. Later he became friendly with Taubman, the *New York Times*' new critic, and wrote an introduction to one of Taubman's books.

Rodgers won a Tony Award for his score and was given a special Tony for his achievements in the theater. Shortly after *No Strings* opened, he celebrated his sixtieth birthday and was given a luncheon in his honor, hosted by Grayson Kirk, president of Columbia University. President Kennedy's special adviser on the arts, August Heckscher, read a telegram from the president: "The musical theatre in our country has reached new heights in considerable part due to [Rodgers'] gifts." Robert Moses, then the impresario for the World's Fair, rose to say, "Thank you for preserving our optimism, our faith and our very sanity in a bewitched, bothered and bewildering world." Rodgers responded briefly by noting that his one-word philosophy was "help"—not as a cry for assistance but as an expression of gratitude for those with whom he had collaborated. Throughout his career he had worked with others who did the real work. "I have never done anything alone in my life," he said modestly.

This was an admirable sentiment, and one he was about to put into practice. Even before No Strings opened, Rodgers had concluded that even if his ego should end up being "lacerated" by that show, it would have healed sufficiently to be placed on the line again—because a man owed it to himself to keep trying. Some years later he expressed the view that No Strings had perhaps been ahead of its time and that a revival might one day be possible. He was particularly pleased by his musical innovations. The show assured him that he could "pick up the pieces of my career and start all over again with new people and new techniques."

He might have continued as a lyricist, except that another Broadway giant was unattached and available—Alan Jay Lerner. Rodgers and Lerner. Two giants!

24

DO I HEAR A WALTZ?

The relative success of *No Strings* was highly therapeutic for Rodgers. It proved that he could if necessary write a musical without Lorenz Hart or Oscar Hammerstein. In many respects it was the high point of his career: he had conceived the idea of the play, recruited the star performers, written the music and lyrics, and introduced several orchestral innovations—all to critical acclaim. But *No Strings* was a false dawn. For the next several years Rodgers suffered a succession of frustrations: an unfruitful collaboration, an unsuccessful show, and, finally, a severe illness. He never regained the luster of the Hammerstein years. There were still a number of fine songs to be written, but as he entered his sixties he was also entering the third and final period of his career.

No Strings pointed up one significant lesson, that in the era of the

musical play, created in large part by Rodgers himself, a solid book was as necessary as good music and lyrics. Throughout his career Hammerstein had written
and talked extensively about the importance of the book. The tepid response to
the book of *No Strings* was probably one reason that Rodgers was intrigued by the
prospect of collaborating with Alan Jay Lerner. He was, after all, the enormously
successful author of *Brigadoon, My Fair Lady,* and *Camelot.* Despite Lerner's break
with the composer Frederick Loewe, he was still brimming with ideas. One of
the shows he had in mind was based on the life of the famous Parisian designer
Coco Chanel; another was about a young lady with extrasensory perception.

In April, even before the opening of *No Strings,* Rodgers had announced his
intention of collaborating with Lerner. They got together through the "under-
ground," as Rodgers described it—that is, each heard that the other was interested. Rodgers was not really interested in the play about Chanel (Lerner would
later write *Coco* as a vehicle for Katharine Hepburn, with music by André Previn),
but he was fascinated by Lerner's idea about ESP and reincarnation. They set to
work on a show tentatively titled *I Picked a Daisy*—Daisy being not only the name
of the female lead but also a play on the slang connotation of "oddball." The
idea was that a young lady enters psychotherapy in order to stop smoking and
in the process reveals several previous incarnations.

On the surface, Rodgers and Lerner seemed an ideal partnership. Rodgers
wrote along the same lines as Frederick Loewe. It is conceivable that Rodgers
could have written the score for *My Fair Lady* or *Brigadoon* and that Loewe could
have written *The Sound of Music,* even though, ironically, Loewe had vetoed Lerner's
proposal for a musical about the von Trapp family. It is also ironic that Rodgers
and Hammerstein worked for a time on an adaptation of *Pygmalion,* which, Hammerstein confessed to Lerner, had proved impossible. But Loewe's temperament
was quite different from Rodgers'. Loewe was content to depart for the Riviera
and the casinos while Lerner was busy with the book and lyrics. Moreover, he
was not eager to embark on new projects and left the initiative to Lerner. When
Loewe was in Paris or the Riviera, Lerner wrote, "the longer I took the better he
liked it."

That was certainly not Rodgers' inclination or reputation, so it is surprising
that Lerner was not more sensitive to this difference. Perhaps he was misled by
the long association between Hart and Rodgers. Lerner, who had known and admired Hart, may have assumed that Rodgers was understanding of his collaborators, regardless of their lifestyle or temperament. Lerner should have reminded
himself that Hart could write extremely quickly and in almost any environment.
Hammerstein was known to be slow and meticulous. Rodgers once commented

to Lerner that Hammerstein had spent three weeks at his farm working on a lyric, adding, "You know it couldn't possibly take three weeks." At that point, Lerner said, he should have known that their partnership was in trouble.[1]

Lerner was notoriously slow and painstaking. In his memoirs he wrote that over a period of eight months he wrote ninety-one lyrics for "On a Clear Day You Can See Forever" and discarded them all! But he was brilliant, and his work was worth waiting for. When he began working with Rodgers he was forty-five years old, a full generation younger than Rodgers, Hammerstein, and Hart. At the time, one of his many marriages had fallen apart, and he had just broken with Loewe. Although this separation was relatively amicable, it must have been traumatic. He had suffered through the uncertain opening of *Camelot*, which took hold only after Moss Hart produced a television excerpt for the *Ed Sullivan Show*.

Aside from the theater, Lerner was also deeply involved in politics; it was he who helped arrange the birthday celebration for President Kennedy in 1962, at which Marilyn Monroe sang her famous version of "Happy Birthday." Later, of course, his lyric for *Camelot* became inextricably identified with the Kennedy years. Perhaps most important, Lerner had become addicted to drugs prescribed by Dr. Max Jacobson, a society doctor who administered injections of a combination of Methedrine and vitamins.[2]

The news of the Rodgers-Lerner collaboration was greeted with surprise and enthusiasm. One New York writer compared it to a merger of the Dodgers and the Yankees. Lerner was asked whether he had any trepidation about working with the nearly legendary Rodgers: "No, not at all. My main emotion is a deep, excited curiosity, and I think that Dick shares my feelings. Rodgers and Hart had a different voice than Rodgers and Hammerstein, and so it will be with us. If we do have different approaches, they will be resolved involuntarily. . . . As we begin to work we will both shift gears instinctively."[3] Rodgers, as usual, was more measured. At that time the collaboration was still a question mark, because he and Lerner realized that a partnership could not be judged until the show was on. Rodgers said, "There is a natural qualm when you embark on a new phase of your life, but it doesn't frighten me. I rather take it as a challenge." It would prove a challenge that neither man could meet.

The show they decided on became *On a Clear Day You Can See Forever*, with music eventually written not by Rodgers but by Burton Lane. For almost two years Rodgers and Lerner worked together—or more precisely, worked apart. Lerner supposedly finished a version of the book, and the partners began thinking about casting. Lerner then decided rewrite the book.[4] During this time Rodgers wrote melodic sketches for seven song titles, some of which were used by Lerner and

Lane. None of Rodgers' melodies seem very inspired, however, and some are rather fragmentary. Obviously, he was waiting for definitive lyrics.[5]

Lerner's explanation for their subsequent failure was too polite and mundane: there were contracts to sign, and the partners had to discuss subsidiary and revival rights, a movie version, and cast albums; by the time that was accomplished, Lerner "didn't have any more strength left to write a show." In fact, the original agreements were signed promptly. The problem was more basic.

Rodgers' version is probably closer to the truth: he said that Lerner had something in common with Hammerstein and Hart—"not liking to work." This was unfair to all three, but Rodgers was understandably indignant: "How dare this young man take up a year of my life. I don't have that much time left."[6] Indeed, it was the prospect of wasting his time that drove Rodgers over the brink. Lerner had told him that he intended to complete some lyrics by working over the Labor Day weekend of 1962. When Rodgers called, however, the maid informed him that Mr. Lerner was in Capri. Rodgers later summed up his views: "Alan was thrown about by an awful lot of things that were bothering him at the time. He had personal difficulties which were enormous. It was almost impossible to get him to work. Not that he didn't want to, and there was nothing about Alan that I didn't like. He's a charming fellow, bright and certainly gifted. But I couldn't get work out of him. And because of the feeling of frustration I just stopped."[7]

On July 25, 1963, it was announced to the press that Rodgers and Lerner had dissolved their partnership. Rodgers wrote to Joshua Logan that he was overcome by a feeling of "freedom and relief." According to the New York Times, they had ended their work two weeks earlier, "because an insufficient amount of Mr. Lerner's lyrics blocked Mr. Rodgers from finishing the score." The report went on to say that Lerner would continue to work on the show with Burton Lane. Lerner apparently bore no grudge. In his book The Musical Theatre, he acknowledged that Rodgers had no kind words to say about him; Lerner was nevertheless certain that had they been engaged in the adaptation of an existing work, rather than an original creation, their work together would have been successful.[8] Curiously enough, Lerner, who had complained of all the contracts he had to sign, retained the rights to the show. On a Clear Day You Can See Forever opened in October 1965 and became successful. Lane commented, however, that it was a "painful creative experience. [It took] two years to write five songs." During this time Lerner "came and went. I never knew when or where."

Shortly before his public break with Lerner, in May and June 1963, the New York City Center held a Richard Rodgers festival, staging productions of Pal Joey, The King and I, and Oklahoma! At the same time, No Strings was marking its five hundredth performance, *The Sound of Music* was in its fourth year, and a new version of *The Boys from Syracuse* was playing off-Broadway. A *New York Times* editorial of May 20, 1963, turned eloquent: "So without any formal celebrations, there is an unexpected Rodgers festival in town. Nostalgia apart, it all adds up to a historic reminder of many of the pioneering moments of American musical comedy."

When Rodgers and Lerner finally parted company, Rodgers had no new show on Broadway and no immediate prospects for one. But he was the new president and producing director of the Music Theater of Lincoln Center, and the Lincoln Center complex was the great new focal point for the performing arts in New York. It included the Metropolitan Opera House, the Vivian Beaumont Theatre, the New York State Theatre, and, directly adjacent, the new buildings of the Juilliard School of Music. The composer William Schuman had resigned from Juilliard to become the general director of Lincoln Center. The Beaumont Theatre was intended for nonmusicals, and during the normal theater season the New York State Theatre was occupied by the New York Opera Company and the New York City Ballet. So that the State Theatre would not be dark during the summers, the board decided to use it for revivals of Broadway shows. Rodgers was the logical choice for producer.

Rodgers undertook the project as he did everything, with professional care and zeal. The idea was to produce two shows each summer and to attract theater-goers of all ages by charging modest prices. In July 1964, Rodgers inaugurated the program with a production of *The King and I* (again starring Yul Brynner), followed by *The Merry Widow* in August, both of which were successful. The following year Rodgers produced *Carousel*, with John Raitt in his original starring role, and in 1966 came a high point, the revival of *Annie Get Your Gun*, once again starring Ethel Merman, for whom Irving Berlin wrote his last published song, "An Old-Fashioned Wedding," which stopped the show. Rodgers wrote to Joshua Logan, who had directed the original, that "Ethel was never better in her life and the whole show went fantastically well."

Unfortunately, the theater was so cavernous that only the more elaborate shows were appropriate, and during the 1966 season a grand revival of *Show Boat* sent production costs soaring. The board of directors refused to raise ticket prices and a financial crisis developed, so the program was cut back to only one show per season. The management and operation of the State Theatre was taken over by City Center, and although Rodgers remained executive producer, the new management was eager to complete its plans for the coming season. Rodgers was not used to taking orders; he had been his own producer since *Carousel*, and he chafed at even the nominal direction of others. In January 1969

Rodgers left his position, and, as he had feared, the New York State Theatre was dark that summer.

During this stint at Lincoln Center the Rodgerses also made a momentous change in their personal life. They sold Rockmeadow, their country home in Southport, Connecticut, and moved a few miles away into a house designed by Dorothy. At first, the prospect of such a move was unsettling for Rodgers. The man who prided himself as a great innovator on Broadway resisted change in his personal life. Dorothy worked hard to arrange the new house so that it would be comfortable for both his work and their social life (later she wrote a book about it, *The House in My Head*).

At about the same time, Rodgers was honored by the city of New York: an amphitheater was built and dedicated in his name in Mount Morris Park, near Rodgers' boyhood home. He contributed to the funding, and after the dedication ceremony he and his wife, along with Mayor John Lindsay, walked a few blocks to the onetime home of Dr. William Rodgers. But nothing seemed very familiar; the spacious rooms he remembered had "shrunk in scale."

It might have been an appropriate moment for Rodgers to retire. Gershwin and Kern had been dead for years; Porter died shortly after the opening of *No Strings*; and Berlin was close to retirement. Of the composers of his caliber, only Harold Arlen was still active. Moreover, the world of musicals that he and Hammerstein had dominated was changing. Alan Jay Lerner wrote that the belle époque of the musical theater had come to an end in September 1964 with the opening of *Hello, Dolly!*

Rodgers insisted that his experience with Lerner had not lessened his "resolve to keep on looking for the right partner and the right property." That proved to be a remake of a 1952 play by Arthur Laurents, *The Time of the Cuckoo*. It was a poignant story of an American tourist's brief encounter with romance in Venice. The lead had been played by Shirley Booth. Geraldine Page, in her first Broadway role, was cast as a young American wife living unhappily in Venice with her artist husband.

The original story, oddly subtitled a "Comedy in Two Acts," was set in the Pensione Fioria, run by Signora Fioria, an "intelligent, sardonic women in her forties" (played by Carol Bruce in the musical). Her guests are the young American couple and two other tourists, Mr. and Mrs. McIlhenny. The new arrival, also an American tourist, is Leona Samish: in the original she is described as "well into her thirties, blondish, plump and pleasantly attractive." For the musical Leona became a "brightly attractive woman lost in her thirties." She meets Renato Di Rossi, the proprietor of an antique shop, who is "forty odd and so handsome that it never occurs to anyone that he does not always tell the truth."

He is attracted to Leona. She is wary but yields to his romantic overtures, even though she knows that he is married and has a family. Soon, she is disillusioned and they part. In the end she realizes her mistake in not seizing the moment, but by then it is too late. Put off by her suspiciousness, Renato has lost interest. She seeks his reassurance that he was genuinely attracted to her, and not simply because she was supposedly a rich American. He reassures her, but they part.

Laurents always thought the story had possibilities as a musical, though one wonders why. There are few appropriate moments for a song, and the characters seem unlikely subjects for a musical, even in Venice. The American couple, Eddie and Jennifer Yeager, are quarreling. Eddie is lured into an affair with the owner of the pensione, and a tipsy Leona informs Jennifer that her husband has been unfaithful. Leona herself is torn between her desire for romance and her fear that she will be betrayed. She conceals her longings under a veneer of flippant indifference. Renato's wife seems to understand her husband's extramarital activities, and his grown son reveals to Leona his father's liberal arrangement. Venice is represented by a street urchin, Mauro, an endearing con artist. None of this was the sort of material that Rodgers preferred.

Laurents had earlier approached Hammerstein with the project, but Hammerstein thought that the movie version, *Summertime* (1955), was still too new. The film had been directed by the incomparable David Lean, who virtually excluded Laurents from participation. In 1964, Laurents contacted Rodgers, who recalled Hammerstein's interest in the play. By that time Laurents had scored major successes as the librettist of *West Side Story* and *Gypsy*, working with Stephen Sondheim on both. For the show with Rodgers, he again enlisted Sondheim, but Sondheim was reluctant. Just before he died, Hammerstein had asked Sondheim to keep an eye out for Rodgers, who would need a new lyricist. Hammerstein wrongly felt that Rodgers would profit by working with a younger partner. After Hammerstein's death Rodgers had indicated to Sondheim that they might work together one day. To be polite, Sondheim had agreed, saying that he would be willing to collaborate if a suitable project could be found. In fact, he did not want to work with Rodgers, particularly because he did not want to be limited to writing only the lyrics.

Sondheim, a student of the composer Milton Babbitt, wanted to write both lyrics and music, as he had done for *A Funny Thing Happened on the Way to the Forum*. After that show he and Laurents had collaborated on *Anyone Can Whistle*, which was a calamitous failure. He was persuaded to write lyrics for Laurents, in part by Rodgers' daughter Mary, who was a close friend of Sondheim's. Later Rodgers wrote, "Steve was opinionated but terribly self-critical and totally dedicated to his craft, and I thought it would be especially challenging to work with someone so thoroughly trained in music as he was."[9] Rodgers was not pleased when he learned that Sondheim had had to be persuaded to work with him.

At first they worked "closely and well," Rodgers wrote, though they had no particular arrangement. "It's all very flexible," he remarked. Sometimes Sondheim would complete an entire lyric, and sometimes Rodgers developed a melodic theme for which Sondheim wrote the words. If the words and music did not fit, they would agree on how to fix the problem or discard the song entirely, according to Rodgers. But Sondheim complained that compared to his relationships with Jule Styne and Leonard Bernstein during *Gypsy* and *West Side Story*, he had little contact with Rodgers.

There was great publicity for what seemed a magic combination of Rodgers-Laurents-Sondheim. They spoke admiringly of one another in interviews, as if "shining each other's halos," Rodgers commented. In a joint interview with the *New York Times* (November 6, 1964) about the forthcoming show, Sondheim acknowledged that he preferred to write music but that Rodgers was the "best man for this score." Rodgers said that he would be the last one to dispute that. Sondheim also remarked that he wanted to puncture the myth about how fast Rodgers wrote: "The truth is that he thinks about a tune a great deal. . . . It took him a number of weeks to find the ending for one song." Defensively interrupting the interview, Rodgers explained that during that time he had been working on other numbers as well.

But there were problems. For one thing, Sondheim did not like the book. Laurents had adapted his own play, staying quite close to the original and retitling it *Do I Hear a Waltz?* The title is from Leona's comment that she would recognize true romance because she would hear a waltz. Sondheim said that metaphorically the character of Leona did not "sing" and that it was therefore impossible to write music for her.[10]

Leona, as played by Shirley Booth in the original and by Katharine Hepburn in the movie, was a spinster desperately in search of romance. But for *Do I Hear a Waltz?* the part was given to Elizabeth Allen, who was too young and too attractive. Laurents disagreed, insisting that the part, as he wrote it, was for a young woman who could not give herself emotionally, not for an aging lady who could not contemplate sex. Rodgers at first defended Laurents' concept; he said that many actresses could and would play the part if the musical became established. Renato Di Rossi was played by Sergio Franchi, whose voice was similar to Ezio Pinza's—large, full, and booming, almost a caricature of an Italian street singer.

Although the play was melancholy, Laurents decided to remain true to the spirit of the original in the musical. Accordingly, there was to be no dancing. During rehearsals, however, they realized that at least one scene in the Piazza San Marco called for some movement and gaiety. Rodgers and Sondheim wrote a new song, "Here We Are Again," and discarded "Two by Two." The choreographer Herbert Ross was brought in for this scene and immediately clashed with the director, John Dexter, who had little experience directing musicals, let alone American ones. He was an associate director of the British National Theatre and had just directed Shaw's *Saint Joan*. Laurents wanted a "dry and tough interpretation," whereas Rodgers wanted more sentimentality. There were also more than the usual conflicts of personality among the director, the cast, and the writers.

Rodgers and Sondheim eventually clashed openly. At one point, according to one version, Rodgers, in front of the entire company, was handed a Sondheim lyric and, on glancing at it, remarked, "This is shit." [11] One reason for the tension was that Sondheim had thought that he had been recruited by Laurents to write both the music and lyrics. By the time Laurents had decided to enlist Rodgers, Sondheim had already written some music. He even had the temerity to give Rodgers both the music and words for the title song. Rodgers turned him down and wrote his own version of the melody, which is much better than Sondheim's draft. Rodgers and Sondheim also disagreed over "We're Gonna Be All Right," sung by the American couple who are determined to overcome their mistakes and differences. The melody is lively and happy, but Sondheim's original lyrics were cynical. Not surprisingly, Rodgers threw them out; the final version is much more optimistic. [12] Two songs were cut: one, entitled "Philadelphia," had Sondheim lyrics that began "Philadelphia/There isn't a finer spot"; the second, "Perhaps," was not particularly impressive.

Rodgers disagreed with both Sondheim and Laurents on the story. While the show was still in rehearsals Rodgers described the story as a clash of moralities, two ways of looking at life, just as in *The King and I*. This comment was for public consumption, because Rodgers objected to Leona's betrayal of the liaison between Eddie and Signora Fioria on the grounds that this outburst made her too unsympathetic. Laurents and Dexter, and sometimes Sondheim, were allied against Rodgers, so that his suggestions were disregarded on almost every point. The more they worked on the changes the more estranged Rodgers became. Rodgers had always enjoyed the camaraderie of the theater, as everyone—the cast, writers, directors, and musicians—prepared for a production. But in this show such camaraderie was impossible. They all ended up hating one another. [13]

According to Laurents, Rodgers seemed to be afraid of Sondheim, "afraid of his own talent not being what it was." Perhaps because of this, Rodgers was

Arthur Laurents, Richard Rodgers, and Stephen Sondheim
preparing for *Do I Hear a Waltz?* (1965). Although Sondheim was nominated for a Tony, his collaboration
with Rodgers turned out to be difficult.

"foul" to Sondheim.[14] In fact, Rodgers admired Sondheim as a lyricist but disliked his music. In a 1973 interview Sondheim said that his mentor, Oscar Hammerstein, was a man of infinite character but limited talent, whereas Rodgers was a man of "infinite talent—but limited soul." At the time Rodgers refused to respond, commenting only that the less said the better. But earlier, before the show opened, he had said, half-jokingly, that since their first meeting during *Oklahoma!* he had watched Sondheim grow from "an attractive little boy to a monster."

These conflicts led to an inevitable breakdown in communications. When Rodgers came into the theater some cast members would acidly comment, "Here comes Godzilla." He was intimidating, to be sure, but he was the producer—unlike Laurents and Sondheim, he had not just written a major failure. One of the assistant directors commented that among these brilliant minds there "wasn't an ounce of communication. It was most exasperating."[15] A reporter's account of the final rehearsals in Boston indicated that Rodgers was, as usual, working "slowly, patiently, and without the slightest trace of the panic that frequently mars the final out-of-town week of an incoming show."

Do I Hear a Waltz? was the most eagerly awaited musical of the season, and it opened on March 18, 1965. The reviews were strained, and Rodgers was subjected to some severe criticism. One noted that there was really no music: "Richard Rodgers has written songs, all right, but they add up to the flattest score the old master has produced in years." Martin Gottfried took him to task for his crass commercialism, "condescending to the theater—and the public—that gave him his reputation in the first place." Although he did mention Sondheim, commenting that his lyrics "will embarrass him whenever he is reminded of them," Rodgers was the main culprit in the failure.[16] Gottfried insisted that despite Rodgers' abilities he had written a series of "formula tunes" that might have been composed twenty years earlier. Rodgers was no longer interested in new developments, Gottfried said, because "he no longer cared." This, of course, was absurd. Rodgers always cared. Walter Kerr concluded that even though Rodgers was still "king of the hill," his songs were too detached from the play. The music was "musical-comedy generally of a high order," but musical comedy songs could not carry an entire evening when the show was not a musical comedy, and perhaps too abrasive even for light opera.

The score was far from Rodgers' best, but it has been relatively neglected. Several years after the show Rodgers cited the title song as an example of fitting the song to the play. Leona will recognize true love only when she hears a waltz, so Rodgers had to give the music "such a vivacious lilt that everyone would be swept along with Leona's thrilling discovery."

The first love song, "Someone Like You," is unusual for Rodgers and belies the criticism that he was writing formula tunes. It was probably written before the lyrics. Perhaps, as Laurents once implied, Rodgers was determined to prove that he could write in Sondheim's more advanced style, hence the exotic harmonies, thirteenth chords, flatted fifths, and other devices of this song that are rarely heard in his other music. Unfortunately, Franchi's full-throated rendition of "Someone Like You" and "Take the Moment" undermined the charm of these songs. A more typical Rodgers song is "We're Gonna Be All Right," a bouncy number with a slight swing to it, reminiscent of Rodgers and Hart.

Although Sondheim's lyrics are usually glossed over by his admiring biographers, on the whole they are not bad. In "This Week, Americans" Signora Fioria sings the praises of her new American guests and ridicules other nationalities:

You can keep the Germans

. . . .

Good eggs, the English
Rotten legs, the English.

. . . .

This week the Americans,
I love Americans,
The pleasure is mine!
Remember: no breakfast after half past nine.

At the end of the play, as the Americans are leaving, she switches sides:

Last week Americans,
Who can bear Americans?
Wash and wear Americans.
Two faced Americans.

But this week the Britishers,
Educated Britishers . . .
Thank God for Britishers
You aren't like them.
And welcome till Saturday at three P.M.

Another clever Sondheim lyric was "What Do We Do, We Fly," a recitation of all the woes of transatlantic flight. The music was routine, however, and one suspects that Rodgers did not take the number seriously.

Sondheim seemed inclined to write short, punchy lyrics, such as

Take the moment
Let it happen

that were not conducive to Rodgers' style. Rodgers tended to write four- or eight-bar phrases that were either based on a longer statement of the lyrics or could be adapted to such lines. This was true of the essential melodic line of "Do I Hear a Waltz?" but Sondheim's lyrics are often choppy:

Can it be?
Is it true?
Things are impossibly lyrical!
Is it me?

DO I HEAR A WALTZ?

No, it's you!

I *do* hear a waltz!

Rodgers accommodated these lines (which are reminiscent of *West Side Story*) by inserting a tedious repetition of the same three-note phrase, which badly interrupts the flow of the main melody. In most of the numbers there is an obvious tension between the lyrics and the melody.

Sondheim's evaluation was that the show had no excitement, no real energy: it was a "workmanlike, professional show. Period. And it deserved to fail." [17] Ironically, Sondheim (and Rodgers) received Tony nominations for this show. Of course, Sondheim went on to great fame on Broadway.

Rodgers' conclusion, three years later, was that it was a good idea gone wrong:

> I think the insistence on the part of the author in making the heroine unsympathetic just made it impossible for that show to be received by the public. Women hated it, and that's always bad. The character of the girl was very unpleasant, and the love affair in the play was abortive, and unpleasant in its own way too. I think this all hurt it.
>
> I don't think it was a terribly good score, either. There was one song called "Do I Hear a Waltz?" which is still played quite a lot, but that's about all. The lyrics were brittle, and not loving at all. I don't think that helps. . . . The music has to reflect the content of the lyrics and the book. I'm not trying to cop-out, as they say, and blame the fact that the score wasn't terribly good on somebody else. I know it wasn't very good. But it was preceded by a good score, perhaps a number of good scores. [18]

The show closed in September 1965, after 220 performances. Once again Rodgers found himself without a show on Broadway and without collaborators or a new property. His prominence in the entertainment world, however, continued in other media. The film of *The Sound of Music* was released two weeks before *Do I Hear a Waltz?* opened. It was a huge commercial success, and some found it an improvement over the original because of the gorgeous scenery and the presence of Julie Andrews. Rodgers had written two new songs for it.

An odd episode that occurred about this time caused concern about Rodgers' health. For a while he worked with the writer A. E. Hotchner, a confidant of Ernest Hemingway and, later, his biographer. Hotchner, who had wanted to write a musical, met with Rodgers to talk over ideas. Rodgers supposedly said that he had always wanted to do a show about Queen Nefertiti and King Akhenaton. The subject interested Hotchner, and they agreed to proceed. But Hotchner found that too often meetings and discussions had to be canceled because of Rodgers' health. Hotchner finished the first act, and Rodgers, who had already begun work on some of the songs, commented that they had a good show in the making. The *New York Times* even reported the new partnership; the story noted that Rodgers was uncertain whether he would do the lyrics, and it mentioned Diahann Carroll as the possible lead.

Then, according to Hotchner, the situation changed. He delivered a scene that he and Rodgers had previously discussed but that Rodgers insisted he knew nothing about it. They worked out a new outline, but at their next meeting Rodgers "seemed vague and uncharacteristically confused about what was happening in the script. His energy level was very low and I had difficulty hearing him when he spoke," Hotchner wrote many years later.[19] Thereafter Rodgers' condition fluctuated: one day he would be sharp, later "vague and remote." Hotchner suspected that Rodgers had suffered a stroke. In any case, Hotchner decided that it was hopeless to continue and told Rodgers that he had to quit the project to work on a new book. Rodgers did not object because he had to turn to the revival of *South Pacific* at Lincoln Center, which was staged in the summer of 1967, after *Do I Hear a Waltz?* Apparently Rodgers had suffered a slight stroke while in his office, but it was not serious enough to warrant hospitalization. He never mentioned working with Hotchner. One can only wonder whether he paid much attention to it, in that many writers were taking him drafts of their ideas.

Whatever his health problems, in fall 1967 Rodgers was well enough to write another television score, this time for a production of Shaw's *Androcles and the Lion*, with his friend Noel Coward playing the part of Caesar. The teleplay was written by Peter Stone, a rising young librettist; Robert Russell Bennett did the orchestrations; and Rodgers wrote his own lyrics. Rodgers and Stone worked out an outline for musical numbers; one intended song was supposed to resemble "If I Loved You."

Adapting any work by Shaw was a nightmare, and Stone had to engage in a long war with the "Shaw Committee," submitting all changes, which the committee would then cross out, even though it had approved them in the first place. In an interview with a young journalist named Gloria Steinem for the *New York Times* (November 12, 1967) Stone explained the process: "If you put me on the rack right now, I couldn't swear that the [Shaw] committee exists. We only deal through a woman in London who says she represents the committee — its membership is kept secret — but who could be the whole thing herself. Or maybe it's

Shaw's ghost. Remember the 'My Fair Lady' poster? Maybe he's smiling up there in the clouds, manipulating us all with strings." After the show was taped in Brooklyn, some of the actors and television staff speculated about its chances of becoming a Broadway show, with the addition of a few more songs. Forget the show, a studio guard warned them. "You'll be lucky to get a taxi out of Brooklyn." [20]

Rodgers had eight songs in the show; the best was "Strangers," and the most charming "Don't Be Afraid of an Animal." The show aired in November 1967, and the reviews were generally favorable: most of the critics liked the score as well as the adaptation. Jack Gould noted in the *New York Times* that the score was "not out of the top drawer by any means, but contained hints of melodic pleasure." Noel Coward was ill during some of the filming but nonetheless thought that the show went well, in spite of his hatred of television. Rodgers turned out to be one of the harshest critics; he was displeased not only with the production but with his own efforts: "I think it was overdirected, moved too much and you can't get too far away from the people who are singing your songs. It's a purely technical thing. You move back 20 or 30 feet with your cameras, and all you see is a little speck on that screen, because the screen is so small. That happened a great deal too much. There was too much movement. It was just overdone. It should have stayed closer to Mr. Shaw's work." [21]

For the next two years Rodgers wrote very little. He spent much of his time in his office, supervising what had become a major business. The Rodgers and Hammerstein organization—he was quick to point out that it was not a corporation—had the entire floor of an office building on Broadway. One half of the office had become a rental library of their shows, which had become a lucrative business. Groups or organizations that wanted to put on *The King and I*, for instance, were shipped all the necessary materials—scripts, orchestrations, instrumental parts, and the like. Once a production was complete, the materials were returned, checked, repaired as necessary, and rented again.

Rodgers used the other half of the office for his current work, much of which was now related to revivals. He had retained a veto over casting and therefore had to (or wanted to) attend cast calls, rehearsals, and performances.

On his sixty-fifth birthday, ASCAP gave him a gala party at the Alvin Theatre. The tributes were endless; a column by Howard Taubman in the *New York Times* was almost reverential. The evening was an emotional moment for Rodgers. There he stood, he remarked later, the lone survivor of Rodgers and Hart and Rodgers and Hammerstein. He realized that he gave the appearance of being unsentimental and matter-of-fact, but that, he claimed, did not reflect his feelings: "That isn't true. I can't help my appearance. There isn't much I can do about that."[22]

These remarks, recorded during an interview for the Columbia University Oral History Program, are remarkably frank. Rarely had Rodgers admitted any sensitivity to his appearance, and indeed he even enjoyed being thought of as a tough-minded s.o.b. Here, however, as he recalled his sixty-fifth birthday, his guard came down for a moment.

During this period he toyed with several projects, including a new musical. An agent had teamed him with the novelist Erich Segal, whom Rodgers called a "clever and energetic" young man. Rodgers had said that he might be ready to start work on the music and the lyrics for a new show in preparation for the fall 1968 season. Then the project simply faded away; it is not clear why.

In late July 1969, just after turning sixty-seven, Rodgers called his doctor to complain of a shortness of breath. Dorothy and Mary were in the Soviet Union at the time. The doctor immediately admitted him to Lenox Hill Hospital, where he lost consciousness. The next morning he learned that he had suffered a major heart attack; that it took place in the hospital probably saved his life. By the time his wife and daughter returned home he had partially recovered. He left the hospital on August 17, 1969.

Years earlier, before his operation for cancer of the jaw, Rodgers had pounded the table in anger after learning of his condition. He insisted that he was not afraid; he was determined to survive and return to the theater. And he did. Now, a decade later, he again insisted that he had no fears. He was still a survivor.

Rodgers had faced the uncertainties of his profession with a good deal of confidence in both his and his partners' abilities. Success after success must have reinforced his belief in his destiny. He recognized that if one came to bat enough times, as he put it, some failures were likely, but the prospect of failure seldom deterred him. He was, in a sense, Godzilla, the monster who courageously quit Hollywood in disgust and returned to the wilds of mid-Depression Broadway; the monster who did not shrink from experimenting with the morally questionable Joey Evans or from trying something entirely new with an untried partner in *Oklahoma!*

Rodgers had the will not only to persevere but to succeed. Personal, physical, or professional setbacks stimulated him. Before his heart attack he had agreed to start a new show based on Clifford Odets' *The Flowering Peach*, to be written by Peter Stone, with lyrics by Martin Charnin. Once again it seemed that success would be assured—especially after Danny Kaye was hired as the lead.

25

TIME

The story of Noah and the ark would seem an unlikely basis for a musical. But when the lyricist Martin Charnin suggested an adaptation of Clifford Odets' *The Flowering Peach*, Rodgers found the idea intriguing. Charnin had not yet scored his triumph with *Annie* (1977), but he had written some lyrics with Mary Rodgers, who introduced him to her father. Rodgers chose Peter Stone to adapt the play. Stone had just achieved a major Broadway success with *1776*, and he had worked with Rodgers on *Androcles and the Lion*. In June 1970 the group announced their project to the press.

The Flowering Peach, which dated to December 1954, is the story of the building of the ark, the great flood, and the survival of Noah's family and the animals he took on board. The original dialogue was an amalgam of modern slang, wisecracks, and Jewish jokes. The basic theme is the importance of family relationships, yet there are conflicts within this far-from-saintly family, conflicts that seemed closer to the Bronx than to the Bible. Noah is an autocratic father who dominates his family; his son Ham is a womanizer; another son, Shem, is greedy; and his third son, Japheth, is rebellious and covets his brother's wife. The female characters include Noah's skeptical wife, Esther; Leah, Shem's quarrelsome wife; Rachel, wife of the unfaithful Ham; and Goldie, a girl from a nearby village whom Ham takes on board the ark.

The play is a broadly allegorical story about the threat to humankind's survival and the family members' response to impending destruction by the flood, the biblical equivalent of the atomic bomb. There are philosophical debates over how to assure their survival—whether the ark needs a man-made rudder or whether the family should trust its fate to Divine Providence. Noah finally learns humility, but only after his wife dies.

Some critics found Odets' play a disconcerting jumble of the modern and the biblical and criticized its "wordy philosophizing." Followers of Odets, however, considered it one of his best works, if only because of its sharp protest against the indifference of the human race to the horrors of the atomic age. Brooks Atkinson went even further: he thought it was Odets' finest work.

The material turned out to be rich in musical potential, both comically and dramatically. When God informs Noah in a dream that the world is to be destroyed by a great flood and that he is to save his family, Noah responds with a song, "Why Me?" When Noah tells his family of the dream, his sons are derisive and Esther is irritated. "You had enough to drink," she says. Then she wonders, Why should *we* be saved? "Our sons and their wives, they're such bargains?" Finally, the sons and Esther decide that Noah is too old and sing, "Put Him Away." Convinced of Noah's vision, however, Japheth wonders whether it is better to die with others or to challenge an avenging God. Before he leaves the ark and his family in protest, he sings that God must love "Something, Somewhere."

As the ark is being built, the animals appear, two by two, thus providing the title for the show and the title song. God assists Noah by transforming him from a six-hundred-year-old to a young man of ninety (fifty in the play). Noah celebrates in a song, "Ninety Again."

Noah tries to persuade Japheth to return to the ark, and Esther insists she will not go if "Japhie" does not. Japheth, however, is in love with Ham's wife, Rachel, and he finally returns and confesses his love to her in the show's best song, "I Do Not Know a Day I Did Not Love You" (reprised in the second act). The storm begins, the flood comes, and the ark is in danger of sinking, until Noah agrees to put back the man-made rudder.

The flood subsides in the second act, "When It Dries." And in "You," Noah reassures Esther that everything will turn out all right. The doves return with a leaf from an olive tree, but Esther dies in Noah's arms as he sings a touching song, "Hey, Girlie." Shem and his wife, Leah, grudgingly decide to stay together, reconciling in "As Far as I'm Concerned." Ham and Rachel separate, and Ham takes Goldie as his mate; Rachel and Japheth decide to marry. The family leaves the ark, but Noah will not get off without a little guarantee, and so he proposes a bargain: if God will not devastate the world, they will not forget His name. Then, if humankind destroys itself, it won't be God's fault. Noah sings:

> Now it is in man's hands to make or destroy the world
> You will be definitely off the hook.

He pleads for a sign from God, and as the music soars, he turns to see a rainbow.

Obviously, the part of Noah would make or break the musical. The cast was to be small—only eight people—and only one set was called for. The producers and writers considered various candidates, Zero Mostel among them. Rodgers was friendly with Danny Kaye and invited him to hear some of score. Kaye had not been in a Broadway musical since he made made his mark there in 1941, in *Lady in the Dark,* which was followed by *Let's Face It,* with music by Cole Porter. His career took him to Hollywood, where he became a superstar. In the late 1960s he starred in a four-year television series on CBS, and from time to time he made personal appearances doing a vaudeville-type routine. Later he claimed that he had become too "comfy" and wanted something challenging.

During a meeting with Rodgers, the director, and the writers, Kaye said that he saw the play as the story of a generation gap, and everyone politely agreed. He claimed that he did not want to return to Broadway in a conventional musical like *Applause,* then starring Lauren Bacall. He cautioned the authors that the play had to be either a huge success or the bomb of all time. Nevertheless, he was not very interested until he learned that the part involved a six-hundred-year-old turning into a younger man, and then turning back again—just the sort of part Kaye reveled in. His wife and musical mentor, Sylvia Fine, offered to do special material, as she had done thirty years earlier in *Let's Face It.* Cole Porter had not objected, but Rodgers declined her offer.

The director, Joe Layton, remembered that after witnessing Kaye's outsized ego, everyone was scared to death he would accept. He did, and his lawyer negotiated a contract for fourteen thousand dollars a week, the same amount Lauren Bacall was receiving for *Applause*. Charnin considered Kaye's involvement an enormous coup.[1]

Discussions then began. One problem was how Jewish to make the play, especially since in the original Noah had been played by a star of the Yiddish theater, Menasha Skulnik. Rodgers feared that if the play was too Jewish, they would lose the audience. Kaye volunteered to find a way to make it more acceptable to Jewish and non-Jewish audiences alike (which he did). As rehearsals began, after each run-through the director would turn to the authors and say, "I know, more Jewish." Kaye developed an ingenious argument: in an interview he said that because there were no religions in biblical times, the play was really about a universal group. Peter Stone commented on the tensions that soon developed: "The show didn't work because every one of us was working on a different show. Charnin and I were doing one show, which was the Odets concept of Noah's family being a lower-middle-class Jewish family from Queens. Rodgers wanted something less Jewish, less lower class, more lyrical, which was his experience. Layton wanted stage magic and brought in concepts that only hurt the show. And Danny Kaye was interested in being Danny Kaye."[2]

In the advertising, Kaye's name towered above the title: "Richard Rodgers presents DANNY KAYE In a New Musical TWO BY TWO." The advance sales were massive before the November opening at the Imperial Theatre. In addition to Kaye, the cast included Harry Goz as Shem, Joan Copeland as Esther, and Madeline Kahn as Goldie; Japheth was played by Walter Willison, Rachel by Tricia O'Neil, and Leah by Marilyn Cooper. The musical director was Jay Blackton, and the orchestrations were by Eddie Sauter, who had worked with Rodgers on *The Valiant Years*. The dance and vocal arrangements were handled by Rodgers' old colleague Trude Rittmann. Rodgers was the producer.

In the initial staff meeting, Sauter, who was a big-band musician and arranger, treated Rittmann rudely, or at least she thought so. During a brief break in the meeting, she asked Rodgers why Sauter was so hostile; Rodgers replied that Sauter was afraid of her, adding, "Sometimes so am I." Rittmann, who had worked on most of Rodgers' earlier shows, beginning with *Carousel*, found that he had mellowed by the time they began *Two by Two*. Although Rodgers was still careful about his songs, he was now more inclined to leave the musical details to Sauter and Rittmann, who eventually worked well together. Rittmann, however, found Kaye impossible to work with in a disciplined routine.[3]

Everything seemed to go well. Rodgers praised Kaye in an interview: "All the artistry, humor and energy that is Danny Kaye is essential to the role of Noah."

TIME

In turn, Kaye said that "to work with Dick Rodgers, who is a giant, and writing so great, stimulated me." Later he said, "Dick's songs are in a different earth, a new soil, in this play. Of course, nobody is coming to a Richard Rodgers show expecting to hear acid rock. . . . But gorgeous melodies? My God, Dick's melodic sense won't quit."[4]

The reviews were enthusiastic about Kaye and about Rodgers' score but far less charitable toward the play itself. In the *New York Times* (November 11, 1970), Clive Barnes was critical of two of Rodgers' decisions: the first, to hire Peter Stone, and the second, to settle for Stone's version of the book. But Barnes also wrote: "Having made two mistakes the producer then did a very smart thing. He hired himself to write the music. . . . And Mr. Rodgers has delivered some very good numbers. This is not going to go down as his best musical score, but neither is it going down as his worst. He can still write a ballad better than anyone around." Walter Kerr, writing a Sunday column in the *New York Times* (November 22) after the opening, provided some shrewd insights to Rodgers' role:

> A musical comedy should be able to walk on music, as this one does. Whenever movement is needed — and it is needed quite often to overcome Peter Stone's long-winded book — Rodgers seems to know precisely the quality of sound that will cleave the gathering air. . . . "I Do Not Know a Day I Did Not Love You" is one of the very best, surely, that Rodgers has ever written. But more than that. It has dropped its featherweight sounds, then reached its full swell at precisely the moment it was needed to keep us caring. . . . This is music functioning as the life blood of a show.

To be sure, there were sharp dissents. Brendan Gill, in the *New Yorker*, found the show "as nearly dead as a musical can be and Danny Kaye's attempt to make his own superb vitality mask the lack of it in the book, music and lyrics . . . is heroic and in vain." Similarly, John Lahr, in the *Village Voice*, wrote it off as "one of the saddest evenings I have ever spent in the theater." John Simon, of *New York* magazine, was more ambivalent: "The music is by Richard Rodgers and there are three mouth-watering songs in it ['An Old Man,' 'I Do Not Know a Day I Did Not Love You,' 'As Far as I'm Concerned']. . . . The rest are fair to piddling, and include the musically senile 'You' and the mawkish 'Hey, Girlie.'" Surprisingly, Martin Gottfried, who had been highly critical of Rodgers in earlier shows and who wrote a biography of Danny Kaye, cast a different vote: "Rodgers has provided his finest score since *No Strings*. Here once more were lilting, surprising melodies, singing out with no apologies to current musical theatre sophistication, nor any need for them."

Everything seemed set. At a party after opening night, Rodgers commented that Kaye had been "truthful in every scene" and "didn't fool around." He played his part and "never succumbed to the obvious temptations." Kaye chimed in that it was not a one-man show.

The play had been running for nearly three months when disaster struck. On February 5, 1971, in the first act, Kaye tore ligaments in his ankle and suffered a hairline fracture. He was hospitalized for four days, and the show closed while his return was debated. Supposedly he insisted on returning. "Danny Kaye will be back in the cast," read the clever press release, and on February 18 he did return—in a wheelchair with his leg in a cast. Kaye's friend Joanna Simon later commented that Kaye was tired of being an entertainer and that he was terribly bored. His return proved to be unfortunate for all concerned. Kaye gradually transformed the musical into his vaudeville act. He ad-libbed outrageously, sometimes talked to the audience, and tried to break up the other actors by poking them with his crutches or mimicking them. He uttered a particularly vulgar remark to Walter Willison, unzipped the dress of Joan Copeland, and once made a speech to the audience after the curtain, remarking that he was glad they were there and not the authors.

The committee in charge of selecting Tony nominees passed over Kaye, perhaps because of his antics. After this snub Kaye began to play more tricks on stage. According to a cast member, his unpredictability was frightening.[5] In general, the audiences seemed to enjoy his unorthodox performances, though a letter to the New York Times charged that Kaye was making a perfect ass of himself. Kaye explained that since he had hurt his leg he had had to turn the show into an entertainment: "People like it better than they did before—I can tell by the audience reaction and what people say." The only person capable of disciplining him was the producer, Richard Rodgers, but he was quoted as saying, "I have no objections. People seem to like the show as it is, and tickets are being sold." In his autobiography, however, Rodgers wrote that Two by Two "left a sour taste in my mouth not because of the mixed reception (it ran almost a year and showed a small profit) but because of Danny's behavior after the show had opened in New York. . . . [He] began improvising his own lines and singing in the wrong tempos. . . . There was nothing I or anyone else could do about all of this. Danny simply could not take criticism. The minute someone faulted him, he'd just sulk and slow down, and figuring that slowing down was worse than cutting up, we reluctantly said nothing."[6]

TIME

Charnin commented that Kaye could have called the cast together and said, "We're going to make it, let's continue." Instead, he became one of the "most singularly selfish human beings I've ever confronted in my entire life." When Kaye's contract ran out in September 1971, the show closed. After the last performance, Walter Willison watched Kaye go back on the darkened stage, take the cast off his leg, fling it into the audience, leap off stage, and run up the center aisle and out of the theater. Kaye never worked on Broadway again.

Rodgers must have been humiliated to see his work mocked because of Kaye's disregard for professional standards. His own work, as the critics pointed out, was middling. The romantic ballads showed the touch of the younger Rodgers. "I Do Not Know a Day I Did Not Love You" has proved more durable than the rest of the score.

Rodgers seemed to be suffering more and more from the loss of Hammerstein, who now had been dead for a decade. Not only was he deprived of Hammerstein's fine lyrics, but he also missed his sure hand on the production side. It is inconceivable that Hammerstein would have allowed the Odets book to degenerate into Kaye's gags. Hammerstein and Rodgers had prided themselves on having their music and words advance the story, explain characters, and function as an integral element in the production. In both *Do I Hear a Waltz?* and *Two by Two*, Rodgers had moved toward songs that were more entertaining than elucidating. Meanwhile, with no new show in the works, Rodgers wrote some melodic themes for the first part of an ABC television series called *The American Idea*, which was telecast on March 18, 1973.

Again, however, Rodgers was struck down by serious illness. In early 1974 he complained of a sore throat, which was diagnosed as cancer of the larynx. That August he underwent surgery. The operation was successful, but for six months Rodgers could not speak and thereafter had to rely on esophageal speech. He spoke slowly and with difficulty, in a low, gravelly voice. Rodgers had been known for his quick wit and lively repartee, but now conversations proceeded without him, and some of his fair-weather friends began to avoid him. Dorothy Rodgers said that it was painful to watch him struggling to master the new mode of speaking. His determination, she said, was extraordinary. He claimed to feel fine and was "more active than at any other period during the past ten years."

That statement appeared in the last chapter of his autobiography, *Musical Stages*, which he wrote with a friend, the critic Stanley Green. Published in 1975, it was more forthright than most autobiographies, though not a kiss-and-tell account of his life. The review in *Newsweek* described the book as "impeccably good tempered" and "judiciously written." Richard Rodgers was a man, *Newsweek* con-

TIME

cluded, who emerges as all of a piece; a man who knew what he wanted, who got it through a dedication to work that has been "total but dispassionate," and one whose supreme gifts as a writer of popular songs "remain a mystery — above all to himself."

By the time the book was finished Rodgers was already at work, watching over a pleasing and nostalgic interlude produced by his distant cousin Richard Lewine, who had produced *Cinderella*. An elaborate revue, titled simply *Rodgers and Hart*, played on Broadway in May 1975, coinciding with the fiftieth anniversary of his success with *The Garrick Gaieties*. Rodgers played no direct role, and the critics were kind to Hart and him — "what fun to have them back" — but not so kind to the revue. The consensus was that too many songs (ninety in all) were presented in rapid-fire succession. "Slaughter on Tenth Avenue," for example, was introduced with six notes and then abandoned. Some cleverly updated passages were added, however, such as a young man in a leather jacket singing "Zip," from *Pal Joey*.[7]

One by-product of this revue was the reminder to audiences and critics of the "exhilarating growth" of Richard Rodgers the composer. Walter Kerr, who obviously had become a Rodgers fan, criticized the revue for blurring Rodgers' progress as a creative artist: "We are given almost [no chance] to chart the highly sophisticated changes Mr. Rodgers wrought in his work during the twenties and thirties. After all, the brittle, pink-champagne brightness of the 'Girl Friend' is a long way from the rolling chords of 'Connecticut Yankee' . . . and the sound of 'Connecticut Yankee' doesn't in the least prepare us for the haunting adventurousness of 'The Boys from Syracuse.' . . . Rodgers' immensely productive restlessness should not be reduced to a blur" (*New York Times*, May 25, 1975).

At about this time Rodgers was asked whether he ever forgot his melodies. He had forgotten some of the verses, he replied, but not the songs: "I recognize the style." This style was obviously something that Rodgers had begun to worry about: not whether he could continue it himself but what might happen to it after he had departed. He wrote his will in 1975 and included an instruction to his executors and trustees (Dorothy and Mary) that included the following statement: "The artistic integrity and reputation of the musical compositions and lyrics written by me and the manner in which my works will be performed or otherwise presented after my death is of great importance to me." He added instructions forbidding performances of his work unless, in the judgment of his executors, he would have found them appropriate.[8]

By spring 1975, Rodgers had already turned to a new show, the first one since *Carousel* that he did not plan to produce himself. Richard Adler, who had written

the successful *Damn Yankees* and *Pajama Game*, had learned that Rodgers was looking for a new project, and over lunch he explained his idea for a musical about
Henry VIII, with Adler as producer. Rodgers agreed, and Adler enlisted Sheldon
Harnick as the lyricist for the show, called *Rex*. Initially, Jerome Lawrence and
Robert Lee (the team responsible for *Mame*) were to write the libretto, but they
were replaced by Sherman Yellen, who had worked with Harnick on *The Roth-
schilds*. Rodgers was pleased, especially since he thought so highly of Harnick's
work on *Fiorello!* and *Fiddler on the Roof.* It is possible that Rodgers wrote one or
two songs before his operation; his music manuscripts suggest a hiatus from
late 1974 until the spring of 1975. In any case, Rodgers commented that "what's
important to me is that I have a new show and there's no feeling like it. Nothing matches the exhilaration of helping to conceive, plan and create something
that has no purpose other than to give people pleasure." The statement sums up
Rodgers life better than any long analysis.

Originally, the Shubert Organization proposed to finance part of the show
if Adler could get Michael Bennett to direct. Adler backed out, however, because Bennett's price was too high; Hal Prince also turned him down. Ed Sherin
was finally hired as director, a decision Adler later regretted, because as things
turned out, hiring Bennett at any price would have been worth it.

The first act of *Rex* concerns the travails of Henry Tudor and his various wives,
especially Catherine and Anne Boleyn. In the second act, his heirs become a
problem, particularly his daughter, the future Queen Elizabeth I. Because two
of his wives, including Elizabeth's mother, Anne Boleyn, had been beheaded, it
was not ideal fare for a musical comedy. For the lead Adler was determined to
recruit the British stage actor Nicol Williamson, whom he considered one of the
world's great actors. Adler traveled to England and met Williamson at lunch near
Stratford-on-Avon, where Williamson lived. Adler thought that Williamson—
"redheaded, virile, reining in regal energy and fire"—personified Henry VIII.
They agreed on terms, and Adler thought that the meeting was a good omen.
Stratford, after all, was the home of Shakespeare's theater.

For the female lead Penny Fuller was chosen. She had played the devious Eve
Harrington in *Applause*, winning a Tony nomination. She portrayed both Anne in
the first act and Elizabeth in the second. Perhaps one of the most notable aspects
of the show (in retrospect, of course) was the appearance of Glenn Close in the
role of Henry's daughter, the princess Mary. *Playbill* noted that she was making
her musical debut but that she had won "acclaim" the previous season for the
Phoenix Repertory's *A Member of the Wedding*. She was given one song in *Rex*.

The story of Henry VIII was scarcely new to audiences. The BBC had produced a multipart television series devoted to his wives, with Keith Mitchell as Henry. It was shown on American television. And, of course, Charles Laughton had put his indelible imprint on the character of Henry in the fine old film.

From the start, according to Penny Fuller's recollection, there was a conflict between the musical comedy group and the "legit" theater group over the proper tone for the play. She thought that the show was doomed but admitted, at the time, that she could not believe these "giants" of the theater could be wrong. Her concerns were in fact shared by Adler, but he too believed that these "true professionals" could pull it off. Adler discovered, however, that Williamson was highly erratic and undependable; his "incredible antics" were "fueled by copious amounts of wine mixed with brandy."[9]

Wary of the prospect of replacing Hart and Hammerstein, Sheldon Harnick was at first reluctant to join Rodgers. Mary Rodgers urged him to do the show but warned him that her father could be difficult. Gradually, however, Adler concluded that Harnick found working with Rodgers too intimidating; as a consequence, Adler believed that Harnick's lyrics were attuned to Hammerstein rather than written in his own original and brilliant style. Rodgers admired Harnick's work. According to Adler's memoirs, Rodgers' genius, if not at its peak, was in "plentiful evidence"; he wrote "incessantly and easily."

The basic problem, nonetheless, was the book. After the first out-of-town tryout in Wilmington, Delaware, a frantic effort was undertaken to change the entire show. The production was so loose that Rodgers found himself writing song after song; of the twenty-six he wrote, only half were used. The last one was written in April 1976, a few days before the New York opening. One of his best songs was changed three times, in the form of new lyrics or a different placement in the show.

He had given up his leverage as producer of his own work, but it is difficult to imagine a younger Richard Rodgers conceding to write and rewrite this much. (This was the same man who had become indignant when Joshua Logan turned down a song for *South Pacific*.) Indeed, it is sad to read the many horror stories about *Rex*. A critic who observed and chronicled the history of the show noted that Rodgers was "keeping an eye on things." Although his walk had been slowed (reportedly by another stroke), he worked as hard as ever, it was reported. "He's amazing," said Fuller. "He writes a song and if they don't like it, he goes up to his room and writes another one." Obviously, it was not that simple, but Rodgers uttered some optimistic sounds for inquiring reporters. He claimed that the audience reaction was good and getting better. Nevertheless, the pile of discarded music in the copyist's room at his hotel was getting higher and higher.

When *Rex* tried out in Washington, D.C., Rodgers' score was praised. Richard I. Coe, the dean of reviewers in the nation's capital, wrote in the *Washington Post* (March 5, 1976): "Richard Rodgers' score is the immediate pleasure, his mellow, melodic music is wholly treasurable." Another reviewer, David Richards, noted that Rodgers was wasting his music on hunts, masques, and pavannes while the audience yearned to hear songs that told what was happening to the main characters. The book was criticized as too serene and terribly repetitious: "*Rex* lacks the lust and luster of the lusty Henry VIII." It concentrated too much on Henry's heirs. Coe wrote that he missed the material that put Anne in context and explained her relationship with Henry. Unfortunately, the producers decided to remedy this gap by putting the burden on Rodgers, who was asked to write new songs to explain the blank spaces in the plot. Some of these ended up being long dirges telling the story of how the Tudors won the War of the Roses or how Henry VIII succeeded to the throne, to marry his brother's widow. Even Rodgers could not make much of these historical narratives. Walter Kerr also concluded that it was unfair to saddle Rodgers with historical details; explaining Henry's theological, political, and astrological beliefs should have been left to the book. Consequently, though Rodgers had written a great deal of material, it did not function as music: "They are loading Mr. Rodgers down with expository work."

By the time the show reached Boston in late March, it had virtually collapsed. A cry went out to Harold Prince to doctor the show and save it. Attempting to justify this rescue effort, Adler claimed that the show had only a "cough," not cancer, and could be salvaged. The nasty character of Henry was the main problem. Williamson said that he could feel the hostility of the audience rolling over him. Moreover, Henry's first wife, Catherine, as originally portrayed in the musical, was young and gorgeous and seemed an unlikely candidate for divorce. So Henry's personage was softened, and Catherine became a dowdy housewife, preoccupied with mending his shirts. That, however, took away the drama of her confrontation with Henry.

Prince performed major surgery: some songs were kept, some were rewritten, and some were cut. Although the reviewer of an out-of-town preview called "The Pears of Anjou" one of Rodgers' finest songs ever, it did not survive. The orchestrator, Irwin Kostal, had won Academy Awards for his orchestrations of the movies *West Side Story* and *The Sound of Music*. At first he tried to create some Elizabethan sounds for Rodgers' melodies, which he thought were too "Broadway." He was encouraged with the initial results but then had second thoughts; after all, the name on the marquee was Richard Rodgers. If the pro-

Richard Rodgers and Sheldon Harnick working on the score for *Rex* (1976).
Rodgers, then in his seventies, was still writing poignant love songs.

ducers wanted Elizabethan music, they should have hired an Elizabethan. His orchestrations were nevertheless criticized as pseudo-Tudor.

Adler commented that no show in his experience had been more thoroughly revamped on the road.[10] Prince and Harnick argued pleasantly about various lyrics. Yellen was writing and rewriting under conditions similar to the Tet Offensive, noted a reporter. As the show left Boston for New York, two new songs were even slated to be added before the opening. One of them, "From Afar" (also titled "So Much You Loved Me"), incorporated part of a melody of yet another song, "Would I Not Love You." Such tumult must have been painful for the careful and well-organized Rodgers. Nonetheless, he remained calm and resigned. Following his operation his doctor had advised him to avoid unnecessary strains. Consequently, Rodgers did not speak up in production meetings, nor did he complain about the book. At one point, when Harnick apologized for Williamson's demands for new songs, Rodgers simply replied, "This is nothing. You never worked with Danny Kaye."

TIME

At first Rodgers agreed to work according to the demands of the moment, either writing the music first or waiting for the lyrics. As it turned out, however, he was unable to supply any music on his own. Harnick believed that Rodgers' various illnesses made it difficult for him to concentrate on abstract subjects. On one occasion, Harnick said, he discussed a song with Rodgers, who could not comprehend what was needed until Harnick set down a lyric: "Once he saw the dummy lyrics and how everything was supposed to be laid out, he knew how to write the music." [11]

Nevertheless, the reality was that he was getting old and beginning to show it. Some of the cast encountering him for the first time had somehow expected the Richard Rodgers of *Oklahoma!* and *Carousel*. One cast member who knew him from a much earlier show was also prepared for the awesome Richard Rodgers of old, but he was in fact a "frail old man with a cane." [12] Harnick recalled, however, that Rodgers remained eager and enthusiastic throughout the ordeal. It was as if songwriting rejuvenated him. He became particularly excited by new harmonies, as if he was using these chords for the first time. As their work progressed Harnick could see the years fall away from Rodgers. Yellen recalled that "Away from You" and "No Song More Pleasing" were among Rodgers' best work. It was unfortunate, he said, that the failure of the show prevented these two songs from getting the attention they deserved. Andrew Lloyd Webber agreed that "Away from You" was a typical Rodgers melody; and Lloyd Webber's father, a well-known classical musician, thought that "Away from You" was as good as anything Rodgers ever did. It turned out to be more or less his swan song.

The show finally opened on April 25, 1976, at the Lunt-Fontanne, with Rodgers in a new, lesser position on the billing. The advertisement read: "Richard Adler presents NICOL WILLIAMSON in The New Richard Rodgers Musical—REX." In *Playbill*, Rodgers was listed on the same credit line as Harnick and Yellen, below the title. Not surprisingly, the show failed drastically. The reviews were downright bad. Clive Barnes in the *New York Times* found that the "show has almost everything not going for it." Rodgers' music was a hodge-podge of "airy-fairy madrigals, lute songs jazzed up for a Broadway orchestra, a sort of mixture of Benjamin Britten and Irving Berlin. . . . We appear to be hearing an anthology of songs from *Camelot* that were ditched on the road." "The music," wrote Brendan Gill in the *New Yorker*, "has been lent a certain factitious vigor by the orchestrations of Irving [sic] Kostal," but "none of the tunes resemble those of Mr. Rodgers' long prime." Harnick's lyrics were neatly rhymed and "occasionally touching," and the cast "all worked hard in a lost cause." Gill offered them his sympathy.

TIME

Rex closed after forty-nine performances—Rodgers' worst failure since Chee-Chee, forty-eight years earlier. The show had the dubious distinction of being not only the least admired of Rodgers' many scores but, like Chee-Chee, one of the most neglected. Some of the songs that were cut are better than those that survived, and some of the melodies are a shade too dramatic and Elizabethan. But the love songs are poignant and fetching: "No Song More Pleasing" is a vintage Rodgers waltz. "As Once I Loved You" and "Away from You"—written when he was seventy-three!—are as valid as any melodies from his post-Hammerstein shows. Nevertheless, he was drawing down on fixed capital; there is no innovation or freshness to the score. It was good by Broadway standards but not by the standards Rodgers himself had established over the years.

Dorothy Rodgers recalled a poignant moment associated with this show. At a preview performance of Rex, Rodgers left his seat at intermission. Dorothy, who had remained seated, heard the sound of applause, and assuming that the audience had spotted a movie star, she turned to look. There, walking slowing up the aisle with the support of his cane, was Richard Rodgers. He was being given a standing ovation.

Rex was not the end of his career—at least not quite. In 1977 he marked his seventy-fifth birthday and celebrated a highly successful revival of The King and I, featuring Yul Brynner in the role he had created. Rodgers claimed to interviewers that he had a "project" in mind but would not disclose it. He was asked about contemporary popular music and responded characteristically for a man who was rumored to have walked out of the second act of Hair (he was known not to return after an intermission on occasion, but he never walked out of a show, a gesture he detested). He said that he had been taught that music has three components: melody, harmony, and rhythm. Modern music, however, dropped the melody and most of the harmony, leaving only one-third of those elements. As for rock music, as far as he could determine, all of the lyrics consisted of the word "baby."

The honors continued to pile up. In December 1978 he was one of the first five artists selected for the prestigious Kennedy Center Awards, conferred on him by President Jimmy Carter at a White House reception and then celebrated at the Kennedy Center, with performances by Mary Martin, John Raitt, and Florence Henderson. The other artists honored were Arthur Rubinstein, George Balanchine, Marian Anderson, and Fred Astaire. In his citation the president said that the quantity of Rodgers' work could be matched only by its "uniform, sustained quality."

By this time Rodgers had already begun work on his final show. There was an

TIME

ironic touch to the selection for this farewell production: The first nonmusical that he had produced with Oscar Hammerstein had been John Van Druten's play *I Remember Mama*. Now, thirty-five years later, Rodgers was working on the same play, but this time as a musical. The idea had been conceived by Charnin and Thomas Meehan, who had collaborated on the book for *Annie*. They had adapted Van Druten's play and then turned to Rodgers for the music. Charnin wrote the lyrics and directed the production. The producers were friends of Rodgers', Alexander Cohen and his wife, Hildy Parks, who had produced shows in both London and New York.

The surprising news was that the stage and screen star Liv Ullmann was to play the lead role. The Norwegian actor was best known for her films with Ingmar Bergman and her interpretations of Ibsen. She was appearing in Eugene O'Neill's *Anna Christie* when she was approached to do the musical version of *I Remember Mama*. She had no experience in musical comedy but was delighted by the opportunity. Her recruitment was apparently Charnin's idea. She relished the idea of appearing in a Richard Rodgers musical, because she "grew up on him." [13] (This turned out to be a press agent's concoction, but she did vaguely remember "Blue Moon.")

Rehearsals started in March 1979. Unfortunately, the show faltered. The basic story had been thoroughly exploited: first on the stage, then as a movie starring Irene Dunne, and most recently as a television series starring Peggy Wood. Van Druten's original play consisted of a series of character studies and an exposition of family relationships. The musical required more of a narrative. It was so heavily rewritten during tryouts that there seemed to be two musicals, the one being performed on stage and the one being rewritten. Charnin's idea was that the play should be a "valentine" to the American family. Rodgers seemed the ideal composer because the show was conceived as a throwback to the Rodgers and Hammerstein era. Alexander Cohen claimed that enlisting Rodgers was his idea, after Charnin had approached him with the general idea for the play, whereas Charnin insisted that he had offered the show to Rodgers. Charnin also claimed credit for persuading Ullmann to star in the show.

The producers started feuding with Charnin, who they claimed had reduced the play to a comic strip. Charnin and Ullmann also clashed. Charnin said that he had conceived the show as an ensemble performance, not as a star vehicle; he described Ullmann as a "transient" in the musical theater who was miffed because she was not receiving enough attention. In turn, she claimed that he had "stabbed" her in the back. After the preview in Philadelphia, Cohen said that they had to go for "radical surgery" or close the show. He replaced Charnin

Liv Ullmann, Martin Charnin, and Richard Rodgers
during rehearsals for I *Remember Mama* (1979), Rodgers' last
Broadway show.

with the director Cy Feuer. Charnin stayed on briefly as the lyricist, but he was
soon replaced by Raymond Jessel, a television writer who had worked with the
producers on another show. Both Feuer and Jessel, of course, wanted to make
extensive changes, first to the book and then to the musical numbers.

For the first time in his career Rodgers found himself working with two
lyricists in the same show. Rodgers wrote twenty-six songs, fourteen of which
were kept. Several songs were cut during tryouts and during the New York previews, which ran for almost a month. New ones were added, but in the final
score, only four of the lyrics were by Jessel. Rodgers claimed that he did not
mind working with different lyricists; they simply gave him the words and he
wrote the music. He added, politely, that working with more than one stimulated his own musical variations. According to a reporter who traveled with the
show, Rodgers projected "youthful high spirits and confidence" to the rest of the
company throughout all of the troubles.[14] Charnin later remarked that despite
Rodgers' physical discomfort, he "cranked it up." When asked for new songs,
he somehow found the "energy and strength" necessary to produce them. (At
one point he was asked to write six in two weeks.) It's more likely that he was
resigned and no longer really cared about the show. He was not inclined toward
confrontation, however, so once again he wrote song after song.[15]

TIME

In the end the show included some fine Rodgers creations. "Easy Come, Easy Go" is an old-fashioned two-step. The lyrics are by Jessel, though they are reminiscent of Charnin's "Easy Street," from *Annie*. Another excellent Rodgers melody is "Ev'ry Day," one of those songs that could have been set in *The King and I* or *The Sound of Music*. One can easily imagine Anna or Maria singing it. The lyrics are by Charnin. "Maybe, Maybe, Maybe," a song that was cut, was much better than its replacement by Jessel. Interestingly, of the first four lyrics Charnin sent to Rodgers on Christmas Day 1977, three stayed in the show.

One of them was Rodgers' favorite in this show, "You Could Not Please Me More." This was one of his last major songs, and an appropriate bookend to his long career. At one end was "Manhattan," the charming, lilting melody and lyric written by two lively young men, Rodgers and Hart. At the other was the melancholy but moving (and surprising) melodic line of "You Could Not Please Me More," which had overtones of Rodgers and Hammerstein but was still pure Richard Rodgers.

The show opened on May 31, 1979, at the Majestic, the site of *Carousel*, his favorite show, and closed on September 2, after 108 performances. Some of the reviews were churlish and mean-spirited about Rodgers' age. He can only "tarnish his own honor," wrote the critic for *Time*. Richard Eder of the *New York Times* found that the play contained very little beyond "stale wit and mobilized sentiment," although Rodgers' score included several "nice pieces." *Variety* concluded that despite all the rescue attempts and changes, "it was no use," but that Rodgers remained an "indomitably creative composer." Clive Barnes, who had switched to the *New York Post*, was more complimentary: "Liv Ullmann sings Richard Rodgers—and it is the real Liv Ullmann and, to a remarkable extent, the real Richard Rodgers. So you will remember I *Remember Mama*. . . . The best news of the musical—apart from Miss Ullmann—is the way it finds Rodgers, one of the supreme artists of our musical theater, back in a superbly lyrical vein. . . . The score definitely recalls *The Sound of Music*." Charles Michener, writing for *Newsweek*, found that Rodgers was back in the land he understood so well, "the land of milk and cookies."

Rodgers' friend Stanley Green attended one of the final previews. He recalled that although the play was not successful, that particular performance drew a standing ovation. After the curtain he and Rodgers embraced. As Green walked up the aisle, he glanced back and saw people converging around Rodgers, whose eyes were "beaming." That was his life.

Nevertheless, Rodgers' career was at an end. Perhaps as an unintended compensation for the failure of I *Remember Mama*, a revival of *Oklahoma!* directed by

William Hammerstein, Oscar's son, opened at the Palace on December 13, 1979. The reviewers were ecstatic. Walter Kerr was particularly enchanted, and after suggesting some changes (it was too long for contemporary audiences), Kerr closed with an admonition: "No one should touch the music though. All that incredible music."

Shortly before his seventy-seventh birthday, Rodgers told an interviewer that he had nothing in mind: "I just want to sit for a while." The last original melody by Richard Rodgers heard on a Broadway stage was "Time," from I Remember Mama. It was, quite fittingly, a waltz. The song ended with Martin Charnin's lyrics: "Oh, Time, Time to let go."

Richard Rodgers died at home on December 30, 1979.

NOTES

Chapter 1: Campfire Days

1. Rodgers, *Musical Stages*, chaps. 1–4; Rodgers' first meeting with Lorenz Hart is described on pp. 26–27. Nolan, *Hart*, chaps. 2 and 3. Ewen, *Richard Rodgers*, chaps. 3 and 4; Rodgers' first meeting with Hart is described on pp. 64–65.

2. Rodgers, *Musical Stages*, p. 6.

3. Dorothy Rodgers, *A Personal Book*, p. 32.

4. The music for "Campfire Days" is reproduced in Taylor, *Some Enchanted Evenings*, p. 23.

5. Quoted in P. G. Wodehouse and Guy Bolton, *Bring on the Girls* (New York: Limelight, 1984), p. 102.

6. Rodgers, *Musical Stages*, p. 20.

Chapter 2: Fly with Me

1. Fordin, *Getting to Know Him*, p. 28.
2. Ibid.
3. Nolan, *Hart*, pp. 3–19.
4. Rodgers, *Musical Stages*, p. 28.
5. Ibid., pp. 30–31. Nolan, *Hart*, pp. 23–24.
6. Rodgers, *Musical Stages*, pp. 30–31.
7. "The Parodoxian," Camp Paradox Newsletter, August, November 1920. Rodgers Collection, Library of Congress, Washington, D.C.

Chapter 3: Melody Man

1. Palmer, *Composer in Hollywood*, pp. 160–67.
2. Percy Goetschius, *Lessons in Musical Form: A Manual of Analysis* (Boston: Oliver Ditson, 1914). George Martin, *The Damrosch Dynasty* (Boston: Houghton Mifflin, 1983), p. 296.
3. Rodgers, *Musical Stages*, p. 47.
4. Leavitt quoted in Marx and Clayton, *Rodgers and Hart*, pp. 40–43.

Chapter 4: The Garrick Gaieties

1. Rodgers, *Musical Stages*, p. 61. Nolan, *Hart*, p. 63.
2. Rodgers, *Musical Stages*, p. 65.
3. Ibid.
4. *Theatre Arts Monthly* (Apr. 1936): 274.
5. Rodgers, *Musical Stages*, p. 72.
6. Lynn Farnol Group, *Fact Book*, pp. 30–32.
7. Hammerstein, *Lyrics*, p. xi.
8. Edith Meiser quoted in Hart, *Thou Swell*, pp. 40–41.

Chapter 5: The Girl Friend

1. Lynn Farnol Group, *Fact Book*, pp. 38–40.
2. Ibid., pp. 45–47.
3. *New York Herald Tribune*, Mar. 26, 1926; also quoted in Nolan, *Hart*, p. 76.
4. Rodgers, *Musical Stages*, p. 88.
5. Ibid., pp. 90–91.

Chapter 6: Peggy-Ann

1. Rodgers, *Letters*, pp. 14–15.

2. Rodgers, *Reminiscences*, p. 113.

3. Rodgers, *Letters*, p. 18.

4. Barrett, *Irving Berlin*, pp. 54–55. Marx and Clayton, *Rodgers and Hart*, pp. 102–03.

5. Rodgers, *Letters*, p. 23.

6. Ibid., pp. 33–35.

7. Jessie Matthews, *Over My Shoulder* (London: W. H. Allen, 1974), pp. 112–13. Marx and Clayton, *Rodgers and Hart*, pp. 106–07.

Chapter 7: A Connecticut Yankee

1. Mark Twain, *A Connecticut Yankee in King Arthur's Court* (New York: Signet Classic, n.d.). *Mark Twain's Notebook* (New York: Harper and Bros., 1935), p. 171.

2. Lynn Farnol Group, *Fact Book*, p. 84.

3. Rodgers, *Musical Stages*, p. 108.

4. Rodgers, *Letters*, p. 51.

5. Musical sketchbook in the Rodgers Collection, Library of Congress.

6. Rodgers, *Letters*, p. 61.

7. Ibid., pp. 65–66.

8. Ibid., p. 70

Chapter 8: Simple Simon

1. Rodgers, *Letters*, p. 79.

2. Nolan, *Hart*, pp. 133–34.

3. Lynn Farnol Group, *Fact Book*, pp. 103–04.

4. Ibid., p. 111.

5. Rodgers, *Letters*, p. 92.

6. Barrios, *Song in the Dark*, p. 236.

7. Ibid., p. 109.

8. *New York Times*, Mar. 6, 1930.

9. Dorothy Rodgers, *Personal Book*, p. 80.

10. Ibid., p. 84.

11. Rodgers, *Letters*, pp. 103–09.

12. Ibid., p. 114.

13. Dorothy Rodgers, *Personal Book*, p. 87.

Chapter 9: Hollywood

1. Wilder, *American Popular Song*, pp. 190–91.

2. Rodgers, *Reminiscences*, pp. 137–38.

3. Ibid., p. 139.

4. Rodgers, *Musical Stages*, p. 165.

5. Rodgers, *Letters*, p. 183.

Chapter 10: On Your Toes

1. Burns Mantle, ed., *Best Plays of 1932–33* (New York: Dodd, Mead, 1933), p. v.

2. Brooks Atkinson, *New York Times*, Nov. 22, 1934. Notes to recording of *Anything Goes* (EMI CD 498482).

3. Rodgers, *Reminiscences*, pp. 161–63.

4. Abbott, *Mister Abbott*, pp. 177–78.

5. Rodgers, *Musical Stages*, p. 175.

6. Rodgers, *Letters*, p. 214.

7. Wilder, *American Popular Song*, p. 203.

8. Lynn Farnol Group, *Fact Book*, p. 153.

9. Ibid., p. 161. Brooks Atkinson, *New York Times*, Oct. 12, 1954.

10. Rodgers, *Reminiscences*, p. 167.

11. Rodgers, *Letters*, p. 223.

12. Lynn Farnol Group, *Fact Book*, pp. 169–70.

13. Forte, *American Popular Ballad*, p. 203.

14. Rodgers, *Reminiscences*, p. 240.

15. Ibid., pp. 138–39.

16. Vera Zorina, *Zorina* (New York: Farrar, Straus, and Giroux, 1986), p. 210. Richard Buckle, *George Balanchine: Ballet Master* (New York: Random House, 1988), pp. 100, 110–11.

17. Wilder, *American Popular Song*, p. 209.

18. *Time*, July 6, 1942.

Chapter 11: The Boys from Syracuse

1. Logan, *Josh*, pp. 100–106.

2. Walter Kerr, *Thirty Plays Hath November* (New York: Simon and Schuster, 1969), pp. 192–95.

3. Hart, *Thou Swell*, pp. 125–26.

4. Vernon Duke, "The Theatre Music Mart," *Theatre Arts Monthly* (Apr. 1937): 212–14.

5. Richard Rodgers, "A Score of Years and One," *New York Times*, May 5, 1940.

Chapter 12: Pal Joey

1. Hyland, *Song Is Ended*, chap. 19. Richard Rodgers, notes to recording of *Pal Joey* (Columbia ML 4653), 1950.

2. Richard Rodgers, " 'Pal Joey': History of a Heel," *New York Times*, Dec. 30, 1951.

3. Bruccoli, *O'Hara Concern*, pp. 160–65.

4. Rodgers, " 'Pal Joey.' "

5. Brooks Atkinson, *New York Times*, Jan. 4, 1952.

6. Hart, *Thou Swell*, p. 158.

7. Ibid., pp. 159–63.

8. Fordin, *Getting to Know Him*, p. 174.

9. Joshua Logan Collection, Library of Congress.

10. Rodgers, *Reminiscences*, pp. 193–94.

Chapter 13: Oklahoma!

1. For background, see Wilk, *OK*, and Hyland, *Song Is Ended*, chap. 22.

2. Wilk, *OK*, p. 30.

3. Langner, *Magic Curtain*, p. 369.

4. Riggs, *Green Grow the Lilacs*, p. vii.

5. Phyllis Cole, *Haunted by Home* (Norman: University of Oklahoma Press, 1988), p. 97.

6. Oscar Hammerstein, "In re Oklahoma!" *New York Times*, May 23, 1943.

7. Undated Theatre Guild press release, New York Public Library, Performing Arts Library (Lincoln Center), *Oklahoma!* file.

8. Musical work sheets, Rodgers Collection, Library of Congress.

9. Hammerstein Collection, Library of Congress, *Oklahoma!* file.

10. Jule Styne, notes to recording of *Oklahoma!* (RCA RCDI 3572), 1980.

11. Easton, *No Intermissions*, pp. 201–07.

12. De Mille, *Dance to the Piper*, pp. 324–26.

13. Ibid., p. 324.

14. Aljean Harmetz, *The Making of "The Wizard of Oz"* (New York: Bantam Doubleday, 1977), p. 68.

15. Fordin, *Getting to Know Him*, pp. 199–200.

16. Nolan, *Hart*, pp. 308–12.

17. Ibid., p. 314.

Chapter 14: Carousel

1. Hammerstein Collection, Library of Congress.

2. Logan Collection, Library of Congress.

3. Easton, *No Intermissions*, pp. 220–21.

4. David Richards, *New York Times*, Mar. 25, 1994. Ethan Mordden, *New York Times*, Sept. 12, 1993. *Time*, Apr. 4, 1994. Frank Rich, *New York Times*, Mar. 31, 1994.

5. Swain, *Broadway Musical*, pp. 99ff.

Chapter 15: Allegro

1. Rodgers, *Musical Stages*, p. 246.

2. Barrett, *Irving Berlin*, p. 239.

3. Easton, *No Intermissions*, pp. 268–71.

4. Suskin, *Opening Night*, p. 43.

5. Lynn Farnol Group, *Fact Book*, pp. 556–57.

6. Cecil Smith, *Theatre Arts Monthly* (Nov. 1947): 13–15.

7. Oscar Hammerstein, preface to *Allegro: A Musical Play* (New York: Alfred Knopf, 1948), pp. v–xviii.

8. Ibid.

9. Rodgers, *Reminiscences*, pp. 281–82.

Chapter 16: South Pacific

1. Wilder, *American Popular Song*, p. 222.

2. Rodgers, *Reminiscences*, pp. 219–20.

3. Ibid.

4. Logan Collection, Library of Congress.

5. Logan, *Josh*, p. 233.

6. Rodgers, *Reminiscences*, pp. 298–99.

7. Michener, *World Is My Home*, p. 295. John P. Hayes, *James P. Michener: A Biography* (New York: Bobbs-Merrill, 1984), p. 85.

8. Hammerstein Collection, Library of Congress, *South Pacific* file.

9. Logan, *Josh*, p. 227.

10. Ward Morehouse, "Romance for the Middle-Aged," *American Mercury*, December 1951, pp. 114–18. Harold Clurman, *New Republic*, April 25, 1949.

11. Rodgers, *Reminiscences*, p. 304.

Chapter 17: The King and I

1. Norman Sherry, *The Life of Graham Greene*, vol. 2, 1939–1955 (New York: Viking, 1994), p. 313.

2. Rodgers, *Musical Stages*, pp. 270–71.

3. Richard Rodgers and Oscar Hammerstein, "About The King and I," *New York Times*, Mar. 23, 1951.

4. Richard Rodgers, "The Background Is Pure Siam," *New York Herald Tribune*, Mar. 25, 1951.

5. Payn and Morley, *Noel Coward Diaries*, pp. 148, 154.

6. Nathaniel Benchley, "Off Stage," *Theatre Arts Monthly* (July 1951).

7. Hammerstein Collection, Library of Congress, letter to R. J. Kaplan, in *The King and I* file.

8. Rodgers, *Musical Stages*, p. 273.

9. John Van Druten, *New York Times*, Sept. 14, 1952.

10. Hammerstein Collection, Library of Congress, *The King and I* file.

11. Logan, *Josh*, pp. 245–46.

12. *New York Times*, Oct. 26, 1952.

13. Jack Gould, *New York Times*, Oct. 27, 1952.

Chapter 18: R&H

1. Richard Rodgers, "In Defense of Common Sense," *New York Times*, June 29, 1952.

2. Brooks Atkinson, *New York Times*, Jan. 13, 1952.

3. De Mille, *Promenade Home*, p. 235.

4. Ibid., p. 236.

5. Mary Rodgers, *Musical Stages* (1995), p. vii.

6. Benjamin Feiner, Jr., "This Week," *New York Herald Tribune*, Nov. 9, 1947.

7. Dorothy Rodgers, *My Favorite Things*, p. 95.

8. *New York Times*, Oct. 23, 1950.

9. Hammerstein, *Lyrics*, p. 19.

10. De Mille, *And Promenade Home*, p. 238.

11. Marx and Clayton, *Rodgers and Hart*, pp. 269–70.

12. Hammerstein, *Lyrics*, pp. 15ff.

13. De Mille, *And Promenade Home*, p. 236.

14. Green, *Rodgers and Hammerstein Story*, p. 14.

15. George Jean Nathan, *Theatre in the Fifties* (New York: Alfred Knopf, 1953), p. 234.

16. Mary Rodgers, *Musical Stages* (1995), p. vii.

17. Oscar Hammerstein and Richard Rodgers, "An Optimistic Appraisal of Our Theatre," *New York Times*, Jan. 1, 1950.

Chapter 19: Me and Juliet

1. Seymour Peck, *New York Times*, May 24, 1953.

2. Hammerstein Collection, Library of Congress.

3. Saul Pett, *Philadelphia Inquirer*, May 31, 1953.

4. *Cleveland Plain Dealer*, Apr. 16, 1953. *New York Times*, Apr. 21, 1953.

5. Abbott, *Mister Abbott*, pp. 246–48.

6. Zinnemann, *Autobiography*, p. 146.

7. Easton, *No Intermissions*, pp. 342–46.

8. Shirley Jones and Marty Engels, *Shirley Jones and Marty Engels* (New York: S. P. I. Books, 1993), pp. 143–44.

9. Steinbeck and Wallsten, *Letters* (New York: Penguin, 1989), p. 511.

10. Ibid., pp. 514–15.

11. Helen Traubel, with Richard G. Hubler, *St. Louis Woman* (New York: Ayer, 1977), pp. 257–58.

12. Steinbeck and Wallsten, *Letters*, pp. 516–17.

13. Brooks Atkinson, *New York Times*, Dec. 11, 1955.

14. Eric Bentley, *What Is Theatre?* (New York: Atheneum, 1968), pp. 192–93.

Chapter 20: Cinderella

1. Richard Rodgers, *New York Times*, Mar. 31, 1957.

2. Hammerstein Collection, Library of Congress. Rodgers, *Musical Stages*, pp. 291–92.

3. Rodgers, *Musical Stages*, p. 293.

4. Mary McCarthy, *The Group* (New York: Harcourt, Brace, World, 1954), p. 329. David Hellerstein, "Letting Go of Payne Whitney," *New York Times Magazine*, Nov. 6, 1994.

5. David Roberts, *Jean Stafford: A Biography* (Boston: Little, Brown, 1988), pp. 254–55.

6. *New York Times Magazine*, Nov. 6, 1994.

7. Mary Rodgers, *Musical Stages* (1995), p. vii.

8. Joanne Stang, *New York Times Magazine*, Nov. 21, 1958.

9. Logan Collection, Library of Congress.

10. Bruce A. McConachie, "The 'Oriental' Musicals of Rodgers and Hammerstein and the U.S. War in Southeast Asia," *Theatre Journal* 46 (1994): 385ff.

Chapter 21: The Sound of Music

1. Draft lyrics for *The Sound of Music*, Hammerstein Collection, Library of Congress.

2. Ibid.

3. *New York Times*, Nov. 15, 1959.

4. Ibid.

5. Martin, *My Heart Belongs*, p. 239.

6. Payn and Morley, *Noel Coward Diaries*, p. 455.

7. Stephen M. Silverman, *The Fox That Got Away: The Last Days of the Zanuck Dynasty at Twentieth Century–Fox* (Secaucus, N.J.: Lyle Stuart), pp. 116–25.

Chapter 22: Words and Music

1. Fordin, *Getting to Know Him*, p. 343.

2. Rodgers, *Musical Stages*, p. 303.

3. *Rodgers and Hart Songbook*, foreword by Oscar Hammerstein II (New York: Simon and Schuster, 1951), p. xi.

4. Forte, *American Popular Ballad*, pp. 177ff.

5. Anthony Storr, *Music and the Mind* (New York: Ballantine, 1992), p. 86.

6. Martin Gottfried, *A Theatre Divided* (New York: Little, Brown, 1967), pp. 171–81.

7. A. J. Gurney, *New York Times*, Sept. 8, 1996. Mordden, *Rodgers and Hammerstein*, p. 215.

Chapter 23: No Strings

1. Rodgers, *Musical Stages*, p. 306.

2. Samuel Chotzinoff, *A Little Night Music* (New York: Harper and Row, 1964), pp. 99–115.

3. *New York Times*, Nov. 20, 1960.

4. *New York Times*, Sept. 22, 1960.

5. Brooks Atkinson, *New York Times*, Dec. 5, 1961.

6. Rodgers, *Musical Stages*, p. 307.

7. Carroll, *Diahann*, pp. 109–10.

8. Rodgers, *Reminiscences*, pp. 198–200.

9. Richard Rodgers, Author's Note, *No Strings* (New York: Random House, 1962).

10. Incidental lyrics from Rodgers Collection, Library of Congress, No Strings folder.

11. Lewis Funke, *New York Times*, Mar. 11, 1962.

12. Carroll, *Diahann*, p. 112.

13. Funke, *New York Times*, Mar. 11, 1962. William K. Zinsser, "Rodgers & Rodgers," *Life*, Mar. 9, 1962.

Chapter 24: Do I Hear a Waltz?

1. Lerner, *Street Where I Live*, p. 160. Lees, *Inventing Champagne*, p. 210. Citron, *Wordsmiths*, p. 232.

2. Jablonski, *Alan Jay Lerner*, pp. 207–09.

3. Lees, *Inventing Champagne*, p. 210.

4. Ewen, *With a Song in His Heart*, pp. 178–79.

5. Rodgers Collection, Library of Congress.

6. Lees, *Inventing Champagne*, p. 213. Nolan, *Sound of Their Music*, p. 229.

7. Rodgers, *Reminiscences*, p. 7.

8. Alan Jay Lerner, *The Musical Theatre: A Celebration* (New York: McGraw-Hill, 1986), p. 213.

9. Rodgers, *Musical Stages*, p. 318. Nolan, *Sound of Their Music*, p. 229.

10. Zadan, *Sondheim & Co.*, p. 100.

11. Ibid. Nolan, *Sound of Their Music*, p. 230.

12. Lyric sheet in Rodgers Collection, Library of Congress, *Do I Hear A Waltz?* folder.

13. Zadan, *Sondheim & Co.*, p. 104.

14. Ibid., p. 102.

15. Ibid.

16. Martin Gottfried, *Opening Nights* (New York: Putnam, 1969), pp. 122–24.

17. Zadan, *Sondheim & Co.*, pp. 106–07.

18. Rodgers, *Reminiscences*, p. 374.

19. A. E. Hotchner, *Choice People* (New York: William Morrow, 1984), pp. 387–95. Rodgers was involved in a number of projects that simply faded away. He was approached by many writers with ideas for shows and even publicly announced some plans. A musical version of a novel by Earl Hammer, *You Can't Get There from Here*, adapted by Erich Segal, was supposed to go into production in the winter of 1968. During this time Rodgers put up all the money ($125,000) for a nonmusical play by Samuel Taylor, *Avanti*, that failed in February 1969 and lost money.

20. *New York Times*, Nov. 12, 1967.

21. Rodgers, *Reminiscences*, pp. 10, 376. Payn and Morley, *Noel Coward Diaries*, p. 654.

22. Rodgers, *Reminiscences*, p. 335.

Chapter 25: Time

1. Gottfried, *Nobody's Fool*, pp. 288–93.

2. Bell, *Broadway Stories*, p. 150.

3. Trude Rittmann, interview with author, 1996.

4. *New York Times*, Nov. 8, 1975.

5. Gottfried, *Nobody's Fool*, pp. 299–300.

6. Rodgers, *Musical Stages*, p. 323.

7. Jack Gould, *New York Times*, May 14, 1975.

8. Rodgers also specified that no new lyrics could be added to any of his songs. In his seventy-four-page will, with six codicils, he left one-half of his estate to Dorothy and one-half in trust for his family. His daughters received cash bequests of $250,000 each. For probate purposes, his estate was valued at more than $500,000, but according to "informed sources" it was worth "many millions" (*New York Times*, Feb. 17, 1980). When Dorothy died in 1992, Christie's valued the paintings she still owned at about $10 million (*Los Angeles Times*, Sept. 25, 1992).

9. Adler, *You Gotta Have Heart*, p. 268.

10. Caryl Rivers, *New York Times*, Apr. 25, 1976.

11. Kasha and Hirschhorn, *Notes on Broadway*, p. 166. *Richard Rodgers: The Sound of His Music*, public television program on *Great Performances*, 1990, produced by WNET, New York.

12. McGovern and Winer, *Sing Out Louise!*, p. 13.

13. Liv Ullmann, *Choices* (New York: Bantam, 1984), p. 15.

14. Ralph Tyler, *New York Times*, May 27, 1979.

15. Martin Charnin's comments in the television program *Richard Rodgers: The Sound of His Music*.

BIBLIOGRAPHY

There are two primary collections of manuscripts and papers concerning Richard Rodgers. Musical holographs for almost all his work have been collected and deposited in the Music Division of the Library of Congress, Washington, D.C. This collection of songs extends from his campfire days through his very last Broadway shows. It also includes musical notebooks and sketches for songs that were never completed or not published. The librarian, Mark Horowitz, has provided valuable notes to the collection.

Also in the Music Division of the Library of Congress is a collection of the papers of Oscar Hammerstein II. It covers almost all the shows he wrote with Rodgers and includes drafts, librettos, and lyrics but has not yet been catalogued.

There is no similar collection of Lorenz Hart's works. *The Complete Lyrics of Lorenz Hart*, edited by Robert Kimball and Hart's sister-in-law, Dorothy Hart, has been published, however (Knopf, 1986). As noted in that publication, some of his lyrics have been lost.

The Library of Congress also holds the musical collections of two of Rodgers' orchestrators, Hans Spialek and Robert Russell Bennett. The papers of the director Joshua Logan are deposited in the Manuscript Division.

A four-hundred-page interview with Rodgers, conducted in 1967 and 1968, can be found in the Oral History Collection of Columbia University. It is available on microfiche.

Three books are of special note. First and foremost is Richard Rodgers' autobiography, *Musical Stages*, published in 1975 by Random House and reprinted in 1995 by Da Capo Press, with a new introduction by his daughter, Mary Rodgers Guettel. It is franker than most autobiographies and, of course, indispensable, although it ends before Rodgers' last two shows.

Also of great value is Hugh Fordin's biography of Oscar Hammerstein, *Getting to Know Him* (Random House, 1977), which is sympathetic but well researched and admirably written. The author was given access to family memoirs and private papers.

Equally valuable is Frederick Nolan's biography, *Lorenz Hart* (Oxford University Press, 1994); it too is indispensable, but, unfortunately, this work does not include any lyrics because of a dispute with the Hart estate.

A selection of Richard Rodgers' letters to his wife has been published: *Richard Rodgers: Letters to Dorothy, 1926–1937* (New York: New York Public Library, 1988). Additionally, there is a Richard Rodgers collection in the Library of Performing Arts, Lincoln Center, a division of the New York Public Library.

Finally, there is the so-called "Black Book," *The Rodgers and Hammerstein Fact Book*, edited by Stanley Green and published by the Lynn Farnol Group in 1980. It is a compilation of information about every show written by Rodgers and includes an extensive bibliography. The *Fact Book* was published shortly after Rodgers' death.

Richard Rodgers

Ewen, David. *Richard Rodgers*. New York: Henry Holt, 1957.

————. *With a Song in His Heart: The Story of Richard Rodgers*. New York: Holt, Reinhardt, 1963.

Green, Stanley. *The Rodgers and Hammerstein Story*. New York: John Day, 1963.

Kaye, Milton. *Richard Rodgers: A Comparative Melody Analysis of His Songs with Hart and Hammerstein Lyrics*. Ph.D. diss., New York University, 1969.

Kislan, Richard J. *Nine Musical Plays of Rodgers and Hammerstein: A Critical Study in Content and Form*. Ph.D. diss., New York University, 1970.

Lynn Farnol Group. *Rodgers and Hammerstein Fact Book*. Edited by Stanley Green. New York: Lynn Farnol Group, 1980.

Mordden, Ethan. *Rodgers and Hammerstein*. New York: Abrams, 1992.

Nolan, Frederick. *The Sound of Their Music*. New York: Walker, 1978.

Rodgers, Dorothy. *The House in My Head*. New York: Athenaeum, 1967.

———. *My Favorite Things*. New York: Athenaeum, 1964.

———. *A Personal Book*. New York: Harper & Row, 1977.

Rodgers, Richard. *Richard Rodgers: Letters to Dorothy, 1926–1937*. Excerpts edited by William W. Appleton. Foreword by Dorothy Rodgers. New York: New York Public Library, 1988.

———. *Musical Stages: An Autobiography*. New York: Random House, 1975. Reprint, New York: Da Capo, 1995.

———. *Reminiscences of Richard Rodgers*. Oral History Collection of Columbia University, 1968. Available on microfiche from Meckler Publishing.

Rodgers and Hammerstein. Facet, F/Compact Disc 8108. Recorded interviews with Rodgers and, separately, Hammerstein by Tony Thomas, 1960.

Suskin, Steven. *Berlin, Kern, Rodgers, Hart and Hammerstein: A Complete Song Catalogue*. Jefferson, N.C.: McFarland, 1990. An extremely useful compilation of Rodgers' songs based on copyright deposits at the Library of Congress.

Taylor, Deems. *Some Enchanted Evenings: The Story of Rodgers and Hammerstein*. New York: Harper and Bros., 1953.

Lorenz Hart

Hart, Dorothy, ed. *Thou Swell, Thou Witty: The Life and Lyrics of Larry Hart*. New York: Harper and Row, 1976.

Hishchak, Thomas S. *Word Crazy*. New York: Praeger, 1991.

Kimball, Robert, and Dorothy Hart, eds. *The Complete Lyrics of Lorenz Hart*. New York: Alfred A. Knopf, 1986.

Marx, Samuel, and Jan Clayton. *Rodgers and Hart: Bewitched, Bothered and Bedeviled*. New York: G. P. Putnam, 1976.

Nolan, Frederick. *Lorenz Hart: A Poet on Broadway*. New York: Oxford University Press, 1994.

Oscar Hammerstein

Citron, Stephen. *The Wordsmiths: Oscar Hammerstein 2nd and Alan Jay Lerner*. New York: Oxford University Press, 1995.

Fordin, Hugh. *Getting to Know Him*. New York: Random House, 1977.

Hammerstein, Oscar. *Lyrics*. New York: Simon and Schuster, 1949. Reprint, Milwaukee: Hal Leonard, 1985.

Riggs, Lynn. *Green Grow the Lilacs*. New York: Samuel French, 1931. Reprint 1958.

Rodgers, Richard, and Oscar Hammerstein. *Six Plays*. New York, Random House, n.d.

Steinbeck, John. *Sweet Thursday*. New York: Penguin, 1986.

Abbott, George. *Mister Abbott*. New York: Random House, 1963.

Adler, Richard. *You Gotta Have Heart: An Autobiography*. New York: Donald I. Fine, 1990.

Alpert, Hollis. *Broadway: 125 Years of American Musical Theatre*. Museum of the City of New York: Little, Brown, 1991.

Atkinson, Brooks. *Broadway*. New York: Macmillan, 1970.

Barrett, Mary Ellin. *Irving Berlin: A Daughter's Memoir*. New York: Simon and Schuster, 1994.

Barrios, Richard. *A Song in the Dark: The Birth of Musical Film*. New York: Oxford University Press, 1995.

Bell, Marty. *Broadway Stories: A Backstage Journey through Musical Theatre*. New York: Limelight, 1993.

Bergreen, Laurence. *As Thousands Cheer: The Life of Irving Berlin*. New York: Viking Penguin, 1990.

Block, Geoffrey. *Enchanted Evenings*. New York: Oxford University Press, 1997.

Bordman, Gerald. *American Musical Comedy: From Adonis to Dreamgirls*. New York: Oxford University Press, 1982.

————. *The American Musical Revue: From the Passing Show to Sugar Babies*. New York: Oxford University Press, 1985.

————. *American Musical Theatre: A Chronicle*. New York: Oxford University Press, 1986.

————. *American Operetta: From HMS Pinafore to Sweeney Todd*. New York: Oxford University Press, 1981.

————. *Jerome Kern: His Life and Music*. New York: Oxford University Press, 1980.

Bowers, Dwight Blocker. *American Musical Theater: Shows, Songs and Stars*. Washington, D.C.: Smithsonian Institution, 1989.

Bruccoli, Matthew J. *The O'Hara Concern: A Biography of John O'Hara*. New York: Random House, 1974.

Carroll, Diahann, with Ross Firestone. *Diahann: An Autobiography*. Boston: Little, Brown, 1986.

de Mille, Agnes. *And Promenade Home*. New York: Little, Brown, 1956.

————. *Dance to the Piper*. New York: Little, Brown, 1952.

Easton, Carol. *No Intermissions: The Life of Agnes de Mille*. New York: Little, Brown, 1996.

Engel, Lehman. *The American Musical Theater*. Rev. ed. New York: Collier, 1975.

Ewen, David. *The American Musical Theatre*. New York: Henry Holt, 1958.

Fordin, Hugh. *The World of Entertainment*. New York: Doubleday, 1975.

Forte, Allen. *The American Popular Ballad of the Golden Era, 1924–1950*. Princeton: Princeton University Press, 1995.

Furia, Phillip. *The Poets of Tin Pan Alley*. New York: Oxford University Press, 1990.

Gaenzl, Kurt. *The British Musical Theatre*, vol. 2, 1915–1984. London: Oxford University Press, 1986.

Gottfried, Martin. *Nobody's Fool: The Lives of Danny Kaye*. New York: Simon and Schuster, 1994.

Green, Benny, ed. *A Hymn to Him: The Lyrics of Alan Jay Lerner*. New York: Limelight, 1987.

Green, Stanley. *Encyclopedia of the Musical Theatre*. New York: Da Capo, 1976.

———. *Ring Bells, Sing Songs: Broadway Musicals of the 1930s*. New Rochelle: Arlington House, 1971.

———. *The World of Musical Comedy*. New York: Da Capo, 1980.

Hamm, Charles. *Yesterdays: Popular Songs in America*. New York: Norton, 1979.

Hyland, William G. *The Song Is Ended: Songwriters and American Music, 1900–1950*. New York: Oxford University Press, 1995.

Jablonski, Edward. *Gershwin: A Biography*. New York: Doubelday, 1987.

———. *Alan Jay Lerner: A Biography*. New York: Henry Holt, 1966.

Kanter, Kenneth. *The Jews on Tin Pan Alley*. New York: Ktav, 1982.

Kasha, Al, and Joel Hirschhorn. *Notes on Broadway*. Chicago: Contemporary, 1985.

Langner, Lawrence. *The Magic Curtain*. New York: E. P. Dutton, 1951.

Laurents, Arthur. *Do I Hear a Waltz?* New York: Random House, 1966.

Lees, Gene. *Inventing Champagne: The Worlds of Lerner and Loewe*. New York: St. Martin's Press, 1990.

Lerner, Alan Jay. *The Street Where I Live*. New York: Norton, 1980.

Lewine, Richard, and Alfred Simon. *Songs of the American Theater*. New York: Dodd, Mead, 1973.

Lindsay, Howard, and Russel Crouse. *The Sound of Music*. New York: Random House, 1960.

Logan, Joshua. *Josh: My Up and Down, In and Out Life*. New York: Delacorte Press, 1976.

McCabe, John. *George M. Cohan: The Man Who Owned Broadway*. New York: Da Capo, 1973.

McGovern, Dennis, and Deborah Grace Winer. *Sing Out, Louise!* New York: Schirmer, 1993.

Martin, Mary. *My Heart Belongs*. New York: William Morrow, 1976.

Mast, Gerald. *Can't Help Singing: The American Musical on Stage and Screen*. New York: Overlook Press, 1987.

Michener, James A. *The World Is My Home: A Memoir*. New York: Random House, 1992.

Mordden, Ethan. *Best Foot Forward*. New York: Grossman, 1976.

———. *Broadway Babies*. New York: Oxford University Press, 1983.

———. *The Hollywood Musical*. New York: St. Martin's Press, 1981.

———. *Rodgers and Hammerstein*. New York: Harry N. Abrams, 1992.

Morehouse, Ward. *George M. Cohan: Prince of the American Theater*. New York: Lippincott, 1943.

Morley, Sheridan. *A Bright Particular Star: A Biography of Gertrude Lawrence*. London: Pavillion, 1986.

O'Hara, John. *Pal Joey: The Libretto and Lyrics*. New York: Random House, 1952.

Palmer, Christopher. *The Composer in Hollywood*. New York: Maron Boyars, 1990.

Parini, Jay. *John Steinbeck: A Biography*. New York: Henry Holt, 1995.

Payn, Graham, and Sheridan Morley, eds. *The Noel Coward Diaries*. New York: Little, Brown, 1982.

Rosenberg, Bernard, and Ernest Harburg. *The Broadway Musical: Collaboration in Commerce and Art*. New York: New York University Press, 1993.

Rosenberg, Deena. *Fascinating Rhythm*. New York: Dutton, 1991.

Schuller, Gunther. *Early Jazz*. New York: Oxford University Press, 1968.

Smith, Cecil. *Musical Comedy in America*. New York: Theater Arts Books, 1950.

Steinbeck, Elaine, and Robert Wallsten, eds. *Steinbeck: A Life in Letters*. New York: Penguin, 1989.

Suskin, Steven. *Opening Night on Broadway: A Critical Quotebook of the Golden Era of the Musical Theatre*. New York: Schirmer, 1990.

Swain, Joseph P. *The Broadway Musical: A Critical and Musical Survey*. New York: Oxford University Press, 1990.

Whitcomb, Ian. *Irving Berlin and Ragtime America*. New York: Limelight, 1988.

Wilder, Alec. *American Popular Song: The Great Innovators, 1900–1950*. Edited by James T. Maher. New York: Oxford University Press, 1972.

Wilk, Max. *OK: The Story of Oklahoma!* New York: Grove Press, 1993.

———. *They're Playing Our Song*. New York: Zoetrope, 1986.

Zadan, Craig. *Sondheim & Co.* 2d ed. New York: Harper & Row, 1986.

Zinnemann, Fred. *An Autobiography: A Life in the Movies*. New York: Scribner's, 1992.

DISCOGRAPHY

A picture may be worth a thousand words, but even a thousand words cannot do justice to a song. In recorded music, one faces the problem of authentic reproduction, capturing compositions as they were written and first performed. Some modern recordings have attempted to replicate the sounds of the 1920s and 1930s—for example, the recent recordings of Hans Spialek's original orchestrations for *Babes in Arms* and *On Your Toes* (see below). But even original recordings that have been salvaged and reworked by the magic of modern electronics are suspect. Unfortunately, many of the surviving recordings feature second-rate orchestras and performances.

A guide to recordings of all of Rodgers' shows can be found in David Hummel, *The Collectors Guide to the American Musical Theatre*, 2 vols. (Metuchen, N.J.: Scarecrow Press, 1984).

Also valuable is Tommy Krasker and Robert Kimball, *Catalog of the Ameri-*

can Musical: Musicals of Irving Berlin, George and Ira Gershwin, Cole Porter, Richard Rodgers and Lorenz Hart (n.p.: National Institute for Opera and Musical Theatre, 1988).

Original cast recordings were made of all Rodgers' shows, beginning with Oklahoma! These have been reissued on compact discs. Rodgers' last show, I Remember Mama, has been recorded and issued as a compact disc (TER CD TER 1102); it is not by the original cast, however.

In addition to the original cast albums, the following recordings seem to be the most notable:

- The Song Is Rodgers and Hart (Living Era CD AJA 5041). Includes Jessie Matthews singing the two songs she introduced, "My Heart Stood Still" and "Dancing on the Ceiling." Also includes a jazz version of "Thou Swell" by the legendary Bix Beiderbecke.

- Music and Songs of Rodgers and Hart (Conifer CD HD 223). Includes "Here in My Arms," sung by Phyllis Dare and Jack Hulbert, who introduced it in London; "Isn't It Romantic?" and "Love Me Tonight," sung by Jeanette MacDonald and Maurice Chevalier; "The Bad in Every Man," sung by Shirley Ross, the first version of what would become "Blue Moon"; and"Ten Cents a Dance," sung by Ruth Etting, who introduced the song in Simple Simon. Many of the same versions are included in Rodgers & Hart: With a Song in Their Hearts (Avid, AVC 538).

- American Musicals: Rodgers & Hart: Pal Joey, The Boys From Syracuse, and Babes in Arms (Time-Life Records, 1981). Cassettes.

- The Boys from Syracuse (Broadway Angel, Broadway Classics, ZDM 764695 2, 1993), a twenty-fifth-anniversary production, off-Broadway version. Also The Boys from Syracuse (Sony Broadway, SK 53329), a CD reissue of a 1953 recording by Columbia Records. Modern recording produced by City Center Encores (DRG 947 67).

- I Married an Angel (AEI, CD 002). Not the full score but includes some of the songs as they were recorded by the Liberty Music Shop in New York, during the original run of the play.

- On Your Toes (TER CDTER 1063). Includes original orchestrations by Hans Spialek.

- Babes in Arms (New World Records, NW 386–2). Includes original Hans Spialek orchestrations and excellent notes by Theodore Chapin.

- Pal Joey (DRG 94763A). Modern recording produced by City Center Encores; includes many of the original orchestrations.

- Ben Bagley's Rodgers and Hart Revisited (Painted Smiles Records, PSCD 116). Nineteen songs that are rarely heard.

- My Funny Valentine: Frederica von Stade Sings Rodgers and Hart (EMI/CDC 7540712). Notable for the use of some original orchestrations.

- This Funny World: Mary Cleere Haran Sings Lyrics by Hart (Varese Sarabande VSD 5584). A modern recording, but includes some songs seldom heard.

- Richard Rodgers: Three Ballets: Slaughter on Tenth Avenue, Ghost Town, and La Princess Zenobia (TER Classics, CD TER 1114). A new recording (1994) of the original orchestrations, conducted by John A. Mauceri.
- Victory at Sea and More Victory at Sea (RCA CD 9026–60963–2 and 60964–2). Robert Russell Bennett conducting the RCA Symphony.

Select Musical Anthologies

Most of Rodgers and Hammerstein's songs are still generally available. Rodgers' music with Hart, as well as his post-Hammerstein music, is somewhat harder to find. With a few exceptions, some version of every song written by Rodgers exists in the collection at the Library of Congress.

Williamson Music has published vocal selections as well as piano-vocal scores for all the Rodgers and Hammerstein shows as well as for the some of the post-Hammerstein shows.

Piano-vocal scores and vocal selections are commercially available for only some of the better-known Rodgers and Hart shows, for example, Babes in Arms, On Your Toes, The Boys from Syracuse, and Pal Joey.

A comprehensive cross-section of his music is found in The Richard Rodgers Collection (New York: Williamson Music, 1990), with a preface by Dorothy Rodgers. Sixty-two songs are included.

The most prominent Rodgers and Hart songs are collected in Rodgers and Hart: A Musical Anthology (distributed by Hal Leonard Publishing, 1984), with a foreword by Dorothy Rodgers.

The Rodgers and Hart Songbook (New York: Simon and Schuster, 1951), with an introduction by Richard Rodgers and a foreword by Oscar Hammerstein, includes the opening song from the first Garrick Gaieties.

The Rodgers and Hammerstein Songbook (New York: Simon and Schuster, n.d.) is a coffee-table book.

Rodgers and Hammerstein Revisited, with an introduction by Richard Rodgers (Williamson Music).

Rodgers & Hammerstein Rediscovered, with notes by Theodore S. Chapin (Williamson Music); includes music and lyrics to songs cut from Oklahoma! and South Pacific, as well as the very first Rodgers and Hammerstein song, "There's Always Room for One More."

CREDITS AND PERMISSIONS

"My Girl Back Home." Copyright 1958 by Richard Rodgers and Oscar Hammerstein II. WILLIAMSON MUSIC owner of publication and allied rights throughout the world.

"Now Is the Time." Copyright 1949 by Richard Rodgers and Oscar Hammerstein II. WILLIAMSON MUSIC owner of publication and allied rights throughout the world.

"Something Wonderful." Copyright 1951 (renewed) by Richard Rodgers and Oscar Hammerstein II. WILLIAMSON MUSIC owner of publication and allied rights throughout the world.

"The King's Song." Copyright 1951 (renewed) by Richard Rodgers and Oscar Hammerstein II. WILLIAMSON MUSIC owner of publication and allied rights throughout the world.

"Why? Why? Why?" Copyright 1951 (renewed) by Richard Rodgers and Oscar Hammerstein II. WILLIAMSON MUSIC owner of publication and allied rights throughout the world.

"It's Me." Copyright 1953 (renewed) by Richard Rodgers and Oscar Hammerstein II. WILLIAMSON MUSIC owner of publication and allied rights throughout the world.

"My Favorite Things." Copyright 1959 by Richard Rodgers and Oscar Hammerstein II. WILLIAMSON MUSIC owner of publication and allied rights throughout the world.

Extracts of lyrics by Richard Rodgers (music by Richard Rodgers) have been used with permission: Copyright Williamson Music. Copyrights renewed. International copyrights secured. All rights reserved.

"The Sweetest Sounds." Copyright 1962 (renewed). WILLIAMSON MUSIC owner of publication and allied rights throughout the world.

"Look No Further." Copyright 1962 (renewed). WILLIAMSON MUSIC owner of publication and allied rights throughout the world.

"Maine." Copyright 1962 (renewed). WILLIAMSON MUSIC owner of publication and allied rights throughout the world.

Extracts of songs by Richard Rodgers, music, and lyrics by Stephen Sondheim have been used with permission: Copyright Williamson Music and Burthen Music Co., Inc. (Warner Brothers Music). Copyrights renewed. International copyrights secured. All rights reserved.

"This Week, Americans." Copyright 1965 (renewed) by Richard Rodgers (administered in the United States by Williamson Music) and Stephen Sondheim (Burthen Music Co., Inc., owner of publication and allied rights throughout the world, Chappell & Co. sole selling agent).

"Do I Hear a Waltz?" Copyright 1965 (renewed) by Richard Rodgers (administered in the United States by Williamson Music) and Stephen Sondheim (Burthen Music Co., Inc., owner of publication and allied rights throughout the world, Chappell & Co. sole selling agent).

"Philadelphia." Copyright 1965 (renewed) by Richard Rodgers (administered in the United States by Williamson Music) and Stephen Sondheim (Burthen Music Co., Inc., owner of publication and allied rights throughout the world, Chappell & Co. sole selling agent).

Lyric excerpts from the following songs, music by Richard Rodgers and lyrics by Lorenz Hart, have been used with permission: Copyright Williamson Music and Warner Brothers Music. Chappell & Co. rights for extended term in United States controlled by estate of Lorenz Hart (administered by WB Music Corp.). Copyrights renewed. All rights reserved.

"Any Old Place with You." Copyright 1919 (renewed) by Williamson Music Co. (for the interest of Richard Rodgers in the United States) and Warner Bros., Inc. Rights for extended renewal term in United States controlled by estate of Lorenz Hart (administered by WB Music Corp.).

"Bye and Bye." Copyright 1925 (renewed) by Williamson Music Co. (for the interest of Richard Rodgers in the United States) and Warner Bros., Inc. Rights for extended term in United States controlled by estate of Lorenz Hart (administered by WB Music Corp.).

"War Is War." Copyright 1985 by the estate of Richard Rodgers (administered in the United States by Williamson Music Co.) and Chappell & Co. Rights for extended term in United States controlled by estate of Lorenz Hart (administered by WB Music Corp.).

"Sweet Peter." Copyright 1925 (renewed) by Williamson Music Co. (for the interest of Richard Rodgers in the United States) and Warner Bros., Inc. Rights for extended term in the United States controlled by estate of Lorenz Hart (administered by WB Music Corp.).

"Six Little Plays." Copyright 1986 by the estate of Richard Rodgers (administered in the United States by Williamson Music Co.) and by the estate of Lorenz Hart (administered by WB Music Corp.).

"Mexico." Copyright 1986 by the estate of Richard Rodgers (administered in the United States by Williamson Music Co.) and by the estate of Lorenz Hart (administered by WB Music Corp.).

"Give That Little Girl a Hand." Copyright 1927 (renewed) by Williamson Music Co. (for the interest of Richard Rodgers in the United States) and Warner Bros., Inc. Rights for extended term in United States controlled by the estate of Lorenz Hart (administered by WB Music Corp.).

"Ladies and Gentlemen, We're Here Again." Copyright 1986 by the estate of Richard Rodgers (administered in the United States by Williamson Music Co.) and by the estate of Lorenz Hart (administered by WB Music Corp.).

"It's Got To Be Love." Copyright 1936 (renewed) by Williamson Music Co. (for the interest of Richard Rodgers in the United States) and Chappell & Co. Rights for extended term in United States controlled by the estate of Lorenz Hart (administered by WB Music Corp.).

"Falling In Love with Love." Copyright 1938 (renewed) by Williamson Music Co. (for the interest of Richard Rodgers in the United States) and Chappell & Co. Rights for extended term in United States controlled by the estate of Lorenz Hart (administered by WB Music Corp.).

"Give It Back to the Indians." Copyright 1939 (renewed) by Williamson Music Co. (for the interest of Richard Rodgers in the United States) and Chappell & Co. Rights for extended term in United States controlled by the estate of Lorenz Hart (administered by WB Music Corp.).

"Glad To Be Unhappy." Copyright 1936 (renewed) by Williamson Music Co. (for the interest of Richard Rodgers in the United States) and Chappell & Co. Rights for extended term in United States controlled by the estate of Lorenz Hart (administered by WB Music Corp.).

"Everything I've Got." Copyright 1942 (renewed) by Williamson Music Co. (for the interest of Richard Rodgers in the United States) and Chappell & Co., on behalf of the estate or Lorenz Hart (administered by Warner Bros. Music Corp.).

"Bewitched." Copyright 1941 (renewed) by Williamson Music Co. (for the interest of Richard Rodgers in the United States) and Chappell & Co. Rights for extended term in United States controlled by estate of Lorenz Hart (administered by WB Music Corp.).

"Take Him." Copyright 1951 (renewed) by Williamson Music Co. (for the interest of Richard Rodgers in the United States) and by Chappell & Co. Used by permission of Warner Bros. Publications, Inc. (for the estate of Lorenz Hart [administered by WB Music Corp.]).

"Zip." Copyright 1951 by Williamson Music Co. (for the interest of Richard Rodgers in the United States) and Chappell & Co. Used by permission of Warner Bros. Publications U.S., Inc. (for the estate of Lorenz Hart [administered by WB Music Corp.]).

Lyric extracts of songs by Richard Rodgers, music, and Lorenz Hart, lyrics, used by permission of Carlin America, Inc. Copyright 1925 by Edward B. Marks Music Co. Copyrights renewed. Used by permission. All rights reserved.

"Manhattan"

"Gilding the Guild"

"Soliciting Subscriptions"

Extract from "The Most Beautiful Girl in the World" Copyright 1935 by Polygram International Publishing, Inc. Copyright renewed. Used by permission. All rights reserved.

Unpublished letter dated April 9, 1953, from Oscar Hammerstein II to R. J. Kaplan. Reprinted by special permission from the Rodgers and Hammerstein Organization.

Quotations from "Reminiscences of Richard Rodgers" used by permission of Columbia University, Oral History Research Office.

Photographs courtesy of the Rodgers and Hammerstein Organization.

INDEX

"Baby Sequence" (Rodgers), 224

Bacall, Lauren, 193, 294, 295

Bad Habits of 1925 (Rodgers, Hart, H. Fields), 27

Baker, Belle, 57–58, 59, 60

Baker, Edythe, 63

Balanchine, George, 106, 108, 112, 115, 124, 305

"Bali Ha'i" (Rodgers, Hammerstein), 184, 199, 250

Ball, Lucille, 122

Ballard, Kaye, 237, 240

Ballet Russe de Monte Carlo, 123

Baravalle, Victor, 22

Barbour, Joyce, 74, 86

Barer, Marshall, 248

"Barking Dog Never Bites, A" (Rodgers, Hart), 124

Barnes, Clive, 162, 296, 304, 308

Barnes, Howard, 151

Barnet, Charlie, 271

Barrett, Ellin, 59

Barrios, Richard, 83

Bayes, Nora, 24

Behrman, S. N., 95

Beiderbecke, Bix, 43

Bell, Book and Candle (Van Druten), 157, 196

Benchley, Robert, 33, 47, 70, 71, 76, 88, 110, 120

Bender, Milton "Doc," 13, 15, 106

"Beneath the Southern Cross" (Rodgers, Hammerstein), 206

Bennett, Michael, 300

Bennett, Robert Russell, 22; Rodgers' initial recruitment of, 64; as orchestrator of *A Connecticut Yankee*, 67; as orchestrator of *She's My Baby*, 71; as orchestrator of *Heads Up*, 81; involvement in *Annie Get Your Gun* of, 166; as orchestrator of *South Pacific*, 180, 184; as orchestrator of *The King and I*, 196–97;

as conductor, 205; as orchestrator of *Androcles and the Lion*, 289

Benny, Jack, 235

Bentley, Eric, 233

Berg, Phil, 96, 114

Bergen, Edgar, 235

Bergen, Polly, 229

Bergman, Ingmar, 306

Bergman, Ingrid, 157

Berkeley, Busby, 67, 69, 73, 74, 86, 110

Berlin, Irving, 46, 82; Rodgers contrasted with, 24; ragtime as influence on, 37; American themes favored by, 42; as composer of "Blue Skies," 59; as celebrity, 75; film career of, 91; as composer of *As Thousands Cheer*, 96, 101; as composer of *Annie Get Your Gun*, 164–66, 280

Berlin Stories (Isherwood), 157

Berman, Pandro, 102

Bernstein, Leonard, 248, 283

Bessie, Alvah, 30

Best Foot Forward (Blane, Martin), 133

"Best Things in Life Are Free, The" (De Sylva, Brown, Henderson), 45

Betsy (Rodgers, Hart), 57–60

"Bewitched" (Rodgers, Hart), 129, 130–31

"Big Black Giant, The" (Rodgers, Hammerstein), 221

Bigley, Isabel, 221

Bikel, Theodore, 253, 254, 255

Billion for Boris, A (Mary Rodgers), 248

"Birth of the Blues" (De Sylva, Brown, Henderson), 70

"Black and White" (Rodgers, Hart), 31

Blackbirds of 1928 (McHugh, D. Fields), 43

"Black Diamond" (Rodgers, Hart), 97–98

Blackton, Jay, 227, 295

"Blah, Blah, Blah" (G. Gershwin, I. Gershwin), 83

Blaine, Vivian, 155, 156

"Joy Spreader" (Rodgers, Hart), 31

Juilliard School of Music, 5, 19, 20

Jumbo (Rodgers, Hart), 102–4, 108

"June Is Bustin' Out All Over" (Rodgers, Hammerstein), 160

Kahn, Gus, 70

Kahn, Madeline, 295

Kalman, Emmerich, 149

Kalmar, Bert, 51, 70, 71, 92

Kander, John, 191

"Kansas City" (Rodgers, Hammerstein), 142–43

Kaplan, R. J., 199

Katz, Elsa, 7–8

Kaufman, George S., 112, 113, 201

Kaufman, Harry, 102

Kay, Hershy, 265

Kaye, Benjamin, 27, 29, 30

Kaye, Danny, 291, 294, 295–98

Kazan, Elia, 143

"Keep It Gay" (Rodgers, Hammerstein), 222

Kelly, Gene, 108, 127, 128, 177, 243, 244, 245

Kennedy, John F., 278

Kern, Jerome, 41, 77; Rodgers contrasted with, 9; as composer of Stepping Stones, 22; Dreyfus as promoter of, 25; as composer of Sally, 26; ragtime as influence on, 37; American themes favored by, 42; as composer of Sunny, 44; many collaborations of, 45–46; as composer of Show Boat, 58, 250; on "Ten Cents a Dance," 82; film career of, 83, 91; as composer of Roberta, 101; as possible collaborator on Oklahoma!, 137–38; as composer of Centennial Summer, 154; as possible collaborator on Annie Get Your Gun, 163–64; film biography of, 175

Kerr, Deborah, 204

Kerr, Walter: on The Boys from Syracuse, 121; on Pal Joey, 132; on Me and Juliet, 223; on Pipe Dream, 231; on The Sound of Music, 255; on No Strings, 274; on Do I Hear a Waltz?, 286; on Two by Two, 296; on Rodgers and Hart, 299; on Rex, 302; on Oklahoma!, 309

Kiley, Richard, 268, 269, 271, 272, 273–74

King, Dennis, 114, 120

King and I, The (Rodgers, Hammerstein), 181, 193–204, 207, 208, 216, 224, 225, 262, 279, 280, 305

Kirk, Grayson, 236, 274

Kiss Me Kate (Porter), 187, 201

Klingenstein Brothers, 2

Kneisel, Franz, 23

Kolodin, Irving, 123, 240

Kostal, Irwin, 256, 302

Krehbiel, Henry, 23

Kroll, William, 24, 26

Kron, Willy, 133, 152

Kroopf, Milton, 16

"Ladies of the Evening" (Rodgers, Hart), 120

Lady Be Good (G. Gershwin, I. Gershwin), 50, 61

Lady in the Dark (Weill), 147, 193, 294

"Lady Is a Tramp, The" (Rodgers, Hart), 110, 111, 176

Lahr, John, 296

Lake, Harriet, 88

Landon, Margaret, 193, 195

"Land Where Good Camp Songs Go, The" (Rodgers, Fields), 18

Lane, Burton, 278–79

Lang, Harold, 132

Lang, Phil, 165

Langdon, Harry, 95

Langner, Lawrence, 30, 138, 139, 157, 224–25